Child of the Covenant
and
Promised Land

Child of the Covenant

and

Promised Land

Michele Guinness

Hodder & Stoughton
LONDON SYDNEY AUCKLAND

British Library Cataloguing in Publication Data
A record for this book is available from the British Library

ISBN 0 340 90866 1

Typeset in Bembo by Avon DataSet Ltd,
Bidford-on-Avon, Warwickshire

Printed and bound in Great Britain by
Clays Ltd, St Ives plc

The paper and board used in this paperback are natural recyclable
products made from wood grown in sustainable forests.
The manufacturing processes conform to the environmental
regulations of the country of origin.

Hodder and Stoughton Ltd
A Division of Hodder Headline Ltd
338 Euston Road
London NW1 3BH
www.madaboutbooks.com
and www.hodderbibles.co.uk

Child of the Covenant

For Joel and Abigail,
children of the covenant twice over.

Acknowledgements

By their support and encouragement more people have been involved in the writing of this story than I could begin to mention. But a special thanks to David Lewis and Sue Rosseter, who reading the original draft made me go home and start all over again – with many useful tips.

I owe a great deal to my parents. Without their extraordinary courage and humour the tale could never have been told. My Canadian mother-in-law ruthlessly corrected my English grammar with the precision of a true colonial. I am indebted to her perfectionism and red pen!

My husband said he wished for no acknowledgement and that just about says everything about him. Only by the self-sacrificial nature of his love have I been able to write.

Glossary

Rosh Hashanah	The Jewish New Year
Yom Kippur	The Day of Atonement
Succoth	Booths, the Harvest Festival
Pesach	The Passover
Purim	The Feast of Esther
Chanukah	The Feast of the Dedication of the Temple
Shabbat or *Shabbas*	The Sabbath

* * *

afikomen	The middle piece of the three matzos used in the Passover service (Symbolises the Paschal lamb)
Bar Mitzvah	A boy's becoming an adult member of the community
Beth Din	Central body which dictates and regulates the dietary laws
bimah	Synagogue platform

7

charoseth	Substance made of apples, wine and walnuts used at the Passover and meant to resemble mortar
Chasidim	An ultra-orthodox Jewish sect
cheder	Hebrew classes
chollah	Plaited Sabbath loaf
chuckele	(Yiddish) 'pet' – term of endearment
chuppah	Canopy of flowers under which Jews are married: a tradition dating back to their desert wanderings
Cohanim	The priests
davening	Swaying at prayer
frumm	(Yiddish) very orthodox or religious
gefüllte fish	Chopped (usually fried) fish balls, traditionally served on the Sabbath
Goyim	The Gentiles, or non-Jews
Haggadah	Service book used at the Passover (lit. 'The narration')
Kaddish	Prayers recited at a funeral and house of mourning
Kiddush	The Sabbath prayer and ceremony
kosher	According to the dietary laws
matzo	Unleavened bread

menorah	The nine-branched candelabra used at the feast of *Chanukah*
minyan	The ten men needed before any official prayers may be said
Seder	Passover service in the home
sheitel	The wig worn by an orthodox Jewish woman
Shemah	The morning and evening prayers. *Shemah Yisrael* means 'Hear, O Israel', a proclamation of the Jews' faith
shivah	The seven days of official mourning after a bereavement
shochet	The ritual slaughterer
shofar	The ram's horn
Siddah	Jewish prayer book
simcha	A time of celebration
tsimmes	A sweet eastern European stew
Yiddishkeit	The traditional Jewish way of life
Yiskedal	First word of Kaddish, prayers for the dead

1

I do like pedigrees! They convey such a sense of continuity and destiny, almost of immortality. My husband's is most impressive. He can boast of brewers, bankers, millionaires and even peers of the realm in his family tree. Would that mine were as illustrious! I could of course say that Abraham, the patriarch, was my goodness-knows-how-many-great-grandfather, that Moses must figure somewhere, but that was a long, long time ago. Our recent history was not quite so brilliant, although it does have its moments.

'But you're not really British, are you?' people say to me, and it makes me mad. I want to wave my passport under their noses.

'As British as you are – well, almost.'

I am the second generation to be born in this country and though I may not look the classic English rose, I feel very British as well as Jewish inside. This was the dream which inspired my great-grandparents. I am its fulfilment, or at least, I would have been, had not things turned out very differently from what we all expected.

I was twelve years old when my maternal great-grandparents died. I knew it was an event of major importance for the family, because everyone wept, argued and fought in a way I had never seen before, but it did not particularly bother me as I hardly knew them. Fortnightly visits to their dark, melancholy house with its extraordinary smell of damp and lavender had seemed more like a punishment than a pleasure. Great-grandpa never moved from his fireside chair. His black skullcap perched on his wizened little polished apple of a head, he would mutter to himself in Hebrew, plunging the piece of lemon up and down in his tea in a kind of rhythmical accompaniment. Great-grandma would be bent over

11

the stove stirring some concoction in a huge copper pot, cackling merrily over some private source of amusement.

'Dirty jokes,' my mother told me when she thought I was old enough to understand. 'Your great-grandmother's sense of humour has always thrived on the basics of life.' I did not have a clue what she meant.

'Come on my little *chuckele*,' Great-grandma would say. She always used that Yiddish term of endearment or its Geordie equivalent, 'little pet', then nipped my cheek between her bony fingers until tears welled up in my eyes with the pain of it. 'Eat up.'

'But Grandma, I'm not hungry. I've already eaten.'

'You want to grow into a big girl, don't you?'

'Not too big,' interjected my mother. Mother's enormous size as a teenager was a family proverb, a warning to all of the dangers of Great-grandma's cooking.

'Eat half,' Mother whispered to me, 'and put the rest over there.' She pointed to a pile of dirty plates at the end of the table. One more would not be noticed.

How I wish I had known then what I know now, what a wealth of adventure and experience lay behind that withered, shrivelled appearance. So many things I would have asked them, so many stories I would have begged to hear. But in all our many visits I never exchanged more than a sentence with them. The room was always so full of aunts, uncles and cousins chattering loudly all at once that I could hardly ever hear what they were saying. And when I did, it was such a strange mixture of Yiddish and broken English with a Newcastle accent that I found it hard to understand anyway.

It was not until I was a teenager and spent occasional weekends with my grandmother, the sixth of their eight children, that I began to realise all my great-grandparents had been through.

One night, long after everyone else was asleep, I saw Gran, in dressing-gown and curlers, slip into the kitchen for a last cigarette. I followed her and while she sat warming her hands round a hot cup of tea made her tell me about her parents.

'They came from Lithuania,' she said, flicking ash into her saucer and watching it slowly disintegrate into the tea slops.

'Where?'

'Russia.'

'Why did they come here?'

'They thought the streets were paved with gold, that a young man could grow rich and famous.'

'And they couldn't in Russia?'

'Oh no. Tsar Nicholas, of "Nicholas and Alexandra", you know . . .'

'They were baddies?'

'Not exactly, just weak. He allowed his Cossack soldiers to ride rough-shod over Jewish settlements, looting, pillaging, killing as they went. You were lucky to stay alive, let alone make a living or build a future for your children.' Gran looked up, but not at me. In her eyes was the fond admiration of a little girl for her proud, handsome father.

He arrived without a penny in his pocket. The overcrowded boat offloaded its herd of immigrants on the Tyne quay. 'Name?' shouted an official. My great-grandfather looked round at his compatriots, each more lonely and bewildered than the last. It was he who was being spoken to. He stated his name. The official looked blank. How many times would he have to repeat it, spell it, and what was it worth now anyway? He looked around for inspiration. A man was selling fish from a barrow on the quayside. Great-grandpa pointed to a pile of debris left behind by the filleting.

'Fish skin?' said the official quizzically.

'Fishkin,' nodded Great-grandpa, and set off with a new name into a new life.

'How did he meet Great-grandma?'

The question startled Gran out of her silence. A smile formed on her lips, which grew into a chuckle. 'He was given an introduction to another Jewish family already living here. It was the accepted thing. After all, he was totally alone. He knew no one. Someone back at home had scribbled the address of a Landsleit, a distant relative long since settled in Newcastle, on a scrappy piece of paper. A name and address in your pocket was more valuable than gold. Mind you, Father was not to know whether they were in any position to offer him assistance, but he was in luck. The gentleman in question was the local *shochet*, the ritual slaughterer, a man of learning and standing in the small community. He could teach him English, and provide him with a dowry which would start a business, for it just so happened there were many marriageable daughters in the family. But Father never intended to marry Mother. It was Kitty, her younger sister, he wanted. You should have seen her. She had violet eyes and long auburn hair.'

'Then what happened? Why couldn't he have her?'

'She had an elder unmarried sister, and in those days you did what custom dictated.'

'Is that why he and Great-grandma argued so much?' I had learnt at an early age that not all the Yiddish I had heard them speak could be repeated in polite company.

Gran laughed. 'Don't believe all you see,' she said. 'They enjoy their quarrels, it keeps their minds active. And besides, they've always shared a bed, and that's saying something.' Gran stubbed out her cigarette and was about to stand up.

'And did he forget Kitty?'

She sat down again, and went silent. 'No, he never did,' she said after a while. 'Kitty married a worthless charlatan. They thought he was a count. What a match! But he was a nobody. He abandoned her during all her five pregnancies. She bore him four sons, then died giving birth to a daughter. I vividly remember the day the letter came telling us of her death. Father took it with him into his study and laid it on his desk. I crept in a few moments later. He had his head in his hands and was weeping bitterly.'

The country of his adoption did not fail Great-grandfather Fishkin. Like many of his kinsmen, he made his fortune in the rag trade. On a Saturday evening when the sun had set and the Sabbath was over, the doors of his vast old house were flung open and young Jews came from miles around to eat and dance. Festivities always ended at midnight on the dot when the pianist was issued with a final command, 'Play "God Save the King".' One night, my grandmother, too young to be allowed to attend at the time, was spying through the keyhole. A game of forfeits was under way, and that particular forfeit required the unlucky girl who had picked it to kiss the handsomest young man in the room. A striking young man stepped forward. 'That's me, I believe. I'm the handsomest man in the room.'

Gran drew in her breath and pressed her eye as closely to the hole as she could. 'He is too,' she thought. 'I'll have him one day, and bring him down a peg or two.' She did just that!

'Mother's own marriage made her a stickler about one thing,' Gran confided in me at another of our late night encounters in

14

the kitchen. The stillness of the hour and a s̶ always had a strangely liberating effect on our con̶ marriage could be made to work, whatever the ci̶ She paused, the steaming kettle in her hand poised over ̶ and turned to look at me, as if debating whether to contí̶ story or not. Then her face relaxed into a grin and she gig̶ . 'You'll never guess what I did on my wedding night. I ran away!'

'You what? Why?'

'Well I wasn't having any of . . . that, was I?'

'You mean, for all her apparent broad-mindedness Great-grandma never actually told you about the facts of life?'

'She wouldn't have dreamed of it, but she did that night, when she found me on the doorstep.'

'What did she say?'

'She sent me home to Grandpa. Told me to get on with it, that I was lucky it wasn't an arranged marriage like hers or some of my friends.'

'What did you do?'

'Did as I was told, just as we all did and always have done, until she died. As brothers and sisters we've had our differences, but she kept the family together. Now I seem to be falling out with everyone. If only one of us had been more like her.'

I waited in silence, not daring to interrupt her flow, desperately hoping that Gran would explain what she meant. What was so special about that strange old lady? Gran sighed, swirled the teabags round in the pot with her spoon in a distracted sort of way, poured the steaming black liquid into a cup and then sipped thoughtfully.

'You see, she was a good Jew. I mean she was a really good woman.' I must have looked quizzical.

'Well, for example, after she died and we were sitting *shivah* for her, you know, the ritual one week of mourning, one evening just before prayers your mother happened to tell us that whenever she went to the house Mother sent her down the road with a hot meal for a certain Miss Weinberg, an old lady who was infirm and bedridden.

' "You took hot meals to Miss Weinberg? So did I!"

' "So did I, but she made me promise not to tell anyone!"

' "Me too!"

'Well, it turned out that each of the grandchildren had taken meals to Miss Weinberg every time they called and that in all

...ty Miss Weinberg had had a good hot meal every day ...her life. That was Mother all right, that was her Judaism, she lived and breathed it.' Gran stared wistfully into her empty teacup.

'I'm not like that,' she said slowly. 'I try, God knows I try. I keep the festivals, I keep the laws, well most of them, I keep a strictly *kosher* kitchen, just as she taught me to. Have you ever had meat with dairy produce in this house? Of course not. But somehow it's not the same. She and Father, they were on familiar terms with the Almighty. They spoke to him like you speak to a friend. But I've never seen him like that. I can't. Life's far too complicated. My brother, your uncle Joe, he's a clever man, he reads, he studies the Torah, the Talmud and other holy Jewish writings, perhaps he can make sense of it all. Well,' Gran started suddenly, 'none of us has inherited their simple kind of faith and there's an end to it.' She rinsed her cup and saucer without a word and then headed for the door. She stopped and turned round slowly. 'Perhaps,' she said thoughtfully, 'perhaps it's something you're given when you specially need it, you know, in all the troubles they had to face. And perhaps with all this,' she waved vaguely at her beautiful fitted kitchen, 'we no longer need it, well not in the same way. Who knows?' She shook her head and disappeared into her bedroom. The door clicked shut and the still house seemed very cold and empty.

How can I describe my father's family? If I said that they were rich, romantic and prosperous, alas, it would merely be wishful thinking. They were from Latvia, then a Polish state, and of much less volatile, more serious and solid stock. In fact, relationships with fellow Lithuanian and Austrian immigrants were often severely strained. They might well all be Jews but there were still marked differences.

'Ach, a Pole she wants to marry, a Litvak,' my great-grandfather lamented when my mother told him of her choice.

Not all Jews have the Midas touch. My father's family proves it. That is not to say they did not dream of material glory, but somehow their dreams always disintegrated in the light of circumstances.

Great-uncle Isaac took a job on the railways and was not looking one day when a train passed by. Great-uncle Mark went gold-prospecting in South Africa, found nothing and lost every penny he had in the first place. Their sister, my grandmother, followed them over here ostensibly to clean and keep house. She had already met and fallen in love with her future husband, but their parents thought it an unsuitable match. He was a mercenary and a mercenary's future is always unpredictable. She had been left a semicripple by a childhood fall and might not be the sort of wife a man needs. He pursued her to Britain, they were married, and my grandfather began to build the first charabanc business in Teesside. He did very well too, until one night his partner disappeared with all the profits. If fate never smiled on my father's family, it actually seemed to leer at my grandfather, who was a gracious, gentle man.

Their eldest child, my aunt Vera, was the most gloriously eccentric person I have ever met. She always wore purple, which was her favourite colour, and I mean wore purple – shoes, stockings, hat, gloves, even eye-shadow. When she bought shoes, another great passion of hers, she bought them in triplicate, one pair in purple, one pair in gold and one pair in silver, if possible. I once asked her if I could borrow a pair of gloves for a special occasion. I imagined a neat little pile of three or four pairs, squeezed into the corner of a chest of drawers, as mine were. Instead, she opened her wardrobe door and began to heave at an enormous sack, which would not budge until we both pulled. She opened it, and taking a deep breath, heaved it upside down and tipped its contents on the floor. There before my eyes appeared the most enormous rainbow-coloured mound of gloves.

'Help yourself, darling,' she panted, then chortled when she saw my face, 'that is, if you can find a matching pair.'

Money meant nothing to her (she is still the only person I have ever known to stew best grilling steak). But despite the love and generosity she showered on me I knew she was unhappy, and not just because she could not have children.

Uncle Solly was a surly man, unable to show affection, the only one to be amused by his own jokes.

'Why did she marry him?' I asked my father, after one of our regular Sunday afternoon visits. Their sniping and bickering had been worse than usual and Aunt Vera seemed to have doubled the number of cream cakes she normally landed on my plate. I felt decidedly queasy. 'Did she love him once?'

'Oh yes, at least she thought so. She was totally infatuated.'

'And did he love her?'

'I don't know, dear, but I don't think so. He needed money badly, to help him finish his studies in medicine and set up in practice somewhere. In those days the only way to do that was to find a girl with a decent dowry.' Father went quiet. He put down the medical journal he had been reading, and there was an expression of great sadness on his face. 'Do you know,' he said after a while, 'that so-and-so came to the house a few days before the wedding and said he wouldn't marry her unless Father gave him two hundred pounds more.'

'Did Aunty Vera know all that?'

'Know it! She was standing outside the door with her ear to the keyhole.'

'Then why did she do it? How could she?'

'Because,' my mother intervened harshly, as if she had been through the conversation so many times that it wearied her, 'your grandmother wanted a doctor for her daughter, and a doctor she'd have at any cost.' Father nodded reluctantly. 'But my word,' continued my mother, with an air of private satisfaction, 'did they live to regret it!'

Father waited for her to leave the room, then turned to me and said, 'The day Father's business collapsed, who do you suppose was the first on the doorstep demanding what he was promised?' I said nothing. I was horrified that anyone could be so callous. 'But Solly got his money all right,' Father continued, 'every penny. Father begged and borrowed, then returned to the only skill he had ever learned back in Latvia, tailoring. He worked all day and sometimes all night too to pay off the debts he'd incurred. And he did it, because he was a man of his word, but it cost him his health. He was paralysed down one side for two years before he died. He was only fifty-five.'

I looked at my father's face for some time, trying to imagine what depths of hatred for Uncle Solly must lie behind his distant expression, but he simply said, 'You would have liked Father so much. I wish he could have seen you three children.'

I realised then how many of his own values were modelled on his father's. He seemed to me a man incapable of harbouring bitterness and rancour and I loved him for it. The shattering realisation of the wealth of regret and self-reproach which lay behind that controlled exterior dawned slowly and much much later.

My grandmother was desolate after my grandfather's death. She had no choice but to swallow her pride and move in with her daughter and son-in-law. She was never welcome in their sitting-room. She sat alone in her self-imposed imprisonment in one room of my aunt's large house, a frail little old lady with hunched shoulders and a permanently wrinkled forehead.

'They think I don't know that they fry bacon. Well I may not be what I once was but I still have a nose.'

'Smoked beef, Mother,' my father would reassure her.

Nothing made her smile any more, not even my clowning, dressed up in her best Sabbath hats, with their long, drooping, bird-of-paradise feathers. The world had turned sour on her. One day she took the only revenge she could, and ended her own life.

Come to think of it, my family had quite a flair for posthumous revenge. Aunt Vera's will left every penny to her brother, my father; a fact which her husband, Uncle Solly found very hard to explain, and the solicitors found impossible to enforce.

So to my parents! Strange how one can never imagine one's own parents' romance. It seems a bit indecent that they should have their moment of passion, though we grant it to everyone else. My father said it happened like this.

He was at a Jewish wedding, which happens to be a very good hunting ground, as every Jew knows. He was fast approaching thirty, the age at which a man has had his fling and needs a bit of tender loving care, someone to warm his underwear in the morning, just like his mother did. He had rarely dated Jewish girls, but marriage was a different proposition, it had to be *kosher*! He was just dancing a suave little military two-step, when a lady's heel from behind lodged itself in his trouser turn-up and dragged both him and the lady in question to the floor. She was furious, he was charmed. With such an introduction what could the chivalrous gentleman do but prolong the acquaintance?

Mother was seventeen and terribly green. She had never been away from home, never set eyes on a boy who was not Jewish. Along came my father, all five-foot-three of him, and bowled her over with his charm and worldliness. And he was a doctor! Security and social status were no small carrot. Only one little cloud darkened the glorious horizon: he appeared to have little interest in Judaism, except in so far as the traditions reminded him of a happy childhood.

'But darling, there's been a war. I've seen suffering you would never have dreamed of. How can there be a God?'

'Don't talk like that. You can't really mean it.'

'Oh, but I do! "Do unto others as you'd have them do unto you", that's the only Judaism I want. You can keep whatever traditions you care to. I won't interfere.'

Mother pushed the subject to the back of her mind. What did it matter anyway? She would make him a Jewish home, surround him with Jewish traditions, cook him Jewish food, and make a Jewish man out of him by every means at her disposal. Surely that was what God expected of every young Jewish woman, to be the perfect wife and mother? Who wanted a career? There was great prestige in being the first among your friends to marry. She had so many hopes and dreams. No momentary qualm would undermine her determination to fulfil her calling. This, after all, was her destiny. Without doubt she would inspire in the next generation the faith of her ancestors.

2

I was born in Gateshead shortly after the war, in a place called Felling, notable only for its male voice choir. Gateshead was dismal and depressed in those difficult days and Felling was Gateshead at its greyest. Ration books were barely in the dustbin when many of the local pits whirred to a standstill and the dole queue more than tripled.

This was where my father bought his first practice. It was all he could afford. Some budding Jewish doctors could look to their parents for financial help and they were only too pleased to give it. After all, they had toiled, scrimped, scrounged, even starved to see their offspring secure in a well-established profession. For a Jew to be an educated, respected member of society, with a contribution to make, was the realisation of a once impossible dream. But with no father to support him my father struggled through college and was thrilled with the great potential of the vast old stone house he had acquired.

It was hardly what my grandparents had had in mind for their daughter. Each of its seventeen rooms was in a state of total disrepair. They surveyed the general dilapidation, swallowed their horror, and tried to kindle some glimmer of enthusiasm in my mother, who had given way to hysterics at first sight. It was a beginning, wasn't it? Everyone has to start somewhere, and standing there in solitary splendour on the top of the hill, looking down on the rows of cobbled streets and smoking chimneys, it did have a certain dignity. Gran rose to the challenge, supervised a total redecoration, ordered carpets and curtains, interviewed maids and gardeners.

'You see what a little imagination can do?' she urged my mother, who went on muttering about the cellars and the rats and the tunnels to the Tyne. 'Rats never bother humans,' she snapped.

One day Father's surgery was brought to a standstill by a blood-curdling scream. Patients in the waiting-room froze with terror. Mother rushed into the examination room, oblivious of what state of undress some poor patient might be in.

'A rat, a rat, there's a rat in the oven,' she screamed, 'and,' she added, as an injured afterthought, 'it's licked all the custard out of the custard tart I was making for tea.'

'Can't you see how busy I am?' said my father, ushering her out as quickly as possible. 'All this fuss for a little mouse.' Nonchalantly he swung open the oven door. 'You see,' he said, then peered in. 'Good grief!' he exclaimed, and slammed it shut in a hurry. 'It's the size of a cat.' They switched on the gas and waited fifteen minutes, but when the oven door was gingerly opened again, the rat had disappeared as mysteriously as it arrived.

From then on the rat-catcher made a courteous, quiet visit once a month, and took away whatever he found in a black suitcase. The rats never bothered me. Their scuffling and scratching was a bit annoying when I was trying to get to sleep, but that was all. Nor were they my mother's only source of misery. She was often lonely and bored. The days were long and dreary.

Felling provided most of the local collieries with manpower, and the manpower with bronchitis, pneumonia and poverty. When my father disappeared into the surgery early in the morning, he rarely emerged before late evening. There was no such thing as an appointment to see the doctor in those days. Sometimes, especially in bad weather, the queue of patients went right round the waiting-room, out of the surgery door and down the street. Mother was unused to so little Jewish company, and despite the kindness of the people, felt uneasy and isolated. If the house was grand by Tyneside's standards, it certainly was by hers. She began to devote her days to making it as perfect as it could be in every way. No picture was ever crooked, no ornament out of place, every curtain fold measured to the last quarter of an inch. Aesthetics lost their meaning. Everything was valued by how easily it could be dusted.

She was not the only one of her generation of Jewish women to succumb to some obsession about her home. It was almost a cultural hazard. Aunt Vera would stand outside her toilet with a duster in her hand whenever it was in use, waiting for it to be vacated so that she could repolish the seat. Her friends and relatives whispered to each other that that was taking cleanliness to its limit. They giggled and went on with their own particular fads.

A certain Jewish cookbook, instruction manual of many a Jewish bride, suggested that the Jewish home was to run as smoothly as a Swiss clock. It was to be swept, dusted, scrubbed and polished daily, as of course were the children, so that the man of the house could return from work to order, serenity and his favourite meal piping hot on the table.

If a young Jewish woman made what was considered to be 'a good match' it normally implied her husband could provide her with domestic staff. The problem was that this made her semi-redundant and forced her to create some justification for her existence. The growth of Zionism meant there was always fund-raising to be done, that or making her home more immaculate than everyone else's.

Once the glamour and novelty of being a married lady wore off my mother lamented her former carefree life of dances and parties. Charitable works had no appeal at all. She was twenty and her future seemed frighteningly long and empty. Pregnancy postponed most of her misery. I came first, then seventeen months later my brother David was born, to my disgust I am told. I soon warmed to him and we became inseparable companions as we grew up together in that huge house. Hand in hand we rushed down the endless dark corridors pursued by ghosts, hobgoblins and wicked witches. Behind every curtain, in every cupboard, at the bottom of every staircase was a hidden world, peopled with all kinds of extraordinary beings. Sometimes we tripped over my mother on hands and knees, straightening the curtains we had ruffled on one of our daring voyages of discovery.

At all costs Father must not be disturbed, not at breakfast when he opened his post, standing in front of the dining-room fire, not at coffee-time when he and his partners smoked their pipes and laughed together in the study. At lunchtime he was out on his visits, at teatime he was back in the surgery, so we normally ate in the draughty kitchen with the nanny and home-helps around a long, pine kitchen table. The atmosphere depended greatly on the mood and temperament of the adults present and how well they related to one another. Some meals were eaten in oppressive, stony silence. David and I hardly dared look up from our plates. Some were relaxed and happy, others were dominated by the blare of the Light Programme. One thing was sure, the domestic staff never stayed the same for long. Few could keep up with my mother's extraordinarily high standards and the turnover was rapid. No sooner did I become attached to someone, when she disappeared from my world. It was very unsettling.

Bedtime was always the same. Father popped upstairs in his white coat between patients to tuck us in and say goodnight.

'What shall we have tonight then, kids?'

'Anything but "Oh Yes, We Have No Bananas" again, Dad.'

'Dash it, I've forgotten my ukulele.'

'Just tell us a story then.'

Whatever we asked for, we always got a cabaret of all-round entertainment. Story after story flowed from the top of his head. He sang us everything from 'Your Tiny Hand is Frozen' to 'When I'm Cleaning Windows'. I knew few nursery rhymes, but could manage an aria or two from Puccini or Verdi. Sadly my mother's loud abuse whenever my father started to sing hid from us how good his voice really was.

We loved Friday evenings. They were special, the Sabbath. My mother and father never went out and David and I were allowed to stay up late and eat with them. Bathed and scrubbed we would sit in silence waiting for Father to appear. Mother would rush in, look anxiously at the clock, grumble, then rush out again to see to the potatoes. Minutes later she would be back to check the table, which was set for a banquet. She always scrutinised the silver, her eyes darting from one piece to another.

'Lizzie always misses that patch there, right under the handle.' Out of her pocket came the inevitable duster and she would put the home-help's lapse to rights. Some time after seven the surgery door would slam. There was a pause as Father took off his white coat and threw it on to a peg. Then he rushed into the room, donned his skullcap and found the place in the prayer book.

'Is the food spoilt?'

'Is it ever? Isn't it always *gefüllte* fish on *Shabbas*?'

'I wonder who started that particular tradition? Do you suppose Moses' wife inflicted cold fried fish cakes on him every Friday evening?' Father lifted the lid off a tureen and peered inside. 'And salad!'

'Now don't start grumbling. You'll put the children off. I've made it in a dressing just how you like it, especially for you.'

'I don't like salad eith . . .'

David was silenced by one of my mother's terrible stares. She picked up the box of matches, which was the signal that the occasion was about to begin. Slowly and with great dignity, she lit the Sabbath candles, muttering to herself in Hebrew, a distant look in her eyes. As the tiny flames sprang to life, casting shadows on the wall, giving the room a magic glow, she paused, transfixed, so unlike herself that David and I gazed in wonder. What was she thinking about? We supposed she was praying, but never really knew.

'*Vay' erev vay voker yom ha'shishi* . . . And it was evening and it was morning, the sixth day . . .'

I loved the lilting, familiar sound of *Kiddush*, the Sabbath prayer. It was a tradition my father took seriously and one of the few pieces of Hebrew he could read with any fluency, because he knew it off by heart. I knew every inflexion of his voice and could say the words quietly with him. I was not sure what they actually meant, for any attempt my father made at reading the translation simultaneously for our benefit was disrupted after the first line by a command from my mother to 'stop messing about!' But the gist was that God had made the world in six days, rested on the seventh and that was why we had weekends. It seemed very sensible. If only we did not have to spend it visiting relatives! Maybe Mother's brother, Uncle Mark, only four years older than I, would take us up to the attic and show us his new records and train set. And Aunt Vera might let me rummage through her jewellery and make-up boxes. Or even better, perhaps it would be one of those marvellous Saturdays when Mother was too busy to visit the family and Father would take us down to the coast, to Whitley Bay.

'David, stand straight and stop lounging!' David and I jumped at my mother's voice. She had just returned from yet another whirlwind visit to the kitchen.

'Amen,' said Father wearily, and put the prayer book reverently down. 'Perhaps one of these weeks we'll finish without interruption?' He lifted his large silver goblet, waited for mother to slice the *chollah*, the plaited Sabbath loaf, drank, then passed the goblet round so that we could all have a sip. 'Good *Shabbas*.'

'*Shabbat shalom.*'

The festive nature of the occasion suddenly returned. Everyone hugged everyone else. Even my father's non-Jewish partners came in to give us their greetings and get their Sabbath kisses.

When the Sabbath was over, most Saturday evenings my parents went out together. My mother loved dancing and my father indulged her fancy for night-clubs and parties as often as he could. Her sumptuous wardrobe of diaphanous chiffons and glittering sequins was a world of magic for me. Occasionally we saw her in all her splendour, when David and I were summoned to the lounge, a room we never saw by day, and standing in our dressing-gowns were instructed to greet the guests she was entertaining. How we admired her. But when we needed a soft, cosy lap, the home-help had to do.

I should have liked a friend. David was all right, but he was my brother. We drove our trikes to the end of the drive and stared out through the wrought-iron gates at the queue of patients waiting at the surgery door. A huddle of faceless grey figures, a hotch-potch of mackintoshes, caps and headsquares, which never acknowledged our existence. I never knew whether it was because we were the doctor's children or whether they sensed we were somehow different because we were Jews. Mother was always telling us that Jews were different from other people: 'They don't dress like we do. They don't eat like we do. They go to churches and have different festivals and traditions.'

Sometimes she called them 'Christians'. At other times, if she was describing behaviour of which she did not particularly approve, she called them '*Goyim*', a Yiddish word meaning Gentiles. Whatever the reason, our secluded little world was completely separate from the one out there, beyond the six-foot stone walls surrounding our garden.

'Would you like to go exploring?' I asked David one morning, when there was nothing of any particular interest to see through the gate. I was about eight at the time. 'I mean, we could always run away.'

He looked at me in horror. 'We can't. Where would we go? They'd find us and we'd get spanked.'

'No we wouldn't. We won't be long. I've seen a park with some swings and a slide in it from the car window. It's only just up the road there.'

I tried the gate. It opened. No one was around. We ran up the road at great speed, revelling in the extraordinary sensation of freedom. My only fear was that I could not remember to any degree of accuracy where the park actually was and might not be able to find it, but I was not going to tell that to David. To my great delight, after we had been running for what seemed an age and were just beginning to gasp for breath, some brightly painted swings appeared in the distance. My sense of achievement was complete. Such was my exhilaration that I never noticed the car which suddenly converged upon us until a firm hand on the back of my dress whisked me through the air and deposited me on a car seat. Two minutes later we were once again safely behind the six-foot walls. In fact we were in my father's study receiving a ceremonial thrashing with his slipper. The grand adventure ended in ignominy. Never again did David allow himself to be carried along by my insatiable curiosity.

One Christmas the daily help invited David and me to her house on Boxing Day. It was a damp, chilly afternoon and I slid my hands in hers and huddled close as the iron gate clanged shut behind us and we set off down into the town. In the foggy haze of a winter afternoon each street seemed much like the next, row upon row of terraced houses and nowhere any sign of a tree or a garden. We suddenly turned left into yet another tiny cobbled street and stopped abruptly outside a bottle-green door. She pushed it open and for me it might have been the opening of Pandora's box.

Inside was the brightest, cosiest little world I had ever seen, like something from one of the story books I read. No hall, just this tiny living room with its glowing coal fire and in the corner a vast Christmas tree, shimmering with dozens of coloured balls. I had never seen anything so beautiful before. We huddled round the fire, pulled crackers and ate mince pies.

'One day, I'm going to have a home like this,' I told myself, as we went out into the fog and trudged back up the hill to the big house at the top.

When I was nine years old everything changed. We moved away from the constant ringing of telephone and door-bell into a standard semi in what was regarded as a nice part of Gateshead. Vicky, my sister, was born and I suspect she was something of a surprise. My parents promised to provide her with a companion, but she cried mercilessly night after night for years and in penance had to grow up alone. This time there was no nanny. My mother reminded us continually that a doctor's salary did not stretch as far as it once did. We played in the street with other children and got the bus to school by ourselves.

For this tiny glimpse of normality there was a price to pay. The time had come for us to begin our Hebrew instruction. We had never mixed with other Jewish children, and it worried my mother. She rang the rabbi who had married her. Of course we could join his *cheder*, his Hebrew school. There was plenty of room in the beginners' class. Only two hours on a Sunday morning. It was enough to start with. What had kept her so long from taking an interest in her children's Jewish education?

'Two hours on a Sunday morning,' David groaned. 'Do we have to?'

'It does seem a bit much,' my father said mildly.

'Oh you, if it depended on you a right pair of little *Goyim* we'd have.' My mother, like most Jews, interspersed her sentences with Yiddish words when roused. That her children should grow up as *Goyim*, with no knowledge of their heritage, was the worst threat she could hold over my father's head. She had given up on him by now. He kept some of the traditions, such as the Sabbath, to keep the peace and because it was part of our family life, but being a Jew was never allowed to interfere with either his professionalism as a doctor or his leisure. My parents had countless arguments over his Saturday morning surgery and afternoon trips to the football match.

'You want me to give up medicine and peddle cheap souvenirs, do you?' he asked Mother one day in utter exasperation. The veiled reference to one of her closest friends who had given up his medical studies when he married into a very orthodox family and was prevailed upon to accept a partnership in their china business, finally silenced my mother on that point. But every Jewish mother knows there is a time to put her foot down, and that moment had just arrived.

'I may not be as good a Jew as I would have liked,' she said, casting a withering look in my father's direction, 'but my children will be!'

One Sunday morning she straightened David's tie and patted the bow on the back of my dress for the umpteenth time, then deposited us on the synagogue steps, dressed up like china dolls in a glass cabinet. We were ushered by the rabbi's two daughters into a large airy hall, filled with small groups of children whose chatter died away as the strangers appeared.

'Name? Date of birth?' The dark, ferocious-looking daughter with hairy arms recalled my attention. 'Do you know your alphabet?'

'What a stupid question,' I thought. 'At our age, of course we do.' I looked at David. He did not move, and his bright-blue eyes looked enormous. I nodded for both of us.

'Then read me this.'

A large book was shoved under my nose filled with the strangest hieroglyphics I had ever seen. I looked up helplessly.

'Then you don't read Hebrew?'

I bit my lip.

'Ah well,' she sighed, softening a little, 'I don't know what parents are coming to these days. I suppose we must begin at the beginning. Turn the book round, we read from right to left, and let's start with "aleph".'

Aleph, bet, daled . . . After one lesson I could string two or three consonants together with a couple of vowels; after two lessons I could manage a short Hebrew word, and after five or six a short sentence was quite possible.

'When do they teach you what it means?' I whispered to a fellow student when the teacher's back was turned. His friendly face became a total blank. He shrugged in response. I waited and nothing happened, so I asked the teacher.

'Well, my little one, do you want to run before you can walk? As long as you can read your prayer book what else matters? And then, after all, we are only women, you and I.'

I thought of how my mother hated going to the synagogue with my father because he always let her down. She would watch him from the women's gallery, laughing and joking with his friends downstairs, fumbling through the prayer book and digging them in the ribs when he lost the place. Everyone knew that almost everyone else could not translate a word of what they were reading, no matter how fluent it sounded, but they at least read Hebrew well enough not to lose the place. My father never even attempted to hide his unfamiliarity with it all, that was what riled her. A decent show of piety would have kept her happy, but Father enjoyed her annoyance much too much for that. She lived in dread of the day the rabbi would bestow the great honour of inviting him up onto the *bimah*, the raised platform, to read a portion of the law from the silver-encased scrolls. On that day his folly really would be plain for all to see. But I had the sneaking suspicion that should it happen, my father would rise to the occasion as he always did. Besides, our Sabbath attendance was far too spasmodic for that event ever to occur.

'You two had better be good pupils,' she said, whenever we complained that Hebrew classes were boring, 'or you'll end up like your father.'

'Didn't you ever go to *cheder*?' we asked him in wonder.

'Well, your grandmother thought I did,' he said with a grin, 'but I hardly ever got there. There was more fun to be had on the beach at Redcar with our ukuleles. And then, if I happened to catch your aunt Vera in Notoriani's Ice Cream Parlour with one of her young men, she'd have to buy my silence.'

'The beach at Redcar! Notoriani's Ice Cream Parlour! Lucky so-and-so! If I were to truant where would I go? Just my luck to get found out the first time anyway,' I thought as I huddled closer to the paraffin heater in the synagogue kitchen, watching the steam rise from my sodden mackintosh. Mr Rosenberg's class now, that was where being a studious pupil had got me, promotion! Two hours on a Sunday morning was not enough. *Cheder* now devours one hour, three evenings a week as well. My feet squelch in my shoes. I hug my stomach in a vain effort to stifle the inner rumblings. I suppose I could try and do some homework while I wait for the class to start. My fingers are too numb to write. I can hardly see the clock. There seems to be more Tyneside fog in the room than out.

Five o'clock at last! Thank goodness for that – time for prayer drill. Every evening the same! Boys line up at the front facing Israel, girls sit quietly at the desks. The boys are learning to be men. One day they'll wind phylacteries on their arms and foreheads morning and evening and recite the ancient prayers in their homes. Dad doesn't, but Uncle Solly does. I've seen him. In fact he likes us to watch him. He sways about muttering to himself and looking holy. It's called *davening*. I wonder if swaying helps you to pray? Mum says Uncle Solly has bacon for breakfast after he's said his prayers so God never listens to him anyway. I wonder why he doesn't listen to women either. It seems a bit unfair. Bet I could *daven* as well as any of the boys.

'Sir,' said Peter, an outsized boy, who was obviously squeezed into his short trousers every morning and ballooned out of every exit, 'are you sure Israel's in this direction?' He was staring at some graffiti on the beige gloss wall until he was cross-eyed.

'Pity,' he continued, no response forthcoming, 'if it was over in that direction we could face the window.'

Mr Rosenberg looked up and caught sight of the huge piece of pink bubble-gum which bloated the boy's mouth. He watched it revolving round and round as if it were his washing at the launderette, opened his mouth, but said nothing. Either he was mesmerised, or, noticing the tie flung over one shoulder and the skullcap hanging limply over one ear, decided not to take on yet another hopeless case. 'Continue your praying,' he snapped.

As Peter turned back to the wall his eyes met mine. He rolled them to the ceiling, made a strange gobbling sound, then, his back to me, began to rock backwards and forwards. The pages of his prayer book flicked over at an unbelievable speed. Two minutes later, which was the record in our class for a passage in the prayer book which normally takes about fifteen minutes to recite, he stopped instantly, then walked back to his seat with a grin.

'Not bad, eh?' he asked, looking over in my direction. 'I can pray like the rabbi's son too!'

'Open your books at page twenty and we will begin our translation. Abraham, if you remember, is journeying through the wilderness.'

'Not still, Sir. He was doing that last week. In fact, he was doing that last year.' With a self-congratulatory smile, Alan, whose ears stuck horizontally out from his head and served as hinges for his school cap, looked round for our approval. He was always in trouble. I lost count of the times that the broad grin which stretched the whole breadth of his face would be wiped out by a sudden violent slap, when Mr Rosenberg's patience was strained beyond all endurance. The cocky little lad would break out into the most nerve-grating howling, and Mr Rosenberg, embarrassed by his sudden lack of control, and even more by the terrible din, would cover him in kisses.

'Ugh,' he said one day, wiping his face with the corner of his sleeve, 'I think I'd rather have his slaps.'

Mr Rosenberg was reputed to be the most learned Jewish scholar in the North-East. If he was, it was wasted on us. We thought him the oldest man alive, and he was about forty-five at the time. Everything about him was bird-like: his little beak of a nose and balding round head, the grey goatee beard resting on his swollen chest, the tiny, beady, black eyes peering at you through bottle-bottom spectacles which periodically slipped down his nose and were lifted by a sudden facial contortion, so that you never knew if he held you in utter disdain, or had just smelled a rather nasty smell.

'Malchah, continue translating.' Malchah was my Hebrew name after my pious great-great-grandmother, but half the girls in the class were Malchah too. It struck me that Jewish parents must have been a bit hard-pressed to find Hebrew names for their daughters. 'Boys, listen to Malchah. Her translation is always faultless.'

'Little squirt,' murmured Peter, to my immense satisfaction. Only I knew that I could not translate a single word. Mr Rosenberg read the translation at the beginning of the class, and, having a reasonable memory, I simply learnt it parrot-fashion.

The boredom of such an exercise was excruciating. Any avenue of escape was worth a try.

'Please, Sir, can I be excused?'

'You, Malchah? I'm surprised, but of course.'

I ran upstairs, savouring every minute of freedom, dawdling as long as I dared, then ambled nonchalantly back into the classroom.

'And the blessing?' Mr Rosenberg's words halted me in my track back to my desk.

'Blessing, Sir?'

'Yes, blessing, the one for after . . .! You may come to the front of the class and read it for us all.' In Judaism there is a blessing for every occasion, a journey, a visit, fruit from the ground, fruit from the tree. Mr Rosenberg made sure we knew them all, but up until that moment that particular one had escaped my notice. It seemed to me to be the longest in the prayer book. There had to be other ways of killing time.

'Please, Sir, tell us a Bible story.'

'Please, Sir, why do Jewish boys have to have that operation, you know?'

'Please, Sir, who was Jesus Christ?' To my horror the room

went deadly silent. What had I said? Why was everyone looking at me? 'P-p-please, Sir,' I stammered, 'it was only that the girls at school tell me that I killed him, so I was just wondering . . .'

Mr Rosenberg seemed to swell before my very eyes and I thought he was going to burst. I had never seen such anger before.

'Never,' he hissed, 'never let me hear that name on the lips of a Jewish girl.'

I sat down. Mr Rosenberg cleared his throat and the class continued in an uncomfortable sort of a way.

I had a fascination for God and continued to afflict Mr Rosenberg with my endless questioning. The trouble was I do not think he could distinguish genuine searching from the distraction technique we all employed. And so I never received a satisfactory answer.

'Why must we always say the right blessing for everything?'

'Because the essence of Judaism is to show our constant devotion to God.'

'But Sir, what if you don't know whether the fruit grows on a tree or in the ground, how can you say the right blessing then?' Alan butted in and waited for the laughter. He always spoilt things.

'But,' I continued, desperately trying to regain Mr Rosenberg's attention, 'how do we please God?'

'You learn the Torah, Malchah, the five books of Moses, the laws of our people, and you keep them.'

'Five books? But Sir, we still haven't finished the first one. We'll never get there.'

'You worry too much . . . for a girl.'

One day Mr Rosenberg asked me to stay behind after the end of the class. 'Malchah,' he said, wrinkling up his nose so that he could peer at me more closely through his spectacles, 'I have a great privilege for you. Since your translation is so faultless, since you have such a desire to learn, you shall be the first girl to study for my Torah Diploma.'

'Oh, er, thank you, Sir,' I muttered and backed out of the room. I could hardly refuse. What had I let myself in for?

I need not have worried. I soon discovered that the Diploma involved a written rather than a verbal examination of our Hebrew translation, no more than that. While the rest of the class continued to appal Mr Rosenberg with their ignorance, I was sent into the next room with the rabbi's son to transcribe on to paper what was recorded on the tape in my head. Within twenty minutes I marched back into the classroom and proudly presented Mr Rosenberg with my work. He scanned the page, making all kinds of unintelligible grunting noises. Suddenly they stopped and then he gasped, 'Malchah, what have you done?'

I peered at my paper over his shoulder. What had I done?

'There,' he whispered in horror, 'look there.'

I followed the long bony finger and read, 'G.o.d. God. It says God.'

'I know what it says. Please do not add to your shame by letting that word pass your lips. Never, except in the most earnest prayer do we use the name of the Holy One, blessed be he.'

'Oh I see. That's why when we read the Scriptures we call him "*Ha'shem*", the Name, rather than . . .'

'Of course,' Mr Rosenberg snapped, interrupting me before I could say the inevitable '*Adonai*'. 'Nor dare we write it in full in English.'

I watched him take a tiny penknife from his jacket pocket and cut a square out of the paper all round the letter 'o'.

'In future you will write G dash d. Do you understand?'

I nodded and wandered to a seat, dumb with amazement. Did God mind what we called him? Did he really require such a pointless exercise?

Somehow Mother discovered that Mr Rosenberg lived quite near us and it was only polite to offer him a lift to and from the *cheder* on Sunday mornings. David and I were hardly pleased. As if it was not bad enough having him in the car for what seemed an endless quarter of an hour, Father would keep up a constant banter on religious matters. We could tell from Mr Rosenberg's rather uncomfortable shuffle and the fixed smile on his face that he did not quite share Father's sense of humour, but could not be rude because he was getting a lift. He must have known my father was not a very religious Jew, but I desperately hoped he would not see how bad he really was. Sometimes I thought Father set out to shock him deliberately and was almost under the back seat with embarrassment when we drove up to Mr Rosenberg's gate.

One day his wife was waiting to meet him. I was staggered. She was dainty and pretty and looked young enough to be his daughter.

'Oh, Mum,' I said when we arrived home, 'you should see Mr Rosenberg's wife. She's so pretty and has lovely red hair.'

Mother smiled. 'She may do, I suppose.'

'May do? What do you mean?'

'Her hair is not her own. She wears a *sheitel*, a wig. When very orthodox women marry they shave their heads, then keep them covered for the rest of their lives.'

I could hardly take it in.

Mother looked at my horror-stricken face then laughed. 'And her marriage will have been arranged for her. A learned man is considered a good catch amongst the ultra-orthodox.'

Any pretensions I might have had to becoming a more orthodox Jew evaporated in that instant. God could ask too much.

With immense relief I left Hebrew classes after three years, with a Diploma for fluent Hebrew reading, a Diploma in knowledge of the Torah, and a whole load of unanswered questions. David was not so lucky! He had a *Bar Mitzvah* to come. It would be the most important moment of his life, when, in the eyes of the entire Jewish community, he would become a man. On that day, when he stood up in the synagogue before all his aunts, uncles, cousins and distant relatives, to sing a portion of the Torah, he had to be word perfect, an immense undertaking for a thirteen-year-old.

Individual Hebrew instruction was the only concession to his having any importance on the occasion at all. Mother had been rushing around frantically for months, arranging caterers for a Sabbath luncheon, choosing menus and finding a band for a Sunday afternoon tea dance, trying desperately to kindle some interest in my father, who only reacted when he saw the caterer's estimate.

'What am I, Rothschild? With two daughters to see wed, and you want two hundred at a *Bar Mitzvah* tea party? Where do you find so many relatives? All yours, you realise? Hitler put paid to most of mine.'

'Some of the ones that survive are bad enough.'

'Yours are so wonderful?'

'Shut up and pass me the seating plan. Now we can't have Uncle Solly and Uncle Myer at the same table. Everyone knows they haven't been speaking for years. Oh, by the way, there's a bill in the post from Books Fashion House. Well, you do have a wife and two daughters to clothe, and after all, it's father's cousins' business, so we do get a good discount.'

Mother liked to keep her money in the family, and the family liked to keep it there too! We had barely opened the dress shop door, when half a dozen harpies swooped on her and carried her off to the model gowns department. I wandered round on my own, fingering the rows of satin and lace, when suddenly I noticed the dress of my dreams. It was a frothy, frilly creation in royal blue chiffon, just like the dress worn by Snow White in Walt Disney's film. I had never worn frills before. Mother preferred to hide my ever-increasing puppy fat in what she called 'something tailored', usually beige and ugly. I took the dress down from the rail and got it on as quickly as I could, then rushed to find Mother who, clad only in bra and corset, was shouting instructions to the entire department.

'Well, Mum?' I said, and twirled round, waiting for her approval. 'Isn't this just it?'

She stopped in mid-sentence and glanced in my direction. 'It's a bit revealing, isn't it?'

'Not really. It's just that I'm a bit high-busted.'

'She has got a lovely figure for her age,' said one of the harpies, suddenly aware of a possible sale in another direction.

'You mean she's got a big bust?' my mother shouted from somewhere within a sequinned tube. 'Well, you should know. It's your side of the family she gets it from. No, I can't have you looking like a barmaid.'

Eventually I persuaded her to let me have a bit cut off the hem and sewn across the offending cleavage, and by the time we went home, leaving garments strewn all over the shop, everyone was happy.

As the great day approached, presents began to arrive in a steady stream. Five writing cases, seven alarm clocks, nine fountain pens. They all had to be laid out for the guests to see, without Aunty Sadie noticing that her present was an inferior version of Aunty Hilda's. In our more modest house, space provided something of a problem. But for a *Bar Mitzvah* all things were possible. The official photographer, the arranger of plastic flowers, relations, waitresses, caterers with vast tureens of chopped liver and chopped herring which they mixed by hand, all fought their way into every available corner. David and I goggled. We had never seen anyone elbow-deep in chopped liver before. Somehow I could not manage to eat any at the buffet.

'What a big girl you're getting, so like her mummy.'

There it went again, a refrain heard so many times that day that I was tempted to join in.

'Soon there'll be a boyfriend and then, please God, a wedding. That will be the next family do. Nothing like a *simcha* for bringing the family together.'

'She's time enough,' Father answered for me, to my great relief, thinking of his bank balance.

David, scrubbed and cropped, in a suit for the first time, wore a vague expression of, disbelief, as if everything seemed to be happening to someone else. Like a wooden soldier he stuck out an arm to greet his guests, escorted his mother out for the first dance and read his after-dinner speech.

'I would like to thank my wonderful parents for all they have done for me.' Mother had written it! Never mind, she still sat behind a valium-induced haze and lapped up the applause.

I felt sick inside, but why on earth should I? There were relatives here I had not seen for years, some from Israel I had never seen before. This was David's big day and I hated every minute of it. What was it all for, the effort, the expense? David would be the same tomorrow as he was today. There were some things about our religion I really did not understand. One thing was sure. No one else seemed to feel the same. They were all having a good time. Something must be wrong with me. I put it out of my mind, too frightened to delve any deeper.

3

Jewish daughters are supposed to learn all they really need to know, not from classes, but from their mothers. And what else does a Jewish daughter need to know except how to get herself a good catch and keep him happy?

'Your father's not a wealthy man,' my mother said with a regretful shake of the head. 'There's not much of a dowry for you. You'll have to get by on your cooking.'

If all her hard work and effort had been amply rewarded, I should have married a Rothschild at least. By the time I was fourteen there was nothing I did not know about Jewish cuisine and keeping a *kosher* kitchen.

'Stand here and watch . . . Stir this . . . beat that . . . How many times have you salted the meat? Do it again. There must be no trace of blood in the rinsing water . . . Make the Yorkshire puddings – with water, not milk . . . No, we can't have cheese sauce. How many times must I tell you, we can't mix meat and dairy produce?'

In interpreting the law which said, 'Thou shalt not boil a kid in its mother's milk,' my mother never went to the lengths which some of her friends did – separate dishes for milk and meat, separate sinks, separate tea towels, separate dish washers, if you could rise to it – but nevertheless she refused to serve the two together at a meal. She insisted her kitchen should be *kosher* and only bought her meat from a *kosher* butcher.

'Why bother,' my father murmured, whenever she complained about the price of *kosher* meat, 'there's only one way to slit an animal's throat and let the blood drain out, whoever the slaughterer is.'

Yet Mother persisted in the belief that every Jewish man would only know true peace of mind when he was sure his wife kept a strictly *kosher* kitchen and would serve him *gefüllte* fish on the Sabbath. The latter was an unwritten law. Great-grandma always served it on *Shabbas*. So did Grandma. So, inevitably, did Mother. And since our washing was always hung to dry on a rack hanging from the kitchen ceiling, it was just as inevitable that we would go to school on Monday morning smelling like chopped, fried fish balls.

Yiddishkeit, not Judaism, that was what really mattered to my mother and her friends. You could be as ignorant about your religion as you chose, reject whatever ritual you found tiresome, never attend the synagogue, as long as you had that elusive, indescribable feel for the Jewish way of life. Tradition mattered more than piety. All that was required of a good Jewess was to pass on to her daughters the ability to create a real Jewish home, just as it had been for generations. Here was the key to the stability of the Jewish family and the survival of the race.

'Ah, but there is something very special about the Jewish home,' or that is what I am always told. So many non-Jewish people revere and romanticise it that I am sure they know something I do not. And so many Jews succumb to its extraordinary influence, that no matter how old they are, or how far away, they are inextricably bound to it by a thousand emotional threads. How can I explain it? Our home was not exactly average, but nor was it untypical. 'We don't do that, we're Jewish,' was a refrain I heard many times. I did not want to be different. I wanted to be just like my friends, but somehow being Jewish did make me feel special. That was what home gave to me, a sense of destiny, despite the frustrations the feeling that it was rather a privilege to be a Jew, and not just an embarrassing freak of birth. After all, if Hitler had had his way, so I was told, or the many other tyrants and nations who had tried to get rid of my ancestors, I would not have existed at all. I was one of a chosen people, chosen by whom and for what I could not understand, but that did not worry me at first. We had our own festivals and celebrations which none of my schoolfriends knew anything about. They belonged to us and were a secret bond between us, linking us to each other and every Jew, near or far, long since dead, or yet to come.

The only Christian festival for which I envied my schoolfriends was Christmas. The rest seemed terribly dull. I would have loved a Christmas tree of my own, dripping with shimmering baubles, and fairy lights twinkling round the front door. Mother bought a *kosher* turkey, since the occasion was technically a bank holiday, but I was sure it was not quite the same as having crackers and decorations. Then, everyone shared in Christmas; we had parties and a tree at school. So perhaps our festivals were more magic after all.

David and I were at a great disadvantage when it came to understanding what they all meant. Mr Rosenberg reckoned Mother would explain them, but Mother never could remember which was which, or why she was doing what.

'What's this one about, Mum?' we asked her one December, grinning at one another, as she lit her *menorah*, the nine-branched candelabra, checking that each of the tiny candles was absolutely vertical, so that no wax could drip on the brass and ruin the display.

'Er, Esther,' she said vaguely.

'Wrong,' we shouted triumphantly.

'Something to do with the temple?' she asked hopefully.

'Yes,' we prompted.

'Somebody's oil lasted eight days.'

'Whose?'

'Elijah's?'

We looked unconvinced. 'Does Judas Maccabeus ring a bell?'

No glimmer of recognition passed her face.

'Mum, *Chanukah*, the Feast of Lights is all about his heroic defence of the temple. His tiny drop of oil lasted eight days. It was a miracle.'

'Well, whoever it was I wish he'd never started this business, because now we have to do it every year.'

Mother regarded most of the major Jewish holy days as an affliction to be endured. She carried out the traditions as if the appeasement of God's wrath depended on it; not because it gave her any real sense of spiritual comfort, but because that was the way things had always been done in her family. The arrival of September filled her with dismay.

'Three Jewish holidays, three in four weeks, and I haven't started to think, cook, clean or anything.'

Rosh Hashanah, the New Year, is the first of the three and supposed to be one of the most important occasions. Dressed up in our new finery David and I would sit in the synagogue waiting with great anticipation for the weird sound of the ram's-horn. Producing any sound at all on the *shofar* is no mean achievement. I have witnessed very few convincing performances. One New Year the rabbi blew so hard he turned purple and we thought he was bound to collapse, but still nothing happened. Steadying his hat, and summoning every ounce of dignity he possessed, he drew his breath, then gave the thing everything he had got. Out came a shrill, cracked little squeak. The respectful silence was suddenly shattered by the raucous laughter of a child, who could not hold it in any longer. I was glad it was not me. The rabbi removed the ram's-horn from his mouth and fixed the young renegade with a stare, which instantly turned him to stone. We all watched for a further quarter of an hour, twiddled our thumbs, stared at the ceiling, coughed politely behind our prayer books, but the instrument refused to co-operate, so no joyous sound heralded that *Rosh Hashanah*.

Some time during the following week, like most other Jews, we paid our annual visit to the family graves. It struck me as an awfully morbid and boring prelude to *Yom Kippur*, the Day of Atonement. Everyone stood around looking so sheepish. Flowers are never left on Jewish graves, so no one seemed to know what to do with their feelings. They rubbed the gravel with the toes of their shoes, read and re-read the inscriptions on the stone slabs, as if they might have changed since last year.

'Do you think we used the right wording, dear?'

'Have they been dead that long, God rest their souls? Where do the years go?'

When we were small, we sat in the car outside the cemetery and waited. The adults emerged looking very serious and blinking.

'What did you do, Dad?'

'I said a prayer.'

We had driven fifty miles to Teesside, dragged the local rabbi away from his fireside chair on a Sunday afternoon, had hung around for what seemed an eternity on a biting autumnal day.

'Couldn't you have said it at home?'

'Yes.'

No explanation! There never was. That was something I never grew up to accept.

Yom Kippur is the most solemn occasion in the Jewish calendar.

41

It is one of several fast days, but the only one my mother insisted we keep. Once I was twelve no sip of water was to pass my lips from sundown to sundown. It is supposed to be a day for confessing one's sins to God and making New Year's resolutions. I found it hard in my early teens to know exactly what my sins were, so I went to the synagogue for light relief, rather than the right religious reasons. On fast days there had to be compensations. There was nothing to pass the time at home.

'Who do you think will be the first to faint and be carried out this year, David?'

'I bet it's Peter again.'

'He just does it to show off.'

'All right then, how much do you bet?'

We waited with ghoulish anticipation for the first victim of hunger to crumple into a heap. Last year it was a man, it usually was, and we women had a bird's eye view from the upstairs gallery. You knew when it happened. Everything went quiet. Even Gran stopped moaning for a cup of tea. Then the service was resumed with more chatter, shuffling, yawning, stretching and tummy-rumbling than ever.

One part of the service always enthralled me. The chatter died down, the children stopped whizzing their Dinky toys around the wooden seats and an awed hush descended on the congregation. Several of the men downstairs, the *Cohanim*, or priests, covered their heads with their prayer shawls and, swaying in harmony, chanted a blessing on the people just like the priests in the temple of old. No one was supposed to look, but I was fascinated by the haunting sound and uncanny sight of all those writhing pieces of white satin beneath us.

From that moment on, the ladies' gallery began to empty. One mother after another was lured away to her kitchen by overpowering thoughts of roast chicken, chopped herring, luscious desserts and all the ritual preparations for breaking the fast. Food always tasted marvellous on that night. It was amazing how much you could put away, once your tummy had been cajoled into coping with the onslaught by a glass of milk and soda water. What would it be tonight? The drooling anticipation became almost unbearable until at last the ram's-horn put us all out of our misery and the synagogue emptied as it never did on any other day. Why linger to chat when there would be food on the table?

Succoth, the Feast of Booths or Harvest, came just after the New Year and the Day of Atonement and suffered for it. By that time it was very difficult to take yet more holiday from work and school, so it more or less passed us by at home.

'Dad, build us a booth in the garden.'

'A what?'

'Well, a kind of wooden shed will do. All Jews are supposed to have them.'

David and I envisaged moving into it for eight days, the duration of the festival, with sleeping bags and pyjamas to spend several nights under the stars.

'Your father, build a shed! Are you crazy? He can barely even change a plug!'

We looked from Mother to Father, hoping he would defy her words, but no luck. We would have to be satisfied with what *cheder* would do for us. They marched us out, one class at a time, into a rickety, makeshift contraption in the grounds, which looked as if it might collapse if we sneezed. Branches and twigs with bits of plastic fruit and flowers attached to them hung down from above and threatened to throttle you if you did not watch your step. Mr Rosenberg, his little chest puffed out until he looked as plump and round as a well-fed robin, presented each of us with a glass of lemonade and a plain biscuit. The proper blessing said, we were allowed to indulge. We kept our eyes on the lemonade as long as we could, then someone looked up and we all had to hide our helpless, ungrateful giggling behind the plastic greenery.

Mother only insisted we attend the synagogue on major festivals, but since she rarely came with us, even that seemed a bit much at times. One festival was too good to be missed however – *Purim*, the Feast of Esther. The synagogue was quite noisy on most occasions, with people coming and going and kissing their relatives as they came or went, but the rabbi only stopped the service when he could no longer hear what he was saying himself. He would rest his elbows on the pulpit and, tapping his foot with a look of mock weariness on his face, stare at the women's gallery, where most of the noise was coming from, until the realisation dawned that the service had come to a standstill and a temporary, penitent silence would descend. But at *Purim* the more noise the better. As the rabbi recounted the famous story of Esther, we booed with all our might every time the name Haman was mentioned, and cheered loudly for Esther and Mordecai. *Cheder* once inflicted a *Purim* play on the parents. Mr Rosenberg gave me permission to join another class for the great event. I was so excited. Stardom at last! And then I realised I was only wanted as a walk-on extra, a Babylonian soldier. They are not even mentioned in the story.

Of all the festivals, the Passover was the favourite. It made the others seem almost insignificant. Eight days without cake, biscuits or cornflakes, eight days craving for things you never normally ate, eight days of Mother complaining of chronic constipation – I cannot think why I liked the Passover at all, except that the first two nights, known as the *Seder* or 'service' nights, made up for everything. Everybody had to be there, Gran, Grandpa, aunts, uncles, the whole family came together to celebrate the deliverance of our people from slavery in Egypt three thousand years ago.

Every year followed an invariable pattern. That was part of the fun. You knew exactly what was coming.

'We can't start, we can't start,' panted Gran, as she opened the front door. She was back in the kitchen before we were over the front doorstep.

'The meringue isn't risen and Mark's in the bath.'

'He would be, of course,' exploded my mother. 'You get out of· there, and quick,' she yelled, in the direction of the raucous singing.

'All right, dearest sister,' the reply mimicked her voice exactly.

'And stop the racket!'

'Just practising for the occasion, you know.'

The sound of laughter and splashing and scale singing continued. Mother shrugged her shoulders and made for the nearest armchair.

'Let me sit down. What a week! I couldn't stand that again. I'm worn out.'

She flopped down in the armchair next to Grandpa's. He was hunched, as he always was, over the two-bar electric fire, trying to achieve what his circulation no longer could and put some feeling of warmth into his hands.

'Uh-huh,' was all he ever said, but it was enough for his daughter.

'The price of the Passover food this year. And no one ever has everything you want. I went to Cohen's for cheese, and Steinberg's for chocolate, and Bloom's for orange squash.'

David, fired by the thought of the huge cardboard box, packed to the brim with jars, boxes, packets and tins, which had been deposited on our doorstep during the week, suddenly said, 'I thought you could eat anything which didn't have something in it to make it rise.'

'Right,' I said, knowingly, 'we can't eat leaven.'

David was silent, then he said, 'Does cheese have leaven in it, or squash, or jam?'

Father, at the other end of the room, looked up at us over the top of the *Evening News*. 'No, they don't,' he said, with a sideways glance at my mother, 'but at Passover time you can only buy them from shops where they have the special "*kosher* for Passover" label.'

'That means the rabbi has watched it being made and blessed it,' said David, incredulously, 'so what difference does that make?'

'A great deal, it doubles the price!'

Father had very little time for the *Beth Din's* system of sanctioning *kosher* food. 'The Death Bin', he called it. 'They'd sanction anything at a price.'

'Now Manny,' Gran paused at the door, half-way back to the kitchen, 'you know we have to do things properly. I've always expected it of my daughter.' Father disappeared behind the newspaper. 'And incidentally,' she said, looking at Mother, 'you have soaked the glassware, haven't you?'

'Yes, Mam.'

'And changed over to the Passover set of crockery?'

'Yes, Mam.'

'And checked every corner for the tiniest breadcrumbs?'

'Why do you think I'm so exhausted?'

I could not help but smile. One tradition we dispensed with in our house was the father's torchlight search, followed by his children, for any bit of leaven which may have escaped the spring-cleaning. Father regarded it as a futile exercise, since no self-respecting breadcrumb would ever dare defy the daily help's vacuum cleaner or my mother's meticulous inspection.

'Good evening, everybody,' Mark appeared, ruddy and polished. 'A kiss from the children, and then we'll begin.'

'About time,' Mother scowled, resenting the way her younger brother always controlled the evening's events.

We made our way to the table, and what a table it was! The cloth was bleached until it dazzled and crinkled when you moved up against it. The best silver had been polished until you could see your own reflection quite clearly. Each person had a tiny silver wine goblet, which shimmered in the candlelight. An embroidered coverlet, draped over three pieces of unleavened bread, added a startling dash of scarlet and sapphire. David and I took our places, wide-eyed and open-mouthed.

'What's that for?' asked David, pointing at an egg with a burn mark on its shell, lying on the dish of Passover symbols in the middle of the table. We were so used to seeing these peculiarities every year that it was some time before we looked at them and realised we did not have a clue what they meant. Even if an explanation had been given we always forgot it in the twelve intervening months.

'That symbolises the temple which was destroyed many years ago. Some rabbis think it speaks of hope and new life too,' explained Mark.

'And what's that?' David was pointing at the bone which lay next to it.

'That represents the lamb which used to be sacrificed for our sins in the temple at Passover-time. And of course the lambs whose blood was daubed on the doorposts of the homes of the children of Israel.'

'And what's this?' David picked up a piece of parsley.

'That reminds us of the hyssop which daubed the blood on.'

'And this?'

'David, do be quiet and wait,' snapped Mother. 'Where are the *Haggadahs*?' She looked on the sideboard for the books with the evening's service in them, but Mark was already handing them out.

'Don't give me that one, I had it last year and the print is far too small.'

'Who has mine, the one with the wine stain on page fifty-two?'

'Someone scribbled in this one last year.'

'I want the one with the colour pictures of the plagues.'

'Damn, I've forgotten my reading glasses.' Father fumbled in his pockets.

Mother groaned. 'Will somebody please start.'

'All right then, David, off you go,' said Mark, 'ask the four questions.'

'Which four?' said David.

He knew very well which four. In fact this was his moment of glory, when everyone's attention is focused on the youngest male child, whose questions form the basis for the whole evening service. But he could not resist bantering with Uncle Mark.

'Any four you like,' Mark replied.

We opened our *Haggadahs*, the appropriate opening blessings were made, Gran lit the candles, then David read out the famous four questions:

'Why is this night different from all other nights and why do we eat unleavened bread?

'Why do we eat bitter herbs instead of vegetables?

'Why do we dip in the dish twice?

'Why do we eat leaning?'

'And why do you ask the same questions every year?' grinned Mark, 'because you always get the same answer.'

Grandpa began to read the long, learned, rabbinic explanation from the *Haggadah*. The word 'Haggadah' means 'telling', because it tells the story of our flight from Egypt, but I never could remember what all the answers were. He got slower and slower until his words were strung together in one loud snore. I was never sure whether the cushions my grandmother put on his chair to prop him up were an attempt to pretend he was leaning, or a last valiant effort to keep him awake.

'For goodness sake take over,' Gran shouted at Mark, 'or we'll be here all night.'

'Not yet, he's not quite asleep.'

'Ooh look!' David exclaimed, holding up his *Haggadah*. 'Look at this picture of the Egyptian soldiers in the middle of the Red Sea. If I pull this tab, see, the waters roll back over them, and they're all drowned.'

'Gruesome little beggar, isn't he?' Mark said, staring at the pictures with fascination.

There was another snore from the head of the table and then Uncle Mark began to sing – in perfect Hebrew. I could hear Mr Rosenberg's voice: 'Your uncle Mark, how he sings, what diction, what delivery, what pronunciation! He sings in a way I rarely hear today, just like the *Chasidim*, the orthodox of the orthodox, the most beautiful there is.'

He did have a marvellous voice. You could not help but be

impressed. Gran looked at him, one moment full of fond admiration, and the next filled with acute aggravation, as he stopped mid-flow to discuss the latest progress of Newcastle United with my father.

'Continue,' she snapped, and when he did she continued her conversation with my mother behind their *Haggadahs*.

'What a terrible time we had in Egypt,' murmured Grandpa. Everyone looked up in surprise. 'Such things we had to endure.' Strangely enough, it did seem as if it all happened yesterday.

My father suddenly started giggling like a naughty schoolboy. Mark's teasing always had that effect on him. He caught Gran's eye, cleared his throat, then muttered, 'We were slaves in Egypt . . .'

'Manny,' said Gran, with an air of injured dignity, 'you aren't by any chance reading the English translation are you? We don't do that in this house. We're Orthodox, not Reform, here.'

I knew Father had attended the new Reform Synagogue in Newcastle once or twice to see what it was like. Their services were half in English and they only kept the basic Jewish traditions. That appealed to him. He had tried to hide his recent interest but nothing escaped his mother-in-law.

'Dreadful wine this,' Mother chipped in, 'whoever trod on this lot forgot to wash his feet.'

'Well, drink up your second cup, sister dear, because then there's a treat in store.'

It was time for the bitter herbs. Grandpa came to with a grunt, saw everyone staring at the Passover dish and picked up the large piece of horseradish root. He shaved off miniature matchsticks and passed them round. I kept passing them on until I ended up with the tiniest sliver.

'You're supposed to be able to taste it,' Gran said, peering at the tiny speck on my palm, 'and it isn't meant to taste nice. It's to remind you of all your ancestors suffered in Egypt.'

Everyone dipped their horseradish into a bowl of grey mess called *charoseth*. Ugh! It was made of good things like wine, apples and walnuts, but it was meant to be the mortar the Israelites used and to me that was exactly how it tasted.

Then we ate a sandwich of horseradish and *charoseth* between two small pieces of *matzo*. That was supposed to be one of the bricks the children of Israel had made. No wonder it seemed to Grandpa as if the exodus happened last year.

Only one more endurance test before the meal, a bowl of hard-boiled eggs floating in salt water, the eyes and tears of my ancestors. I had to concentrate on keeping it down. I could not bear egg in any form. From now on Grandpa had to be watched. He drew out the middle piece of the three pieces of *matzo* under the coverlet and broke it in half. One half was the *afikomen*, symbol of the Passover lamb. Grandpa was supposed to hide it and we had to find it and sell it back to him.

We gobbled down an enormous meal, chopped liver paté, chicken soup, roast chicken, a sweet stew called *tsimmes*, then fruit and meringues, coconut haystacks and cinnamon cookies, never once taking our eyes off Grandpa.

'Have you hidden it yet, Grandpa?'

'Yes.'

'Not like last year, when you forgot where you'd put it until Mum sat on it, and a fat lot of good it was then!'

We jumped down from our chairs and tore round the house, searching behind every curtain and in every drawer. Mark watched in amusement.

'Here it is,' shouted David, triumphantly waving the piece of *matzo* in the air.

'Decoy!' shouted Grandpa and produced five identical pieces from different corners of the room.

'Come on, Grandpa, this is the real one. Fifteen shillings split three ways, between David and me and the baby!'

'I don't want it this year.'

'But you have to want it.'

'What for?'

'It's . . . it's a tradition.'

Eventually the teasing stopped and mother secured us a reasonable deal. We gathered again around the table and Grandpa took the *afikomen*, broke it, blessed it, and passed it around. No more food must touch our lips that night. Then he took up the third cup of wine and we all drank. Gran went to the front door and opened it for Elijah. David and I stood with bated breath. Would he come this year to drink his goblet of wine and tell us the Messiah was coming? No, he never did. Every year we were disappointed, all except my father, who drank his wine for him in his absence. It did just occur to me that if he came, he would not be able to stand after he had done his first street, but I imagined that like Santa Claus he had ways and means of overcoming such difficulties.

Grandpa prayed for God's anger to come upon the nations that did not believe in him, and then we drank. Somehow Father managed to launch his goblet across the table with the corner of his *Haggadah*. Mesmerised, we all watched the steadily expanding red pool on the table until Gran, realising the service had come to a standstill looked up and rushed out for a cloth.

'Manny, you get the laundry bill this year.'

'But Mam,' my mother said, to our amazement rising to Father's defence, 'he didn't stand a chance. We've knocked the goblets down so many times that their stems are all bent, and they don't stand up straight any more.'

'And whose fault is that?'

'Well,' Mother continued, taking a calculated risk, 'it was you who knocked the wine over last year, if you remember?'

Gran paused. 'Mark, get singing!'

'And a happy *Pesach* to all,' grinned Mark. 'It isn't a real *Pesach* until someone spills the wine.'

He began to sing the traditional folk songs, faster and faster, until David and I gave up altogether. Gran sang different tunes, the ones she sang as a girl. Father, the only one with a real voice, could not follow the Hebrew. The racket rose to a crescendo during 'The Kid Sold for Two Farthings', until suddenly it was all over, and the books slammed shut for another year.

'Next year in Jerusalem.'

'And please God, may British Airways reduce the fare.'

4

My secular education was by courtesy of the Church of England. There was no Jewish day school in existence then and even if there had been my parents would have dismissed the idea as 'too narrow'. They wanted their children to mix easily in the society and culture of the country of their birth, and attend good private schools with reputations for academic success. In my case the Newcastle Church High School seemed to fulfil the necessary requirements. Most of my Jewish acquaintances at *cheder* attended the Roman Catholic Convent School. Their parents thought another minority religious group would have more sympathy for Jews, but Mother had a horror of dark and gloomy convents with their weird religious symbols plastered all over the walls and she hated the idea of my being taught by all those nuns. Besides, she had attended the Sunderland Church High School as a girl – and survived. It had been her only chance to mix with non-Jews, but since there had been three other Jewish girls in her class it had hardly been necessary.

'I had a form teacher,' she told me, as she laid out my clothing for my first morning in the senior school, checking to see that everything had been safely labelled with my name, 'who used to say to us, "In recent years the Jewish people have shown them-selves to have a remarkable brilliance. It is of the utmost disappointment to me that I happen to have four exceptions in my class." '

'Didn't you do very well then?'

'We were always in trouble, for chattering and giggling usually. Well, what was the point of studying? You don't need to pass exams to get married and have babies, do you? Still, times have changed. You have chances I never had.'

If the Sunderland Church High School did little for my mother academically, at least it accepted her religion, albeit grudgingly. Any hint of anti-Semitism was carefully disguised.

'The Church of England is so tolerant. They understand about Jews,' she said.

I set off on that first morning with her words ringing in my ears: 'If they get on to anything religious, say you're Jewish and opt out.' The assembly bell rang. The classroom emptied in a moment, and I was left sitting at my new desk, a carved-on, rickety old thing, the only one left when the other girls had finished choosing theirs. I was obviously the only Jew in my class. The teacher went on marking her register. I wriggled and the desk creaked. She looked up, and, seeing me, frowned.

'Well? Why didn't you follow the others?'

'I'm . . . Jewish.'

'Well, don't just sit there. Jewish prayers, third classroom down the corridor on the left.' Her gaze followed me across the room and out of the door.

Jewish prayers! What on earth were they? I wandered down a long dimly-lit corridor, peering in at every classroom window, looking for something which might look like Jewish girls praying. The idea seemed a bit indecent. I had never prayed with just girls before, in fact I had never really prayed. The men always did it on our behalf.

I found the room, struggled with the doorknob, while five faces stared at me in surprise through the glass.

'Turn it the other way,' the prefect shouted. She was sitting on top of a desk facing the others.

'Come in, don't be frightened. Let's have a look at you. All right, who do you know and who are you related to?'

'Marilyn, shut up and let her sit down.' The prefect smiled and nodded at a chair beneath the desk she was perched on. I sank into it. 'Have you brought your prayer book?' she asked kindly.

'No.'

'Tomorrow, then.'

I made a mental note to ask Mother where my ivory bound *siddah*, a bridesmaid's present, was.

'We're bound to be cousins. I'm related to everybody,' Marilyn whispered over my shoulder.

The other three girls said nothing, and kept their heads down.

52

One of them was twisting her prayer book round and round on the desk.

'Sharon!' She jumped at the prefect's voice. 'Your turn to read.'

'Er . . . what shall I read?'

'Something from the morning service, of course.'

Nervously, Sharon flicked through several pages of Hebrew. 'It's very long,' she gulped, 'where shall I start?'

'Anywhere you like,' the prefect snapped with exasperation. 'It's all the same.'

'Page eight, Sharon,' Marilyn chuckled, 'the paragraph that thanks God we're neither Gentiles nor women.'

Sharon began to read in Hebrew haltingly, faltering over every other word. I sighed with relief. At least when my turn came I could read more fluently than that. The prefect yawned. Marilyn giggled.

'Something funny, Marilyn?' asked the prefect.

'Oh, just passing thoughts,' she said, her head on one side, surveying the older girl for a few moments. 'Guess who I was with last night?' She rolled her chewing gum under her tongue and held it there. 'Danny Greenstone. He took me to Grey's Club.'

'I don't believe it, he never takes anyone out.'

'He says his cousin likes you.'

Marilyn stretched out her legs to one side of the desk. Her black tights were full of holes and the circles of white flesh they revealed were ringed with red nail-polish. I could not imagine why any boy should want to take her to a night-club.

'He hardly knows me. Er, Sharon,' the prefect snapped, 'keep reading, anything, quickly, here comes the teacher on duty. Let's at least look as if we're praying.' Sharon droned on in a dull expressionless voice for a few minutes. We did not dare look up. Heavy footsteps moved slowly past the door.

'Amen,' shouted Marilyn, interrupting Sharon's efforts. She slammed her prayer book shut, kissed it, and tossed it on the desk. I caught a momentary expression of hurt on Sharon's face and felt sorry and embarrassed for her.

'Well, his mother told my aunt Phyllis that he'd especially asked at Lisa's wedding who you were.'

'Come on girls, the doors are open, time for the notices.' The prefect jumped up in a fluster and rushed into the assembly hall.

'Where do we go now?' I asked Sharon, disappointed that the fascinating conversation I had witnessed had come to such an abrupt end.

'Just follow the latecomers and Muslims.'

'Do they have Muslim prayers?'

'Of course not. They do their homework.'

Then why, I wondered, as we marched into the silent assembly hall and lined up in a row beneath the stony stare of the head-mistress and staff, were we made to perform such a charade? I never found out. Was it the same at all church schools? I had my doubts. I only knew it made me feel horribly conspicuous when I would have far rather just been like everyone else.

That was the problem with the 'Kosher Dinners', the *kosher* school meals service organised by several ladies at the local synagogue. I had to tramp round the corner on my own in my lunchtime so there was no chance to socialise with my school-friends. And then I sat and ate on my own as the other children there were not from my school and I hardly knew them. The food was appalling. Eventually one day we were served fried eggs on lumpy mashed potato – and that for a fortune – and Mother relented. I could have school meals.

Despite occasional feelings of isolation I was happy at school on the whole. The creaking floorboards and stone steps were worn down by the relentless tramping of sensible schoolgirl shoes, the long corridor walls were covered with old photographs, children long since mothers and grandmothers. It was like being part of a big, old machine, whose cogs ground on year after year, turning out one generation after the next, the production works of Tyneside's young ladies. We wore bottle-green tunics and Wedgwood-blue blouses, brown socks and mackintoshes tied like sacks in the middle which did nothing for a figure struggling with puppy fat. Hats were compulsory, felt pudding-basins, bought two sizes too large because they shrank in the rain. We tied them under our chins with a tickly piece of black elastic, and whipped them off quick when we saw the boys from the local grammar school in the distance.

Non-Jewish boys! They were my mother's continual nightmare. What if I should meet one, like one, and – horror to end all horrors – marry one?

'You're of an age now,' my mother said to me, when I was

fifteen, 'when you must understand that you can't go to your schoolfriends' parties.'

'But why not?'

'Because they invite . . . boys.'

'What's wrong with boys?'

'Nothing, as long as they're the right sort for you, the *kosher* sort.'

'But I'm not going to get married yet.'

'So don't ask for trouble.'

I was rarely able to mix with my schoolfriends outside school anyway. On Saturday afternoons we always went to my grand-mother's in Sunderland and in the morning there was the shopping to do. Sometimes I hung around for an hour, waiting for the list. Mother's brain worked strictly in a chronological fashion and it might be eleven o'clock before it reached shopping. Boredom bred resentment.

'I thought we weren't supposed to shop on the Sabbath,' I muttered at her, as she chewed the old pencil she always carried round in her overall pocket.

'We're not,' she said distractedly.

'But you won't let me play on the hockey team, or be in the school play because rehearsals are on the Sabbath.'

'That's different.'

Different! How was it different from Father doing a Saturday morning surgery, or our going to Sunderland by car? Different because it only spoiled things for me, not them. I sometimes sulked all the way to Gran's, staring out of the car window, stubbornly refusing to enter into conversation. We passed small groups of bearded men in long frock coats and shiny black hats, taking a Sabbath afternoon stroll.

'See where fanaticism gets you?' my mother said, turning to me, then jerking her head in their direction. 'I can't be like that, but certain standards I must maintain.'

'I wish they'd realise this is Britain, not Poland,' Father muttered, 'and it's the twentieth century. No wonder there's still anti-Semitism about. I fought for this country you know.'

'Haven't I polished your medals often enough?'

We drew up at my grandmother's door. Mother turned round and saw the patchwork bag on my knee.

'Shelly, you haven't brought your knitting? On the Sabbath!

What will Gran say? She'll think I don't know how to bring you up.'

I clutched it defiantly and went into the house. Since Mark had gone to London to study sociology I had nothing else to help relieve the monotony.

The noise of the Saturday sports commentary filled the house. Grandpa was slouched in an armchair in front of the television, snoring loudly.

'Wait till the horses come on,' Gran grumbled, 'He'll soon wake up then.'

'Had a little flutter again, has he?'

'A flutter you call it? Well you know your father.'

'I thought we were forbidden to watch television on the Sabbath,' I said self-righteously.

'That's nothing compared with gambling,' Gran retorted.

'Listen who's talking, with her cigarette hanging out of her mouth.' Mother laughed.

Gran shrugged her shoulders and settled down into her armchair. The doorbell went and she nearly jumped through the ceiling. 'Quick, quick, where can I put it? I bet that's Moishe and Pearl.'

Moishe and Pearl were renowned in our family for their orthodoxy. They even had their house wired so that the lights would come on automatically on the Sabbath. Gran ran over to a plant pot and stuffed the ash and fag end into the soil. Grandpa stirred and groaned. 'No wonder I can never grow anything.' I kicked my knitting under the chair and sighed. I could not let the family down.

'This Jewish Law,' I thought, 'I can't work it out. Is it just something adults impose on children to spoil all their fun? Can you grow out of it?' After all, if you were rich enough like Moishe and Pearl, you could get round it anyway. God did not seem to mind the little lapses of most of the Jewish adults I knew. They broke the Sabbath, ate non-*kosher* food in restaurants, only went to the synagogue when they felt like it – and no thunderbolt from heaven. Even our local rabbi gave up and told the congregation they could park outside the synagogue instead of in the next street, because everyone knew everyone else had come by car anyway. Did these things really matter to God? Supposing I tried terribly hard to keep as many of the laws as I could remember, I still could not keep them all, and even if I did, I had the strong suspicion it would not help me feel any closer to God. Where was he and who was he anyway that he was worth such an effort?

I went to the synagogue one day to find God. I did not know where else to look. I thought that a religious atmosphere might give that mysterious being, who hid behind the clouds, a chance to communicate. I needed to know more than that he had made me and chosen me. I wanted to know that he was there and interested in me. I wanted to feel his presence. Someone dug me in the ribs, and whispered.'Have you seen John Greenbaum down there? Cor, I don't half fancy him.' I turned away.

Behind me, just loud enough for me to hear, a large lady said, 'Why must Mrs Davidman wear those ridiculous hats? They do nothing for her.' I tried to shut out the chatter and gossip going on all around.

'You, beyond the gilded vaulted ceiling, are you there? Can you hear me?' Silence! The doors of heaven were shut. I felt nothing and went home disappointed.

There were times when life seemed very silly and meaningless. I was sixteen years old, studying frantically, night after night, to get my 'O' levels, so I could do 'A' levels, so I could go to university, get a good job, earn good money, to eat, to work, to eat, to work, to die one day. What if you died never knowing why you had lived? What a miserable existence, what a waste!

Mother thought I was becoming terribly morbid.

'Mum,' I said one day, watching her straighten the candlesticks on the sideboard for about the sixth time that day, 'what's life all about?'

'Well,' she said, moving one candlestick a sixteenth of an inch to the left with the tip of her finger, 'you meet a nice Jewish boy, have a nice home, children, cars . . .'

'And then what?'

'When?'

'When you get all that, what then?'

'What more do you want? Oh, you and your questions. Why can't you just accept things as I did!'

Mother's great ambition was to see me married under the *chuppah*, the canopy of flowers erected in the synagogue for every bride. With this end in view, and to provide a little 'safe' social life,

I was packed off to the Jewish Youth Club, dressed up for the kill. The trouble was, everyone else's daughter was dressed up for the kill too! Still, I bagged my first rabbit in practically no time at all, and took him proudly home.

'What did you say his name was?' Mother asked, when the interview was over and the front door safely shut. 'It rings a bell. Wait a minute, I know who his father is. Underwear business! No good! You can do better.'

I tried again.

'You can't marry him. Something always disappeared at the parties his father went to when I was a girl.'

I tried again.

'Family's too orthodox.'

And again.

'Mother's only half-Jewish.'

When eventually I did drag home a satisfactory conquest called Samuel, a budding solicitor with no conversation, everyone was pleased except me. By that time I had been round most of the boys at the club, and fallen out with most of the girls, so there was little left to go for. There were parties and discos. I spent my life waiting for the next great event, then hating it because it never lived up to my dreams. The real fun was getting ready for them, the long, luxurious bathtime soak, the meticulous work with hairbrush and tongs, the master-stroke with lipstick and mascara wand, the silky feel of new tights. The work of art complete, you make your entry in an expensive haze of perfume and talcum powder. You look furtively round to see who has noticed the great arrival. No one has! Everything is just the same as it always is, same people, same music, same small talk, and you wonder why you bothered.

'There just has to be more than this, but if there is, where is it, and how do I find it?'

My question began to be answered in a most unexpected way. There was a girl in my class at school called Mary. For years I politely ignored her, and when I did not, I was anything but polite. She had long pigtails, wore National Health spectacles and her skirt flapped around her sensible shoes. Mine had made a temporary halt just above the knees, and that only because school required it. Mary hated pop music and I reckoned myself a real 'teenybopper'. She was the daughter of missionary parents. We were worlds apart. Suddenly I began to notice her. I could not think what it was that attracted me. Perhaps it was something to do with that look of gentle pity in her eyes whenever I teased her or laughed at her. There was no reproach, no sulking, no snappy reply, just a certain quiet dignity, which made her stand out from all the other girls.

'Mary?'

'Mmmmm?'

We were in the cloakroom, struggling into our hockey boots. Her ample form was bent over, bottom towards me. She looked round at me, and straightened up, panting slightly.

'Oh I do hate this awful game.'

'Yes, I've noticed. You do tend to run in the opposite direction when you see the ball coming.' She grinned sheepishly. I tucked my knee under my chin. Instinctively she moved over to the wooden bench and sat down beside me. Our heads were half-hidden by the green mackintoshes which hung from the pegs above us.

'The new French teacher, she goes to your church, doesn't she?'

'Yes.'

I paused. How could I put into words what I wanted to ask? 'She seems . . . a very happy person.'

'Yes, she is. Amazing, isn't it, when you think how she nurses an invalid father?'

'Well, what has she got to be happy about?'

'She's a Christian.'

'I don't see what difference that makes. You have no choice in the matter. You're either born a Jew, or born a Christian.'

'Oh, no, you don't understand. You can't be born a Christian, you have to decide to become one.'

I looked at Mary in silence. What she was saying did not make sense. 'What is a Christian then?' I asked after a while.

She took a deep breath. 'Come to my church and find out.'

I shrieked with laughter. The idea of it. Me, go to a church, with my face, for everyone to stare and think I had missed the synagogue? 'No thanks,' I said, grabbed my hockey stick, and rushed out on to the playing field.

But I could not get Mary's words out of my head. Several of my other schoolfriends began to go to her church and they definitely improved as a result. They seemed happier, kinder, more confident. Was I missing something? What if I went to her church too? Just once, just to see what they got up to, that was all.

5

It was a cold, wet evening, just the night for curling up by the fire in front of the television. I stood at the church gates for ages, looking up at the vast grey building protruding sharply up into an angry sky. The lighted windows beckoned me in, the granite stone walls bid me stay out. 'Go away,' they seemed to say, 'you've no business here.'

I took a deep breath, paused to let the hammering in my ribcage subside a little, then let my feet carry me reluctantly across the flagstones, up the time-worn steps, into the gloomy, vaulted interior.

Silence! I can hear myself breathing. There is a vague smell of beeswax, of age and decay. Dead saints glower at me from their gloomy, stained glass windows. Well it's certainly not like the synagogue. No satin and velvet, no crimson and gold. A small pile of books is thrust into my hands. 'Oh, thank you.' Now what do I do with these? I'll just slip into the nearest pew and pretend I'm not here. No, that would look too conspicuous. The back pews are empty and everyone is down at the front. I keep going, on tiptoes. Heads turn. I am confronted by a sea of staring eyes and curious faces. I wish they would mind their own business. I suppose I must be late, but I really couldn't help it. As usual, Mother insisted that I bath Vicky before I went out, and I could hardly say, 'Sorry Mum, not tonight, I'll be late for church.' She wouldn't have let me out at all. So I just said, 'I have to be at the Club early tonight,' and she wasn't really satisfied with that. Well, the Club is only two minutes walk away from here. I'll go there afterwards, and then I won't have told any lies.

Here's an empty pew, right at the end of the row. If I sit here I won't disturb anybody. Arrange your little pile of books in a neat row on the ledge in front of you, like everyone else. Good, that looks impressive. I have the strange sensation of being watched, but when I look up, can't catch anyone actually looking at me. The drone at the front suddenly stops. Long pause, everyone shuffles. Now what? They are all on their feet, chanting something or other. I wish I could find the place. I could pretend I know it or look helpless. Don't know which. Thud! The prayer book has fallen to the floor with a clatter which rings round the building. A hundred pairs of eyes follow my fumbling underneath the pew. I wish my PVC mackintosh would stop making that awful crinkling sound. Why on earth did you wear it today anyway, and the matching hat? You're not exactly a chameleon! I emerge and everyone else has disappeared. They're kneeling. I have never knelt in my life. I'd better have a go. If I don't do the same as everyone else, they might be offended. Which is the quickest way out of this place? Barr! It's so cold and dreary. I really don't belong here.

The service ended and I was out of my seat and heading for the door when my exit was cut off by a group of friends from school.

'Great you could make it. Coming for coffee?'

'Er, actually I'm just off to a dance at the Jewish Youth Club round the corner.'

'Just five minutes.'

'Oh, go on then, just five minutes.'

They led me round to the church hall, a drab, dingy little building with bare floorboards and peeling paintwork, pushed a thick white china mug of steaming coffee into my hands, and introduced me round. The coffee tasted terrible, but the welcome seemed genuine enough. It surprised me. I mean, why bother to make an outsider feel at home?

They persuaded me to stay for the young people's meeting and I enjoyed it enormously. Someone showed some slides of missionary work in Africa. It was a revelation to me. I knew virtually nothing about anything beyond my own little world. Geography had been abandoned in the third year because it bored me stiff. How could such misery and poverty exist? And how could anyone care so much that they would give up their own comforts, leave the people they loved and go out there to do something about it? It made gyrating at discos and the mindless chatter that went with it seem selfish as well as pointless.

'I could be happy at a youth group like this,' I thought. You could talk to people, sit down and discuss all kinds of interesting things.

'Are you coming on the hike on Saturday?' Mary asked, as she escorted me to the door.

'I've never been on a hike before.'

'The vicar's a fanatic,' she giggled, 'so everyone has to go.'

'I'd like to, but I'll have to ask my parents.'

What would I say, I wondered, as I walked round the corner to the Jewish Youth Club, how could I make them let me go? I pushed open the door, and the blast of pop music drove away any chance to think straight. I hung up my coat in the girls' cloakroom, then joined the row at the mirror with my comb and lipstick.

'Have you seen Marcia in those Lurex trousers? With her bottom! I wouldn't be seen dead in them.'

'Ruth looks better tonight than she's looked for ages. That's what I like about her. She tries so hard.'

Just like school. The same mindless, bitchy small-talk. My mind was made up!

'Mum, some of the girls at school are going hiking on Saturday. Can I go too?'

'Whose car are you going in?'

'Er, I don't know. One of the fathers', I expect.'

'You know how I hate you going out on the Sabbath.'

'Oh, let her be, dear,' Dad said mildly, over the top of the *Reader's Digest*, 'it can't do her any harm.'

'Can I wear an old pair of trousers?'

'You haven't got an old pair of trousers.'

'Well, something that won't spoil if it gets dirty.'

'Clothes are not made to get dirty. I don't spend money on clothes for you to ruin them on one stupid hike.'

What did it matter. They were going to let me go. That was what counted. My heart thumped with excitement and relief that the inquest was over.

Saturday came, warm and sunny, a marvellous day for an adventure. I was sure Mother would find an excuse to keep me at home, and felt sick by the time we set off. Within three quarters of an hour we were in the heart of Northumberland. We abandoned the cars and slung our picnics over our shoulders. I really did not think I would enjoy walking, but was in for a big surprise.

I quickly lost track of the time and distance, caught up in the extraordinary beauty of the scenery all around me. At every turn in the path the view was more exquisite than the last. It took my breath away. Why had I never noticed it before? My parents were not great ones for the countryside. 'A little breath of fresh air' at the coast was the usual family jaunt, and although I had a passion for the sea and the turbulent drama of its many moods, I had never yet experienced the gracious serenity of the countryside. I stood still, revelling in every new sensation, the wind in my hair, the sun on my back, the gentle bleating of the sheep, the luscious green of the rolling hills and wide open spaces, the exhilaration of being miles from civilisation. Surely there had to be a God who had made all this and given it to human beings to enjoy? Was it really so silly to hope that this God might even want to get in touch with me and help me to understand why he had put me on this earth at all? Looking around me I could not believe that I should have to die one day never knowing anything more about the meaning of my existence than the dreary monotony I had experienced so far.

We found an idyllic spot for a picnic. I could have stayed there for ever. We played around on some stepping stones over a brook. I fell in, got wet and dirty, borrowed trousers a size too large and laughed as I never had before. Someone, curled up inside me, who had been sleeping for years, was stirring. It was exciting and frightening all at once. Instinctively I knew that here, just beyond the grasp of my understanding, was the sort of life I had always wanted, but if I pursued it, what then of that other life, the only one I had ever known? That day I had a tiny glimpse of a joy I never knew existed and I could not let it go.

For several months my existence was schizophrenic. I was caught between two worlds. On a Sunday evening I rushed out to the Church Youth Fellowship, and to church too, if an excuse to get out early presented itself. Then I ran round the corner to the Jewish Youth Club, hitched up my skirt several inches and was ready for the disco. Gradually, the world I was supposed to belong to drew me less and less and attendance there became an irritating drudge, a necessity enforced upon me by my guilty conscience about lying. But church services, though still alien and strange, had an increasingly irresistible attraction.

'Have you ever read the New Testament?' Mary asked one day.

'I don't suppose I have,' I said, surprised that after several months of slipping surreptitiously into church, the idea had never occurred to me.

'Well, you believe the Old Testament, don't you?'

I nodded. She seemed so certain. Memories of endless translation practice, of Abraham and his desert wanderings. I hardly knew the Old Testament, but I believed in God. Perhaps that was good enough.

'Well, here's a little booklet to help you. Begin with John's Gospel, that's the best place to start.'

I took the little booklet of notes out of my handbag that evening and went in search of my old school Bible. It was hidden away in a book cupboard, not exactly dusty, Mother would never have stood for that, but certainly unopened for many years. She had been furious when we bought it for Scripture lessons, that we could not find an Old Testament on its own. 'We're Jewish,' she shouted, in a voice which resounded throughout the shop, 'we don't want this end bit.' I had tried to disappear under the counter. I could not have cared less at the time, but now I was glad to have the entire Bible in my hands. I tucked it under my arm, ran upstairs and hid it under the bedclothes.

That night, in the dark, I waited to hear the gentle, even snoring from my sister's bed, then drew it out and flipped through the pages by torchlight. 'The Gospel according to John,' that must be it. I opened the little booklet, 'Pray,' it said, 'and ask God to help you understand what you're reading.'

'O God,' I prayed obediently under my breath, watching the shadows flickering across the ceiling, 'if you really are there, please let me get to know you, because I don't know how else or where else to find you.'

I began to read, slowly at first, struggling with the quaint, archaic language, then faster as the story began to unfold, until, almost despite myself, I was so enthralled that I could not stop, but read on and on into the night.

That was my first encounter with Jesus Christ. I knew virtually nothing about him. Vicky, who attended Hebrew classes at the Reform Synagogue (such was now my father's influence over my mother's weakening orthodoxy), had informed me that Jesus Christ was one of our best prophets; not God, that was a Christian travesty, but a very good man. My father referred to him by some rude Yiddish name. 'Jesus, our brother,' said one of my cousins. Whatever they thought of him, they actually visualised a cold, lifeless statue with glazed eyes and a pitiful expression. Jesus, the Gentile God, an idol created by the Church to satisfy the imaginations of those poor Christians who could not believe in anything invisible.

Yet despite everything he had always had a secret fascination for me. Years ago Mother had taken me to see the film *Ben Hur*, and to her utter astonishment I wept buckets at the sight of Christ, despised and abandoned, bearing his cross to Calvary.

'Jewish girls don't cry at this bit,' she hissed loudly.

I gulped and stifled the next sob, but it was no good. Nothing would ever erase from my mind the extraordinary expression of love and compassion I saw in that face.

Although my mother had expressly forbidden New Testament lessons at school, I sometimes lingered at my desk longer than I should, taking an age to gather my books and leave the classroom. Or I stood with one ear to the closed assembly hall doors. I wanted to hear more about Jesus. He did not seem to have done any wrong that Jews should treat him so disparagingly. In fact all I had managed to piece together was the picture of one of the most extraordinary beings who had ever lived. Christians revered and worshipped him. Could they all be misguided? When it came to numbers they had more right on their side than we did. Mother said proudly that that was because we Jews did not proselytise like the Christians. We did not want converts, but I was never convinced that that was the answer.

That night, as I read about him for the first time, Jesus Christ lived for me. This was no remote historical character of two thousand years ago, but someone who was vibrantly alive now, in the present. He became as real to me as the people I sat next to on the bus every day, with the difference that none of them was like this man. He was utterly unique, totally compelling. Every gesture, every word mattered, not just because they made sense out of the mess our world seemed to be, but because they spoke directly to me. That was what was so extraordinary. The more fascinated I became the more I felt our relationship was reciprocal.

'Don't be a fool!' I told myself. 'A man who died all those years ago! How can he read your thoughts?' Yet everything he said confirmed the growing feeling that he knew me with a startling intimacy. Nothing seemed hidden from him, no question, frustration or longing, none of the nasty pieces of selfishness that went on in my little head. It was an uncomfortable feeling but I neither wanted to run away nor defend myself with a protective covering of self-righteousness. What was the point? For Jesus, mankind was obviously an open book. Besides, instinct told me he would not reject me, but rather, unbelievably, that he loved me and had been waiting for me to give him my attention all along.

I was thrilled that when he dealt with the Pharisees he seemed to understand completely how I felt about hypocrisy. It made him angry too. If I had religion it would have to be genuine, and somehow I could not conceive that this man would offer me anything less.

I read on until one particular statement which Jesus made halted me with a start:

'In my Father's house are many rooms; if it were not so, would I have told you that I go to prepare a place for you?' (John 14:2).

I read it over and over again to make sure I had read it properly. I could hardly believe that here was the answer to the one question which had haunted me for years. No one, not even the rabbis, had ever spoken to me confidently about heaven before. 'Do your best,' they said, 'and then one day; perhaps, who knows . . .' A 'maybe' was not good enough for me. If there was nothing beyond the grave, then death made a mockery of every day we lived. Why do your best for something that might not exist? Why live at all?

Was it possible that Christ was right, that there was such a thing as life after death, that he had room in heaven for me too one day? No, it was too good to be true, a fairy story. Who was I to say that generations of Jews had been wrong? What did I know about theology? Still, I could reason it all out as well as anybody else. If there was no heaven or hell, Christ was a liar. How could a man who spoke so much that rang true for me be a liar? He might have been deluded, suffered hallucinations. Then he would have been locked up somewhere for safety. What if Vicky's teacher at the Reform *cheder* was right, that Christ was a great man, another prophet? But he seemed to suggest he was God. No other Jewish prophet had ever done that before. That was blasphemy. What was left? Only that he was who he said he was, the Messiah, the one my people had been awaiting for so many years.

I shut the Bible, thrust it under my pillow, switched off the torch and tried to get some sleep. My mind was racing. 'Take up your cross and follow me.' What did it mean? If I followed Christ, would I have to say goodbye to my family, friends and traditions, the only life I had ever known? They would certainly say goodbye to me. Oh no, God, no, not that, I can't.

Get a grip on yourself, stop being so silly, who are you talking to anyway? A God who lives way beyond the galaxy in untouchable splendour. As if he cares about a tiny dot like you!

The next night I got my Bible out and began to read again. Philip, the disciple, seemed to put my dilemma into words:

'Lord, show us the Father, and we shall be satisfied' (John 14:8).

That was it, what did God look like? I had never dared formulate a mental picture of God before. There are never any paintings of him in Jewish books or synagogues. That would be a transgression of the commandment never to make a graven image. Somehow that had transferred itself to painting pictures in my imagination too. Christ's reply took me aback:

'Have I been with you so long, and yet you do not know me, Philip? He who has seen me has seen the Father' (John 14:9).

I understood. The very things which attracted me to Christ reflected the personality of God, his Father. At last I could give my imagination the freedom it longed for. I could begin to see God.

I never realised how disconcerting that kind of an exercise could be. My conscience had never particularly bothered me before, but now I felt as if a pair of unseen eyes was watching everything I did. The long hours spent snogging at parties filled me with distaste. Words and deeds over which I would never have thought twice began to affect my peace of mind.

'Dodging the busfare, that's stealing!'

'Telling lies again?'

'That was a hurtful, catty remark!'

I felt that God was sitting in heaven, judging everything I did, and everything I did was such a miserable failure. Could he ever forgive me? Would I ever be any different?

Some six months after that first tentative venture into a church building, a school trip to York was arranged to see the Mystery Plays. A weekend away with friends was a rare treat and as the coach set off from Newcastle my pulse raced with anticipation.

By evening the rain had benevolently acknowledged our pleadings and petered out to a light drizzle. Waterproofed to the hilt as only the English know how, we trundled in a straggly crocodile into the floodlit castle grounds, then found our places amidst dozens of other school parties. Someone handed out the toffees and chewing contentedly we huddled closer together to keep out the chilly evening air. I had not realised that the Mystery Plays were medieval interpretations of biblical stories from creation to the end of time, but somehow seeing the Bible portrayed like that as a whole made me realise just how much the New Testament was a continuation and completion of the Old.

As darkness fell and the lights on the immense stage beneath us were turned up, the munching and wriggling slowly stopped and the performance took on a magical quality. The crowds around me ceased to exist. The hard wooden bench which moments earlier had seemed to bite into my backside no longer vied for my attention. I was entranced, aware only that as we moved inexorably on to the crucifixion we were reaching the climax of the evening. Christ was on trial, was booed, hissed and rejected. A vast cross was dragged across the stage and the Roman soldiers stripped him and nailed him down with blows which resounded right across the York Castle grounds. As the cross was hoisted into the air with Christ stretched out upon it, suddenly everything fell into place for me, and I understood what I had been reading for the last few weeks. I wanted to leap up and down and shout, 'That's it! I've got it! That's why Christ had to die, for me, for my sins, so that I can be forgiven and have eternal life,' but I held on tight to the bench instead.

I was dizzy with excitement. All the self-reproach, the sense of failure and emptiness which had weighed me down for years and made me feel unable to look God in the face was offloaded onto that cross and hung there with Christ. This was the real freedom he spoke about. Blow the cost, I would follow him whatever it meant.

The performance ended. People got up, laughed and chattered. I sat very still. I did not want to move. I wanted to hold on to every minute for as long as possible, to try and make some sense of it all. Someone dug me playfully in the ribs with the end of an umbrella. In a daze I followed the other girls back to the guest house, almost unable to speak for the strange gurgling sensation in the pit of my stomach. I wondered whether to stop one of them, Mary perhaps, but what would I say? 'Something very important has happened to me tonight.' It sounded a bit forced, even a bit corny, so I said nothing and sauntered along in my own little world, blithely oblivious of everything around me. Besides, I had neither the comprehension nor the vocabulary to explain whatever it was that had happened to me that evening, although I knew I should never be the same again.

6

'Mary?'

'Yes?'

We had been heading for the ice cream van in the ten-minute interval of the Mystery Plays. Mary had been gingerly stepping on the grassy-looking bits of the field to avoid getting mud all over her shoes and tights, but without much success. She looked up at me distractedly. Her glasses had slipped to the end of her nose.

'What's the Holy Spirit?'

'Who, you mean.'

'OK, who?'

'Well,' she took a deep breath, then sighed heavily, 'you do ask difficult questions at such funny times. I'll tell you later, when we get back to the guest house.'

She kept her word, and later that evening, when the six of us who shared the rather dowdy guest house bedroom were in our pyjamas and tucked up in bed, she padded over to me in her furry slippers. She picked up my Bible, opened it at the beginning of the Book of Acts and said, 'Read that. If there's anything you don't understand, ask me tomorrow.'

I wanted to tell her what had happened to me, but did not know where to begin. I opened my mouth, but she was half-way into bed. I read for a while, and when I next looked over at her, there was a loud snoring sound coming from her open mouth.

'I still don't understand about the Holy Spirit,' I said the next day, after a rather restless night.

Mary sat down on her bed. It sagged several inches. 'It's like this,' she said, 'the Holy Spirit is part of the Trinity.' Trinity! It was an alien word. I shuddered slightly. 'I mean, he's the third part of

71

God. He comes to live inside us, when we're Christians, to help us live a Christian life.'

'So that's all right for Christians,' I murmured, 'but what about me? I don't know what I am any more. I suppose I'm nothing now. I don't belong anywhere.'

The room went very silent. The four girls who were sprawled on their beds, recovering from a service in York Minster and Sunday lunch, looked up incredulously. Joanna, the head girl, put down her book. She always spoke with great authority. 'Oh, but you are something! You are a Christian.'

A Christian! How could I be a Christian? I was a Jew. What made her say that? Was it because I now attended a Bible study group she and Mary had started at school? I had never realised before that you could actually discuss the Bible and learn something from the mistakes of men like King David. Or was it that driven by an inexhaustible curiosity to know about God, I had started to creep like a criminal into morning assemblies, feeling conspicuous and uncomfortable as if I were betraying a sacred trust and everyone knew it? I had always sensed that Joanna sympathised with the agonies of conscience I had had to overcome in order to do it.

But Jews did not become Christians! The very word was a contradiction of all that being Jewish meant. I felt confused and my face must have registered my struggle for comprehension. Everyone watched me for a while. No one spoke. I allowed my mind to wander back to the previous evening and relived that extraordinary moment when both Old and New Testament had come together and I had gazed on a tapestry woven with great harmony and precision, instead of a tangled mass of skeins. The crucifixion made sense of everything. Christ had received the punishment I deserved so that I could be forgiven. God's forgiveness was the missing piece in the jigsaw puzzle which I had been searching for all along. That was what Judaism had been unable to promise me.

'Yes,' I said slowly to Joanna, breaking into the silence, 'you're right, I am a Christian.' Their faces suddenly stretched into the most enormous beams. I watched her and Mary and waited. 'I'm a Christian,' I repeated a little more confidently. It still seemed a very strange thing to be saying. 'Oh horrors!' I gasped as the full realisation of what I had just said finally dawned. 'What will my parents say?'

'Don't be in too much of a rush to tell them,' Mary said wisely. 'Let them see the change in you and they will ask the questions.' She was right, of course, I was a different person. They would be stunned by the startling transformation. I would be loving, helpful, patient. After all, the Holy Spirit lived in me now. He would do it all!

For a few weeks I floated through the house on air. Sheer joy made washing the dishes and making the beds quite bearable. But gradually the ever-increasing list of tasks which mother's fanaticism for tidiness imposed on the household stirred up such a mass of frustration that I could not swallow it any longer. I exploded with rage. I managed not to throw anything, and thought that must be a sign of progress, but I still felt awful. I said so many things I never meant to say, and I was a Christian! I had ruined everything.

I was still in a state of dejection as Christmas approached. My first Christmas as a Christian. What a failure I had turned out to be! God could not possibly still love me. On Christmas morning I was at my post, by the bedroom window, wash leather in hand. Mother insisted that every window in the house be wiped down with three different cloths, three times a day. She had a horror of condensation. The tiniest patch could so easily turn into a drop of water, that drop become a trickle, the trickle a flood and the flood would damage the curtains and ruin the carpets!

I stood still and stared out at the people slowly making their way to the church at the top of our street. The intense longing to rush out and join them welled up inside into a terrible ache. I made myself continue wiping, my fingers so frozen that I could hardly feel the cloth. Suddenly I became aware of an invisible presence standing right next to me, so close that I was afraid to reach out a hand, or breathe, or move at all, lest it vanish. I was overwhelmed with the sense of comfort and joy. It was as if Christ himself had opened his arms and drawn me into them, holding me tight, just as my father had done when we were younger. Somewhere inside me a voice seemed to whisper, 'I am Emmanuel, God with you, God very close to you. This is the only Christmas present you need.' I held on to the moment as long as I could, dreading being left alone again. Yet long after the wonder of it had died away, I knew that Christ was still beside me.

He understood what I was going through, and knew I was not always to blame for the outbursts I could not control. He would share the boredom, the loneliness, the frustration and the tears. I would tell him exactly what I felt, and he would help me to cope. He was right. To know that he was close by was all I needed.

Day after day I wrestled with the growing inner conviction that I would have to tell my parents what had happened. My stomach turned over and I felt slightly nauseated at the very thought. They would never understand. It would seem a betrayal, the worst thing I could possibly do. I could not hurt them like that. The stigma in the Jewish community alone would be terrible. I could almost hear the gossip and see my parents slinking away in shame.

'Their daughter . . .'

'Did you hear?'

'Isn't it tragic?'

'Who would have ever thought?'

In my bed at night countless agonising scenes would act themselves out in my mind in glaring Technicolor and I would bury my head in my pillow desperately trying to shut them out.

'Christ is with me, Christ will help me,' I repeated to myself over and over again, but I had no idea how. 'Oh let them see the new me,' I prayed. 'Let them make some comment about it, and then I shall say, "It's Christ who's done that, he makes the difference," and they might just be the tiniest bit glad.'

But the day never came. It was no good wriggling out of what I had to do. We were close enough as a family for me to hate the deceit and lies. Finding excuses to get out early on a Sunday night was becoming an impossible strain. Besides, I sometimes felt that my parents knew what I was up to. A bit like the proverbial ostrich, they stuck their heads in the sand. Suspicion was easier to live with than truth. Only a year to go until I left home to go to university. I would wait until then. It seemed by far the most sensible idea. If things turned out for the worst, at least I would have a bolt-hole.

I hung on to the prospect of university like the survivor of a shipwreck to the piece of timber he hoped would carry him to the distant shore. Studying French was a small attraction compared to my deep need for freedom and independence. 'Durham,' I wrote as my first choice on the university application form.

'Durham?' my French teacher queried. She had taken to spending a few moments alone with me whenever possible, sometimes to explain a Bible passage I had been reading and did not understand, at other times to listen to my tales of woe and advise me if she could. 'Durham's only twenty minutes away by car. Shouldn't you be exploring further afield?'

How could I explain the panic I felt at the thought of leaving everything and everyone I loved? It vied constantly with my longing to escape and be myself, two entirely conflicting emotions in a desperate struggle for supremacy. In Durham I thought I had found a compromise.

'Where else would you like to go?'

'Well, I'd like to do drama as well as French and that's only possible at Hull, Manchester . . .'

'Manchester? Put Manchester down as your second choice.'

'Oh, I don't really want to go there.'

'Yes, but it has a good French department by reputation, and . . . I don't know why, it just has a certain "feel" about it.'

I did as I was told, it could do no harm. Durham was bound to accept me. A letter came from Manchester with the offer of a place. They demanded high 'A' level grades, but it was a place. I waited. Then one morning there on the mat lay a long white envelope with 'University of Durham' written in black letters along the top. My fingers felt like lumps of Plasticine and the few seconds it took to tear the envelope apart seemed interminable. The letter was simple, but as I read it, I felt stunned, as if someone had landed their fist sharply across my jaw.

'We regret we are unable to offer you a place . . .'

Disbelief gradually gave way to anger and I flounced into school that morning in a fury. Mary emerged from the sixth form cloakroom and peered over the banisters to see whose arrival was making the wooden staircase creak more than usual.

'Oh, oh,' she said and disappeared back into the cloakroom. I followed her, flung my mack over a hook, and rammed my outdoor shoes into a cubbyhole. She watched me in silence, a rather bemused expression on her face. It was by no means the first of my rages she had witnessed. I went to the mirror and attacked my hair with a comb.

'Durham,' I said, between bared teeth, 'have rejected me.'

'That doesn't surprise me.'

She was behind me and I could see her face in the mirror. She was smiling. I refused to comment.

'Look,' she said impatiently, 'did you or did you not give your life to Christ? Don't you think he has the right to say "no" sometimes?'

'But I want to go to Durham,' I shouted, threw down my comb and marched into the classroom, with the sound of Mary's gentle laughter behind me.

She was right of course, but I did not discover that until later; there could be no possible compromise between my need for security and the search for self-discovery. The former would have swallowed up the latter and destroyed any chance I might have had of maturity as a Christian, let alone as a person. I had to go further from home. Looking back with the wisdom of hindsight I was thankful that God did sometimes say 'no', not just to thwart me and spoil my fun, but because he understood the intricacies of my emotions better than I did myself. The objective nature of his love for me enabled him to make by far the most sensible decisions for my future. And so I packed my ample belongings into an enormous trunk and set off for Manchester University.

I spent my first day trailing around identical high-rise factory buildings, searching in dozens of dark corridors for obscure room numbers, sitting in endless queues, filling in piles of administrative paper, thus proving I was intelligent enough to become a fully-fledged undergraduate. Then we 'freshers' were let loose on the Union building and told to present ourselves to the societies of our choice. The surging mob carried me up the steps and pressed on ahead while I lingered to read a sign which said, 'Entry Forbidden to Those under the Age of Eighteen.' I was seventeen and not used to ignoring instructions. I gingerly stepped inside and was immediately catapulted in a world which was louder, more garish and belligerent than any I had ever seen before. Every available inch of wall was plastered with cheap posters, bearing weird names and even weirder drawings. The corridors were lined with makeshift stalls made out of trestle tables, each representing a different society, each manned by students determined to lure in the innocent and the unsuspecting. I was bombarded with hand-outs and deafened by the hullabaloo.

The floor, littered with discarded advertising, almost felt like a carpet beneath my feet. I wandered around in a daze feeling lost and very alone. Where should I start? The French Society or the Drama Society? But there appeared to be dozens of drama societies and I didn't know which to choose. Then I remembered that when we had said goodbye Mary had warned me it would be like this.

'Make sure you look for the Christian Union,' she had instructed me in a maternal sort of way. I had nodded obediently. 'I don't want you falling by the way. And anyway, they'll have your name. I've sent it to them already.'

'She's certainly taking no chances,' I thought.

Standing in the middle of the Union building I felt more like running away than falling away. 'Excuse me,' I whispered to a young man in faded, frayed blue jeans who was leaning idly against a wall, but the blast of pop music drowned me completely and he went on tapping his foot to the instant drum–beat, totally oblivious of my presence. 'Excuse me,' I tried a bit louder, 'could you tell me the way to the Christian Union stall?'

He suddenly realised there was something at the height of his elbow which was not going to go away and looked down, 'Eh?'

'The Christian Union,' I shouted. The sound of my own voice startled me and I shrunk another inch.

'Down there,' he sneered, jerked his head, then turned away. 'In with all the other religious nuts.'

Religious nuts! His contempt took me aback. As a Jew I had come to live with disdain, as a Christian it was totally unexpected.

I followed the general direction of the jerk of the head and eventually came out into a quieter, sunny room. It was full of stalls: Methodist Society, Baptist Society, Catholic Society. The Anglican Fellowship. It suddenly struck me how strange and sad it was that Christians divided themselves up into these silly groupings. A Jew was a Jew however he chose to worship, but there were countless brands of Christians.

My reflection was disrupted by the sound of laughter from the other side of the room. A group of people were chattering with great animation around one particular stall. I looked at the wall above it and read 'Manchester Inter-Faculty Christian Union' in huge red letters. They stopped their conversation and looked at me quizzically as I approached, then broke into smiles of greeting when they realised I really had found the stall I was looking for.

'Hallo, where are you from?'

'What's your name?'

'Which hall are you in?'

'What are you studying?'

'Just fill in this card, will you?'

Someone handed me a pen. I obediently filled in the card, then the pen was taken from one hand, the card from the other. The latter was studied with great interest by a girl with enormous brown eyes and an infectious grin. 'I'm Hilary. I see you're in Langdale Hall. Ruth is the rep there. She'll look after you.'

'Rep?'

'Yes. She's responsible for organising the Christian group in your hall. She'll tell you all about Bible studies, prayer meetings and the like. Now, here's a Christian Union programme too. We've some fantastic speakers coming this term. Are you coming on the hike on Saturday by the way? Oh good, you'll soon get to know lots of people.'

I could have hugged her with relief, but felt a little too overwhelmed at that precise moment. As I turned away I suddenly noticed the neighbouring stall for the first time. The large blue Star of David on the white cloth draped over the trestle table was unmistakable. I did not need to look up and read 'Jewish Society' on the wall. A dark-haired girl manning the stall caught my gaze and stared at me with marked curiosity. I averted my face, but knew I was still being watched.

'She knows I'm Jewish,' I thought. 'I could have picked *her* out as a Jew anywhere.'

I was tempted to go and speak to her, drawn by a sense of belonging and mutual understanding, but instead I turned round and walked away, feeling a strange mixture of guilt and embarrassment. Her eyes burned into my back. Why could I not join them? I had every right to do so. Blind panic told me that if they knew that I was a Christian they would not accept me. I would end up in another horrible maze of lying and deceit. And anyway, I had been seen at the Christian Union stall. The truth could not be concealed for long. Whether my fears were well-founded or not I could not risk the possibility of having to justify myself or of their rejection, not then. Too many changes were taking place both within and outside me. Too bad if it seemed like running away. There was so much to get used to. I needed time.

That first year in Manchester was a great adventure. Life was so hectic that after the first week I had little time to feel homesick. I loved the city itself, the glittering metropolis with its elegant buildings, theatres and concerts, which for a Geordie lass had all the glamour of London. And I had the freedom to succumb to its many attractions. The university was just near enough to the city centre to pop in for an hour's shopping between lectures or a curried salad lunch at the Ceylon Centre.

I did not manage much work, just stared helplessly at endless booklists and wondered where to begin, but the social life was better than anything I had ever imagined. For the first time I met Christian boys! The church youth group back in Newcastle was virtually all female. Any specimen of the male variety of the species who actually came to church never dared to brave such a gathering for two weeks in succession, but the Christian Union was full of them. There were the handsome, the charming, the shy, the awkward, the considerate and the masterful, an endless variety from which to choose. My head spun.

And then there was the rapture of being able to attend any Christian meeting I wanted, without the shame and fear of being found out, without planning explanations all the way home. The term became a whirl of Bible studies, prayer meetings, planning meetings, coffee parties, houseparties, parties of all kinds. I was not going to miss anything. Like a sponge I soaked up every drop of Christian teaching available, all the more so as the prospect of the first vacation loomed nearer and nearer.

My parents were proud and thrilled to have a daughter at university. Manchester too, where we had those nice relatives with the eligible son! They missed me, and were greatly looking forward to the vacation. I walked back into the house for the first time after several months with a sinking feeling in my stomach. I looked round at all the familiar objects, all in their usual places, pill bottles in neat little rows, cups upside-down on saucers, ready for the next drink, cold coffee in an old metal coffee pot, ready to be reheated for the next morning's breakfast. The dog rushed out to greet me, wagging his tail furiously. I bent down and stroked his head. He stayed very still and I wondered if he sensed my mood. This was it! Better get it over with as soon as possible, but what on earth was I going to tell them? How could I bring such disruption to their world and destroy all the high hopes they had placed in me?

Over supper I was bombarded with questions. How were Aunty and Uncle? And what was their son like, the one who was studying medicine? Did I like university? Was I settled? I answered their questions briefly, reassured them I was enjoying Manchester very much and went on eating my meal. Mother looked slightly troubled, shrugged it off and began to clear away the dishes.

'Mum, dad,' I said quietly. My hand was shaking and I tried to control it. 'I've something to tell you.' Mother put the dishes down and dropped back on to her chair. She would not look up at me. My father wiped his mouth on his table-napkin and put it on the table. 'I've . . . I've become a Christian.'

No one spoke. I looked at them, and could hardly bear the pained expressions on their faces. I tried to say, 'But this doesn't really change anything, I'm still Jewish, I'm still your daughter, I still love you,' just as I had rehearsed it dozens of times, over and over again in my mind, but the words refused to come.

'You've been going to church, haven't you?' my Mother demanded.

'Yes.'

'That it should ever come to this, a daughter of mine going into a church.'

'Now don't get into a state, dear, it's these friends of hers. They've influenced her. She'll grow out of it, won't you?'

I shook my head.

Father looked suddenly bewildered. 'Where did we go wrong? How have we failed you?'

Mother broke down and wept violently. 'No *chuppah*! Never to see my daughter married under a canopy. I'll be the laughing-stock of the entire community.' So that was what really mattered, what the relatives thought. Anger broke through the hurt I felt at what I was doing, and gave me the resolve to stand firm and weather the immediate crisis.

It was the first of many during that vacation. My mother spent most days wandering miserably around the house, muttering, 'What are we going to do?' 'She'll survive,' I thought. My father worried me more. He was unnaturally quiet and thoughtful, and I often caught him looking at me with great tenderness and pain in his eyes.

'We can't go on like this,' he murmured, after yet another scene, with everyone pleading and weeping their way through the box of tissues. 'We're not getting anywhere, so let's be sensible about the whole thing. "Honour thy father and thy mother" is one of the Ten Commandments, isn't it?' I nodded, blowing my nose and drying my eyes. 'Well, I can't help but feel you'd give up this "Christian" business if you really believed that. Still. I think you'll grow out of all this. You're not twenty-one yet, so we still have some say. While we can't demand it, we want you to promise not to be baptised, or to go to church.'

'Or take that bread and wine they eat,' Mother interrupted, 'and we'd like you to see a rabbi, I've rung him already, who'll teach you more about Judaism, and answer some of your impossible questions. Oh, and we want you to stop reading your Bible, and please,' tears flowed again copiously, 'don't go out with any non-Jewish boys.'

I weighed up their words carefully. They had a right to see that I still loved them and wanted to honour their wishes. 'I agree to everything,' I said, swallowing the lump in my throat, 'except that I must read my Bible.'

'You'll read as much Old Testament as you read New?'

I nodded. They sighed with relief, and gave me a hug.

'Well,' said Father, 'let's get on with life, shall we?'

There was a letter waiting for me when I got back to my hall of residence in Manchester. Rabbi Gold would like to have a little talk with me, at my parents' request. I explained everything that had happened to the small Christian group who met in hall to pray and study the Bible together. It was such a relief to share it all.

'Pray for me, girls,' I said, 'because God only knows how I'm going to survive the next three years without going to church or going out with boys. And what on earth shall I say to this rabbi?'

My tummy felt tight and I was breathless when I tapped at the rabbi's door. A secretary ushered me into the waiting area outside his study. I sat chewing the skin round my nails, reminding myself over and over again of the Bible verses my friends had given me!

'And when they bring you before the synagogues and the rulers and the authorities, do not be anxious how or what you are to answer or what you are to say; for the Holy Spirit will teach you in that very hour what you ought to say' (Luke 12:11–12).

He emerged moments later, not as I imagined a rabbi, a tall, gaunt, clean-shaven man, with a prominent nose and small, penetrating eyes. He had his arm around a younger, rather good-looking man, and as he showed him out he called after him, 'Don't forget, let me know how you get on.'

A nod seemed to suggest that I follow him, and another that I take a chair. I perched on the edge, bracing myself for the first assault.

'So why have your parents sent you to me?'

He knew why, surely. I was not playing 'cat and mouse'. 'I've become a Christian.'

'How does a Jew become a Christian?' he asked slowly, with a hint of mocking irony in his voice.

I told him my experience as briefly as I could. Was it my imagination, or did he seem slightly shaken?

'The boy,' he said, 'the one you saw, who was in here before you, he said exactly the same things.' He paused a while, and stared unseeingly out of the window. I prayed he was reckoning me a hopeless case and would let me go. 'Well, well, what do you want to ask me?' The tone became dismissive.

I tried to think up some suitable questions. 'Isaiah, chapter fifty-three?'

'The Suffering Servant, yes?'

'Well it says that the Messiah would be "wounded for our transgressions, and bruised for our iniquities". That describes Jesus Christ on the cross. It's obviously Jesus Christ. He fulfilled the prophecy. That makes him the Messiah.'

The rabbi smiled and shook his head. 'I think not. The Suffering Servant is Israel, the nation.'

'How can Israel be "a man of sorrows and acquainted with grief"?' I asked, genuinely puzzled.

'In the Scriptures Israel is often referred to as a person.'

'Oh.' I was not satisfied, but had no means to argue. 'God answers my prayers now.'

'And mine too.'

'I don't know what to say. All I know is that before I was utterly miserable, but now I have something which makes life seem worthwhile.'

'And you know what this is doing to your parents? It will be the death of your grandparents.'

I nodded and got up. I had to get out.

'Before you go, I have a friend, a Church of England minister, who will help you appreciate what it means to be a Jew. Will you see him?'

I shook my head. I could not stand any more. I ran out into Albert Square and walked round and round, until I felt calm enough to get on a bus. Though I did not know it, I had just turned down a premature opportunity to meet my future father-in-law.

One clergyman I did see was the minister of the church I attended in my first term. He had been contacted by the vicar in Newcastle and invited me round for a little chat. Once again I found myself sitting in a clerical study walled with books from floor to ceiling, feeling slightly intimidated. But this man was fatherly and kind.

'I hear you've promised your parents that you won't go to church until you're twenty-one?'

'Yes. I want them to see that I'm bending over backwards to honour them.'

'But you can't go on like that, not for more than a month or two.'

'But I must, I've promised.' I was beginning to feel the hot prickly sensation at the back of my neck I was coming to associate with pressure, however gentle.

'You need fellowship, the support of others, Christian teaching.'

'But I get it all in the Christian Union without breaking my word.'

Smiling he got up and showed me to the door. 'I'll give you a month,' he said, 'then see you back in church.'

As the door closed behind me I made up my mind to be guided only by an inner voice. If I listened to everyone else I would end up torn in a hundred pieces and strewn across Manchester from church to synagogue.

For most of my time at university I managed to keep my parents' wishes. I was quite relieved to have an excuse for not going to church. I still did not feel at ease in that environment, and found that the multiplicity of meetings laid on by the Christian Union more than made up for what I missed. In fact, as I grew more confident about being a Christian, I realised that Christian meetings could swallow up every bit of available spare time, that one's horizons could become very narrow and restricted, and so I ventured out into the secular world, joined a drama society, acted in plays at the university theatre, got involved in student local radio and became captain of the hall table-tennis team. There was hardly time to breathe and I tried to push home to the back of my mind. It made the vacations harder than ever.

'Yes, Samuel, she is free tonight. I'm sure she'd love to go out with you.' I hung over the banisters, shaking my head furiously, as Mother put the receiver down. 'Such a nice boy,' she said smugly, 'he seems so keen on you. Do go out with him. It'll be good for you, take you out of yourself a bit.' I gave in. I felt so helpless. Poor Samuel. If he only knew how he was being used. Then suddenly I had an idea.

'Samuel,' I said that evening, as we drove up to the house in the dark after a lavish meal, 'there is something I have to tell you. I'm not what I seem.'

'Oh?' He wriggled uncomfortably.

'I think Jesus is the Messiah. I mean, I'm a Christian, so you won't want to see me any more.'

'Are you going into a convent?'

'No, but it means a lot to me. My life is so different now. We're miles apart.'

'You can believe what you like. It doesn't bother me.'

'OK. Well, see you around. Thanks for a lovely evening.'

I rushed into the house and breathed a sigh of relief. He never rang again. Mother was puzzled.

'You know,' she said one day, 'I'm sure it's because you never gave him a goodnight kiss. I watched you from the window. Boys like a little bit of that.'

We jogged along in an uneasy truce for a number of years. Mother watched me anxiously, desperately hoping for a sign that the crisis was over, then giving way to utter wretchedness when she saw that the Bible was still on my bedside table. I said nothing, and kept the Christian side of my life very much to myself. In Manchester I joined a group of students who met to worship together on a Sunday morning. They attended house churches when they were at home and did not like institutional church services. I identified with that, and enjoyed the informality and spontaneity. We were regarded as something of a dissident group by the rest of the Christian Union.

'Don't go there,' I was warned. 'They're very extreme. They speak in tongues.'

I was on my guard and did find the garbled, muttering sound which went on as people prayed under their breath very strange at first. Their ecstatic expressions and raised hands made me feel uncomfortable too, but what drew me was that they seemed to love God in a way I did not. I appreciated him for the things he gave me, forgiveness and the peace inside that went with it, eternal life and the promise of a place in heaven, but loving him for himself alone, that was something different altogether. I read a chapter from the Bible every day, but it no longer thrilled me like it did at first. Praying, too had become very routine. 'Are you filled with the Holy Spirit?' they asked me. 'Well, I received the Holy Spirit when I became a Christian, didn't I?' 'Yes, but there's much more than that. You need to be baptised in the Spirit, filled full to overflowing.' What did they mean? Whatever it was, if there was a dimension I had missed, I meant to have it. 'I haven't fought all this way to get only half the goods,' I thought. 'Fill me with your Holy Spirit, Lord,' I asked, 'because I do want to love you like they do.'

He answered when I least expected. No noisy emotional 'whizz-bang' experience! But one day, when I bumped into Hilary on the Union steps and quite spontaneously we had decided to find a quiet little room upstairs to spend some time praying together, in the stillness I became aware of God's presence in a way I had only once experienced before, that Christmas Day years ago, when I had been drying the windows. Only this time the sense of God's nearness did not fade. It became increasingly real. His love seemed to flow in waves all around me and I relaxed and allowed myself to be carried along in the ocean.

'So this is what heaven is really like,' I thought, 'this utter rest and peace, this endless warmth and comfort and enjoyment of God's presence!' I did not want to return to reality, fearful that the moment would evaporate into nothingness, but it did not. The new awareness of God's love and greatness stayed with me, transforming my routine Bible study and prayer life into the language of a love affair, making all I thought I had sacrificed seem paltry and insignificant. Worship came easily, I wanted to spend time with God.

'You couldn't call that Sunday meeting "church",' I told myself. 'You are still keeping your part of the bargain.' Or was I? The niggling at the back of my mind refused to go away. I was twenty-one. Had the time come to reopen the old wounds?

I moved to a flat in Didsbury and began to attend the local Free Church there. The agreement with my parents was a thing of the past. I realised with a heavy heart that we would have to talk again. Besides, the church had a baptistry. I watched several of my friends being baptised and knew it was only a matter of time before I would have to follow. I kept putting it off. I told myself it was an unnecessary extra, that it was unreasonable to hurt my parents again. One day, as I was reading through the Book of Acts, a verse almost rose off the page, as if it were illuminated: 'And now why do you wait? Rise and be baptised' (Acts 22:16). I could not go on running away from that inner voice. 'All right, Lord, you win,' I shouted, 'but I can't tell my parents, not now, with my final exams on the horizon.'

'You know what baptism means, don't you?' The minister looked down at me with an air of gravity and compassion. 'It's a public demonstration that you belong to Christ.'

'I know.' I hung my head. He put his hand into his pocket.

'Here's the key to the vestry. Help yourself to the telephone.'

I wandered across the half-empty church in a daze. Unfortunately the key slid into the vestry door lock without the slightest effort. The room smelled musty. I sat down weakly beside the phone, lifted the receiver, and waited a while for my heart to stop pounding. My fingers trembled on the dial, then somehow found the right numbers. It was ringing. Oh, let them be out, please!

'Hello! Oh, it's you darling, how are things?'

'Mum. I'm going to be baptised.' The silence seemed interminable. 'I said . . .'

'I know what you said.' The voice was cold and hard. 'Never come home again. You're no longer our daughter.' Click! The line was dead. I put the receiver down slowly. When the minister appeared at the door a few moments later, I looked up and saw to my horror mascara-stained pools of tears splodged all over his crisp white writing paper.

I was baptised on Whit Sunday with little elation and a great deal of pain. 'I'm doing this because you ask it,' I whispered to God, 'not because I want to, so don't expect me to enjoy it.' Everyone around me seemed thrilled. They fussed me, hugged me, petted me, but I felt numb. Afterwards, I went back to my little flat and sat alone in the dark. 'O God,' I whispered, 'why didn't you make me a Gentile? It would have been so easy then.'

7

I would sometimes study my face in the mirror, sigh and think how nice it would have been to see a blonde, Scandinavian-type goddess staring back. But there she was, that rather swarthy looking character with the dark, unruly curls, the olive complexion, that nose infuriatingly large compared to other small features. I tried fluttering my eyelashes and pouted for effect. She pouted back and looked, I thought, passably sultry and continental. But I was sick of being asked if I were foreign. I never knew what to say.

'No, actually, I'm English,' never seemed to convince anybody, except once in a crowded restaurant. A studious-looking gentleman at the next table peered at me through the spectacles on the end of his nose. When he had finished his meal he leant across and said, 'My dear, permit me to say what fine Celtic colouring you have.'

The friend I was with giggled into her table napkin. 'No Celt here, mate,' she whispered to me.

'Semitic actually,' I said to the gentleman, smiled sweetly and went on eating my chocolate mousse.

'What I want to know is,' I confided in the mirror, 'when people pass me in the street can they tell that I'm Jewish?'

'Does it really matter?' the reflection enquired.

'Of course it does. Let's be honest. If people say "Jew" at the first glance, their preconceptions will affect how they see me before I open my mouth.'

I never forgot an experience which happened when I had only been a Christian for a matter of weeks. I was with a group from school, on our way to a Bible study at the local boys' grammar school, when a boy passing us in the corridor stopped, pointed a finger and jeered. 'Look at that Yid.' The corridor, one moment raucous with end-of-schoolday noise, suddenly seemed very quiet. My clothes stuck to my body. I felt awkward, conspicuous, too humiliated and stunned for anger, as if I had been slapped across the face. I could not respond. To my annoyance no words would come. Then there was a peal of laughter and he and his friends disappeared. My friends pretended not to notice and continued our chit-chat.

Becoming a Christian so radically shook my sense of identity that it became imperative for me to discover what being a Jew really meant to me. It never mattered before. It was a fact of life, something to be embraced alternately with joy and resignation.

'You're still a Jew of course, aren't you?' my Christian friends said to me, but which part of me was 'still a Jew'? How could I be so sure? It was illogical, irrational, but reason did not enter into it. I knew I was a Jew because I still felt Jewish inside. It was an entirely emotional response, yet here, unwittingly, I had discovered why even the least-practising Jew will adhere belligerently to his radical, if not religious, identity. What matters is what I feel, not what I do.

If there was one phrase I heard more than any other as a child it was, 'I'm not a good Jew, but I am a proud Jew.' It was said with such gusto, such assurance, that I thought being a proud Jew must earn you such a vast tick on your credit column that when the Almighty balanced the books it wiped out all the debits of deliberate law-breaking. One day I suddenly understood. There are times when people repeat a phrase over and over again with great certainty and dogmatism in a desperate bid to convince themselves of its truth. Jews are not always fearless of what others might think of them. Deep down inside, perhaps at a subconscious level, many must have felt as I did that day in the boys' grammar school, small and very worthless. The real terror is not that others might abuse us, but that they might be justified in their abuse. Debase and despise a people for long enough and they will almost be convinced they deserve it. That was the hangdog attitude which drove six million Jews into Hitler's gas chambers with barely a murmur or a protest. We were helpless, defeated.

No Jew can come to terms with being Jewish without coming to terms with the Holocaust. I could look at it objectively as a historic event, be appalled at the degradation of human behaviour, even grieve for the relatives I never met, but that was not enough. Amongst Jews genetic bonds are very strong. Each Jew seems to carry in his bones the tragedy and sufferings of his entire race. It was not enough to wonder what it would have been like if I had been there, then bury the feelings in the depths of my subconscious when they became unbearable. One thing was certain, if I had been born twenty, even ten years earlier, in Germany, Poland, Holland, Czechoslovakia or France, I would have been transported to a concentration camp. In that it happened to my people it happened to me, and I had to allow myself to experience the absolute hell of it. Nightmare followed nightmare for several months, as my emotions wrestled to resolve their inner turmoil. I felt the terror of that uncertainty in the overcrowded cattle-trucks, the ache and pain of bereavement, the humiliation of becoming a faceless, nameless piece of human flesh, the stench of hatred and loathing exuding from the bodies of our persecutors. Then the dreams stopped. I had reached a total acceptance of what it meant to be Jewish, the conscious awareness that time and time again throughout history one has had less value than horse manure.

How one uses that knowledge is crucial. It has produced the dedicated Zionist, convinced that a homeland is the only solution, the aggressive Israeli who has discovered that for the first time a Jew can actually fight and win, the materialistic entrepreneur, seeking security and acceptance in wealth, and the extraordinary cultural and intellectual achievement of the Jewish people in recent years born of centuries of brokenness and rejection. I too had a choice to make. I could allow my Jewishness to have a negative influence, read anti-Semitism into the most meaningless word and gesture, or I could use it positively, learning to trust and forgive. Ironically, it was my experience of the Church which drove me to the crisis point and forced me to a definite decision.

For three years I had honoured my parents' wishes and did not attend a church, but nor had I mixed in a Jewish environment either. I temporarily postponed making any real decision about who I was or where I belonged. I clung tenaciously to my experience as a Christian and my identity as a Jew without emotionally being able to bring the two into any kind of inner harmony. I had not grown up. As I became more involved in the rather conventional Free Church where I had been baptised the realisation suddenly dawned upon me that while Christians patted me on the back and whispered soothingly, 'Of course, you're still Jewish,' it meant nothing at all. In fact, although it was never actually said, I began to feel that most people hoped I would settle down and become a Gentile as quickly as possible. I could hardly blame them. After all, the early Church was not sure how to cope with the problem of converted Gentiles and the Jewish Christians wanted them to become Jewish as quickly as possible too.

It was a great temptation to blend like a chameleon into my new environment, to be safe, secure, wanted, to pretend that I had never known any other life. I could wipe out the pain of my parents' rejection, hack off my Jewish past, throw it into the deepest recesses of my subconscious and begin again, a totally different person. It would never work. The process would have involved a radical amputation, leaving me scarred and mutilated, not whole at all. Besides, pretence is a dreadful strain to live with. The past would have haunted me like a restless ghost, making unwelcome appearances at the most inconvenient moments. That was not the abundant life Jesus had offered me. He was a Jew himself, he had accepted me as a Jew, surely Christians could as well. Was it really fair of people to criticise me for being 'too emotional', 'too independent', 'too outspoken', 'too noticeable', 'too unconventional'? I was sick of being taken into a corner and being told that for my own good, I really ought to know that certain church members had expressed concern that . . .!

The problem was that this was my first real encounter with the institutional Church, albeit in its Free Church disguise, and we did not get on too well. Occasional church attendance had been one thing, commitment was another altogether. I suddenly realised that a 'take it or leave it' attitude was no longer possible. Somehow when I took Christ and made him mine I also managed to acquire the institutional Church, a bit like Jacob with his Rachel and his Leah, and I definitely had not expected that part of the bargain.

'Free Church services will be much freer than the Anglican services you remember,' I told myself, 'much more spontaneous and informal.' But there it was, week in, week out: hymn, prayer, hymn, reading, hymn, sermon, hymn; a triple-decker sandwich with the minimum weekly variation in the filling. The sermon was always excellent, but how I wished it did not seem that in order to get there we had to dispense with the rest as quickly as possible. I thought worship was supposed to be important. Was this it, this standing, singing, sitting, slouching, in strict obedience to the voice at the front, this dull, dry ritual enacted by a hundred marionettes devoid of every indication of human emotion? It left me cold, unmoved, unable to participate. Even a smile could freeze on your face. Religion is a serious business! I thought it false and hypocritical to hide behind a mask of piety during services.

The Victorian décor did not help matters. Coloured glass windows set in mullion stone, coated on the outside with the grime of years of Manchester traffic, shut out the daylight. The low timbered ceiling, though pine, had been painted with the dark brown varnish so fashionable at the turn of the century. In my flights of fantasy I would climb up there with a tin of paint-stripper and a brush. How many months would it take to restore it to its original golden beauty? But it would be worth it. The wood-panelled walls were caked with dark brown varnish too. The loose wooden blocks in the parquet floor clattered and squeaked when someone shuffled on their chair. I sometimes felt I was enclosed in an airless, dark brown wooden crate and had to fight the urge to get up and run outside into the sunshine.

Where was the noise, the colour, the emotional vibrancy of the synagogue? I had never realised how much a part of me they were, the haunting quality of the Hebraic chant, the easy natural alternation between prayer, song and chatter, the dazzling shimmer of the scrolls as they were carefully removed from the crimson-curtained ark, then lovingly carried round so that the men and children could kiss their prayer shawls, then reach out and touch them. In the intensity of my search for God I had been so full of Judaism's inadequacies that I had forgotten its sheer joy and beauty, until I was deprived of it. In the middle of church services memories would flood over me in a huge, irresistible wave, filling me with a sudden, terrible panic.

'What am I doing here? How did I get here? I don't belong. Let me out, please.'

And then I would remember I had nowhere else to go. The festivals with their gaiety and laughter, the family traditions I loved so much, had gone forever. At my baptism I thought I had found a new family, but it did not quite work out as I expected.

Sunday after Sunday I walked home from church alone and sought refuge in my little flat; interminable Sundays, full of hurt and loneliness.

'It wouldn't be like this in the Jewish community,' I moaned. 'Someone would have invited me home on the Sabbath.'

The more I grieved for the world I had lost, the more I sunk into a morass of self-pity and anger, with the Church as the primary object of my resentment. Christians could not do anything right. Like a porcupine, I was all wound up inside and covered with protective prickles on the outside.

'In Ephesians,' says the preacher from the pulpit, 'in chapter two verse twelve, Paul tells the Gentiles that they were alienated from the commonwealth of Israel. That speaks to each one of us today.'

I squirm on my chair. 'Speak for yourself.'

'When the Jews crucified Christ . . .' the preacher continues.

That makes me really mad, but there is worse to come.

'Now that God has finished with the Jews, we Christians are the chosen people, the new Israel.'

Finished with the Jews! Well, why am I sitting here? Why have we been so persecuted? If God doesn't still love us, who does? Just wait until the service is over. I'll tell him a thing or two, and anyone else who happens to be in range.

To the credit of my Christian friends, they endured my tempers, tantrums and explosions, as I wrestled for my identity, with more grace than I deserved. If only they knew how much I hated my own behaviour. I did not understand it. I could not seem to control it. I wanted to bite my stupid tongue off. Patience was supposed to be a fruit of the Holy Spirit. If only it would plop, like a windfall, into my lap. I would do better next time! And then someone had to discuss Middle Eastern politics with me. So kind of you to take the time to explain the Arab point of view. I'm sure they have one, but do you really expect me to see it? My people have never had a land to call their own before. We don't belong anywhere. No one ever wants us. Inside me a voice was crying, 'And do you, a Gentile, really want me, a Jew, in your Church?'

There seemed no outlet for my Jewishness at all, and it was an immense frustration, particularly as I was constantly discovering how Jewish Christianity was.

'Look,' I said excitedly at a home group one day, as we were exploring the meaning of Jesus' words, ' "For where two or three are gathered in my name, there am I in the midst of them" (Matt. 18:20) Don't you see? In Judaism no act of public worship is valid without a *minyan*, a quota of ten men. Jesus is saying, "Forget it, two is all you need for my presence to be with you." '

'Oh yes, very nice,' everyone said, and smiled at me indulgently.

Certainly New Testament passages were real for me in a way I could see they were not for others. I could never hear the verse, 'For he [Jesus] is our peace, who has made us both [Jew and Gentile] one, and has broken down the dividing wall of hostility' (Eph. 2:14), without wanting to leap off my chair in a paroxysm of joy. But my smiles only met blank stares. I could have shaken the congregation one by one and shouted, 'Don't you see what Christ has done? Here we are together, though normally we'd have nothing in common, and years of mistrust would have held us miles apart.' But they did not see it, and sadly I wondered whether in taking my being a Jew for granted, they did not take the extraordinary reconciliatory work of Christ on the cross for granted too.

What was I to do? I could not continue like this, writhing on my chair in the agony of believing I could preach better sermons than those I was hearing. I sat down one night in the quiet of my little flat and weighed up all the possibilities. I had tried to conform, to be what everyone seemed to expect of me, but that had not been the answer. I could not sustain the performance for more than a week. Or I could fritter away my life lamenting my lost past, just like the children of Israel in the wilderness, looking wistfully back over their shoulders, idealising the Egypt they had left behind: '. . . the leeks, the onions, and the garlic' (Num. 11:5).

'Let's face it,' I thought, 'if Judaism was that wonderful, why was I converted in the first place?' Just like the children of Israel my persistent moaning was blinding me to the many good things in my new inheritance.

The only remaining possiblity was to learn to live with myself, explore the riches my Jewish background had given to me and seek, somehow, to share them with the Church. That sounded good, but how could it be done?

'Oh God,' I pleaded in desperation one night, 'here I am, feeling such a mess inside. I want a Christianity which really works, so please sort me out, will you, and while you're at it, do something useful with my life.' Slowly, very slowly, he answered.

Several months after my baptism I rang home for the first time.

'Er, Mum? It's me, I've got my degree.'

'Oh yes?'

'Will you come to the graduation?'

'We'll see. We'll let you know.' Click! The phone went dead. They said they might come, there was a glimmer of hope. I hung on to it and was rewarded. There, among the last cars to swing into the car park, was the familiar shiny white Volvo.

My heart pounded as I went to meet them. It was a hot day. I felt wet and sticky beneath the weight of my gown. Mother checked me over from head to toe with a glance, straightened my hood, then frowned when she noticed my tangled, limp curls. We walked in silence to the graduation ceremony, then afterwards stood together on the steps of the Arts building and smiled for the official photographer.

'Where's your luggage?' she demanded, when the ceremony was over. I could hardly believe my ears. 'Get the car,' she barked at my father, 'it's time to go home.'

'I presume you went through with it?' Mother asked in a very controlled voice, after we had journeyed in heavy silence for some half an hour. She did not even turn her head.

'Yes,' I whispered from the back of the car.

I saw her reach out and pat my father's knee with her hand. 'We might have been so proud of you today, and instead, this. You come home as a stranger, you realise, not our daughter.'

That first evening I was sitting alone. The house seemed very silent. Father appeared at the sitting-room door, wearing his skullcap. 'Have you a moment?' he asked.

'Of course.'

I followed him up to his bedroom, and saw his prayer book lying open on the bed. He picked it up uncertainly.

'I've been trying to pray,' he said, the words choking him slightly. 'Funny, isn't it, me, an agnostic, wanting to pray? I need someone to pray with and don't know who else to ask. Will you pray with me?'

He took up the prayer book, and we read together, in English. I slipped my arm through his and saw that there were tears in his eyes.

'You're a great comfort to me, you know,' he said.

Gradually my parents and I rebuilt our shattered relationship, but not as it was before. To my amazement it was much less fragile, stronger, more stable, based on their acceptance of my adult decision to live my own life. No more blind dates, no more playing their 'Fiddler on the Roof' record in the hope of creating some sudden, emotional return to the fold on my part. They let go, and as they did I discovered a freedom to love them I had never known before. I loved them for accepting me despite everything their consciences told them, I loved them for making no further demands despite their own pain.

I felt a great need to be alone with God, to walk, to think, to understand this unexpected gift he was giving me. As I did so memories came flooding back, many adolescent and childhood scenes which had caused great hurt, words which had left unhealed scars, just waiting to open and ooze again. The feelings of rejection I associated with becoming a Christian had much deeper roots than that. They were buried in my subconscious. I felt as if God were opening a hundred tiny doors to the corridors of my mind, which I had kept tightly shut for years, and inviting me to go with him on a guided tour of inspection. A small group of close friends sat with me and prayed as a whole series of incidents from childhood and beyond, of which I could have no conscious recollection, enacted themselves before me. The hurt was almost unbearable, but the healing God seemed to pour into those gaping wounds made the temporary discomfort infinitely worth it. Anger, resentment, pain were carried away by copious tears.

'My daughter, let me have that chip on your shoulder, that feeling of utter rejection. Do you want to know where it comes from?'

'Where, Lord? Show me.'

I heard an inner voice as if I were a little girl:

'The *Goyim* don't cook like we do, the *Goyim* don't live like we do. Never trust a *Goy*. They despise us. And even if you marry one he'll call you "dirty Jew" in the end.'

'But I don't really believe that, do I Lord?'

Rationally, of course I did not, but something of that attitude remained deeply embedded within me like a cankering sore, inhibiting my ability to feel at ease in the Church, and form open, trusting relationships there.

One Sunday morning, during a time of open worship in the morning service, an exciting and refreshing innovation for the church, I falteringly asked for forgiveness for all the bitterness I had felt. If it had not been for Gentile Christians I would never have found Christ at all. If it had not been for their love and perseverance my survival as a Christian might have been in jeopardy. I am not sure the apology was understood, but it was graciously accepted.

I was determined from now on to use my Jewishness positively and enrich the Church in whatever small way I could. If there are hundreds of years of pain and rejection locked in the heart of every Jew, there are also hundreds of years of worship buried there just waiting to be released when the Messiah comes with the key. I had not discovered a new religion or a strange new God, but the God who had always been there, with my ancestors down through the centuries, with me in the rituals of my childhood, only I had not recognised or known him. If I was Jewish through and through so was the Church, from its founder and foundations to the book that inspired it. One day it would wake up and begin to explore the Hebraic cultural roots it had ignored for so long. I wanted it to happen overnight, that was my mistake. But happen it would and I was going to do everything in my power to help it: introduce feasts, festivals, celebrations, all the treasures of the Jewish heritage. Besides, the wind of change was now in the air. Charismatic Renewal began to affect the whole Church and not just a few individuals on the fringe. Old preconceptions were shaken, some conventional attitudes overturned. There was a new interest in Hebraic music and dance. The time was ripe for innovation.

I now began to find the confidence and freedom I needed to make a point of going home for the major religious festivals. Besides, Judaism had begun to make sense in a new way. The ritual of eating bread and drinking wine on the Sabbath Eve was a small foretaste of the Communion service. Kindling the *Chanukah* lights at the Feast of the Dedication of the Temple was a visual reminder that Christ was the light of the world, come to give light to all men. But it was the Passover which thrilled me most of all. It was the same old service I had loved as a child. But now, as we read and sang it together, I imagined Christ eating his last meal with his disciples, his own heart heavy because he knew what was coming. Yet he used the rich symbolism as an audio-visual aid, so that they would understand why he had to die, that he was the real Passover lamb, the *Afikomen*, broken for the sins of the world.

He took: 'In the same way also the cup, after supper, saying, "This cup is the new covenant in my blood"' (1 Cor. 11:25). The cup taken after the meal was the third cup, known as the cup of blessing. Christ's blood was shed so that death would forever pass his children by. I gazed at Elijah's goblet with gratitude. In every Jewish home it would always stand untouched. The Messiah had already come.

Two places at our Passover table were conspicuously empty and Gran wept her way through the entire service. The new joy I found in the traditional words and symbols was checked by her terrible pain and our loss as a family. Grandpa died after a stroke had left him paralysed and speechless for two years. When his only son, Mark, was born, so totally unexpectedly, seventeen years after my mother, Grandpa had exclaimed with enormous satisfaction, 'Now I have my *Kaddish*.' Only a son can recite those special prayers for the dead and keep alive his father's memory by having his name and taking his place in the synagogue. Mark came home for the funeral from Peru, where he was a journalist. For seven evenings, the duration of official mourning called *shivah* after the Hebrew word for seven, his glorious voice resounded round the house as he sang those ancient words, '*Yis kedal va'yis kadosh sh'may raboh . . .*' (*Glorified and sanctified be God's great name . . .*)

Six months later he was dead too, after a tragic accident. He was twenty-seven and had no son to say *Kaddish* for him. His coffin was flown home for burial in the Jewish cemetery in Sunderland. Only my father could bear to lift the lid and look for the last time at the sleeping face, wrapped in the prayer shawl he had so often worn in the synagogue. For the second time in six months the rabbi took a pair of scissors and made long cuts in the clothing which Mother and Gran were wearing, an old tradition dating back to the time when people rent their garments in grief and despair.

'Why?' Gran shouted at the ceiling. 'Why, why? There isn't a God! There can't be a God!'

The women sat together trying to comfort her, as David led

the men in the all too familiar prayers in the next room. They mourned a life cut short, wasted potential, the children Mark would never beget. As the sound of their lament drifted through into our room Mother turned to me, looked at me inquisitively for a while, then said, 'If only I had your faith.'

'You can,' I whispered, desperate to bring her some kind of hope. But she just shook her head sadly and looked away.

Prayers ended and one by one the visitors filed past the bereaved to pay their respects.

'What's this I hear about you then?'

To my embarrassment I realised that Geoffrey, one of my mother's cousins, was addressing me.

'You've become a Jehovah's Witness or something? I know Mark defended you to the hilt. He was adamant you should be allowed to follow your own conscience.' To my surprise Geoffrey's smile conveyed genuine interest, not paternalistic indulgence.

'I've become a Christian actually.'

'Really? Tell me about it, won't you? I'd love to chat.'

This was a conversation I had never anticipated. I had become so used to a negative response that it took me some time to lower my defences.

Being a Christian in a Jewish environment and a Jew in the Church began to be extremely enjoyable. When it came to the latter I discovered there could be great advantages in coming into the Church without any denominational bias, without any knowledge of long-standing Christian traditions. One could have a very objective approach to what was valid and biblical, and what were extraneous cultural additions.

'It must be marvellous to be free from the law,' gushed a well-meaning middle-aged lady after she had heard me speak about my conversion. I was always being asked to 'give my testimony' in church after church *ad nauseam*, until I felt a bit like a combination of a freak specimen and a prize poodle.

'Oh yes,' I said, anxious not to quash her enthusiasm but embarrassed by my own hypocrisy.

'Free from the law,' what did it mean? Jewish laws had not really been an encumbrance to me. It was impossible to remember all of them, let alone keep them. If Jews really believed that keeping the law earned them God's favour they would be much more careful. In observing those we chose to observe and ignoring the rest, the law had served us. How could I explain that in the few seconds of a snatched conversation? 'Yes, thank you, I do enjoy an occasional pork chop now.' We had always gone out to restaurants for our pork chops anyway! How could I make her see that in fact some Christians had a system of laws more terrible and tyrannical than anything I had ever known as a Jew, a veritable evangelical Torah?

'Thou shalt not smile in church.'

'Thou shalt not wear make-up.'

'Thou shalt not date without intent to marry.'

'Thou shalt not go to the theatre, the cinema, dances, nor anything which may be classed as worldly.'

The whole lot could be summed up in one glorious commandment: 'Thou shalt conform.'

Sometimes the Church felt like a vast machine which swallowed up its members, ground them to powder, then pumped them out again, model Christians, numbered and coded without any personal identity or individuality. I fought the process with all I had. Why give in to a puritan, Victorian anachronism?

One incident which happened while I was still at university made me smile whenever I thought about it. It was a Sunday evening and I was unpacking my suitcase in my little box of a university hall of residence bedroom after a weekend at home. I was in a turmoil of a hundred different emotions and very tired. Mother had bought me a lovely new dress, bright red and cut away at the shoulders. I could not resist wearing it for the journey back to Manchester. There was a timid little tap at my door.

'Come in.'

It opened slowly, and Ruth, who was in charge of the hall Christian Union group, peeped round it. 'Can I come in?' she murmured, staring at the floor.

'Of course you can. Why the formality all of a sudden?'

She did not answer, or look up, but shuffled sheepishly into the room. Those ridiculous old slippers!

'Seat?' I nodded at a spare bit of bed next to my suitcase. She perched on the very end and examined her fingernails.

'Shell?'

'Mmmm?'

'I, er, Sylvia told me to come. She thought, and I did as well, that I ought to talk to you about, er, the way you dress.'

Sylvia was vice-president of the University Christian Union. She was wise, she was spiritual, she gave up her fiancé because he was not a Christian. She spoke and we obeyed. I felt hot and sticky all of a sudden. 'What bothers you in particular?'

'Well, your hemline for a start. It's barely decent. Christian men have a hard time keeping their thoughts pure. With you around it's twice as difficult.'

I looked down at my knees. They were nothing marvellous. I wondered whether to feel flattered.

'And just look at that dress.' Ruth was warming to her subject. 'Look where the stitching goes. Talk about suggestive.'

For the first time I noticed two rows of white topstitching making two circles on the front of my dress.

'Ooh, yes. Is that bad? Will it upset somebody, do you think?'

'Sylvia and I, we think that you should succeed me in leading the hall group, but really, it does depend on your behaving more as a Christian girl should.' She got up and began to back to the door. In a funny way I respected her for saying what she felt she had to. She had not found it easy.

'OK Ruth,' I said, too weary and stunned to say anything else, 'I'll try.'

'Oh, and by the way,' she delivered her parting shot from the safety of the doorway, 'even your nightie's red and frilly.'

'Well, drat,' I thought, 'she's even been peeping under my pillow.'

I flopped down on the bed and sat there thinking for some time. I had to admit it was a bit daring, not to mention a bit chilly, almost to reveal my underwear. My legs were too short anyway. It was just that some of the girls in the Christian Union were a bit old-fashioned, even dowdy, and I did like to shock. But then I never had a boyfriend like some of my Christian friends. So many Christian men seemed dreadfully mild and timid. I had a sneaking suspicion that they were frightened of me. I was either too foreign, or too fast, and looking down at my hemline and the circular stitching on the bodice of my dress, it was not hard to guess which. I should have to reform a little, I decided, for the sake of happy, open relationships, not because someone had held out the carrot of position and responsibility. Hang ambition! It was not exactly Christ-like, hardly a virtue worth the cost of conforming. I would be true to Christ and what I understood to be his will and true to myself.

God had used his creative skills to make me with all my foibles and idiosyncrasies, a Jew who was a Christian as well. I could look him straight in the eye exactly as I was. Let the minister's wife say, 'If God had intended you to have green eyelids you would have been born with them.' If God had not intended her to have a shiny nose why was she not born with it ready-powdered?

I lost a great deal of excess weight and for the first time in my life felt very glad to be me. There was just one problem. I had a degree, but no job, and no certainty of what I wanted to do either. One thing alone was clear.

'Oh God,' I said one evening, watching various huddled shapes pass beneath my flat windows in the twilight drizzle, 'let me never forget what I've felt like these last few years, and let me bring the joy and wholeness you have given me to those who feel as lonely and insecure as I did once.'

8

I never meant to fall in love. It was an added emotional complication I could have well done without, especially in my final year at university. But there he was, that tall, rather composed sort of character, with the gentle voice and brown velvet eyes, smiling at me across the room in a Christian Union meeting. My stomach turned cartwheels. Suddenly all my noble aspirations to serve God in whatever way he wanted were overtaken by a host of uninvited daydreams, of romance on desert islands, white wedding veils, and terry nappies hanging on the washing line.

Then came the devastating blow. It was painfully obvious that my affections were not reciprocated. I could not believe it. How could God let this happen to me? Had I not given up enough for him: home, family, community? How dared he refuse me the man I wanted too? I yelled and raged at the Almighty, wept and stamped my foot. It was not fair. It was all his fault. I never wanted to feel like this.

'It's so easy for you,' I told him, 'you can make Peter fall in love with me in a second, or make me stop. So why don't you?' I suppose I thought he was some kind of celestial Eros, who, having misdirected a fiery dart, would say, 'Sorry dear, my mistake,' and either pull mine out or shoot one at Peter too. There was no response from the heavens. What was the use of telling God that he would never again find anyone as suitable as me, that Peter's family have been interested in the Jews for generations, that we had so much in common? He would neither be bulldozed nor blackmailed into giving me what I wanted. I would somehow have to trust that he did know what was best, even if it was beyond my comprehension, even though Peter moved into a flat barely a quarter of a mile away from mine and started to attend the same church. At least I could still have his friendship, his presence at various social occasions, his figure to stare at surreptitiously from behind my hymn book every Sunday morning. But that was all I had for a very long time.

Since there was evidently no immediate prospect of marriage on the horizon I still had to discover what I was meant to do with my life. I might have to watch Peter walk down the aisle with somebody else one day. I might never marry. The idea filled me with horror, but all around me were single Christian women in their thirties and forties. Why should God not ask it of me? Although it was not easy, better face it and accept it than spend years mooning around waiting for Mister Right. After all, there were some positive advantages in having no ties and few responsibilities.

'Have your fling, dear,' my father said with a knowing wink.

'Fling?' my mother expostulated. 'Who needs a fling? At her age I was a mother.'

She had taken to making loud comments about 'young, glamorous grannies', and 'the blessing a grandchild must be', whenever I was within earshot on social occasions. To my parents' despair the only 'children' I acquired were anything but desirable. I became a youth worker.

Working with delinquents and drug addicts had seemed romantic to some of my friends, but never to me. I had intended being a teacher, but felt very unsure about it. In my final year at university I applied to do a certificate in education, mainly because everyone else did, and set up a record in the French department of being rejected by all six colleges of my choice. If I was not meant to teach, what was I meant to do? I staved off any decision by working for two years for a Master's degree, and never got it. Fascinating though Wagner's influence on French literature might be, I was soon fed up with musty libraries and nothing but books for company.

I only called at the Manchester Youth Services out of vague curiosity. Helping at a Youth Club occasionally might bring me the fulfilment which research did not.

'What experience have you of working with young people?'

'Summer camps.'

'None at all. I see.'

'I once stopped a girl committing suicide on me.'

'Fascinating. How about doing the real thing, say helping at a youth club for one or two evenings a week, to see if you like it?'

'Fine.'

I felt my face coming under intense scrutiny, and I knew what was coming. 'At a Jewish Youth Club?'

'Great!'

'There's one just round the corner from where you live and the youth worker happens to be the best in the Manchester area, in my opinion. He'll train you well, if youth work's what you want to do.'

That evening I walked round to the synagogue and stood for a while outside the huge wrought-iron gates. From my flat window I had watched the congregation come and go, and wanted to join them, but had never dared. Well, here I was after all. The gates creaked open with a little pressure, and I followed the stream of light and blast of pop music into a large hall full of teenagers who immediately stopped what they were doing to stare at the stranger who had just slipped in. I looked around at the many faces, some swarthy and very Jewish, others fair and light-eyed. Some were open and animated, full of expectation, others were hostile, bored already, suspicious of anything new. Eight years vanished in a moment. I was transported back in time to my own adolescence with all its anxieties and insecurities. I might have been back at the youth club in Newcastle. It was a decidedly uncanny feeling.

'Come into my office, darlin'.' The high-pitched voice with its strong Cockney accent startled me back into the present. So this was Ernest Bates, the youth worker. 'D'yer smoke?'

'Me? No.'

'Good, ruins the natural body odours. What do yer do?'

'Er, a bit of drama.'

The tiny eyes, which never left my face, reminded me of two black beads stuck into a round wooden ball on which someone had painted lips and cheeks. Everything about the little middle-aged man, from his shorn haircut and baggy tweed suit to the briefcase, which dwarfed him, was conventional to the point of old-fashioned. A more obvious Gentile in a room full of Jews would have been hard to find.

'I'm a *Goy*, yer know.'

'Yes,' I muttered, convinced he was reading my thoughts.

'But I don't stand for any nonsense. If any non-Jewish

youngsters come in here, they keep their hands off the opposite sex. No marrying out. It's more than my job's worth.'

'There's something I'd better tell you then.'

'Oh yes?'

'I am a Jew, but I'm a Christian too. I became one a few years ago.'

'Oh gawd, not one of them. I've met your sort before. Trust my luck to get landed with one. Yer not going to convert us all, are yer?' He laughed so raucously I thought he would be heard above the music in the next room.

'If I'm asked about it, I can't lie.'

'All right darlin', you do yer own thing, only don't cause me any trouble.'

Ernest Bates lived up to his reputation for training youth workers. Once I had got used to his rather strange sense of humour I was grateful for his astute and honest assessment of my progress, or the lack of it. With all expenses paid for by the Association of Jewish Youth, I joined a training course he had organised for several volunteer workers.

'Where did you say you were based?' the other students asked, disparagingly. 'A Jewish Youth Club? You can't call that the real thing, can you? I mean, those kids are hardly socially deprived. They're middle-class, they've got money, too much of it. A good spanking would be more use to them than your help.' I thought of Simon, struggling to cope with eighty per cent deafness; Jackie, a spastic neglected by her parents, desperate to prove she was as intelligent as anyone else; Julie, an adopted child, bewildered and confused, not looking at all Jewish, but raised in an extremely orthodox home, and the others, all with their own particular anxieties, trying to come to terms with belonging to a minority culture, most of them living with enormous pressures: to achieve, to marry well, to please parents and community. How could anyone be stupid enough to suggest that their needs were less than anyone else's, that they would be spared the trauma of growing up?

I was just beginning to be trusted at the club, to feel I was of some use, when the crisis occurred. A journalist from one of the local Jewish newspapers popped into the club to see what went on. 'What exactly do you do?' he asked me.

'Well, I seem to sit in the Ladies' most of the time. The girls like to chat while they put their lipsticks on.'

'Youth Worker Spends Her Evenings in Ladies' Loo,' went the headline. The kids spread the newspaper out on the bar and shrieked with laughter when they read it.

The editor of the rival Jewish newspaper was not so amused. He had heard me speak on Radio Manchester about being a Christian, noted the name, and when he saw the article, knew he had a scoop. This time I was given a front page spread: 'Christian Youth Worker Proselytises Our Youth'. I could not believe it, it was so untrue. I dashed to the telephone.

'So it's you, is it?'

'Oh, Ernest, I'm so sorry.'

'How could yer do it? How could yer give the man an interview?'

'He tricked me. He said he wanted to talk to me about youth work.'

'I could have told you what he was like. Don't suppose you've read the editorial?'

I had. It began, 'How long must we employ a Gentile youth worker . . . ?'

'It's me they want rid of,' Ernest bellowed. 'Ah, well, I've weathered worse storms than this. But do me a favour, don't show yer face round here again.' When next I heard of Ernest he had a lecturer's post in youth work at a polytechnic.

I wished I had been able to say goodbye to the kids, to offer some kind of explanation, rather than slink off like a criminal. A few days later the phone rang. 'Michele? It's Julie. Hope you don't mind my ringing. Can I meet you in town? I'd like to talk to you.'

We sat in the Kardomah Café two days later. Julie giggled into her Cona coffee.

'If Dad knew I was meeting you he'd kill me.'

'I can imagine.' Dad was quite a bigwig on the Synagogue and Youth Club committees. He must have loved me! I studied Julie for a while. She was striking already, with her long blonde curls and vivid blue eyes. She created havoc among the boys, who found her English-rose attractions quite irresistible. The girl who seemed to have everything, but behind that bounce and sparkle was someone who felt very lost and very unloved. Suddenly she became grave, struggling for the right words.

'That article in the newspaper,' she said, then looked straight at me, and for the first time I saw the hurt, and the tinge of anger in her face. 'Was it true? I mean, did you really only help us to get converted?'

'What do you think, Julie?'

'I don't know. I'm so confused. Everyone says you did and they feel betrayed. They're furious, but I don't ever remember you trying. That night, when I was so upset and you sat with me, I thought, here's someone who's really interested in me, but now I don't know any more.'

'Julie, I do care. I've become very fond of all of you.'

'Then why? What made you convert anyway?'

'Well, I suppose, just like the article said, I was looking for something I didn't find in Judaism. I was fed up with religious hypocrisy, and like you, I was fed up with the superficial social routine, and I felt that something was missing, that I wanted to know who God was. I read the New Testament, and though it's hard to explain, when I read about Jesus Christ he seemed the most real, the most honest person I'd ever come across. The things he said made Judaism make sense at last. Realising he was the Messiah was the missing link.'

'You amaze me. You're quite nice looking. You could marry a nice Jewish boy, settle down, have a pleasant, easy life, but instead you chose this.'

'Funny, isn't it? Sometimes it amazes me too, but I wouldn't change things. When you find something that answers all your questions about why you exist at all, it's worth any price you might pay. And I suppose, had any of you asked me about it, I would have told you. I can't actually convert anyone. I can tell you what happened to me, but then it's up to you. You have a mind of your own.'

'I think I understand a little.' Julie was smiling now. 'Can I see you again?'

'I'd like that a lot.'

Julie was the first of several youngsters from the club to seek me out and demand some kind of explanation. The editor of the Jewish newspaper achieved more than he dreamed of! I was thrilled, but it still did not alter the fact that my research grant had run out, I was unemployed and had to find money for food and rent. I scoured the newspapers for a job, but nothing seemed right. 'Something will turn up,' I said. Was it faith or fatalism? I think it must have been the former, because my confidence was quickly rewarded. A couple of days after I had given up looking, the telephone rang.

'Hello, my name's Frank White.' The voice on the other end of the receiver was warm and friendly, and its soft, Geordie lilt aroused my instant affection. 'I've just come to Manchester to work for the Catacombs Trust, a Christian detached youth work project. It's grant-aided by the local authorities, who are represented on the committee by Ernest Bates. I told him I wanted a colleague and he tells me you're just the girl I'm looking for.'

It sounded like a proposal.

Although we knew before we met that there were too many coincidences involved already for me not to be the right co-worker for Frank, he still needed to see flesh and blood to be finally convinced. I chose my wardrobe carefully, not too trendy, but not too conventional either, and felt a total anachronism as I walked into the Manchester City Mission. No mortal had been at pains to redesign its mournful interior since Queen Victoria ended her glorious reign. The chapel was tiled in green and white like a public lavatory, hushed voices floated eerily out of several tiny offices, two old tramps huddled up with misery sat in a corridor, waiting to be attended to. I wondered if Dickens had been here once and found inspiration.

'I'm up here.' Frank was leaning over a rickety wooden staircase. 'Come up. This attic's the office.'

As he looked down at me I saw curiosity give way to a quickly suppressed smile of approval. A face which gave everything away, that was a good sign!

The office was tiny, barely big enough for one desk, a filing cabinet and two people. 'How do you bring kids in here?' I asked.

'You don't,' he grinned. 'One look at this place and they'll be off. They'll think it's haunted.'

I sat down on the one chair and Frank perched on the end of his desk. 'Well, all I have to do now is persuade the committee I need you.'

'And do you?'

'Oh yes, a man out alone at night on the streets of Manchester! I can't approach a girl, and I'm just discovering I can't approach a boy either.'

His look of comic indignation made me laugh. I liked him

enormously straight away. He was relaxed and easy. With his tattered khaki hat pulled half over his eyes, he reminded me of a stray mongrel, and that touch of the vagabond added to his charm.

'Yes, you do have a problem,' I admitted, 'and I'd love to help you solve it.'

The committee was convinced. How much pay did I want? I hadn't a clue. I thought of a minimal figure and they seemed quite satisfied. No one knew where it would come from, but it would come. Frank and I walked out into Piccadilly Square feeling slightly dazed. This was now our home, this bewildering hotch-potch of vast grey buildings and endless streets, full of jostling, surging, anonymous people. Simultaneously we took a deep breath. What on earth had we let ourselves in for? We had no base, apart from a tiny office, no youth club, no ready clientele, no experience, no professional identity, no authority. Whatever work we did we would have to create. We had to go out there, on to the streets, and find young people in need, then persuade them that they needed us, and ultimately, that they needed Christ. The latter seemed the easiest prospect. At least Christ could perform miracles. Help, Lord, where do we start?

'The first thing we do,' Frank said, with greater confidence than I thought he felt, 'is to patrol the streets.'

'What do we do that for?'

'To find out just what goes on.'

He must know. He had the university diploma in social work and I did not. So inch by inch, hour after hour, night after night, we trod the pavements, until the soles of our shoes were so worn down that I reckoned Manchester City Council deserved what we were paying in rates. We saw it all: pubs, clubs, casinos, brothels, gay bars, there was hardly a den of iniquity in Manchester which had not either ejected us or made us want to leave in a hurry. We went home feeling sad and soiled, but no nearer creating a day's work for ourselves.

One evening, it must have been late that first autumn because our breath was beginning to freeze in the night air, I stepped over a large human bundle on the pavement and walked on.

'Where do you think you're going?'

I turned round. Frank had stopped to survey the heap at his feet.

'Oh, Frank, it's only a drunk, leave him, for goodness sake.' I was tired and irritated. I hated walking around in endless circles and I hated damp weather. It made my curly hair frizz.

'We can't just leave him,' Frank retorted. 'The next bobby who comes along will book him, and that's a night in the cells.'

The stench of alcohol and vomit was beginning to waft in my direction. 'Good, he has it coming to him.' Frank looked at me in hurt surprise. I felt ashamed, but after all this was not what detached youth work was all about. It was romantic, glamorous, exciting, Christian Sir Galahads out rescuing the perishing!

'Would Christ have left him lying there in the gutter like that?'

Blow Frank! Blow his Christian charity!

'I'll take his arms and you take his legs. Where do you want to be, pal?'

'Hotel Piccadilly,' murmured the semi-conscious form.

'Phew, we've got a posh one here,' whistled Frank.

Somehow we managed to manoeuvre the heaving, retching dead weight through the streets to the doors of his hotel, then standing him on his feet, propped between us, we nonchalantly dragged him past the pages and porters, into the lift, along to his room where we dumped him on his bed and left him to snore in peace.

It was a relief to walk out into the sharp night air. I felt clean.

'Frank?'

'Yes?'

'You don't half smell.'

'Thanks.'

We giggled. 'You won't find any more like that, will you?'

'I'm not promising anything.'

It was just as well he didn't. In the months that followed I lost count of the number of drugged or drunken youngsters we dragged home. But from that night on, it never bothered me. I had learnt something. The resources are within us to do whatever Christ would have done in any situation.

Not being a natural walker, and not given to enjoying the bracing winter air, I soon tired of Manchester's streets and found a little coffee-bar where I could sit in peace and while away the hours at my crochet. Occasionally one or two youths came in to shelter from the cold and I began to recognise some familiar faces. One day one of them watched me out of the corner of his eye as he shredded his paper coffee-cup. Suddenly he stopped what he was doing, caught the attention of his mates, then swaggered over to me.

'OK then, show us how to do it.'

'Sit down and I'll show you.'

Jamo never did learn to crochet, but from that day on Frank and I rarely again had a peaceful moment. Through one lad we made contact with about two hundred young people, white, black, half-caste, unemployed, delinquent, homeless; all found a kind of refuge in the anonymity of Manchester's city streets and markets. We spent our days in the social security offices, law courts, coin arcades and VD clinics, but mainly hanging about on street corners, dodging police orders to 'move on' just as the kids did. Some of them thought it was great. The novelty of having their own private social worker really appealed. Others were indifferent. Most were totally mystified.

'What do you really do?'

'We're here to help you in whatever way we can.'

'Man, why bovver? No one ever 'as before.'

'Because we're Christians.'

'What da you know about anyfing? Ya don't know what it's like to be black, always in da minority.'

'I do know. You see, I'm a Jew and I reckon my people know even more about prejudice than yours.'

'Man, you really are mixed up.'

We were not exactly popular with anyone. The police were suspicious of us, the authorities found us a nuisance, the coffee-bar proprietors blamed us for the kids' vandalism and called us misguided do-gooders. There were days when I almost felt I could not face it any more. There seemed to be nothing around me but aggression, violence, injustice and gross exploitation. The world was a sickening place, divided into prey and predators. The kids were easy prey. The predators were those who plied them with booze, drugs, gambling, cheap sexual thrills and the like, all for money.

Then suddenly there were those rare moments which made everything worth while, like one evening at the weekly bop at Belle Vue. We were with a group of kids we had got to know well. Booze money had run out and they were bored silly. Sprawled over their chairs, the boys were discussing ways of livening up the evening.

'Ah fink ah'll go and give dat Charlie somefing 'ee won't forget. 'E makes me sick, always nicking my girls. Oo's comin' den?' Darren looked slowly round, but no one looked up. Someone even yawned.

'How about turning the other cheek for a change, Darren?'

Frank's quiet words made him freeze on the spot. He grinned sheepishly. 'Eh? Wot daft bugger would do that?'

'Christ would.'

Darren's mouth fell open and a damp, half-chewed fag-end fell out. Gary, his mate, whose head had been resting on his folded arms, looked up at Frank slowly and blinked, as if he had seen an apparition.

'Ya don't take all that stuff serious, do yer, Frank?' he asked.

'Are them two goin' on about Jesus again?' laughed Maggie, and pulled up a chair between us.

Half a dozen more kids drew their chairs in closer, so that they could hear the conversation. Suddenly everyone was wide awake and full of questions. Who was Jesus? What did he do and why did he do it? What difference could he possibly make to the here and now? We talked on and on into the small hours of the morning. The music stopped, the bar closed, the dance hall emptied, but no one moved away from our table. They were oblivious of everything except this new world which was opening before them.

'Christ said, "If any man asks for your jacket, give him your coat as well." '

'Did 'ee, Frank?' said Gary. 'Well, give us yer jacket then.'

Frank stood up obediently, took off his worn, patched old jacket and handed it over, wallet, car keys and all. My heart sank. We would never get home tonight. Gary strutted off and was gone for the next half-hour. He reappeared with a quizzical look on his face and handed the jacket back.

'Thanks, pal.' Frank put it on without a flicker of emotion and sat down.

'Yer money's all there, Frank.'

'Great.'

'So's yer car keys – and yer car.'

'Great.'

Gary stared at Frank in disbelief. 'You really trusted me, didn't yer? No one's ever trusted me before. Maybe you two got somefin' after all.'

How did that 'something' become real for these kids? For two years I struggled to find an answer. I had the distinct impression that there was a key, that though it dangled in front of our noses and was there for the taking, it belonged to the Church as the body of Christ, and not just to me as an individual. On our own Frank and I were fairly helpless. We could introduce the kids to Christ, tell them what he had done and said, and it certainly made some kind of sense to them. After all, he had mixed with the underworld of criminals and prostitutes they knew so well. The problem came when they said, 'OK then, I'll give it a try. I'll follow Christ.' As long as they frequented the old haunts and mixed with the old company they did not stand a chance. They desperately needed an alternative, a Christian community which would love and want them. Few churches were that. If they survived one service it was a miracle. Some could not read, let alone follow a hymn book. They felt bored and awkward; they did not belong. I remembered the feeling only too well, and did not try to prevent their escape. The only comfort was that God was bigger than the families and inadequacies of any Christian institution. We gave the kids what we could and he alone knew what they made of it all.

The intensity of the job, its utter relentlessness – a night's sleep could be disturbed at 3 or 4 a.m. by a homeless waif or two standing on the doorstep – made a long summer holiday imperative. In the Corfu sunshine a thousand bricks seemed to fall off my shoulders. I could breathe again, could exist, without glancing over my shoulder, clutching my handbag or preparing the words to deflect the next crisis. Needing some quiet I went down to the seashore in the early morning and sat on a rock, my feet dangling in the sea. Somehow I knew that my time with the Catacombs Trust would soon be at an end.

'But what then, Father? Another youth work post? I have no real ambitions or qualifications.'

'What would you like to do?'

The question took me by surprise. 'Well, if you really want to know . . .'

I did not have to tell him. I sensed that if I could have seen his face, there would have been a real twinkle in his eye.

9

Four years had passed since my affections were first engaged and their object was no nearer making any response now than he had been then. If anything Peter was colder, more remote. He was not unaware of my intentions and a certain stiffness had entered our relationship. He made very sure that our eyes never met across the church, that we would not end up alone together for any length of time. I found a very effective, albeit melodramatic way of coping with the situation. I imagined that in my bedroom was a little stone altar such as Abraham might have built when God asked him to sacrifice his only son Isaac. Whenever I felt I could no longer hold out Peter to God on the open palm of my hand I ran to that altar and gave him back to God again.

'He's yours, Father, and whether he's ever mine is for you to choose.' Kate and Paula, my two flatmates, learnt to respect the sanctuary of that room on many a Sunday evening.

Nonetheless, those years were anything but miserable. In fact they were very full, and often very happy. Kate, Paula and I created a real home out of our flat. Admittedly my youth work sometimes tested their patience to the very limit, such as the time we provided shelter for two homeless waifs and they left behind the two guest beds full of dead body-lice, but Paula even had the grace to comfort me. 'Don't worry, darlin',' she spluttered, disappearing in a cloud of insecticide, 'this stuff they gave me at the town hall should do the trick. And if not, well they're all God's little creatures, after all.'

Kate was a whizz at sniffing out eligible men and inviting them back for a meal. We had quite a social life. I even received some proposals, but always my heart told me I should never love anyone as I loved Peter. It was maddening. Why could he not disappear from my life, get another job and move? Slowly the idea dawned that perhaps that was what *I* should do.

'Lord, this isn't an ultimatum,' I said on my return from Corfu, when the sight of Manchester city centre was hardly endearing, 'just a means of preserving the bit of sanity I have left. If there's no sign of a thaw by Christmas, I'm packing my bags and leaving Manchester.' I meant it too. I had had enough.

Christmas approached, the shops glittered with goodies and the kids kept helping themselves. I was never away from the magistrates' courts. Some season of goodwill! I dreaded it. I always felt more rootless and lonely than at any other time of the year.

'Let's put up a few decorations, it'll cheer us up no end!' Kate was on hands and knees in front of the fire, sorting out a tangled heap of baubles and paper chains. The phone rang. 'I'll go,' she said, jumping up, 'you never know, my prince may have found me at last.'

When she came back into the room, I could tell from the expression of disbelief on her face that this was no ordinary telephone call.

'It's for you,' she said, breaking into a huge grin. 'Guess who.'

My legs wobbled as I walked out into the hallway. Kate followed me. 'Hello, yes? Yes, I'd love to go out for a meal. The twenty-third is free.'

Paula appeared at the top of the attic stairs, drawn irresistibly by something in the air, her mouth wide open. I put down the receiver and we stared at each other in silence for a while, letting the impact of what had happened sink in. 'He's asked me out for a meal,' I whispered, as if the Prince of Wales himself had phoned. 'He doesn't usually do that, does he?'

Simultaneously we all broke out into shrieks of laughter and cavorted round the little hallway, until the landlady's banging on the ceiling reminded us of her presence. Kate rushed to my wardrobe and rummaged around. 'What are you going to wear? You'll have to buy something.'

Paula was still sitting on the stairs, recovering from shock. 'Well, darlin',' she said, shaking her head incredulously, 'there must be hope for us all.'

Within a few weeks our engagement was official. Once his mind was made up, Peter worked with the same speed and determination which had earned his beer-brewing ancestors their millions.

'I knew I must be in love,' he said, 'I've never spent so much on a night out in my life.'

'But how did it happen? I've hardly seen you in months.'

'I don't really know. Seeing you at church every week was always an embarrassment. I knew you had designs on me and I thought, "Poor girl, she's wasting her time." That was why I ignored you, to help you get over it. Then, a few weeks ago, I began to dislike my bachelor state. I mentioned it to God and asked if he had anyone in mind for me. I was blank at first and then I kept thinking about you, until by the end of the week I was totally distracted. It did occur to me that you might not still feel the same about me, but I was ready to take that chance.'

'Not feel the same!' I hardly knew what to do with myself I was so ecstatic. I could not eat, could not sleep, was a lousy youth worker. I had only one worry. My parents! How would they feel? Had I already committed the ultimate crime, or was 'marrying out' still far worse?

'Poor mum,' I thought, as my train shunted jerkily the last few yards over the River Tyne into Newcastle Central Station, 'things never do seem to go her way where I'm concerned.' There were the five bridges! I was nearly home, but this time, despite the usual apprehension, everything was different. There was someone back in Manchester thinking of me, waiting for me. I was not on my own any more.

'Still picking up yobbos out of the gutter and dropping them back, dear?'

'Yes, Dad.'

Supper conversation had not changed much in two years. My father, half amused, half wistful, shook his head. 'If only you'd been a doctor like me. You would have made a marvellous doctor.'

'What's more to the point,' Mum intervened, 'any boys on the horizon, any nice boys?' I paused. It looked as if this was the moment.

'Yes, actually. A very special one. In fact I'm going to marry him.'

'Now dear, don't get upset,' my father said, patting Mother on the arm, before she had time to react.

'Not Jewish, I suppose? I hardly need to ask.' She was rather pale, tight-lipped, but very calm. 'Well, I can't say I didn't expect it. Marry him, you don't need our permission, so don't expect a blessing either. When I think of all the dreams I've had for you.'

Father waited for her to leave the table, then he turned to me. 'Give her time,' he whispered, 'she's ready for it, she'll accept it.'

I nodded, amazed at how prepared she seemed to be.

'It's strange how things work out,' Father continued. 'Do you know, I had made up my mind to talk to you this weekend. I was going to say, "Don't stay single just for us. If there's a nice non-Jewish boy you want to marry, marry him. You'll have a life to live long after we're dead and buried. Don't sacrifice yourself for us." However, I do have one quibble. Did you have to pick a *poor* member of the Guinness family?' Mother came back into the room and I hugged them both.

'We can't come to any church service, you realise,' she said, 'but we will attend a reception.'

It was more than I dreamed possible.

'Now, how shall I tell all the relatives?'

'You mean, I can bring him home to meet everyone?'

'I didn't say that. No, I'm afraid you can't. I have your brother and sister to think about. If I just give in to you they'll think they can just go and marry out if they please and it won't make a scrap of difference to us. I must set an example.'

She noticed my crestfallen expression and relented a little.

'Once he's your husband and nothing can be changed, then you can bring him home. Until then, we'll have to find a convenient meeting place somewhere half-way between Newcastle and Manchester.'

One Sunday, a few weeks later, Peter and I slipped out of church before the end of the service and drove to Harrogate to meet my parents for lunch. He chattered away easily, but I felt uneasy and tense. 'If only he knew them like I do,' I thought. 'They'll either love him or hate him, but there's no in-between.' Besides, the odds were hardly in his favour.

They were already there and having a drink in the bar when we arrived a little late. I hugged them stiffly, formally introduced my fiancé and to my relief they greeted him with genuine warmth. 'What a height,' my mother gasped. To my amusement I noted that Peter was almost bent double so that she could talk to him without straining her neck. 'How tall are you?'

'Six foot four, I think. My family are all tall. Never mind,' he smiled, 'marriage with yours will bring us down a peg or two.'

We went into lunch and there was gammon and pineapple on the menu, Peter's favourite. I wondered what he would do and watched his face with interest.

'Lamb, please,' he said, then his eyes widened and his mouth fell open as father turned to the waitress and said, 'And I'll have a pork chop.'

'Blow it!' he whispered to me after the meal. 'I could have had gammon. I was being so careful not to offend.'

That was a minor surprise compared with what was to come. Over coffee my parents really got down to business. They had saved a certain amount of money to give away with their daughter, not exactly a dowry, but a little 'help'. Now, what had Peter to offer? How much had he saved, what did he earn and what were his prospects? I wanted to disappear into a hole. I knew that marrying off one's children still involved a financial arrangement for most Jewish parents, but I never imagined it would apply in our case. Peter looked stunned, then he rallied.

'Actually, I've saved about five hundred pounds,' he said proudly.

'Nothing at all! I see,' my mother sighed. 'And what prospects has a schoolteacher?' She shook her head. 'Well, you're not exactly all we wished for our daughter, but I suppose you'll do.'

A few months later we were married in the Free Church we attended. I was disappointed that my family could not be there, especially that Father did not give me away, but our church family took us to their hearts and made it a very special service. We walked out of church as man and wife on a muggy Manchester day to the tune of '*Hatikvah*', 'the Hope', the Israeli national anthem.

To the horror of both our mothers, we bought a little wreck of a house in Didsbury, reduced it to bricks and rubble, and spent our first few years together proving to everyone that we could make it a cosy, interesting home. My parents often came to stay, especially once the first grandchild had arrived.

'You know,' my mother said one evening, 'I never intended to like Peter, let alone love him, but somehow he just crept up on me.' Little did I guess to what extent that love was to be tested over the ensuing few months.

We had barely painted our final skirting-board, when Peter

made an announcement which rocked my contented, little existence.

'Love, I think I may be called to the Church of England ministry.' He was stretched out on the bed, hands under his head, staring blankly at the ceiling. I was searching for some new fascination for our one-year-old, who was never fascinated by anything for longer than two minutes.

'Great, love,' I said distractedly, 'a deacon in the Free Church, they'll welcome you with open arms.'

'I'm serious. I've been thinking about it for ages. You know when we got married I always said I'd be in some kind of Christian ministry one day.'

'Yes, but you never mentioned the Church of England. You said you didn't know what you'd do but you knew we'd never be rich. That was the day you went out and bought me the sewing machine.'

There was no response. I began to feel really disturbed.

'How can we leave our church and the people we love so much? We've been members there for eight years. When I think of all that's happened in that time it hardly seems the same place.'

Peter still made no reply. I allowed my mind to wander back. How rich those years had been. We were such a funny hotch-potch of a congregation, all from totally different backgrounds, Brethren, Pentecostals, Calvinists, Charismatics, Baptists. Everyone had an opinion about the church and the right to have it heard. People wrote papers on everything from 'Living in a Christian Community' to 'Perfect Church Government and Structures'. We passed them round, studied them, debated them at General Meetings and usually decided that since there was no blueprint in the Bible we should have to agree to differ. Relationships were forged, some were severely strained, and yet a remarkable sense of commitment to one another prevailed. Changes were made, some of them quite unusual for a Free Church. The Communion service became the weekly focal point for our worship, and not a monthly additional extra. Freedom was given for an extended time of extempore prayer. We learnt to be sensitive to each other, to choose appropriate hymns, to differentiate between an awkward and a reverent silence. The spontaneity and vibrancy I had longed for had become a reality. How could I leave behind what we had wept for? How would I ever cope with the Anglican liturgy, with

120

a whole set of cultural traditions which meant nothing to me at all?

'So,' I said out loud, 'we just say, "Thanks for the last eight years. We really appreciate you all very much but we've just had this sudden revelation we're meant to be Anglicans."'

'But love,' Peter said, in the supplicatory tone of voice I had come to recognise as saying, 'I've made my mind up, so do try and accept it.' It made my toenails curl. 'I've explored the Free Church ministry but no door ever seems to open. I'm thirty, I can't sit around waiting any longer, not when the Church of England has issued us with such an open invitation.'

'Has it? I hadn't noticed.'

'Of course. Don't you remember?'

I was blank at first and then it came to me, that weekend in Rugby! We rarely went away for weekends. Peter was the deacon in charge of the church fabric and committed to ensuring that the entire building was in perfect working order. Then close friends in Rugby invited me to speak at their church one Saturday afternoon and of course we stayed for Sunday. It just happened to be the Sunday that Dr Coggan the Archbishop of Canterbury's appeal for men to come forward for the ministry was read out in every Anglican church, and we just happened to be sitting in one.

If ever a man's ears pricked up, Peter's did. His rigid attention made me feel slightly uneasy. After all, he was the son of an Anglican clergyman and I think I had always known where his roots really were.

'Wasn't that extraordinary?' he said as we walked back to Sunday lunch.

I feigned innocence. 'What was?'

'That we should hear the Archbishop's letter.'

'Ironic, yes.' I had laughed and put the incident right out of my mind.

'But I'm no Anglican,' I shouted, as the first awful awareness seeped like an icy pool into my consciousness that perhaps my husband was better acquainted with God's will for our lives than I was, 'and I don't want to be a vicar's wife.' I had visions of dowdy clothing, awful hats, of running women's meetings and organising jumble sales.

'More and more this seems to me to be the right way forward, love. We'll have to start attending the local Anglican church, of course, but we've friends there, it won't be too hard. It will give us a chance to think about it. See how you feel.'

For the next few days I wandered round the house feeling miserable, unable to think of anything else. There was the Victorian pine dresser, built into the kitchen wall, which we had stripped with such loving care, and the Georgian window in the dining-room. Peter had made every joint by hand, and the little brick hearth in the front room, which we had designed ourselves, leaving the bricks to set overnight, balanced round an arched piece of curtain rail. We had rushed down in the morning to see if it had survived the night. How could I leave it all behind, to live in properties which other people had designed and decorated, never to have our own house again? It was so easy to follow Christ, wherever he asked, when there was not a lot to lose. Suddenly I realised that despite all my promises to the contrary, materialism had crept up on me without my noticing. I was enjoying a comfortable rut like so many Christians I had been quick to criticise. Giving up our home, our friends and a reasonable salary might be madness, but at least it was not boring.

'That does it, Pete, we'll go,' I announced as he walked in from work a few days later. His eyes opened wide with surprise. 'Quick, get in touch with the Bishop before I change my mind. After all, what is this place except bricks and mortar! God will give us another heap of stones somewhere else. There is just one thing, though, I'll try to be an Anglican, but suppose I don't really settle?'

He took me in his arms. 'You will,' he said, smiling down at me, 'I know you will. After all, it isn't the first time you've had to make some major adjustments.'

'Well then, I suppose I'd better go and make a purple Crimplene suit. Isn't that what clergymen's wives wear?'

'You dare!' he laughed.

'Oh, by the way,' I called after him. He was half-way out of the door, a huge grin stretching from ear to ear. 'You can tell my parents!' The grin dissolved in an instant. We stood looking at each other for a while, then he took a deep breath and nodded.

My poor parents coped a great deal better with our news than we ever anticipated.

'I knew it! I knew it! I knew you'd do something like this to me,' Mother raged.

'Well, after all, a clergyman is a professional man,' my father reassured himself.

'Hardly one of the professions Jewish parents wish upon their children!' my mother snapped.

Then gradually, despite the pain, the elasticity of their love prevailed and stretched to encompass this new shock. Mother's face slowly relaxed into a smile.

'Hmm! Mein-Sohn-in-law, the vicar! Who'd have ever thought? Well, I may yet be mother-in-law to the Archbishop of Canterbury. What would our rabbi say to that?'

A few months later, when Peter had been accepted as a prospective ordinand, and we had begun to plan our two years at theological college, my parents treated us to a few days at the seaside. The car was packed and we were ready to go, when I had an afterthought.

'Love, go and get Grandma's ring out of its hiding place. I'll wear it while we're away.'

'Peter,' my mother commanded, 'you heard the vicar's wife, she wants to wear her diamonds.' When mother applied Jewish humour to a situation it was a very positive sign. 'Oh, and by the way,' her voice followed me out to the car, 'when I die and you inherit my wonderful furs, which I've collected so carefully, I suppose you'll wear them to the parish fêtes?'

'Mother, what on earth would I want with your furs?'

'You see what I mean? That's the point. Well, don't sell them at the jumble sales, that's all, or I may come back and haunt you!'

10

I pinch myself sometimes, just to make sure the whole thing is not some extraordinary dream. Here I am, an Anglican, Free Church, Jewish Christian, married to a clergyman and a source of theological confusion to everyone, even myself at times. I certainly find it becoming more difficult to convince people that I am not really committed to any one particular denomination. Clergyman's wife or not I still maintain that Christ himself, not the Church of England or any other denomination, is the fulfilment of my Judaism, and if stretched to classify my particular brand of Christianity, I should probably say 'Jewish'. This is not mere facetiousness. Common sense and history make it quite clear that in the event of widespread anti-Semitism, that is exactly how I would be labelled. Earlier this century there were large groups of Jewish Christians in Europe. After the war they were never heard of again. Conversion has never meant an easy escape from persecution. Still, I am quite pleased to be able to take a very minor stand against denominationalism, because it so undermines the credibility of the Church. It is one thing to have preferences in worship, for choice brings variety, it is another to believe that only one particular way makes a real Christian. Jewish friends say to me, 'But how can you accept Christianity? Christians don't even agree or get on with one another.' I hang my head in shame. It is no use arguing with them that Jewish people have their feuds too. They do, but it is not the same.

When my father began to pursue in earnest his previous flirtation with Reform Judaism, the family teased him mercilessly.

'Come on, Dad,' David joked, 'you know that isn't the real thing.'

'Not when they have the service in English,' Mother laughed.

'None of my family have ever been Reform before. It sounds more like a church to me.' There was more than just a hint of indignation in Gran's voice. She thought she had delivered the ultimate in effrontery, but my Father refused to be nonplussed. Some of our conversations had rekindled his interest in religion.

'At least I now know what I'm praying,' he murmured. No one could argue the point and Father was left in peace.

The differences between Reform and Orthodox Judaism, and even the wide range of opinion about practice within Orthodox Judaism, are not the same as the differences between the Christian denominations. Argument and debate have been traditional methods of learning for centuries. It is a way of life. Jews can argue furiously, even over religion, they can fight and quarrel, yet remain deeply committed to each other. This is because of a highly developed awareness of their identity as a people. The feeling of being somehow 'chosen', special, and therefore vulnerable, combined with thousands of years of insecurity and suffering, have produced a sense of mutual belonging and interdependence.

I long for Christians to have a similar sense of destiny. To follow Christ is surely a special calling, the greatest privilege that ever man could possess, conferring every right to feel 'chosen', but how quickly wonder evaporates, leaving behind an almost bland ordinariness about the Church. A distinguishing feature or two would help, but the one which Jesus intended to mark out his followers before the world, is the very one which rigid denominationalism throws to the wind: love. No one would wish it but I sometimes feel that until Christians have faced the harassment which has consistently pursued the Jews, they will never grasp how costly a luxury self-assertive disagreement over doctrinal accuracy really is. The threat of persecution might weaken self-reliance a little. Petty dislikes would become relatively meaningless. Christians might not take their foibles so seriously. Gentle self-mockery and humour have always been a safety valve for the Jewish people, for laughter preserves integrity and balance. Many attitudes and priorities in the Church could be radically overturned. For one thing, there would have to be a loosening of dependence upon the building itself and a rediscovery of the value of worship in the home.

Jewish communities have been scattered, their synagogues destroyed, but the faith preserved as strong as ever because it did not need a building, nor even a rabbi to ensure its survival. One Jewish home is all that is required. Christians uphold family life as the key to a well-ordered society. Jews uphold family life as the key to the survival of Judaism. That is the secret of its success.

When Peter was ordained the strains and pressures of the job came as quite a shock. While at theological college we were well prepared for the fact that life would be fairly hectic, that Peter would be out many evenings and I would become a kind of clerical widow, left to my knitting and needlework. The latter was by no means unappealing. What I had not grasped was how much our life as a family would be threatened. But we were not the only ones to suffer. The Church proclaims the joys of family life and undermines it with the same breath. Families rarely worship together. The children are shunted off into Sunday School and endless evening meetings separate spouses or mean a continual stream of babysitters.

'You're not out again, Mum, are you?' Joel asked in desperation one evening. 'Where to this time?'

'Church,' says our two-year-old, barely able to speak.

'This can't be right,' I said to Peter later. 'I don't want the children to grow up thinking the Church takes their parents away from them. That's a sure way to breed resentment. When they're older I want them to associate God with the good memories, not the bad ones.'

I am no more able now to accept things as they are because that is how they always have been, than I could as a teenager. The only difference is that whereas it was once Judaism, now it is the Church. Must the church programme appear to treat children as an infringement of their parents' freedom, to be tolerated as a kind of necessary evil until they are old enough to sit still and keep quiet? And as for my own children, what about their Jewish heritage? Such was the pace of life that it was in danger of being eroded altogether.

One day Granny brought Joel a beautifully embroidered skull-cap from Israel.

He was thrilled. 'Mummy,' he said, examining it carefully, 'am I really Jewish like Granny said?'

I nodded. He put it on and looked very impressive, a real little Jewish boy. 'Yes, you're Jewish, Joel, because my family is. It depends on the mother.'

'But what does that mean?'

I suddenly realised how important it was that he should attend his cousins' *Bar Mitzvahs* and take his place at the synagogue naturally and with confidence. It would be unfair to rob him of his birthright. Peter and I would have to rethink the needs of our family and find a way to hold two contrasting cultures in balance, passing on the best of both to our children.

Fortunately I married a man more convinced of the value of my Jewish heritage than I was. For generations his family had loved the Jewish people and sought to convince Christians and Jews alike of the Jewishness of the Messiah.

'It was always Jews for breakfast, Jews for lunch and Jews for supper in my home,' Peter told me that day we got engaged. 'It was my father's favourite topic of conversation. Little did I guess that I was in for it for the rest of my life!'

From the first, and even more so after his decision to be ordained, Peter was determined we should hold on to my Jewishness, explore and enjoy it for ourselves and more than that, endeavour to apply some of its strengths to the Church if at all possible.

'Maintaining the Jewish culture is so important,' he said to me one day with great earnestness, 'that on principle I really don't believe Jews should marry out.'

I laughed. 'But that's what you made me do.'

'I know,' he said with a twinkle in his eye. 'What a good job I don't always live up to my principles!'

With his encouragement I began to reassess my childhood experience to try and discover which traditions would work for us. I rejected the complex Judaic system of laws, including the dietary laws. There were far too many and they were much too complicated to observe with any measure of accuracy. And besides, I felt they were obsolete. Because of Christ's death, God's favour is a gift, not a reward. But I did realise how much I had valued the Sabbath as a family night and what it had cost my parents to refuse many interesting invitations out. Relying on their time and presence for that one evening, a special meal, familiar rituals and candlelight were part of the security and rhythm of our existence. Despite our hilarity, the festivals, with all their richness and colour celebrated around the mealtable, filled me with a sense of awe and wonder. We never closed our eyes or folded our hands in the formal way the Church often teaches children to pray, but somehow I knew God was there, in the laughter, the singing, the familiar stories and symbols, the God I was determined to discover as I grew up.

I suppose I shall never come to terms with the way Christians split the spiritual from the secular, as if there were some shame attached to being human. It still seems strange to me that there has to be a right environment, atmosphere and stance before prayer is really valid. When we were married Peter and I were told we must learn to pray together. We would spend an hour in deep discussion, then say, 'We must pray about it,' close our eyes and repeat the whole conversation all over again, as if closing our eyes and formal language would make God suddenly sit up and listen. I felt instinctively that prayer should be more natural, as I remembered it from childhood. Christian children learn that prayer requires absolute quiet and total concentration, then grow up banning children from church services because they make a noise.

Of course there is room for silence and solitude in meeting God. It is marvellous when the relationship gets beyond the point where words are necessary and it is enough just to sit in his presence, but a church service is not the best place. The more I see congregations huddled over their pews, each individual locked into his own private world of prayer, totally inaccessible to his neighbour, the more I understand and value the noise and chatter of the synagogue. What mattered was not the individual, but the corporate experience of worship. Physical togetherness was not a necessary misfortune to be endured. It was a vital part of communal life. My need for stillness and quiet as I struggled to feel God's presence was comparatively irrelevant. I could have my own encounter with God at home if that was what I wanted. For the Jew there is no such thing as a private religious life. His whole existence is bound up in the wider community. Every personal anniversary and special occasion from birth to death, whether joyous or sad, is celebrated in public by the entire community. No man's business is his own affair.

My grandfather's greatest pleasure in later life was to sit on a public bench on the cliffs at Roker overlooking the sea.

'Well, what sort of a day, Dad?' my mother would ask him on the way home.

'Bah! No one even sat next to me,' he would say with bitter

disappointment some days, but on other days his whole face would flush with excitement. 'You know who I met? Such an interesting man, a plumber with six children and you know how much he earns a week?'

All men were his friends. Hours wiled away at the synagogue had taught him to make people his hobby. No two Jews sit together at a service then return home without knowing the state of their neighbour's business, his medical history, favourite football team and intimate details about most of his relatives.

I would love the Church to become more of a community, knowing those moments of corporate joy and sadness which drive away loneliness and isolation. Some congregations are becoming warmer, but it is a painfully slow process, especially where there is a longer tradition of British reserve and formality. After all, where else but in church will two people who have already met sit side by side and even share a hymn book while barely saying hello? In the Church of England the only recognition that our neighbour exists at all is in the giving of the peace, a rather formalised greeting which some resent as an intrusion into their privacy anyway. The service ends and everyone dives for the door, enticed away by Sunday lunch and the church warden clanking the keys. Some Sabbath celebration!

At home we have started to celebrate *Kiddush* on Friday evenings. It is our family night, sometimes on our own, sometimes with others joining us from the wider church family. I light the Sabbath candles as my mother did, and hers before her, and sometimes I catch that unmistakable glimpse of wonder in the children's faces. We sing, eat *chollah*, drink from the *Kiddush* cup and read the familiar blessings, thanking God for weekends, but most of all that those simple symbols, bread for man's labour and wine for his rest, now remind us of Jesus. Most Jewish blessings begin reverently, 'Blessed are you, O Lord, our God, King of the universe.' The disciples must have been devastated when Jesus taught them they should call God, '*Abba*: dear Daddy.'

Ideally I want my children to grow up with a Jewish sense of awe for God, and the Christian joy at his nearness. I hope they will be able to express what they feel for him freely and without inhibition, not restricted by rules and formalities, either Jewish or Christian, but praying as they breathe, instinctively, because the Almighty God who made heaven and earth is also their Father.

We have the added bonus of two sets of festivals and they often dovetail. The Jewish ones are a great opportunity to recount the old familiar stories, seated around the mealtable. Christian festivals apart from Christmas seem to me to be greatly underplayed, and we try to make them special too. It is hard work, but well worth it. Easter has a whole new significance when it follows on from Passover. The *Seder* night enables all who participate to experience the last supper and appreciate how fully Christ used the symbolism to demonstrate that he was the climax of the story of man's redemption. Passover is anticipated with the same excitement as Christmas in our home and there are no presents, only an Easter egg given in exchange for the treasured *afikomen*. The Christian symbol of resurrection replaces the Jewish symbol of sacrifice.

Peter's having no Hebrew presented a problem. In addition we received invitations to lead *Seder* nights in one or two churches. The English translation of the *Haggadah* was stilted and archaic, so we drafted our own paraphrased version, eliminating some rabbinic explanation, but closely adhering to the original text, rather than attempting to 'christianise' it. Christians seem to find the evening a novel experience.

'We shall be involved in worship throughout,' Peter tells the participants in his introduction, 'but do feel free to joke, laugh, chat, however the mood takes you. I shall just continue.'

Dozens of pairs of eyes open wide in amazement.

'What got me were the prayers,' said one young man as he shook my hand vigorously on his way out. 'They're just like ours.'

It was my turn to be surprised. 'Well, yes,' I said, 'many of them were psalms.'

'Yes, just like ours,' he repeated.

It has taken me a long time to realise that Christians have so appropriated the Jewish Scriptures and worship, wrapping them round in their own cultural traditions, that they no longer recognise what originally belonged to the Jews. It is little short of pillage and plunder. Sometimes, during Communion services, I am tempted to cry out, 'What have you done to our *Kiddush*?' How did that simple traditional thanksgiving, made regularly in every Jewish home, become a cold, rigid, formal occasion? Jesus never said, 'From now on have a special service once a week.' He simply said, 'When you do this, remember me.'

I often wonder how he would feel about our institutionalised

Church, our Gothic buildings, quaint language and Victorian attitudes. I suspect they would be as much of a mystery to him as they were to me. As a child, although I realised Jesus was a Jew, I never really believed it, not a Jew like I was at any rate. Many Christians have totally dissociated him from his Jewishness because they believed he was against it. But he was fully, truly Jewish, because he kept the spirit of the law perfectly. It was religious hypocrisy he opposed, not Judaism, and I suspect that Christian hypocrisy today would anger him as much as Jewish hypocrisy did then.

The more Christianity is put back into its Jewish context the richer it becomes. Judaism enlightens Christianity and Christianity completes Judaism. The two were never supposed to be in conflict. That is not to say that I do not appreciate the great wealth of historical tradition in which the Church of England is steeped. I imagine the Prayer Book will never call forth from me the same emotional response as the *Shema*, the *Kiddush*, or even *Yiskedal* – the prayers of mourning – yet nevertheless I am slowly learning to value the liturgy. It is good to be part of English history as well. This is still no excuse for refusing to strip away the centuries in an attempt to discover the real essence of the teachings of Jesus and his disciples, without all our cultural additions.

Many years have passed since the days when I thought I must be the only Jew who had ever become a Christian. Now there are groups of Jewish Christians all over the world, in the USA and Israel in particular, but in Britain too. I sometimes gaze at them wistfully over my shoulder. It would be so much easier to preserve Jewish-flavoured worship in a group than in isolation, but the geography never seems to work. Besides, I do enjoy my Gentile Christian family. The cross has ensured that racial differences need no longer hold us apart. And I quite enjoy being a thorn in the Church's side! The apostle Paul felt called to the Gentiles. I hope it is not presumption to identify with such a calling. So there I stand at Passover time at the supermarket checkout with the rest of the Jewish community, our trolleys filled with boxes of *matzos*, theirs to last them eight days, mine one night – at a church *Seder*! I no longer find it a schizophrenic experience. On the contrary, it is twice the fun. Within me two cultures exist side by side, sometimes in tension, yet inseparable, each finding its completion in the other.

I should like to think I am a microcosm of what the Church might be. Christians continually ask me why the Jewish people do not see that Christ is the Messiah when it is so obvious! But it is not obvious to them, and never will be until they are allowed to see that Judaism and Christianity are not mutually exclusive, rather that each extends and enriches the other. For a time their Messiah is hidden from them. This is not because of some failure on their part, but a temporary arrangement, carefully planned by a God who so loved the world he had made that he wanted men of every race to have the opportunity of becoming his children by covenant. But the first agreement with his old friend Abraham will not be forgotten. God has promised the Jewish people a special part in his plans. What a day that will be. The Church had better be ready!

Promised Land

For all my family in 'Grimlington',
a rich source of laughter, tears and inspiration!

Oh please don't cry my darling son
for the things I can't afford
because your dad's on strike lad
for his job and some day yours.
He's too young to retire love,
he's only thirty three,
so that's why there's only a sandwich for your tea.
There's this man called McGregor,
who is some seventy plus,
who's telling men your daddy's age,
'That's it lads, you've worked enough.
We're going to shut your pits down,
slim down the workforce too,
and if you don't agree with it,
there's always the dole for you.'
Well Daddy needs a job, love,
to keep the wolves at bay,
he wouldn't be very happy
sitting here all day.
I know it's hard, my darling,
after all, you're only two,
but Daddy and the other men must win this fight,
     that's true.
So dry your eyes, my angel,
cos when this fight is won,
there'll not be just a job for Dad,
but for you, my darling son.

                                        Nicky Layton

Preface

'I think you should call your book "a turnip-head's guide to a northern church," ' Linda said, 'before the North becomes a distant memory! I mean the theory's all right, if you like reading the heavy stuff, but you should write a story about ordinary people for ordinary people like me.'

The name 'Grimlington' is not intended to be derogatory. By some strange quirk of fate towns in the North do seem to acquire names like Grimsby, Grotton and Foulby, whether they reflect the truth of the matter or not!

Many readers will know where 'Grimlington' is, but that is largely irrelevant. It is 'Everytown', at least every small, industrial northern town, where life has become increasingly uncertain in recent years. Grimlington people are ordinary, yet they have a resilience and humour which makes them as special as the many others in our nation who now have to fight to make a future for their children.

I have also used a pseudonym for the town to cover my tracks and protect the church from public gaze. It is an ordinary parish church, with its usual share of ups and downs. Other churches have far more dramatic, exciting stories to tell. As we struggle to come to terms with the needs and culture of the working man, we still have more questions than answers.

No book is a work of journalism. Had Edward, Anna, or Alicia written it, it would be a different story. My roots go deep into the northern soil. I know nothing else. But for Edward and Anna the transplant has not been without cost and heartache. Life in Grimlington has meant a kind of death for them.

These are my impressions, events seen through my eyes alone. There have been many times in the past when, as a Jew, I have felt culturally alienated from the Church. I felt an outsider, little guessing how many others, Anglo-Saxon and Gentile as they were, felt the same. Unlike the Catholic, Pentecostal or Salvation Army churches, the Church of England, rightly or wrongly, has a certain image and tends to represent a certain kind of churchmanship, at home in a rural or professional environment, but not among the working classes. I realise that my terminology and the division it creates might give offence, but the reality is that Britain is divided into what almost amounts to two tribes, each with its own language, standards and culture. To deny it is to play the proverbial ostrich. The Church must adapt to the local environment. But more than that, it must work for understanding and acceptance. Both cultures have their strengths and weaknesses and much to give to each other, if we would but realise it.

I dare to hope that my Jewishness has invested me with a certain objectivity, which a clergyman's wife might not normally possess. I suppose I shall always feel a little like the outsider looking in, though Grimlington has done more than any church to conquer that feeling. Throughout history the Jew has been forced to wander in search of a land and like a chameleon has learnt to adapt to his environment. While preserving his own identity, he often becomes the greatest defender of the place of his adoption.

1

Grimlington's special charm is not exactly obvious. Those who pass through are hardly aware they have been and do not come back for the scenery. But those born here believe there is no finer place on God's earth. Nowhere else can a man toil his life away underground, then for ever rest his weary bones so peacefully in his old, familiar haunt beneath the soil. A certain charm there is in the gentle whirring sound from the pit wheel which wafts its way across the farmers' fields; in its hooter announcing the end of the shift; in the sight of the distant Yorkshire hills beyond the boundaries of the town, now dwarfed by the growing mountains of slag, black against the horizon; in the terraced cottages, back-to-back with their smoking chimneys, beckoning men to a good fire and good food. For these sights and sounds have the charm of home.

Good food and fires are almost a distant memory today. The High Street is quiet for a Tuesday, market day, the day the Post Office pays out the Benefits. Women, normally glad to stop and chat, warmed by the temporary illusion of wealth, walk quickly, lest if they stop to stare in a shop window the precious coins will somehow vanish from their purses. The greengrocer, a jovial man, loads his wares in crates upon the pavement, succulent oranges, shiny red apples, large bananas firm and tempting.

'Come on ladies, pears are a give-away this week. Leave the price to me.'

The women stop, gaze wistfully for a moment, then drag themselves away.

The butcher's shop is almost empty. There is no demand for meat. Sausage is the only treat since the strike began. Sausage on Saturday, sausage on Sunday.

'If I as much as look at another sausage . . .' says Mrs Whitaker. The butcher nods in sympathy. He could happily strangle any of the poor sausages which hang from the hook in his window, were they not already dead.

But it is midday and what would a man not give for the sight of a sausage, sizzling in the pan. The thought stirs his gastric juices into action. He must stop hallucinating. He must not go home. That way there will be more food for the kids. Company will drive away the hunger pangs. So the men congregate at the bottom of the street in the Market Square at the Spittle rail, so called because there the retired miners always stand every day, leaning against the rail, watching the world go by and coughing up the thick, black stuff which lines their lungs. Once it was known as the 'hitching rail', because, years ago, before the pits existed, the weary traveller would stop, hitch up his horse, fetch it water from the fountain and find himself a pint of ale. The fountain is now a clock, but little else has changed. For hundreds of years all the news and gossip of the world has found its way to and from that spot.

There the retired have been joined by the unemployed, restless, bored and heartsick, finding a comfort in companionship not to be found at the dole office across the road. And now the strike has added many more. They are a familiar sight, and there is reassurance in the sound of their laughter. Life goes on. They say that when the strike is over they will have to erect a bronze monument where Fred Benson has stood these eight months, like a statue, his elbows on the rail, unmoving except for his eyes. The town will not seem the same once he is back down the pit.

Wives, mothers and sisters with buggies full of children stop for a word, blocking the pavement, then trudge up the High Street.

I jostle past as I always do every Tuesday, and go into the market for eggs, almost warm from the farms. Then just a tiny diversion, not to buy, I tell myself, just to peep in the wool shop window. But oh the bargains! Bags of offcuts straight from the local mills, mohair and chunky and cottons, knubbly and crunchy in irresistible emerald, fuchsia and turquoise.

'Tempted again are we?'

I jump. Laughing, hanging half out of the jewellery boutique next door is Betty, the health visitor. It is her lunch hour and the object of this visit is Marjorie, whose brother owns the shop. Cathy, Marjorie's sister, is there too, giggling as she does, like a naughty schoolgirl caught smoking in the toilets.

'I thought I heard a noise. I might have guessed.'

'Join us.'

'There's no room.'

'There's heaps of room for a little one.'

'Does no one have any work to do?'

'Cheeky beggar, isn't she?' says Betty.

Marjorie smiles.

'We're not exactly busy.'

'So we're callin' instead,' says Cathy.

'Callin'', with a flat 'a' as in pally, is a practised art in West Yorkshire. Gossip makes the day pass quickly. The women do it guiltily with the disapproval of the men. The men do it naturally and no one disapproves of them.

A woman comes quietly into the shop and waits at the door. As if it is an unspoken signal Cathy gets down. 'I'm on duty at the park at one,' she says.

'And I've three more visits before clinic,' says Betty. 'See yer, Marj.'

I am about to go too when a silver chain catches my eye, the kind I have been wanting for ages.

The woman slowly approaches the counter, and lifts her left hand, the skin worksore and toughened like animal hide. She eases the gold band off her third finger.

'Will yer tek it?' she whispers, her eyes filling with tears. 'I've nowt else and the kids must eat.'

Marjorie nods and lays the ring lovingly in a tiny box on a bed of cotton wool.

'I'll not sell it,' she says, when the woman has gone. 'I couldn't. I'll keep it safe for her and she'll come for it when the strike's over.'

The silver chain has lost its appeal and I walk on up the High Street. Everything seems the same, the corner sweet shop with huge glass jars of sherbet, mints and gob-stoppers lined up in rows in the window, and the newspaper shop, door propped open, stark, bare and mucky with print. Yet it is different, too quiet, almost as if rumour has it that no food is to be had in the shops today. But the bakery bulges with curd cakes and Sally Lunns, bread cakes and scufflers.

'Mornin', love. Hundred per cent wholemeal as usual?'

The loaf is in her hand already, then in mine, warm and steaming with the smell of new bread.

'Thanks, Gladys. It's quiet in here today.'

'Ay well, what can yer expect? It were a good service though Sunday night.'

'Was it?'

'Weren't yer there?'

'Babysitting.'

'Oh ay, I forgot.'

Gladys, with her smile, warm and wholesome like the bread she sells, who said months ago she wouldn't go to church. She hadn't been for years, wouldn't know anyone. And when she came she knew them all. They bought bread from her and fancy, she never even knew they went.

It was always the same with new people. They crept in and sat at the back or behind a pillar. I tried to speak to them, because, being Jewish, I remembered my first visit to a church, how strange it seemed, how out-of-place I felt.

'Hello. I haven't seen you before.'

'No, I've not been since we had young 'uns christened.'

'Do you know anyone here?'

'I know 'em all, love. I've lived in Grimlington all me life. That's me cousin over there. But I don't know you. Who are you?'

It was a fair question. I often wondered who I was myself. The curate's wife? The role hung round my neck like a dead weight at times and I longed to heave it off and throw it away. The curate's Jewish wife? That was more confusing, and made me more foreign than ever.

'We like you, you know, even though you're a Jew.'

'Thanks!' I said, then smiled to myself and took it as it was offered, an honest token of acceptance. Yorkshire people speak their mind. I could not ask for more. It meant they saw beyond the caricature which role and preconceptions imposed, to me as I am, always a foreigner of sorts, yet now with so much of the town in my bloodstream. Strange that I should see so much of my own struggle reflected in theirs, struggle to resist pressure, refusal

144

to conform, insistence to be what we are, by birth and choice. Who would ever have guessed, when I first came nearly two years ago, that our lives would so intermingle?

Dear old town. When I wash your soot from my hair and the suds turn grey, when I wipe soot daily from my windowsills and watch it appear through the floor-boards in stripes on my carpets, when I see it and can laugh, then I know you have secured a niche for yourself in my heart that nowhere else shall supplant. Rumour has it that land round here belonged to Wilberforce, fighter of slavery. Later, strange irony, its harvest made other slaves, men, women and children, who hacked it day and night, and were just as black and bowed. Land always tugging at my heart strings, once fair, then raped and plundered for its treasure, now abandoned, bruised and scarred, its attractions gone. What will become of it and the men whose destiny is buried in its soil? What will all our striking and starving achieve? Will it preserve the community we love or drive it further towards its destruction?

2

I never dreamed of being a clergyman's wife. Not that I imagine many girls do these days. It just so happened that mine was the strange fortune, strange for a Jewish child, of attending a Church of England girls' school. And there I discovered that some girls, and even certain teachers, are very susceptible to the sight of an attractive young face emerging from a dog collar. Whatever it was that made them weak at the knees, I never succumbed to it.

I never wanted to marry a rabbi either for that matter. Although we kept most of the Jewish festivals at home and Mother's cooking was strictly kosher, yet they were far too pious for us. Besides, rabbis were not attractive. They had beards and their wives wore wigs!

And then events took over. At seventeen I read a forbidden book, the New Testament. And because of that apparently innocent exercise the course of my life was changed. Such are the fruits of curiosity! Mother's plans for me of a hard-working, if not wealthy Jewish boy were doomed from the moment I opened its pages. I became a Christian, but not a convert. How I hated the word! Christ was the logical extension of my Jewishness, not an alternative. Years later, after I had fought my battles to be a Christian and a Jew, I met Peter, not Jewish and only a schoolteacher, but a nice enough boy. Or so my mother thought, until he announced his sense of calling to the Church of England ministry.

She was not the only one to be horrified. She at least saw the funny side. I was devastated. By then we had been married four years, had our own home and up to that moment had been nonconformist! I prided myself on being versatile, especially when it came to the denominations, but there were limits. The vicar's wife could hardly try another church if she did not enjoy the one where her husband ministered. She was stuck for life with one denomination and all its foibles and with her husband's sermons. She had no choice. She fitted in. She did as people expected. She was bland, safe, without opinions and without friends for who would want their private thoughts to find their way back to the vicar?

I pushed my fears away for the two years of training, stimulating, happy years, a chance to read and think, to shake off inherited attitudes I felt were unreal. But I still did not confront my real self and its refusal to come to terms with its destiny, not until that first weekend we drove into Grimlington with a view to a possible curacy. 'For better, for worse', I had vowed only six years ago. And this, I decided, was worse, far worse.

We drove in silence up the one long road which stretched from the motorway to the centre of the town. On either side were rows of uneven, red-brick terraced housing, broken by a side street or a dingy corner shop. I looked for greenery, but there was none: no trees, no shrubs, no sign of spring, though March was almost past. The tiny gardens, separated from the pavement by two-foot high walls, were muddy and bare. It occurred to me that it would take a fairly determined flower to fight its way to daylight through gravy-stained cartons, scrunched up newspaper and empty pop cans.

'Well,' Peter said, breaking into the silence, as we stopped at the traffic lights, 'could you live here?'

So many impressions were flashing through my mind in a confused mass. The impression of 'once had been': a chapel now a warehouse, a cinema now a factory, a thriving, busy town now past its height. Yet also the feeling that in the occasional splash of colour for a front door, the fancy brickwork and hotch-potch of modernisation, bottle-bottom window panes and frilly net curtains, hope and pride survived.

'Oh, it's not so bad,' I said, transported in time to Felling, the little pit town in Gateshead where I had grown up. My father was the local doctor and he loved the little community in his care. Back-to-back terraces, cobbled streets and smoking chimneys were sights I had seen from the window every day. I would watch for hours. And sometimes, our Albert, a retired sailor and postman, who trained the dog, did the garden, collected us from school, sang us to sleep and kept the whole family in order, would take me home with him. Home to his Nelly, a real fire, home-made scones and endless cups of tea. I shook myself back into the present.

'There are far worse places to live,' I said.

'Ashton!' said Peter and rammed the car into gear.

His associations were not nearly as positive as mine. He was an eight-year-old once again, forced to leave behind a lakeside apartment in Geneva for Ashton-under-Lyne where his father was to be the new vicar. For the first weeks the family stayed with the churchwarden. All went down with gastric flu and the only toilet was out in the backyard. Peter did not understand and it was a trauma he never forgot. The Ashton of thirty years ago symbolised for him all that was drab, grey and depressing about small northern towns.

But I never expected to live anywhere else. Two years at theological college in the suburbs of Nottingham were the nearest I had ever been to beautiful surroundings. And while in mad moments of fantasy I dreamed of hearing a divine command to head south to a house on the coast with a sea view, I knew my chances were slim. I could live in Grimlington. But whether I could live there as a clergyman's wife was another issue. That was my struggle.

We turned up a long drive and as if by magic the scene changed into one of almost rural tranquillity. We were surrounded by trees, shrubs and riots of daffodils. A path led through a rustic gate to a rather picturesque old church ahead. For a moment it seemed we had come to the very heart of rural England – until I opened the car door and an acrid, sulphurous smell hit my nostrils and ruined the illusion.

'Pwah!' I said. It never occurred to me that the thick black smoke which poured into the sky from every chimney and hung over the town in a heavy brown pall would smell quite like that.

'I suppose you get used to it,' I said hopefully.

'Ashton!' was all Peter said and sniffed, wrinkling up his nose.

Meeting a prospective vicar is the closest equivalent I know to a blind date. We had been sent to two vicars already and neither seemed right. We were in danger of appearing too choosy. But our whole future happiness hung in the balance. We had a right to be sure. We walked up to the front door of a large, modern vicarage, rang and waited, as the condemned man waits to hear the footsteps of those who will take him to his execution.

The door opened and a striking-looking man appeared. We stood for a while, weighing each other up, wondering, I suppose, whether each was the answer to the other's prayer. For our part the poor man had a great deal to live up to. We had a definite blueprint: someone strong, forceful, determined, warm, caring, enthusiastic, all that and with a sense of humour too. Whether such a mortal, let alone a clergyman, existed was another matter. Given that we were also anticipating a fair measure of theological agreement and a willing partner in our plans to revolutionise the Church of England overnight, Edward Huntingdon was at some disadvantage. Nevertheless when, after half-an-hour's basic probing, he disappeared to fetch the coffee, we nodded to each other in agreement that he was faring quite well on our mental identikit. How we were faring on his remained to be seen.

Anna, Edward's wife, came in with the coffee.

'Cherchez la femme,' they had warned us at college. 'Look out for the wife, the power behind the man.' She was young, with a strong, attractive face. I noticed the firm jawline of someone who knew her mind and stuck to it. She did not appear to be someone whose life would consist of meetings, jumble sales, flower arranging and benevolent visits to the sick.

'I do little in any official sense,' she said. 'Only one committee, and that by choice. We've only been married a couple of years and I'm still getting used to everything. It takes me all my time to cope with the telephone, the doorbell, this big house and garden and a baby.'

I sighed with relief. The last thing I wanted was to provide a church with the sweat, blood and unpaid labour expected of many a minister's wife. I had supported my husband when he was a teacher, been involved in the life of the school, but no one had assumed I would do his job. I hoped it would be the same now.

'I'm warming to this place all the time,' I whispered to Peter as we went into lunch.

Alicia, the deaconess, joined us.

'Oh, this is nothing, dears,' she said, conscious that we were watching her struggle into a chair. 'Spondylitis of the hip. No pain, just a nuisance, a little stiffness.'

Alicia had had years of experience as a deaconess – twelve of them in Grimlington – and left us in no doubt that she regarded it as the third best place after heaven. Second was her native Scottish Highlands, but Grimlington was very close behind. She regaled us throughout our meal with an enthusiastic account of all its comings and goings, births, deaths and the best takeaway food. Edward had only been vicar five months and obviously had much to learn.

'You remember Molly Fairclough, whose sister we buried on Tuesday? Her youngest daughter is married to the brother of the man whose daughter you're marrying on Saturday. The groom is the nephew of Jim Burton, whose wife's sister I went to see this morning. And she's promised to come to church this Sunday.'

The tale was obviously perfectly comprehensible to Alicia and little short of a minor triumph, even if it was lost on Edward, who seemed a thousand miles away and stared abstractedly at a little blond, blue-eyed baby in a high chair, who was plastering food in her eyes, ears, up her nose, anywhere in an attempt to find the right opening. Just like our little Abby.

'Everyone here is related to everyone else,' Anna said, coming to the baby's rescue, 'a fact you may discover to your cost.'

She grinned knowingly at Edward. 'So never be rude about anyone. You'll probably discover you're talking to their mother-in-law, or a fifth cousin twice removed.'

'We wanted somewhere with a strong sense of community,' I said to Peter.

Alicia nodded in agreement. 'Then how,' he asked quietly, 'does an outsider fare?'

Alicia smiled.

'You're an outsider here, darling, if you come from the next town, or the other side of the motorway. Just be yourself. It's sham they've no time for. And I must go.'

She hobbled to the door, and, turning, left us with the ultimate encouragement. 'The bird life is quite exceptional round here.'

I looked out of the window. Birdsong was not a sound I had noticed.

'I mean, we have an ings nearby, reclaimed land filled with water. If you do decide to come you can borrow my binoculars whenever you like.'

No one had said anything yet about the house. College had

buzzed with incredible horror stories of curates' houses, damp, cold and in disrepair. Why did they not mention the house? It did matter. Other people could choose theirs.

'Shall we go and see the house?' Anna asked at last. 'I haven't seen inside it myself yet.'

We drove through the town, a leaden weight of dread resting on my stomach.

'How big did you say the town was?' I asked.

Anna watched my face, amused.

'About eighteen thousand,' Edward said from the front.

'And no Boots, no Woolworths?'

Anna laughed. 'I asked the same questions a year ago. No, no Boots or Woolworths. There were once, but they had to close. Hard to imagine, isn't it? Apparently the turnover was bad, and the service was worse. The pace of life is slow round here. No Sainsbury's either and for a southerner like me that's hard to bear. But don't despair, the town got its first purpose-built supermarket two years ago. It's a Co-op, adequate, if not exciting, as long as you're not an exotic cook.'

We drove on towards the outskirts of the town and into a large area of council housing. No high rise blocks, but only, I suspected, because the planners had run out of money before they remembered Grimlington's existence. There were some advantages in not being strictly inner city.

At the furthermost edge of the town, in total isolation, stood a modern detached house, separated on all sides from every other house by a thousand square yards of grassland. There was no tree to soften its starkness or shelter it from the wind. There it stood, the only private house, the only house without a chimney, looking for all the world like the folly of a man with too much money, who wanted to impress but had made a big mistake.

The car came to a halt and my heart sank. The curate's house, of course, what else? Built to look as if its inhabitants were somewhat superior to the rest of the neighbourhood, either that or carriers of the plague. Edward was obviously struck by its oddity too.

'It was built seven years ago,' he said. 'The idea was to establish a kind of church presence up here where we have so little contact.'

'Then why not rent a council house?' I asked. Living like the lord of the manor could hardly be called identifying with the people and I was not sure I fancied being a presence.

'I think the church members hoped the curate would soon attract a small congregation, then a church would be built on the spare ground.'

'How many curates have lived here?'

'Two.'

'And no congregation?'

Edward surveyed the grassland and shook his head. 'What church members there are want to move down into town. There's nothing here, no shops, no heart to the community.'

The exterior was all that was imposing about the house. Inside it smelt musty and looked pokey, painted as it was in a lurid, midnight blue.

'I'd no idea it was so shabby,' Anna said, looking round apologetically. 'Don't you think a coat of paint will work wonders?'

I tried to summon some rapidly dwindling enthusiasm, but such as there was evaporated when I realised the full extent of its catastrophic design. Some diocesan architect had excelled himself this time. Every room was completely overlooked from outside. The kitchen, apart from having three doors which collided when opened simultaneously, had no space for extras like a fridge. The previous curate's fridge stood where he had left it, in the centre of the room, and we walked round it as if it were a museum piece. There was no dining room, just a tiny square alcove off the kitchen. And the third 'bedroom' was too small to take a bed. The only concession to this being a purpose-built clergy house was a large downstairs toilet.

'The only room big enough for a filing cabinet,' Peter commented.

For two years in our small temporary house in Nottingham I had been forced to climb over his desk, mounds of books and papers and half-written essays to get into bed. It had been a veritable feat of mountaineering. I had dreamed of a house with some space. But here all we should have were two average-sized bedrooms. The children were small enough to share, but how could I invite friends to stay? Leaving so many behind was wrench enough without the added pain of being unable to offer them hospitality.

And my poor parents! I had always said to them, 'Whatever

happens, wherever we go, there will always be room for you.' Where would I put them? In Nottingham I juggled with cots and squeezed them in. It would take more than invention to do the same in this house.

Edward and Anna looked out over the garage roof.

'I wonder if we could extend out?' he asked.

I clung to the idea as to the only strand of hope. And I yearned for Manchester, for our first home, an old terrace lovingly renovated to meet our every need, then left behind when the call came. From now on we were doomed to other people's taste and other people's follies. My stomach turned over. I wanted to say, 'Thank you very much for showing us round but Grimlington isn't for us,' before running as fast as I could back to Nottingham. But something kept my mouth closed and fastened me to the spot. Had I become so inflexible? It was a roof over our heads. And life is more than houses. Though what that 'more' was I could not remember, not until later that evening, when we were introduced to some of the congregation.

3

They came shyly into the room, as frightened of us as we were of them. Edward introduced Marjorie first as one of the church-wardens. She was a warm, motherly woman, round and dimpled, with a shock of white hair which framed a face which must have once been the toast of the town. I felt at ease with her at once, and so did Edward, judging from the merciless way he teased her. But there was respect in his voice too.

'Keeping vicar in order is her hardest job, isn't it Marj?' said a voice behind them.

'And this is Lucy,' Edward said, drawing forward a shy-looking woman with bobbed hair, who nodded at us nervously. She perched on the end of the settee.

'I were just sayin',' she said, in the uneasy silence which followed, 'Council have been after us again about state of our back garden. It's like a wilderness and I can't get Dad to do it. It's getting past 'im.'

'Offer it back to the Council as a cemetery,' Peter suggested, 'and then they'd have to do it.'

She looked at him, shocked, realised he was joking, then laughed uproariously. The ice was broken.

'Oooh, do excuse me,' she said, as a loud gurgling sound filled the room. 'It's Oscar,' she patted her stomach, 'my peptic ulcer. He's always lettin' me down.'

The doorbell went again. Moments later Alicia brought a small, neat woman into the room. A quiet, dignified man stood slightly behind her. She looked round to see who was there, smiled at Marjorie and Lucy with satisfaction, then introduced herself.

'I'm Vera, and we represent the older generation, don't we Arnold?'

Marjorie laughed. 'Hey, Lucy, that makes us spring chickens. I suppose we should feel flattered.'

Anna brought in the tea and suddenly everyone was talking at once. I gave up trying to follow any line of conversation and enjoyed watching them. Peter's eyes were moving backwards and forwards too, like a spectator at a tennis match. Eventually Edward managed to persuade them to tell us one at a time how they had come to be involved in the church. From the deferring looks Marjorie understood that she was to begin. She explained how the church had gone through a time of great upheaval since she had started going. That was years ago, when her children were small. She had an asthma attack one night and nearly died.

'I was in hospital struggling for breath when I felt someone take hold of me hand and will me to live. I thought it were Charlie, me husband. Only he loves me like that. But when I said to him later, "I was glad they let yer stay with me," he said, "They didn't. They thought yer'd had it!" Well this may sound funny to you, and don't ask me how, but I was sure it were Jesus who had stood at me bedside that night.'

There was silence for a time, except for the ticking of the carriage clock, then Marjorie laughed.

'And here I am. Mind you the church was posh in them days. I felt a bit out-of-place. It was so . . .'

'Traditional?' Vera suggested.

'Full of people like us,' Vera added smiling. 'Well, we didn't know any different then, did we, Arnold? We went because we always had. Arnold's father was in trade and it was expected of us. Then one day a team of young people came. They stayed in our homes. And we suddenly realised we'd little real faith at all.'

I watched Arnold, wondering how he felt about this revelation. He was chuckling to himself in recollection.

'We told all our friends,' he said quietly, 'even customers who came into the shop. They think you're in your dotage when you become religious in later life.'

'Although they were churchgoers themselves,' Vera added. 'And they've found all the changes very hard indeed. It's been difficult for us. We're often in the middle.'

'I get my share of complaints too,' Marjorie said, shaking her head.

'Mother to the town, aren't you, Marj?' Edward said.

'I don't know about that.'

'And you, Lucy,' Edward said, suddenly turning to her. She jumped. 'It's your turn.'

'Me? I've nothing to tell.'

'Go on with you,' Marjorie said.

'Well, my speaking to yer now's a miracle. Yer can hear me stammer?'

I had barely noticed it.

'That's nothing. After me twin died I couldn't string two words together. I'd no confidence at all. I suppose I'd say God gave me a voice. Now, well, that one,' she said, pointing at Alicia, 'has me birdwatching, going to opera and all sorts.'

Alicia chortled to herself.

'Alicia has a lot of people doing things they never dreamed they'd do,' Edward agreed, catching Alicia's eye. 'I think it's called the gentle art of persuasion. When I ask people what made them start coming to church the most common reply is, "It was the only way to stop Alicia visiting." '

All this time Arnold had been studying us, watching and waiting with his eyes, like an owl.

'And you,' he said suddenly, 'what brings you to a place like Grimlington?'

Peter shared his chequered history and I shared mine. To be anything less than totally honest would have been an affront to their openness. They had already given so much of themselves.

'So you see,' he said, 'I don't want to come in as the traditional curate, good at almost everything, pretending I can do it all, because I can't. Edward says you need someone with special gifts in youth work and mission. I've neither. All I know is that somewhere there is a church with a Peter-and-Michele-shaped hole. And when we find it we'll know.'

'Well all I can say is that our curates seem to like us,' said Vera, as she collected her things together. 'They stay at least four years.' I was not sure whether that was a threat or a warning.

'Lucy,' I said, before she had a chance to disappear, 'tell me what you do.'

'I pack for Asda. You know them packs of apples wrapped in cling film? Well I put them together.'

'Do you enjoy it?'

She thought for a moment. 'It's a job. And that's something

these days. I'd rather work with people though. Wrappin' apples gets a bit monotonous. But then,' she said, a twinkle in her eye, 'some days, for variety they give us avocados or kiwis. The excitement! We'd never seen them before.'

She got up, went to the door, then came back and put her arms round me. 'Whatever yer decide, tonight's been special,' she said.

As the front door closed Peter and I looked at each other knowingly and smiled. Here were people who did not try to hide their true selves or their feelings and made no attempt to impress. We had found what we were looking for.

'I feel as if I've come home,' I said.

But it was an illusion. There in the vicarage with Edward and Anna we were safe, cocooned. The reality of the situation hit me again with all its force the following afternoon when Peter went to measure up the house. I took the children to play amidst the broken glass, litter, dog mess and dereliction on some swings on the spare ground opposite. From every house coils of black floated up into the air. The smell of sulphur was stronger here than anywhere else. Would I never be able to open my front door and breathe in fresh air again? I suddenly felt numb and desolate. I had not even the energy to push the children. I wanted to cry, but the tears would not come. I sat on one of the swings and rocked backwards and forwards. A child spoke to me and seemed puzzled when all I did was shake my head. I looked at the brick monument in the distance. Today it did not even look imposing, just pathetic, stuck out there on its own, as if it did not know how it got there or where it really belonged. Everything seemed so hopeless. Who would ever pop in for a cup of tea? The whole neighbourhood would know where they were going. How would we ever be accepted or get to know anyone, living such a strange, separate existence? I had always loved having neighbours and hated the isolation of the clergy. My worst fears were coming true. I would have no friends. It was all very well telling myself that if this was where we were meant to be I would have to cope. But what if we agreed to come and my feelings did not obligingly fall into line? I had to use my common sense. I would be no good to Peter as a lonely, quivering heap.

'Say no,' said a voice inside. 'That's all you have to do. Walk over there and tell him to put his tape measure away. He's wasting his time. You're not coming.'

I tucked Abby under one arm and with Joel trailing after me, lamenting leaving the swings behind, I marched up to the house, ready to offload all my misery on my poor longsuffering husband. He was sitting in a corner on the floor. One look at his face told me that he was contending with enough of his own. We looked at each other for a while in a helpless silence.

'Well,' he said, turning to stare out of the window, 'I do seem to ask a lot of you.'

I went over and sat next to him.

'Whatever happens, wherever we go, at least we have each other, and the kids.'

The thought cheered us a little, or at least helped us get ourselves together enough to follow Edward's street map to the other side of the town, where we had been invited for tea. We walked for what seemed an age, then turned into a new estate of tiny, box-like, neo-Georgian semis. 'Superior housing of distinction', we were informed by a large sign, but it was really very little different to the estate we had just left.

We were lousy company. Conversation was an effort and despite the warmth of their welcome, Rick and Julie and Mick and Karen were obviously unsure about how to handle our gloom. They agreed about the house, but were as helpless as we were about a solution. Julie disappeared quickly into the kitchen to make the tea.

'And all this smoke,' I grumbled rudely. I was too fed up to be polite.

'Why does everyone burn coal round here? Haven't they heard of the Clean Air Act?'

Mick surveyed me with the sort of quizzical expression that says, 'What have they sent us this time?' Then he seemed to remember we were foreigners after all.

'They burn it because it's free if yer work for Coal Board, like I do.'

'Then why don't they give them anthracite?'

'They do,' said Mick, with more grace than I knew I deserved, 'but not nearly so much. And none of us can afford to be finicky. It's the only real perk to working down pit. There's not much else to commend it, but at least yer don't have to worry about keeping warm.'

'You're a miner?' Peter asked.

'No, an engineer. There are as many of us, and electricians and joiners, as there are colliers.'

'Do you enjoy it?'

Mick grinned, a warm, infectious grin, with an almost school-boy appeal, and looked round at Karen, who had been sitting quietly at his side, smiling at us sympathetically.

'It's a job,' he said and I remembered I had heard that before. 'There's talk, yer see, rumours, about pits closing. A man's glad these days he's work at all. But what I'd really like to do,' he paused with a faraway look in his eyes, 'is 'ave a recording studio.'

Karen smiled at him, her face a mixture of motherly indulgence and despair. 'Oh Mick,' she said gently, and sighed. 'Him and his audio equipment!'

'No, no,' he insisted. 'I could use it for the church. A man can dream, can't 'e?'

'And he's another one,' Julie said, cocking her head at Rick as she sailed in from the kitchen with a large plate of buns. She was heavily pregnant and it seemed to suit her joviality. 'He'd like to be making music all day.'

Rick, who seemed quite an earnest young man, told us enthusi-astically about a music group he had started in the church. My spirits began to lift slightly. Mick, aware of the fact, weighed us up, then decided to take a chance.

'If you think Grimlington's bad,' he said, 'you should see Ossleforth, other side of motorway. If this country were a human body, Ossleforth would have the haemorrhoids.'

'Oh Mick,' Karen said, tugging hard at his pullover sleeve, but his face broke into an enormous grin and Rick and Julie shook with laughter. We laughed too, and it brought a sudden surge of relief.

Rick's music group were certainly not in evidence at the evening service. It was a laboured, traditional affair, using the old prayer book. A choir of five took what looked like a last stand and tried to rouse a sleepy, unresponsive congregation to worship. I wondered whether it was really as dreary as it seemed or whether it was just my Jewish nature with its love of life and colour playing tricks on me again, when a young couple in front of us who had been shuffling uncomfortably for a while, suddenly got up and walked out. The droning of the psalm had evidently finished them off. I had a deep desire to run after them and apologise for the church. Either that or escape from the boredom as well. 'At least,' I thought with relief as we sang the final hymn, 'on future occasions I'll be babysitting.'

I headed for the door. It had been a long weekend. Arnold was there before me.

'Grimlington's not such a bad place,' he said. 'We once had one of the most important railway stations in Europe. The Queen slept here.'

I tried to look impressed, then noticed the twinkle in his eye.

'In a railway carriage, in the sidings,' he chuckled.

'Which queen was that, Elizabeth or Victoria?'

'Touché.' He laughed, then said seriously, 'If you don't come back, don't forget us, will you, because we won't forget you.'

A lump came to my throat. I turned and went quickly out of the door.

4

We moved on the two most depressing days of the year. The sky was a heavy, leaden grey and the rain poured incessantly, not easing for a moment. The removal lorry with the ramp had broken down and was replaced by one with a tail-gate lift. We watched our furniture, bedding and precious belongings being battered and soaked.

'Never mind,' we said to each other, 'it can't possibly rain like this tomorrow when we offload in Grimlington.' But it did.

I hate moving. It is like turning over the final page of a good book. The experiences, relationships and emotions of that particular story are gone, never to be recaptured in quite the same way again. They disappear into the past, the silent secret of the bare walls and floorboards that make up the empty shell of the house that is left behind. As the last cup is wrapped in newspaper and placed in the crate, the remains of the sugar bowl thrown into the dustbin, a piece of toy, found under the carpet, shoved into a pocket, many scenes and sounds float back eerily, then vanish, gone for ever. It is hard to close the door for the last time and say goodbye to part of oneself.

I wondered how many goodbyes there would be in the future. They would be real separations, final, a kind of death. Clergy rarely haunt an old pitch. Perhaps it would be less painful not to love at all, than love and lose all the time.

I sat in the car, watching our belongings in the lorry ahead, feeling like a caveman's wife, being dragged by the hair where she never wanted to go.

'What sort of a vicar's wife will you make?' taunted an inner voice. 'You can't even say the Lord's Prayer without looking at the book. You're Jewish. You know nothing about the Church of

England. What have you got to give the people in Grimlington?'

Then words came back to me, spoken by a friend when I had admitted my conflict.

'There's buried treasure in that town. Dig for it like a miner.' And the feeling, deeper, quieter than my fear, that told me Grimlington would not be a dead end, but a place of open doors. With a struggle we had said yes to house and all and then discovered it would only be a temporary home. The PCC had decided it was inadequate. They would sell it and buy us another. Our gratitude was enormous. We detected glints of that treasure already.

In the rain Grimlington looked greyer than I remembered and as miserable as I felt. By the time we turned into the estate and pulled up at our front door I was fighting the tears.

'Let's go home,' I said.

'Where's that?' Peter asked.

'I don't care. Anywhere you like.'

I would have happily crept into any hole as long as it was warm and dry.

Peter struggled for a while, trying to fit the key into the strange lock, then he flung the door open.

'Come and see,' he called, with excitement. I followed him half-heartedly, then stared in amazement. The lurid, claustrophobic blue was gone and instead we walked into a light, clean, airy house. The walls had been painted white, the floorboards scrubbed and the paintwork washed. I walked slowly into my new kitchen which sparkled as if it were in a detergent advert on the television. There, filling the entire double bench was the largest food hamper I had ever seen. It was packed to overflowing with tins of steak, chicken, salmon, strawberries and pineapple. There were packets of soup and sauces, jars of jam and pickles. We could have survived a siege for a year. Beside the hamper was a basket of fruit and with a bouquet of flowers was a card which said, 'With love from your new family.'

I could not speak. Peter took the card from me.

'Goodness,' he said. 'This lot will have cost some of them a week's housekeeping.'

The removal men, as bedraggled as our belongings, began to offload them, cramming them into every available space, smearing black stuff everywhere as they did so. As I was directing the traffic,

I noticed a young woman wobbling up to our door on a bike, a fruit flan precariously balanced on one hand. It was an acrobatic feat requiring some precision.

'Hello,' she said shyly, taking note of the chaos, 'I'm Mary. And this is Louise.'

She beckoned to a teenage girl who had biked up behind her and was waiting at the gate.

'Your daughter?' I asked carefully. I reckoned Mary was probably about my age. She was also very petite, smaller than the girl at the gate. She nodded.

'But you don't look old enough.'

Her face showed a mixture of pride and pleasure.

'I've two older than her at home. Anyway, we're not stopping. We've been told not to bother you, so I've just come to give you this.' She shoved the flan into my hand. 'If you need anything, I'm just at the bottom of the street,' she called, jumped on her bike and was gone.

The flan tasted wonderful later in the evening, when a counter had been taken out and the washing machine installed, and we sat down to eat, exhausted and ravenous.

Slowly some of the crates were emptied and others stored in the garage, temporary carpets and curtains were found, we put up pictures and ornaments and began to feel more at home. One or two church members popped in to see if we needed anything and were all right. Then they disappeared fast. There was no chance to find out anything about them or the community. Then one morning the doorbell rang loudly and insistently.

'Someone with determination,' I said to Peter. There on our doorstep was a small, smartly-dressed woman with greying hair and an attractive, lively face.

'Hello, love, I'm Betty,' she said. 'We met at the service when you were here on a visit. I don't know if you remember.'

I remembered her very well, and the large golden earrings that swung jauntily as she spoke, which she did, persistently. To out-talk me was quite an accomplishment. I remembered too that Anna had told me she was one of Grimlington's four health visitors.

'Professional or social visit?' I asked, as she came into the living room and had a good look round.

'A bit of both, let's say. Killing two birds with one stone. Haven't you made it nice?' she said appreciatively, taking in every detail of our plants and pictures.

I was only too aware that our carpets looked like handkerchiefs on the bare floorboards and the curtains stopped several inches above the window-sill.

'A bit makeshift, but since it's temporary it'll do.'

'But it was so dark and pokey before.'

'Well the difference is thanks to you lot.'

'Weren't those dark blue walls awful? It took six coats of white emulsion to cover them.'

I was staggered. Such effort for a temporary house.

'In fact,' she said, following me into the kitchen where I had gone to put the kettle on, 'you see that ceiling up there?'

I followed the direction of her finger and we stood gazing at the ceiling together for some time.

'One evening my Frank was up there and on to his fourth coat. He drove us mad with his moaning. I said to him, "If you can't do it in the right spirit don't do it at all." He stopped dead and put his brush down. I thought yer'd had yer ceiling. Suddenly he started singing hymns at the top of his voice and the ceiling was done in double quick time. I'll never look at that ceiling again in the same light.'

We took our coffee and sat down. After a few thoughtful mouthfuls, which seemed to help Betty warm to her subject, she said, 'What I've really come about is . . . well, sooner or later you might be needing my services.'

I knew what was coming, Anna had warned me, but I could not resist playing the innocent.

'Baby clinic?' I asked. 'Abby is ready for a measles vaccination.'

'Er, yes. What I really meant was family planning,' she said in a conspiratorial whisper. 'I help with the clinic. Now if you need anything, you know, all you have to do is give me a wink and a nod in church.'

'And you'll pass it down the pew?' I asked innocently.

'Go on with you!' she laughed and got up to go. She stopped at the front door and looked round the estate.

'You know,' she said, 'Grimlington's a great place. It's a tight-knit community. Mining people always stick together. But if yer come from elsewhere and the Council stick yer in a house up here, it can be terribly lonely. I feel for some of these girls, so young, tied in with babies and they don't know anyone.'

'It's a long walk into town with a pram,' I agreed. I had tried it. 'But there's nothing up here, no shopping centre or anything. Are there no toddler clubs?'

Betty shook her head.

'Like you say, not up here. There's one fortnightly at church and some girls come to the clinic for company, but it's an almost impossible walk with a pram and a toddler.'

'Playgroups?' I asked.

Betty shook her head again.

'Only one down in the town and it's more than most mums can afford. Then the church runs one two mornings a week.'

'For a town this size? I can't believe it.'

Betty smiled.

'There's nothing, love, only one small youth club, no cinema, no facilities at all. But we survive. We make our own entertainment. And I'm off. Oh, by the way,' she said, as she turned to go, 'your little boy, what's his name, Joel, he'll soon get to know me. We go into school to check their 'eads. In fact I'm known locally as "Nitty Norah, the big game hunter".'

I hardly felt reassured and scratched involuntarily as I went back into the house. Peter was packing his case in preparation for his pre-ordination retreat. When I deposited him in Leeds it would be the last we would see of each other until he emerged from the cathedral four days later, a fully-fledged clergyman.

'We're not allowed to see each other before the services,' he said. 'No chatting and certainly no kissing.'

'It seems daft to me. I can understand you need time for quiet and reflection, but to go to such lengths?'

'I'm in purdah, I'm afraid.' He grinned. 'Don't you remember how in the Old Testament, before special ceremonies the priests of Israel had to stay away from women?'

'I thought the Church of England was Christian not Jewish!'

'I sometimes wonder,' he said wryly.

When he went I felt an enormous void. We had been apart before, but this was different. We were on the threshold of a new existence, in a strange town, where I knew almost no one. I understood his need for quiet reflection. The paradox was that if ever we needed to be together it was now. I resented the Church. It seemed a formidable rival, demanding a total disruption of my life and giving nothing in return. Let there be no doubt, it was my husband she really wanted. I would always count for little.

I made up my mind not to enjoy the ordination ceremony. All the other ordinands had hordes of family supporting them, mothers and aunties in large hats, clucking and cooing and puffing out their feathers as if it were a wedding. I could hardly expect my family to be there, but it was still a source of pain that they never were at the great occasions in our lives. Most of Peter's family were abroad, but his sister and nephew came from Geneva and how we valued that.

Despite myself I found the pomp and ceremony impressive. Peter stood head and shoulders above the rest, looking handsome and dignified in his cassock and surplice. I felt so proud of him, until I remembered that those were probably not the thoughts I should be thinking on such an occasion. I tried to marshall my powers of concentration, when Joel, sitting quietly next to me up until that moment, suddenly tipped the contents of his little brown case on to the pew. I had been too busy to check what he was bringing. Several dozen large, brightly-coloured pieces of Lego hit the polished wood with a clatter which resounded through the building.

'Shhhhhhhh!' came from all sides.

I felt like retorting, 'It's his father being ordained, you know, he has a right to be here,' but decided that our assailants were probably too set in their ways to accept that a child has a place in God's house. Unperturbed, Joel built the pieces into a gun and shot various members of the congregation throughout the service. Our attempts to teach him non-violent games had failed.

Across the cathedral I caught sight of Betty, Marjorie and Lucy smiling and waving. They nodded and winked at me in the sermon when the archdeacon warned the congregation not to expect another curate in the man's wife. I was glad to have them there. Their bright faces were a striking contrast to some of the others around them. More than that their presence enabled me to make the commitment I had been unable to make before.

As Peter publicly swore his allegiance to Church and Queen, as he vowed to pastor and teach his flock, the enormity and folly of what we were doing hit me again. We had given up a secure teaching job with prospects, a reasonable salary, a home of our own and the friends we loved, for what? A crazy job with no prospects, unspecified commitment, unlimited hours, minimal pay and life on a council desert island. All that and the weight of carrying around a role with all the expectations that created.

Yet suddenly I realised that the urge to run away and hide in a hole had gone. I was ready to face the future and commit myself, not to some great and noble vocation, that just seemed a surfeit of piety, but to Grimlington. The town had begun to touch in me emotions of which I was unaware until that moment. It seemed so much like a neglected, unwanted little foster child, spurned by the vast metropolitan borough, passed over when the goodies were handed out: It reminded me of a runny-nosed child with tear-stained cheeks, yet still too proud to be patronised. I would give whatever I could, and that seemed appallingly little. The 'call' when it finally came was bigger than all my resources to fill it.

'Help me, God, you've brought me this far, screaming and kicking all the way. I feel helpless, inadequate, but here I am, for what it's worth.'

The steward put his hand on my shoulder and encouraged me to leave before the masses so that I could see my husband before they did. I joined Peter, took his arm and together we walked out of the cathedral into the warm sunshine.

5

Acclimatising to life in a goldfish bowl was a slow process. We had never exactly been very private people, but nor were we goldfish. Most mornings a row of noses would appear squashed against our downstairs window panes. The school holidays were long, there was nothing to do, and a clergyman was something of a peculiarity. They did not need to come that close. There was a perfectly good view into every room of our house from a radius of about a hundred yards. The bus-stop for the main bus route to Leeds was right outside and when I opened my bedroom curtains in the morning, I frequently found myself staring into the face of an upstairs passenger on his way to work. Even the bathroom window was not opaque and the front door was made of glass.

At first I took care to be decently dressed at all times, but it soon became an effort.

'Blow modesty,' I said to Peter one day, when he was reminding me for the umpteenth time not to provide added local colour. 'If you can't relax in your own home, where can you?'

So he insisted we put up netting like everyone else, but I did not feel more private, just more enclosed. We were only cutting ourselves off completely.

I waited, hoping some of the local people would call, welcome us and see if we were all right, but they never did. Sometimes, particularly if we were working in the garden, I was sure we were being watched from a distant window, but when I looked up only the curtains moved.

But the girls came in their dozens, teenagers and tiny ones, lured by the irresistible attraction of a baby. They waited in queues at the front door, arguing over whose turn it was to take Abby out. There was great prestige in having a pram to push. Some of them were sensible and doing a child care course in their last year at school. The younger ones were not and abandoned the babies while they played on the swings. If I said no they came back a quarter of an hour later and asked again. If there was no reply at the front door they hammered at the back. In fact there was so much ringing and knocking that I had little time to do anything except answer the door.

The local lads, of all sizes, used our outside walls for football practice. They drew a goal then took it in turns to score. Every time the ball hit the wall there was a thud so violent that the house shook and bits of plaster fell off the ceiling. I endured with gritted teeth, especially if I had just put the children to bed. It was a harmless enough pursuit. And most of the boys were bigger than me!

Joel was longing to play with them, but only the girls came to the house, and for Abby, not for him.

'The girls round here are stupid,' he said in disgust. 'All they want to do is push a pram.'

'It's like playing with a doll,' I explained to him, but he was not impressed.

He suffered more than all of us. At first he was thrilled by the sight of so many children playing out in the evening and he rushed out to join in. But it was not like the square in Nottingham where all the children played together. Here he was an oddity. He talked posh. He lived in the posh house. He liked dressing up and playing imaginative games. All they did was stand around doing nothing, he said. And it took him a while to understand their language. He came in one day, shouting, 'Mum, what's a bastard?'

'Why?' I asked.

'Because one of the dads has just called me one.'

'What were you doing?'

'Getting my football from his garden.'

'Well, Joel,' I said and lifted him on to my knee, for a four-year-old is still a baby, no matter how big and sturdy, 'you may be many things, but a bastard you're not.'

He seemed satisfied and ran out to try again.

I had to admire his determination. Day after day he sat around watching the older children playing cricket and football, waiting for a chance to field, or run and fetch the ball for them. I watched him from the window, my heart aching for the little chap, sitting alone on his football, his head in his hands, waiting so patiently. And sometimes they let him have a go and he would come in, his eyes shining and his chest puffed out with pride.

At other times he curled up in a corner of the house and cried quietly for his friends in Nottingham while I felt a heel and reproached myself for what we had done to him. What right had we to make him the innocent victim of what we understood to be God's will for us?

A story from the Old Testament came forcibly to my mind, probably because it was so familiar. When I was a child it was recounted every year at the Passover. My ancestors were slaves in Egypt when Moses went to bring them out and take them to the promised land of their dreams. In typical Jewish fashion the great adventure quickly disintegrated into chaotic schemozzle and a forty-year trek round the desert. And how they moaned!

'We've no food. Our children will die. We should have stayed in Egypt.'

Eventually the Almighty could take no more.

'All right,' he said, 'die in the wilderness, but your children, whom you called innocent victims, they will see the promised land.'

No matter how much I loved my children I could not use them in an argument against God. And perhaps, I told myself, one of these days Joel will look back and be glad that he discovered that relationships are not always easy.

Peter was eased gently into work. Alicia offered to show him the ropes, and that she did, literally.

'Pull, Peter, pull. That's it, harder. Now tie a bowline can you?'

'I've done some sailing in my time, Alicia,' he said, as they hauled the screen for the overhead projector into place. It was an extraordinary feat of engineering, suspended precariously at forty-five degrees over the pulpit and attached by a motley collection of ropes and knots to pillars, beams and the organ.

'Fun, isn't it?' she said, gazing fondly at her invention. 'Jack and I made it. If there are three of us it only takes fifteen minutes to get it up.'

'But Alicia,' Peter said, the words tumbling out despite himself, 'we used the latest equipment at college, out and up in two minutes. Think of the time saved.'

'And the satisfaction missed,' she said, smiling at him benignly. 'Anyway, darling, this is Grimlington. Money is hard to come by and there certainly isn't enough for new equipment. So we make do.'

She examined some of the knots to make sure they were secure.

'Are you sure it's safe?' Peter asked.

She nodded reassuringly.

'Well, I only hope the organist enjoys my sermons,' he said. 'If he doesn't all he has to do is cut a rope and I'm silenced . . . for ever.'

The transition from schoolteacher to clergyman was not going to be easy for Peter. He liked order and organisation, and it was not until our first family service that we realised just how alien both were to the local temperament.

The day began badly. It drizzled. Peter grumbled as he draped his cassock and surplice round the saddle bag of his bike and covered them with polythene. He hated wearing what he called his 'medieval angel kit'. He had never enjoyed dressing up, not even as a child.

'The uniform is only there to separate us from the people and impress them with our superiority,' he said. 'It creates a false impression.' Yet the ministerial garb had cost almost as much as a Belville Sassoon ball gown, and since it had to be worn it would have been a shame to trail it in the mud or catch it in the spokes.

I stayed in bed, warm and dry, then drove down to church in style, by car. Outside stood an excited, noisy band of Cubs and Brownies with banners.

'Strange!' I thought. 'Peter never mentioned a procession. He must know.'

Edward was away, but he had left instructions.

'Be adequately prepared for a service well in advance,' they had told us at college, 'and prepare the church. Allow for an atmosphere of quiet meditation before worship begins.'

Whoever said that had never been to Grimlington.

The noise met me before I reached the door. The church seemed fairly full, but it was hard to tell with so much happening. The music group was tuning up and wrestling with chairs and music stands. Mick was having trouble with the PA and could do little for babies shuffling down the aisles. Children catapulted over pews and tripped over wires or the edge of the carpet. People called to each other across the church and waved to their friends. A small group of older people huddled together, probably for protection.

Peter walked in, looking very much in control and commanded a certain quiet, if not exactly silence. He announced a hymn and the organist struck up a chord. In from the back with dignity and determination marched the Cubs and Brownies. Peter looked up and for a moment his mouth and eyes opened wide with astonishment. He turned to Alicia, who sat smiling at the little gaggle now waiting patiently at the level of his knees, waving their banners expectantly.

'Sorry, dear, forgot to tell you,' she whispered. 'Just ad lib.'

'I never even knew there were Cubs and Brownies in the church,' he said with a chuckle over lunch. 'Good job my dad was a vicar. At least I remembered what to do.'

'I expect that won't be the last time you have to ad lib either,' I said to him.

'No. A congregation isn't a classroom full of kids, is it? You can't organise adults in the same way, especially here.'

I laughed. 'Someone on the way out said to me, "Yer can tell he were a teacher by way he scowls at yer over 'is spectacles."'

'A fat lot of good it did.'

'At least they're honest. One thing we can guarantee, what they say behind our backs will be said to our faces sooner or later.'

Alone in the house that evening, the children in bed, and Peter at the evening service, there was time to think. There had been changes since our exploratory visit in the spring. The new prayer book for one, but also more life and spontaneity. And I had feared cold, reserved, British Anglicanism! I had been sure I would not cope. But what I had seen this morning was much more like the synagogue. Most people seemed relaxed and warm and glad to be there.

'You know I've been thinking,' I said to Peter, when he came in.

'Fatal!' he said and sat down next to me with a mug of Ovaltine.

'The noise this morning, the chatter before the service . . .'

'It was similar tonight,' he said, 'very informal, but the congregation was much smaller and there was more opportunity for quiet without the children there. Still, it is different from our last experience, a welcome surprise!'

'I'm glad you're not tempted to shut them up. I've always thought it was a nonsense to talk about going to church to meet God. That traps him in a building and divides the sacred from the secular. The Jewish idea seems more sensible. Since God is with us all the time, going to the synagogue is an expression of community. On that basis we do go to church to meet each other, to experience corporate worship, otherwise why not stay at home to pray? The British concept of private religion has always left me cold. What's private about loving your neighbour as yourself? It seems only right and natural to say hello to one another and find out how everyone is. That's what they'd do in the High Street.'

'I only wish I could make myself heard,' Peter said wistfully.

'Then you'll have to do what the rabbis do. Either wait for some quiet or carry on despite it.'

Peter shook his head and smiled. He had been amused in the synagogue at the rabbi's struggle to keep control, never dreaming it might happen to him.

'Well, Mick's working on the PA. At least they don't seem to have picked up the cultural tradition that the church is an awesome, holy place where everyone talks in deferential, hushed whispers. I can't bear that. Middle-class propriety disguised as piety. Long may such traditions go on changing.'

'What if it's too late?' I asked him.

'Too late for what?'

'For estates like this. Say there were about two hundred people in church this morning and half that this evening . . .'

'Less.'

'In a town of eighteen thousand! And it's obvious that those who do come don't live up here. Hasn't the Church become such a Victorian, middle-class anachronism that it's been failing them for years? How do we persuade them it's the institution, not the message which is at fault?'

Peter shook his head sadly.

'I don't know. Perhaps our image communicates the wrong message. Only radical change can alter that. And that's a daunting prospect.'

6

Autumn slowly crept up on us. The last few sparse leaves which the trees had managed to produce turned a sickly yellow and tumbled dejectedly to the ground, making muddy, slimy heaps upon the pavement. The grassland around the house and at the play area became a boggy swamp and the children had to wade to the swings in their wellingtons. If they fell their clothes were pasted with a greasy black substance, largely soot and water, which no amount of washing would remove. The farmer whose fields stretched out to the pit, behind the houses which faced our front door, was covering them with manure and the air was ripe with its scent.

'Victims we are of industrial and rural life,' I said to Peter, ruefully, as our nostrils were filled with this latest perfume.

But soon even those fields would be swallowed up. One day, as we took our usual walk, closing our eyes and ears to the sight and sound of the vast iron structure ahead of us, pretending we were miles from civilisation, we noticed the tell-tale, heavy tyre marks, criss-crossing the fields. The Coal Board lorry had been prospecting. The farmer's days were numbered. It was wiser not to become too attached to any hill or patch of green.

On some days the Coal Board lorry moved slowly round the town, dumping mounds of coal in pyramids all over the pavements. I watched fascinated as the women appeared, only to vanish in a black haze, coughing all the while, as they shovelled it into their coal bunkers. On a blustery day the wind whipped up a blinding dust and more fool she who hung out her sheets to dry. In they came, spotted and speckled, and worse than when she started.

But in those chilly late September days Joel made a friend. At first Claire stood around and watched his antics in a bemused sort of way. Then one day I looked out of the window and saw her chasing after him, both dressed up as firemen in kagouls and wellington boots, wearing toy hats and with a mock hose made out of an old vacuum cleaner pipe.

Every evening, after dusk, gangs of older teenagers congregated in the play area and with nothing better to do, wrapped the swings round the top bar so that the little children could not play with them the next day. I watched them from the kitchen window, becoming more and more annoyed, until one evening I could bear it no longer and tore across the road in a fury. I poured out on them all the pent-up anger I had been storing up since our move. Words like stupid, selfish and childish poured out through my clenched teeth in a torrent. Then I ran dry. I paused, hunting for inspiration and to my amazement they grinned at me sheepishly, and stopped. Conscious of them staring after me and feeling a deep, inner satisfaction, I marched back to the house, which seemed to blaze in the dark like a beacon on an island.

The next night they were back. But Peter had a much more charitable solution to the problem. He took a ladder across and unwound the swings. From then on, every afternoon, as soon as school ended there was a queue at our door. 'Would vicar come and get swings down?'

'At least you're in demand with the children,' I said to Peter one day, when we were lamenting the fact that we still knew so few of our neighbours. We had made ourselves as approachable as we could and refused to hide. I sat out in the jungle which was our garden, on a deckchair which wobbled about on the tufts of couch grass and the downhill slope. It was a bit unnerving to be the focal point of attention for such a wide radius. Children came and I gave them squash and sometimes, on a wet day, we read a story. But their parents did not come near.

In fact I was always amazed at how little sign of life there was at all. It was such a contrast to the High Street, where people would stand and chat all day. There was no community centre on the estate. The only place where people congregated for any length of time was at Maggie's, the newsagents.

I had never met anyone who worked as hard as Maggie. She opened the shop at eight and stayed open without a lunch hour

175

until past seven o'clock, seven days a week. In a spare moment she slipped into the back to put the washing on or put tea ready for her two children and elderly father.

'I'll put papers through yer door,' she said.

'No, I'll come in. I like to catch up on the gossip.'

'Ay, yer hear it all in 'ere.'

Everyone who came into the shop knew who I was. They began to tell me stories: what vicar said at our Tracy's wedding, what last curate were like and the lovely funeral 'e give Grandad.

'Leavin' us already, are yer?' Maggie said, the day the For Sale sign went up outside our house.

I tried to explain. We did not want the estate to feel we were abandoning them, but I could see from the cynical expression on her face that my words had little effect.

'There's a lot'll be sorry ter see yer go,' she said. 'We've not much up 'ere, but at least we 'ad us own vicar.'

'A fat lot of good he is to you,' I said.

'We knew 'e were there if we needed 'im.'

I went home feeling sad and torn. She was right. If the Church talked about love it had to show it. But how could I explain to her that I could not cope with being the Church's representative, treated as an object and not a human being. I needed friends too. I hated the deferential look I saw in their eyes as I walked into the shop. 'You're not one of us,' it said, before I had a chance. The Church created a divide no one would let me cross. And yet there was the uneasy feeling too that time, patience and perseverance could break down the years of mistrust. But we were one family alone and in the wrong house.

In the event the house was to be our home for another fifteen months. One or two potential buyers looked round and quickly decided it was the wrong house too. Those months, endless at times, as the price dropped and still no customers came to our door, gave us an invaluable opportunity to discover that on our estate to go to church was almost as alien as a visit to a mosque.

One Saturday night we went to bed early. Peter always needed a lot of sleep and especially before a Sunday.

'I wish several church families would come and live up here,' I said to him, as he settled down, tucking in the bedclothes, 'a sort of mini-community, drawing others in, not a figure-head who poses a threat. That way they'd see the church wasn't just a social service, providing occasional weddings and funerals, but a way of life that has something to offer.'

Peter yawned.

'And who are you going to get to do that? Most of the church members who live up here want to move down into town.'

'Well, I don't know. I suppose no one is willing to do it.'

'Right! If they were they wouldn't have put us up here,' he said and switched off the light.

We must have been asleep barely a couple of hours when we were both jolted from our slumbers by blood-curdling screams. Peter leapt out of bed and pulled back the curtains.

'What is it?' I asked. My heart was pounding.

'It looks like a fight.'

For a few moments there was no sound at all. We held our breath in the strange, unnatural silence. Suddenly the air was split with shrill screaming, then a girl's voice wailing over and over again, 'Yer've killed me dad, yer've killed me dad.'

'It's nasty,' Peter said. 'I'm going to phone the police.'

I went to the window and peeping out from behind the curtain, saw several figures below stagger over to our car, take off their jackets and lay them on the bonnet. Then they took their shirts off too. I blinked, wondering what was coming next. Half-naked, they lurched at each other, swiping and punching and beating with their fists. They butted each other in the stomach. Keeping their balance was such a delicate art that they often missed and landed head-first in a crumpled heap on the ground. When one fell, the others gathered round and kicked his head as if it was some kind of grotesque turnip. I rubbed my eyes. This was not the television. It was real and there was something nauseating and terrible about the sight of naked human aggression.

'We've got to do something. We've got to stop them,' I said to Peter as he joined me at the window. 'They're killing each other.'

'There's nothing we can do, love,' he said, 'except wait for the police. They're so much the worse for drink, they don't know what they're doing. They'd start on us.'

All this time the wailing continued, interrupted only by the occasional hysterical scream. And so did the punching and kicking, but there was no sign of the police. Peter rang them again. They were waiting for reinforcements. Grimlington, although known on citizen band radio as 'Crazy Town', still only had a skeleton police force. I left the window, unable to watch any longer, feeling angry and helpless at the sight of such unnecessary violence. I realised with a sickening awareness that aggression is buried so deeply in the human subconscious that when drink robs a man of reason and control his whole mentality is one of ruthless, angry self-assertion.

After what seemed an eternity, in roared the police panda cars, vans, and motorbikes, lights flashing and sirens howling. The street had been in darkness and I thought that we were the only ones watching. Suddenly lights appeared at almost every window and people were framed in their open doorways. The culprits disappeared into a house opposite and the police pursued them in. One by one a string of silhouettes emerged and were pushed calmly but firmly into the police van. An ambulance arrived and several figures were lifted in. There was a chase as someone tried to make an escape, but they were brought back, handcuffed. The walkie-talkie droned on for another hour and at last, by four-thirty, the street was quiet again.

Peter came in. With an anorak over his pyjamas he had been walking up and down, chatting to people as they stood and watched.

'Apparently it's always the same family. No one seems too upset. Oh, and by the way,' he said, as we crawled shivering back into bed, 'the car only has a few scratches and a broken aerial, again! My salary should include danger money.'

Life the next day was a bit of a daze. We both staggered to the morning service, bleary-eyed. By the time we came home for lunch the curtains at the house opposite were open.

'I think it's time for a pastoral visit,' Peter said, 'before I take my dog collar off.' He took a deep breath.

I waited nervously. He came in half-an-hour later, shaking his head and laughing.

'It was an engagement party!' he said. 'The fiancé came within a fraction of killing his future father-in-law, or at least kicking his eye out. He almost had a cerebral haemorrhage, but never mind, all's forgiven. They sat me down, gave me a cup of tea and laughed in an embarrassed kind of way about the whole thing.'

It was a fortnight later that the doorbell rang and standing shyly on the doorstep was a slim, pretty girl, who backed when I opened the door.

'I'm from 'cross the road,' she said, needing to say no more. 'Am I bothering you?'

'No,' I said, 'come on in.'

But she was not too keen, and kept turning to look behind her like a frightened doe.

'I only want to know if vicar'll marry us,' she said sheepishly.

Peter appeared at the top of the stairs. 'Of course I'll marry you, Carol. But no booze before the wedding!'

She grinned. 'It's a promise.'

'Well,' Peter said, 'and that was the first local person to come to our door!'

We both laughed, but the incident affected us more deeply than either of us cared to admit. For months the slightest noise outside our bedroom window woke me with a start and made my nerves jangle. And never again could either of us bear to watch violence of any kind on the television.

7

A person might be forgiven for coming to the conclusion that life in Grimlington came to a very slow standstill about twenty years ago. The railway station, once its pride and joy, a major junction and a grand, bustling metropolis with arches, mosaics, fine glass and marble, has become a hideous, derelict heap. The restaurant has long since gone. So have the attendants in their high-necked black dresses and frilly white aprons. Now there is not so much as a coffee machine. The entrance hall leaks rain through its broken roof and window panes and the puddles absorb the litter, turning the ground into a dirty, soggy carpet. Timetables hang in tatters from the noticeboard and everything smells dank and musty. Anyone arriving at night in the eerie light of one inadequate electric light bulb might think they had come to a ghost town. The wind which howls down the deserted platforms seems to carry echoes of a distant past, when a thousand employees joked, chatted, blew their whistles and polished the brasses.

'Ay, I drove the steam trains once,' an old man once said to me wistfully as I waited for the pay train to Leeds. 'Beautiful they were and the speed of 'em! All the best trains came through 'ere. The second biggest marshallin' yard in Britain it were.'

The drivers reckoned they were somebody in those days, one cut better than a miner. You could tell a railway worker by the hat he wore, be it a silk topper, brown bowler or a trade cap. Then the railways were reorganised. A thousand jobs were lost. An old elite, an upper working-class, vanished and the trains, mosaics, and marble were removed, to be displayed in the Railway Museum in York.

Going to the doctor's or the dentist's was like stepping back in time. The doctor's waiting room is a large airy cellar with painted bricks and old slatted wooden railway benches for seats. Sitting there the years vanish and I am a little girl again, creeping down the back stairs of our large, old house, peeping round the surgery door to see if the patients have gone yet and my father is alone. The medical care is just as my father would have given too. The doctor is meticulous, insisting on doing the children's vaccinations himself, knowing his patients and giving time to them, the old values of general practice, miraculously kept alive.

I was less at ease at the dentist's surgery with its dark corridors, peeling paintwork and old-fashioned, cracked linoleum, the sort I remembered on our kitchen floor in the fifties. Large posters on the cramped waiting-room wall are a gruesome reminder of the dangers of too much sugar and not enough brushing. But many young people in the town have false teeth anyway or gaping holes where teeth should have been. It was hardly a great encouragement to those who appreciate that part of their anatomy.

Every clergyman is called to make countless unusual errands of mercy. Peter's first left a lasting impression. Cathy, who lived on our estate and had been faithfully popping in to collect and forward the previous curate's post, asked Peter if he would mind taking her husband to the dentist to have fourteen teeth out. Peter was not too sure if his presence was required to hold his hand, carry him out or to say an appropriate blessing.

'You're only young,' Peter said to him nervously, as they drew up at the dentist's door. 'Can't they be filled?'

'Oh ay,' the victim replied, 'but it's not worth it. I might as well get rid of them now, then they'll cause me no more bother and no more money.'

Peter came home, feeling weak at the knees and more determined than ever to hang on to his teeth as long as possible.

Some of the older men, like Lucy's dad, did not bother to wear their false teeth at all. I found their nods and gummy grins endearing as I walked down the High Street, but it puzzled me, until I was enlightened. No collier goes down the pit wearing false teeth. A piece of grit under the palate is excruciating. And they get used to leaving them out.

'Do they just eat baby food for the rest of their lives?' I asked naively.

'Don't be daft, their gums get so hard they can bite through an apple.'

But even so, Dad Barker, Lucy's father, could not manage the celery and apple salad I offered him inadvertently when he came to tea.

'He won't eat unusual things,' Lucy reassured me when I told her what I had done. 'He won't eat what 'e calls "foreign muck", lasagne or spaghetti bolognese. It's got to be pie and chips all the time and it doesn't exactly stretch me.'

I began to realise how little I knew about miners for one who had been raised among them.

'You'll be all right there,' my mother said, when I told her where we were going. 'Miners are the kindest, the most generous people. When food was rationed they came to the house with tins of salmon for the doctor. They'll give away their last penny.'

My father agreed. Although he was a doctor, he was the son of a poor tailor and never forgot his origins. He regarded medicine as a privilege and a responsibility. I learned from him the value of people.

'We who have been shown the greatest intolerance must show the greatest tolerance,' he said, 'otherwise the lesson of the holocaust is wasted.'

Yet he was the doctor and social distinctions were clear. He could mix with other professionals and shop keepers, and the vicar, of course. My father often chose to defy convention. Life would have been colourless without the companionship of Albert, his mate. But the mining community kept themselves very much to themselves.

I remembered the craggy, wrinkled, friendly faces, covered in tiny blue-black marks, but only now did I discover that those were the tell-tale signs of a collier, pieces of grit embedded in the skin of his face, hands and arms. There they were in Dad Barker's face, as I examined it one Sunday after lunch at Lucy's. After dinner he sat warming himself by the open fire, his toothless gums chewing on his pipe and a look of supreme contentment on his face.

'Nothing like a good coal fire, that's what I say, especially after a good, traditional Sunday dinner.'

Lucy caught my eye and shook her head.

'I see you're a man who enjoys retirement,' Peter said.

'What!' Dad Barker snorted. 'Me? I'd give anything to be back down pit.'

182

'They had a trip down pit last year from church, the clergy wanted to see it, and who do yer think put 'is name down to go?' Lucy laughed affectionately. 'Yer'd have thought he'd 'ad enough. Right put out 'e was when they wouldn't tek 'im.'

'I just wanted to see the old place once more,' he said wistfully. 'Yer don't forget yer know, not after fifty years. I were thirteen when I started as a trapper, opening doors for ponies, then I drove 'em. It were two more years before I went on 'note and were a proper collier. Given me chance again, I'd do same.'

'After all that time in the dark and dirt I'd have thought you'd have been glad to see the back of it,' I said.

'Ah, Michele,' he said, with a distant, far-away look in his eyes, 'how can I get yer to understand what it were like, the good times we 'ad, the way we all stuck together and helped each other out? We all lived together too, yer see, up on Crossfarm View, where your estate is now. But in them days we all knew each other. We never locked us doors. Yer could leave anythin' out. Nothing were ever nicked. We shared everything, even a toilet at bottom of street.'

'The key hung on an 'ook in t'scullery. Yer had to be a fast runner in them days,' Lucy said, smiling at the memory.

'Do you miss them, Lucy?'

She thought for a bit, took her pinny off and came and sat down with us by the fire.

'Ay,' she said, 'I suppose I do. Give a man garden walls and a gate and it's never the same.'

She took the poker and banked up the fire. 'I tell you what, though, I wish Council would give us another 'ouse. This one's too big. At least the old cottages were easy to heat. It's perishin' cold and damp. The water trickles down walls. We've been on Council list for ages. Dad retired early because of ill health. I sometimes wonder if 'is chest'll survive another winter if we stay 'ere. Come December I'll be scraping ice off inside o' winders so we can see out.'

I shivered. My back, which was away from the fire was chilled already and it was still September.

'That's other thing,' Dad Barker said suddenly, only half with us and half back in that other world below ground. 'It's changed down there. It were clean work once.'

I looked at him, puzzled.

183

'We carried us own blades. There was no machinery. That's what started all the dust and made our chests bad. Ay, and there were none of these strikes all the time.'

'There were a few Dad, as I remember,' I said.

'But we'd just cause in them days. Yer couldn't live on pay. Now they're just young hot-heads,' he said and puffed at his pipe. 'I tell yer this. I'd not let my sons go down.'

He smiled as if in self-congratulation.

'Now then, that surprises yer. I'd no choice, but they could choose National Service. I told 'em which to tek and they've not regretted it, have they Lucy? No, it's not the same any more.'

We got up to go, thanking Lucy for her lavish hospitality.

'Two puddings was a real treat!'

'I always make two, one for 'im and one for us,' she said, with a grin in the direction of the figure in the armchair, who, with a headful of happy memories and a tummy full of sweet mince pie, was now quietly nodding off.

'It's funny, isn't it,' I said to Peter as we walked up to the estate, 'how companionship can make a heaven out of a lousy job?'

'That's probably the only way to cope with it,' Peter said.

Suddenly it seemed a great many things were clicking into place.

'Hey, all the spitting that goes on in the High Street . . .'

'Pneumoconiosis, the miners' disease. Alicia says that's why there are so many inquests and post mortems in the town. If pneumoconiosis can be proved the Coal Board has to pay the family compensation.'

'It's only right if we rob a man of his health.'

'Ah yes, but life isn't as fair as that, is it?' Peter said.

Life in Grimlington had a slow, unhurried pace, which I found refreshing after the rush and bustle of city life. With its routine, traditions and strong sense of community it still revolved around the pits. People had time for each other. I discovered that any piece of information I let slip in the High Street at ten o'clock was the gossip of the town by eleven. Everyone minded everyone else's business. There was no such thing as a secret. For years every experience, good and bad, had been shared by all. And they had been through much joy and sorrow together.

Everyone still remembered the great day the pit-head showers were opened.

'I were a little girl at the time,' Linda told me, her eyes still sparkling with the memory of it. She was one of a group of young women with small children, who had, I gathered, recently started coming to the church. Her capacity to see the funny in the most ordinary situations provided me with an instant soul-mate. She could send people up mercilessly, especially if they were pompous. With her short fair hair and rather arch way of looking, I could imagine her as a little girl wearing a gingham frock with a bow at the back. She must have been just as her little Tracy was now, a real bundle of mischief.

'I ran down the street shouting, "There's a strange man eating me dad's tea." Well, I'd never seen him clean at teatime before, had I?'

From then on the men developed a taste for gossip. Every young girl lived in fear lest her name be mentioned in the showers and her father overhear it! It ensured very high moral standards in the town.

Many still remember the night the men were having a quiet drink in the Crossfarm Club, when a collier burst in in his overalls, his eyes wild and his face ashen behind the dirt and grime. No one needed to say a word. Every man rose in silence, then ran to collect boots, helmets, belts and ropes. They fought for hours, up to the waist in water, to free brothers, fathers, sons and friends. Many were bereaved that night and rumour has it that five men whose bodies were never found are still up there in the disused pit.

Grimlington had the first Mines Rescue Training Centre, and the first national mining hero, who lost his life leading a rescue team after an underground explosion in Birmingham. But despite the danger, there was a long waiting list for the job. Linda's husband, Joe, was turned down because he was the son-in-law, not the son of a miner, and the pits were closing anyway. I began to pick up a great deal of tension and fear. If jobs went so would a whole way of life.

'Where's it all going to end?' I overheard one woman calling to another, as she laid out a selection of goods on her market stall. There was no modern shopping centre in Grimlington, just this, a new market of makeshift stalls, a token, a courteous nod from the planners in the direction of the nineteen eighties.

'God, I 'ope they don't strike again,' the other woman shouted back. 'It were bad enough in 1971. This stall doesn't make enough to keep us.'

'They won't strike,' the other woman said. 'No one wants to.'

'Yes, but what future is there for our kids?'

And then they were taken up by customers.

If the town struggled with problems of employment, so did we. But our own private struggle was rather different. Peter's job was a source of frustration to both of us. I knew I would have my battles, but I thought he would take to being a clergyman at once. He hated it. His organised mind wrestled with the lack of routine and structure. I could not get used to having him under my feet all day. Neither could the children. He was there, yet he wasn't there. He came in and they leapt with joy. Then he disappeared into his study and closed the door and they howled with frustration. Some Saturday mornings the two of them stood banging at the study door, demanding he come out and play, while I wrestled with the weekend's shopping and cooking.

'My sermon preparation!' he shouted.

'Football!' Joel shouted back.

'Why don't you go to the vestry or the public library?' I joined in. 'Then we'd all have some peace.'

Slowly the realisation dawned on both of us that it was no use lamenting what once was, no more than a clock can work backwards. The steady routine, organised days, relaxed weekends were gone for ever. The new life was here to stay and I would somehow have to make the best of it. I did not mind the evenings in alone. It was the fact that I could hardly ever plan a day out for just the two of us without being disappointed. It was usually a funeral. People did not die to suit my convenience.

Peter popped down to see Mick one night, knowing from the first time he met him that here was someone he could talk to, who would understand.

'It's the lack of job satisfaction that gets me down,' Peter said to him, 'especially after teaching. I get to the end of the day worn out, with nothing to show for it.'

'Join the club,' Mick said. Then, noting Peter's surprise, 'Well, yer never thought anyone worked down a pit or in a factory for job satisfaction, did yer? Yer work to keep the family and try not to think about anything else. Yer'd go mad if yer did. Most of us are lucky to have work at all these days.'

'Yes,' Peter agreed, 'at least I haven't got that to contend with. No redundancies in the Church of England.'

'Ay, if pits go so does my job.'

'What'll you do?'

Mick shrugged, then he smiled, embarrassed. 'Sometimes I think I'd like to work for the church. It's a bit of a dream I 'ave. Karen says I spend so much time there that I do that already and I'm only an engineer in me spare time. She's always complaining she never sees me. So, it sounds as if you and me 'ave a lot in common.'

Peter came home in a pensive mood, but with a much lighter heart. 'That'll teach me to grumble,' he said. 'You know, until tonight I never realised that for most people job satisfaction is a luxury, not a right.'

8

I often wonder what possessed me to start a Drama Group. Perhaps because I did not seem to fit in anywhere else. Although motherhood had its enjoyable moments, it had its days of excruciating drudgery too. If I had any contribution to make to the church I hoped it would have nothing whatsoever to do with babies or children.

In the event, the Drama Group turned out to be my lifeline to sanity. It provided me with that precious commodity I thought had gone for ever, friendship. Every Tuesday night I lay awake in bed with aching sides, from laughter, not exertion.

My dramatic skills were minimal. I had studied it at university, the theory, rather than the practice, in true academic fashion. I took it up again years later, when Peter was at theological college, but then I had to drop out because my pregnant bump limited my versatility, and agility. Yet instinct told me that drama had a vital place in the Church, in a visual age when television had weakened our ability to listen and concentrate. But it would have to be good, not so hick and amateur that our audience squirmed with embarrassment and missed the message.

Uncertainly, I put an announcement in the weekly newsletter. Would anyone interested in forming a Drama Group please come to a meeting on Tuesday evening in the parish hall. And I prayed no one would come. But there were six of them.

'Only one man?' I said.

The girls smiled. So did he.

'The men round here don't go in for this kind of thing,' Jan said. She was petite and fair, with large owlish glasses. Linda had already introduced me to her Canadian friend, but the faint drawl still sounded strangely out of place after weeks of hearing only

Yorkshire. I wondered what had brought her to Grimlington.

'They reckon they're macho, y'know,' she said, flexing her muscles. 'It's not that they're not creative. They just don't dare let it show.'

Her voice had just a hint of, 'believe me, I know from experience'.

'Oh well, it just means we're a bit limited,' I said.

'Why?'

A pair of penetrating blue eyes stared straight into mine.

'A woman can play any man's part, can't she, Frances?'

The girl at her side smiled and nodded.

'Yes, Angela.'

'Even God?' I could have bitten my tongue.

'Especially God! Why shouldn't a woman play God?'

I shrugged my shoulders. Why not? I had no answer. The others grinned nervously. I had noticed that the two women were sitting slightly apart from the others.

'We go to Cuttlesworth,' Angela explained, as if to an unasked question. She was the larger of the two, who I realised were sisters, and there was an almost Amazon-like sturdiness in her build and open intense face.

Cuttlesworth? Oh yes, the daughter church. Peter had said something about a last vestige of traditionalism.

'We haven't seen you there yet,' Angela said, weighing me up out of the corner of her eye.

'Not yet,' I hedged and cursed the need to be political which the clergy-wife role and Angela's teasing manner had imposed.

'Well,' I said, returning safely to the matter at hand, 'we could all meet fortnightly if you like.' 'Once a week'll be fine,' Linda said, looking round at Jan and Dorothy, who had been silent so far. They nodded in agreement.

'You see, Tuesday night's been our night out for years, long before we started coming to church. A woman needs a night away from the kids. We go to the Anchor or the Duck and Partridge, so instead we'll come here. There's no problem. Our men know we're out Tuesdays. And this is what we really want to do.'

I was terrified. In a week I read all I could and tried to drag the rest out of the furthermost recesses of my brain. Their sacrifice and enthusiasm deserved a bit of effort on my part. But I was not prepared for their ingenuity and natural talent. Linda, Jan, Dorothy and I were all still at the baby and nappy bucket stage and arrived exhausted, having cleared up and put the children to bed. Ian was a nurse and worked very long shifts. None of us had done any drama for years, if at all. As we warmed up, the hall was filled with the sound of moaning, groaning and creaking, cracking joints. Games left us lying on the floor in a panting heap, especially Dorothy, who struggled with a little more weight than Jan or Linda.

'No more, no more,' she cried, 'I can't stand it.'

'Come on Dorothy, it's doing yer good,' Linda shouted.

But when we turned to improvisation, clever, creative ideas poured out, as if they had been buried inside for years, and were waiting to be released. And I learned more about life in Grimlington in an evening than I had learned in weeks.

The first simple sketch we put together was based on the parable of the sower.

'What's the story about?' I asked them, as we lay on the floor, our open Bibles in front of us.

'Productivity,' Angela said.

'So where would you set it?'

'In the mines,' she said.

Linda laughed. 'Well I like the idea, and I don't mind playing a miner, but since no woman's worked down pit in recent years, don't you think it would look better in a factory?'

'And we all know what that's like,' Jan said.

The others nodded, all except Ian. Factory work was 'women's work', poorly paid and often available as a temporary measure.

'I don't think I'll ever forget it,' Frances said. 'Nine hours a day sewing elastic into hundreds of pairs of underpants. It nearly drove me mad.'

'By the end of the day the noise and routine make you feel you've become part of the machine,' Jan said.

'What noise does the machine make?' I asked them.

They began to whirr and grind and click, gradually blending the sounds into a steady, monotonous rhythm.

'That's it,' I shouted. 'Keep going. We'll use it as a background.' After a few minutes their faces began to register boredom. Their eyes became vacant and they assumed the mindless expressions of zombies.

'Does this look right?' Frances asked. 'Because it feels right.'

'All we need's the patter now, girls,' Linda said.

And that was no problem.

Ian was the factory manager.

'Good morning, girls.'

'Good morning, Mr Heseltine,' they drawled together, turning up their noses behind his back.

'A fat bonus to any girl who can increase her productivity substantially.'

'You're too nice,' shouted Frances.

Ian looked puzzled.

'You're the politest manager I've ever come across,' she said.

'We're only factory girls remember.'

Ian tried again with a bit of a snarl.

'Who does 'e think 'e is?' says the first. 'If 'e thinks I'm killing myself for 'im 'e's very much mistaken,' and she goes to the toilets for a fag. The 'seed' is devoured by birds before it has time to grow at all.

The second girl starts well, then remembers the cream bun and flask of hot coffee in her bag. She slowly grinds to a standstill. The 'seed' has fallen on rocky ground and has no root.

'Well, I'm going to get that bonus,' says the third girl. 'I could really do with it,' and she works at a great pace, until she remembers her boyfriend waiting for her at the gate. Should she meet him or work late? Blow work, she's got to see him and the 'seed' has been choked by thorns.

The fourth girl works on. This 'seed' has increased production by a thousand per cent. She earns the fat bonus and the commendation of the boss. She seems a bit too good and prissy, but then that's how Christians are seen in the town, I was told.

We were excited and apprehensive about our first performance in public. The open air ecumenical service had been the Council of Churches' only contribution to the town Gala for years. It was conservative enough for those who thought a small dose of formal religion was right on special occasions and dreary enough to confirm everyone else's expectations of what that religion was like. We wanted to invest the service with life, to say that our faith was our life and not just an occasional courteous but cold bow before the Almighty. So we worked hard and had at the end a reasonably polished performance.

191

The Gala weekend was wet. In fact it was a wash-out. Friday evening's excitement as everyone put the finishing touches to their floats and costumes, was carried away in Saturday morning's torrents. By midday the High Street was full of people and still it poured. The street streamers snapped beneath the weight of the downpour and bits of flag hung limply down on to the pavement. The floats were ruined. Crepe paper awnings drooped limply and dripped into scarlet and turquoise pools. Dozens of fairies and elves were smeared up their legs and down their arms in rainbow colours. The rain brought down the soot in greasy black spots and soon everyone looked smutty, dishevelled and irritated.

We turned out in mackintoshes and wellingtons to watch the procession, but the Mayor took one look at the shivering brass band and bedraggled majorettes and cancelled it. The stalls were moved from the park to a piece of wasteland by the station in order to tempt Saturday shoppers to buy.

It was a great disappointment. The Gala is one of the high spots of the year, an old mining tradition. But more important, since Council money is short and there are no grants available, local charities rely on this occasion to raise vital funds. Lucy had been preparing for weeks, collecting toiletries and making gift baskets with them, often out of her own wages, to raise money to provide temporary accommodation for the elderly. In Grimlington the Old Folks' Home is a last resort, there only for those with no child to care for them. No one complains. Looking after elderly parents and relatives is an accepted way of life, part of being a community. But despite the enormous saving on Council funds, there was no provision for caring relatives to have an occasional rest or holiday. Lucy was involved in a project – funded by charity alone – which hoped to provide that desperately needed break. They had managed to buy three large terraced houses, but each needed a fortune in renovation and the money came in very, very slowly. Lucy loved old people and dreamed of the day there might even be a job for her. No more packing fruit and vegetables, or being sent out to sweep the yard or wash the boss's car because there was nothing else to do. She would work for the minimum wage just to feel that her life was useful to someone.

There was rain dripping from her plastic hat, down her glasses and from the tip of her nose, but she was as cheery as ever.

'We've not done too bad,' she called to me, then slipped

something into the hands of a child who had stopped to stare at the stall with large, round eyes.

'If you didn't give so much away you'd make more,' I shouted back.

'Yer know I can't resist a child.'

The other stalls were a quaint mixture of raffles, hula-hoop, pick-a-straw and luscious home-made cakes. There were mounds of second-hand clothing, books, ornaments, bent lamp-shades and the inevitable red and white striped satin curtains. The second-hand trade in West Yorkshire is big business. Every market, as well as every fete and gala seemed to have dozens of white elephant stalls, filling the air with that unmistakable smell of age and use. I found one or two welcome bargains, a curate's salary not stretching as it might, but I could not help but wonder who would be tempted by the shoes. Better than none at all, I supposed.

By the evening the rain had tailed off to a drizzle and the whole town turned out for the firework display. From the top of the hill in the park it was an impressive sight. The children had never seen anything like it. Their upturned faces, lit up in the darkness by the sudden bursts of light, were a mixture of pleasure and wonder. Then, as the last explosion died away, the fair opened at the bottom of the hill in a riot of noise and a blaze of flickering, coloured lights. Children dragged their unwilling parents to the magic sight.

On Sunday the rain began again and the ecumenical Gala service was moved indoors into the Baptist Church. Numbers were depleted, but at least there was no competition from the fairground. The Drama Group waited in an agony of nerves. Only Ian looked calm. He always did. His nursing experience probably. Linda wriggled on her seat and Jan and Dorothy chattered like a pair of parrots. I fidgeted about, then went to find a toilet. Linda grinned at me as I shuffled past her.

'Hey,' she said when I got back, 'I used to think you were a right flash piece. I thought you'd got it all together, and never worried about anything, not the type I'd ever make a friend of. But underneath you're just like the rest of us, aren't yer?'

She winked at me and the service started. Suddenly it was our turn, then it was all over, without a hitch. As we slumped back into the pews with relief, Mo and Eric got up and went to the front. They were new to our church and Edward had thought that members of the other churches would be as thrilled by their story as we were. He was wrong. They told how they had lived together for some years and had two children, and then how they had moved to Grimlington, his home town, where their relationship began to fall apart. She was a southerner and lonely. He was out every night with his mates. They separated, and Eric went to live in Ossleforth, each knowing it was not the answer and feeling as desperate as ever. Without any consultation, hardly knowing why, both were drawn to church, though not the same one. Apart, each struggled with Christianity and what they saw of the foibles, yet obvious warmth, of its followers. Independently both clutched at the last straw, then discovered with amazement what had happened to the other and that they had a basis on which to rebuild their relationship.

'And I'm going to marry 'er,' Eric said, turning to Mo and smiling. She started in surprise at so public a proposal, then blushed with pleasure.

'Disgusting!' said some of the congregation. 'What a display!'

'What was?' we asked in innocence.

'All of it,' they said. 'Drama an' all.'

We were crestfallen, until the Lady Mayoress came and put her arm round Linda. 'That was wonderful, dear. I was a factory girl a long time ago and it took me right back.'

'Well, you can't please everyone,' Linda said ruefully to the group, as we gathered in the porch.

They were still a little deflated.

'You did well,' I reassured them.

'And anyway,' Ian said, 'it's those outside the Church we want to listen, not those inside.'

Everyone nodded and their faces brightened.

'If we can't take a bit of criticism we're not worth much,' Linda laughed. 'And anyway, it'll do us good. Too much praise would only make us big-headed.'

'See you Tuesday?' I asked.

'See you Tuesday,' they all said together.

9

'It's a plot, that's what it is,' Ian informed us the following Tuesday night, when we were trying, vainly, to fit in an extra rehearsal. No one had any free time. There seemed to be church meetings for almost every night of the week.

'Keep 'em all so busy,' he said, 'that they've no time to get up to mischief. So much for converting the natives. It's so long since I've seen me mates they've forgotten who I am.'

'Your mates?' Jan said in her slow drawl. 'It's my husband. He can't understand how I can find so much to do. He swears the church is taking me away from him.'

'Well Joe still goes to his club on Friday nights and I'll not stop him,' Linda said, compressing her lips the way she did when she had made up her mind about something. I was learning to respect her determination. She was always fair.

'So I'm sorry everyone but I can't rehearse on Friday night. It's my turn to babysit. I'll not spoil his night out. You see, Michele,' she explained to me apologetically, 'round here you're born into a club, usually your dad's, and it's like belonging to a big family. It's an old tradition, dating from time when houses were so tiny, living rooms weren't big enough for the whole family, especially when pit clothes were hung to dry over oven. And they were there all the time, since sons didn't always work same shifts as their fathers. The women were glad to see back of their menfolk. It meant they could get tin bath down and soak in peace! The men still love their club. They 'ave a laugh together, let their hair down. If yer stop going all of a sudden just because yer go to church it looks as if yer think yer a cut better than rest. Yer can't mix any more, only with yer own sort. Religious people always seem to live in a kind of a . . .'

'Ghetto?' I suggested.

'That's it. It's not natural. Jesus would 'ave gone into the clubs and mixed, wouldn't he?'

She looked round for approval, then decided it wasn't necessary.

'Anyway, Joe and Eric go down on Friday nights. They get some stick, but that's what it's all about.'

Kelly, Ian's wife, arrived to collect him. They had only been married a few months.

'And I thought the Church was in favour of marriage,' Ian said, as she came into the room. 'Well, it's not doing much for ours. We haven't had a night in together for weeks. We haven't had the chance to get to know each other yet. Imagine how it would sound in a divorce court. "What would you say was the major factor leading to the breakdown of your marriage?" "Please your honour, it was the Church." '

Kelly took his hand coyly, and suggested gently that it was time to go home.

'A-aaaaa,' sighed the assembled company.

'Remember those days eh, Jan?' Linda said, smiling.

'That was a long time ago,' Jan said sadly.

'Come on,' Linda said, throwing her her coat, 'we'd better go home, or we'll all be in trouble.'

The following evening, Wednesday, was the mid-week meeting.

'You go,' Peter said. 'I'm not needed and it'll do you good. Besides,' he said, a mischievous twinkle in his eye, 'why must the clergy always be there and the poor little wife be stuck at home? Let's create a precedent.'

'My, two evenings out in a row,' I said sarcastically. 'Be careful, I might begin to enjoy such freedom.'

'That's all right,' he said, 'I might just enjoy having a night in. At least it's a chance to watch the news and catch up with the world.'

'In that case, you won't mind doing the ironing will you?' I called out as I dashed out of the front door.

'Having a night off, is he?' Frank asked when I appeared at the parish hall. Substituting for my husband at a meeting was obviously quite a novelty. As he stooped to hear my reply, I noticed that Betty was right about her husband. 'Not a grey hair in his head,' she said, 'and no Grecian 2000 either! Makes yer sick!' He did look surprisingly youthful.

I refused to apologise for being second best.

'No, I'm having the night off. He's working tonight, putting the children to bed.'

Frank's face broke into a smile. The point was taken.

Despite shifts, and the strange hours many worked, there was a surprising turn-out, about a third of the congregation. Such was the sense of anticipation that it took Edward some time to call the meeting to order, struggling to make himself heard above the laughter and chatter. I had the distinct impression that for the rest of the evening his hold on the situation was completely arbitrary and might disintegrate at any moment. His topic was 'giving' and he gave himself to the subject with his customary force. But no amount of force or fire was going to impress this audience one bit.

'Give now,' he shouted, 'your money will be no good to you once you're dead.'

'You'll get it all then, Vicar,' Albert said quietly.

The meeting dissolved in laughter. Notwithstanding being cut off in mid-flow, Edward tried again.

'Dear old Lucy here . . .'

'Less of the "old", if you don't mind,' she said.

And so it continued. Edward rose to the challenge, cut, thrust and parried and, like a black preacher, began to use the participation to drive his message home. He enjoyed every minute of it. I had expected the meeting to be sober, restrained, dignified, as so many I had attended in the past in my non-conformist days, where the expounding of the word of God was a solemn, serious business and to speak out of turn might be seen as a breach of respect. Given the increasing informality of the Sunday services and the tendency of the congregation to reply to rhetorical questions from the pulpit, I should have known what to expect, but the entertainment factor was an unanticipated bonus. I only hoped Peter would be able to develop the taste and wit for quick repartee. His teaching experience would help.

He studied my face as I walked into the sitting room.

'Well?' he said, smiling, but then he knew my taste for the slightly unconventional. I kicked off my shoes and dropped onto the settee.

'Well, it's certainly not like any meeting I've ever experienced before. But I like it.'

He grinned. 'I thought that was what you'd say.'

'It was . . . real, I suppose. No masks or pretence, no disguising their real feelings with a show of piety. Mick was feeling lousy tonight, a failure, so he said so. People prayed just as they spoke, an odd sentence, sometimes just a word. It reminded me of when Joel learned to speak.'

' "Sock",' Peter mimicked, 'and "sick".'

We laughed, remembering. Poor Joel had been a very sick-y baby. Hardly surprising it should be his first word.

'Most of the time only we knew what he was saying, but it didn't matter. We were so thrilled. Maybe God feels like that when he hears those prayers.'

'It's a frightening experience,' Peter said, 'especially in a culture where people are not encouraged to take the limelight. That's management's job. So the sound of your own voice speaking out in public can be a shock.'

I sat back for a while. Peter watched me.

'Something's buzzing around in your little head.'

'Yes,' I said slowly. 'Yes. It's just dawned on me what we're doing to people when they become Christians in a town like this. No matter how much the church seems to us to reflect the way of life here, it's still a total change of culture.'

'And that's something you understand,' Peter smiled.

'Yes, it is.' I began to feel excited. 'At least it's very similar. We don't exactly tell them not to go to their clubs, but we don't give them enough time. We expect singing hymns, praying, Bible studies, and saying the liturgy to come naturally, as if they had always done it. But it's another world. It must be as foreign to them as it was to me.'

'It is, if you're not used to reading. I visited a chap the other day who kept insisting he couldn't come. I suddenly realised it was probably because he couldn't read and he didn't want to look daft in front of all those people. The sight of all the books we hand out must send some people into a state of paralysis.'

I got up to go to bed and could not help laughing.

'And to think,' I said to Peter, 'I thought God had got his wires crossed. What use was I, a Jewish clergy wife in a mining town? Maybe it's not as silly as it seems after all.'

I climbed the stairs to bed, congratulating the Almighty on the ingenuity of his arrangement.

I lay awake that night, a thousand thoughts rushing through my head, such a mass of different impressions, yet overriding the rest the sense that I had caught a glimpse of something very special, yet also very vulnerable. Mick's words came back to me with all the pain and frustration they expressed.

'They think there's something wrong with yer at work if yer don't join in all the grumbling, cheating and plotting. There's no trust. I hate the atmosphere. It pulls me down.'

What was it that he stirred up inside me? It was more than sympathy. A certain wistfulness? A sense of awe perhaps. Here was someone not cossetted, protected and safe, as I was, but out in the real world, where it was hard grind, yet still preserving a child-like trust, a faith that was simple, accepting and as tough as the old boots he had to wear. I never accepted anything. I questioned everything, argued with everyone, from God himself to my own shadow. My mother always warned me it would get me into trouble, and when Peter decided to become a clergyman I began to think she was right. Not that questioning is wrong. I had half a suspicion that the Church might not have become so culturally out-of-date if we had questioned our idiosyncrasies a little earlier. But there is also a time to accept, a time to believe and rest in that belief.

'I've let yer down again God,' Mick said. 'I'm sorry.' And that was it. He was ready to face tomorrow.

That treasure we were promised before we came to Grimlington was there all right and I had barely had to dig to find it. With the realisation that night that I might have something to give came another just as certain, that I would receive a thousand times more.

We discovered quite soon that almost every meeting that took place in the church, however resented, from PCC to the Fabric Committee was invested with the same banter and humour. In fact Mick and Karen's home group sounded so entertaining through the breeze block wall that their neighbours thought they must be missing something, and joined them.

There were eight home groups and although they had been meeting for some time they never really seemed to flourish as well as they might have done in an area inclined to more cerebral activity. One difficulty was that people felt extremely anxious about going into each other's homes. That, of course, was the problem on our estate, why no one came to our door. We were clergy, the professionals, and tradition had long dictated that a working man should know his place. But we never anticipated how lasting and widespread the attitude was. The church members were so generous in their hospitality that I had not cooked a Sunday lunch for weeks and I presumed that was the norm, the usual northern warmth I had enjoyed as a Geordie. And I rejoiced that I had fallen on my feet. Then on his visits Peter picked up a constant refrain: 'I won't go to any meeting in a home. I've never been one for going into other people's houses and I won't start now.' And I began to realise that my Sunday lunches out were not to be taken for granted. It took courage to let go of a privacy which had become a way of life. In the back-to-back terraces people had shared their homes and lives, but the tradition died with the houses and fierce Yorkshire pride took over. No one could see your house unless it was perfect. Those lunches were a sign that Christianity was beginning to cut across the self-reliance and independence which masked much deeper, more sensitive feelings.

As people shed their layers of self-protection a great deal of pain and hurt was exposed, and the home groups bore the brunt of it. Many individuals had been treated as if they were of no value and now they believed it. Grimlington had had a large grammar school of reputation. Children came to it from miles around. It offered unlimited opportunity and a golden future, escape from the pit and inherited drudgery. But if, with the failure of one exam, that opportunity seemed to be destroyed, then a sense of failure hung around ever after, dogging the steps of its victims. At eleven, or sooner, a man's destiny might be made final. If it was not, his self-image certainly was. How hard it then was to convince people that they were loved, wanted and valuable, especially when everything around them, from their wages to their conditions of employment, often said the opposite.

From experience Peter and I were both convinced of the healing potential of groups. He warmed to the idea of leading some basic training in group dynamics, and when the first meeting in our home was a training session for home group leaders it seemed his time had come. But this was Grimlington and we had not yet learned that all the best-made plans had a strange way of going awry.

I had invited Mary round for a chat that evening.

'Are you settling down? Are you happy here?'

It was strange how everyone asked us that from the first week we arrived.

'Yes,' I said doubtfully. It was hard to tell. 'It always takes me a while. That's my fault, not yours.'

She looked at the For Sale sign through the window.

'Any sign of a buyer?'

I shook my head.

'Can you blame them? We'd like to move too, somewhere bigger on the new estate. We've our names down on the Council list, though there's not much chance.'

I groaned inside. Another church family wanting to leave this estate. Then I remembered how Mary lived. I visited them once in August in a heatwave. A roaring fire was blazing in the hearth and Phil was sitting in his favourite armchair, the beads of perspiration pouring down his face. Mary had caught my quizzical expression and explained, 'We've visitors coming to stay. We need hot water in case they want a bath.'

My face was still a puzzle and she laughed, caught my arm and gave me a little shake.

'We use coal for everything round here, you idiot.'

It clicked.

'No immersion?'

'Just as well, we couldn't afford electric anyway.'

No, I could not begrudge Phil and Mary what I wanted so much for myself.

'We need the space,' Mary said, 'with the children growing up. Teenagers need a bedroom each, especially with Cheryl coming to live at home. She can be hard to handle.'

'How did it happen?'

'Cheryl? It was a hard birth, me being so small. Hospitals have improved in the last fifteen years, but there were more mistakes then. She were brain damaged. She's God's gift to us all the same, though she drives me mad at times. I tell yer what though, if I had a nervous breakdown, Council would have to find us a bigger house.'

'Any chance of that?' I asked.

'A lot,' she laughed, then our conversation was totally drowned by the sound of raucous laughter coming from the next room. We could not hear each other.

'What did you say they were doing?' she shouted.

I tried to lip read. 'Peter said it was some kind of group exercise.'

'Well there's not that much noise in our street when the pub's just closed.'

'A good meeting, was it?' I asked Betty, as I opened the door for her a couple of hours later.

She stood on the doorstep giggling, waiting for Frank.

'Ooooh, 'e's a one, that man of mine! Frank, where are yer? Get a move on.'

'I'm out here, waiting for you to finish gassing,' came a voice from the darkness beyond the front door, 'and I have been for the past quarter of an hour.'

'Ooooh 'eck,' she said, and Frank walked back up the path, took her by the arm and without a flicker of an eyelid, escorted her firmly towards the car. He turned for a moment and we caught his wink just before we closed the door.

Peter sat down on the stairs and roared with laughter.

'Well, I wonder what that achieved? It was a shambles. I deliberately refused to give a lead, not even to open with a prayer. Alicia, bless her, played straight into my hands. She got quite uptight and said it wouldn't be a proper meeting because we'd missed out a vital piece of ritual. Then everything seemed to disintegrate all at once. Frank and Betty had a private row in one corner, everyone else talked at cross purposes and Rick tried in vain to call things to order. At last I managed to shut everyone up and tried to make them see what happens when everyone comes with their own expectations and no one dares to take the lead. I think they got the point because Rick said, "Now I see what happens in my home group." But then, just as I thought we were getting somewhere Alicia unwrapped one of those mints of hers. It was supposed to be surreptitious, but we could hear the paper crackling all around the room. As she popped it into her mouth, thinking no one had noticed, Frank said, "Alicia, if that had been Jesus he would have shared it with us all." And that was the end of my training session!'

We sat on the stairs laughing for some time.

'I can't see us losing our sense of proportion round here, can you? Betty told me that when Alicia enthused to Frank about the eagle she'd seen when she was last up in Scotland, he said, "Yer've been to Edinburgh zoo, have yer, Alicia?" '

'The PCC's the same,' Peter said, 'so good humoured, not a sour note. It's great to have such support and fun. But occasionally, just occasionally, I wish they'd get down to making decisions of real importance.'

Peter's wishes were to be fulfilled sooner than he ever anticipated, and with a pain and cost he never anticipated either. That was the night they decided to disband the choir. Only then did we understand why the PCC had been constantly postponing major decisions for so many years.

10

Nowhere in England do the old and new coexist in such perilous tension as in the Church. It stands on the one hand as one of the last surviving British institutions, an essential part of our history and heritage, and on the other as the symbol of fossilised religiosity, relevant only to a tiny, dwindling initiate. Its members polarise into those who attend because they always have and find comfort in the old ways, and those whose faith is new and see that tradition means little to the secular masses.

Grimlington was no exception. The feeling in the town was that the parish church was 'not for the likes of us'. Its traditions were the traditions of the professional classes and tradespeople, the posh, the nicely dressed and politely spoken. Their attitude was justified by long, painful memories. Legend told of a previous vicar who would cross the road rather than say good morning to a miner. Only twenty years before the church had still catered for the needs of a sizable, social elite, performing plays and playing whist. The grammar school headmaster had his own pew and read the lessons. Women wore hats. A strict silence was observed at all times. The church was fairly full, but then propriety required attendance. Once that was no longer so, the decline began.

Working men and women were never allowed to mingle their praises with those of management. The majority were nonconformist. The rest attended one of the three daughter churches, less threatening and more like chapel. Subsidence finished what changing customs had started and two closed before they collapsed. The last remaining daughter church, Cuttlesworth, struggled on, a tiny congregation in a dismal Edwardian building, clinging desperately to the comfort of their childhood memories.

By the time Edward's predecessor arrived the church had

become an anachronism. It belonged to another age, long since a dream, before the soft green hills became a tangled mass of iron and steel and the trees were engulfed in waste and slag when the farmers had farmed in safety, and the church was an integral part of rural life, following the rhythm of its seasons. Then the industrial revolution stretched its grip across West Yorkshire. Birdsong gave way to the whirr of the pit and the constant shunting of the steam train. Men came from miles around to find work. The Irish asked for Tommy Cox's Catholic coal factory. They thought coal was manufactured. The Polish went there too. Nonconformists mined at Pope and Pearson's, and the rest at Dom Pedro's and any other pit that would have them. They worked on their backs, their bellies and their knees, hacking the black treasure out of the earth, to fire trains, mills and factories. Women thought themselves lucky to find work in the woollen mills. It was better than pulling trucks of coal underground. Men, women and children worked twelve hours a day, in work that robbed humanity of health and daylight and made them old before their time.

And over the years more and more trees were razed, the fields churned, the natural landscape destroyed to make way for row upon row of tiny terraced cottages with no garden, no green and one lavatory for every dozen houses, all in the name of the Christian principle of prosperity. Pope and Pearson were chapel men. Coal owners went to church just as the landowners had. They were benevolent. They were philanthropists, providing schools and public facilities, but it did not occur to their Christian conscience to improve their employees' conditions of work. In industrial England, as in rural England, all life had its order and the Church upheld it.

But then the Church had no competition in those days; no one questioned its absolute authority. It never had to fight for its life, not until the old ways began to crumble. The great depression of the thirties took its toll. Coal was mined more cheaply abroad. But still the owners refused to modernise. Industry no longer made them rich, so they fled south with what fortune they had left, and the men who had made them rich were left to starve. War provided employment, at least temporarily. But if the first war had made men question, the second confirmed their doubts. The national crisis called for coal. The men worked on Sundays to provide it and never went back to church.

In the forties and fifties the nation took over the mines and hope died as the railways, pits and stations began to close. Communities were rehoused in the name of progress and many of them died. There were pubs, clubs and the cinema for solace. And, more devastating for the Church, there was the television. A man need never be bored or wonder what to do with his leisure time again. And the Church never even realised it had a rival or asked where three quarters of its congregation had gone, until it was too late. But as it had been in the beginning, so it went on, singing the same old hymns, saying the same old services, while most of the town agreed, 'It's just not for the likes of us.'

Edward's predecessor courageously carried his church kicking and screaming into the twentieth century, but, on his own admission, only as far as the nineteen sixties. Then his energy ran out and exhaustion forced him to give way to a man with fresh, vigorous ideas. For a few months Edward waited and watched. The new prayer book was introduced, even at the eight o'clock Sunday morning Communion, lest that service become a stronghold of reactionary feeling, and the church be split into two separate congregations. But as Edward watched and listened it became apparent that far more sweeping changes would be necessary if the town was ever to be convinced that Jesus spoke for the working man of their day and not for the respectable people of previous generations. One major change would affect that most cherished of institutions, the choir!

No one doubted that Grimlington's choir had seen better days. Bob, the organist and choirmaster for forty years, did his best, but it would have taken little short of a miracle to produce anything approaching a reasonable performance with the handful he had left. The four or five remaining stalwarts, whose numbers swelled to nine or ten on great occasions, appeared to rattle round the empty choir stalls. Their robes, colourful and dignified in former years, now looked out of place in a congregation wearing jeans and dungarees. And they no longer made sufficient sound to beat the organ to the back pews. No one expected the standard of a great cathedral, but one night they were reduced to one solitary bass singing his heart out in splendid isolation. He would have had to be little short of superman, or bionic woman, to manage tenor, alto and soprano too. The days of our choir were numbered.

What hurt some of the last remaining choir members was the

sudden, rapid growth of the new Music Group. Rick, who had started it, learned his love of music from the Salvation Army. At the turn of the century 'the Army' in Grimlington had a congregation of five hundred, one of the largest in the town. Now, they no longer had a Citadel and Rick and Julie had been going to Ossleforth to worship. The transference of their allegiance to us was not without a great deal of heartache. Julie was horrified when Rick first told her of his urge to visit the parish church and the increasing feeling that that was where he ought to be making music. Her whole family were Salvationists. The rigid formality of the Church of England left her cold, and one visit confirmed her worst impressions. Little short of divorce crossed her mind. Reason told her it was foolish to split the family and reluctantly, against all the instincts of her upbringing, she followed her husband. Rick began the music group and she began a playgroup. It was probably not the first time that the Church of England was indebted to the Salvation Army – though there were some who would question that debt, when roused from their slumbers after the sermon and prayers by Rick's trumpet accompaniment to the final hymn.

Reading music was not a vital prerequisite to joining the music group, otherwise there would have been no candidates. In fact, unlike the choir, there were no conditions of entry and no audition, so Rick could only hope for a group of people who could sing reasonably in tune. And he found them. Some had not sung since they were at primary school, but it was a start and they loved it. By the time Edward arrived they were confident enough to make quite a contribution to the Family Services. There were rumbles of disapproval at the appearance of guitars, despite the fact that for years everyone had been happily chanting psalms about praising God on stringed instruments. Reading about it was one thing, doing it was another.

So when, during our first autumn in Grimlington, the PCC met to discuss the choir's final demise, feelings were running high.

'We've got to do it, there's no question.'

'But they'll be so upset.'

'They'll say it's that new vicar again.'

'Well they're wrong. We're going to make the final decision!'

'Yes, but I'm frightened. Me Aunty Gladys'll do 'er nut. She's fond of choir. They sang at 'er wedding thirty year ago.'

'Ay, and she 'asn't been since!'

'But what about Bob?'

Bob's feelings were a source of major concern. Not all churches are blessed in their organist. We were. It was impossible to think of hurting him. For forty years he had played the organ at three services every Sunday, sometimes at as many as six funerals a week and fifty weddings a year, forgoing holidays and weekends away. Such was his stamina that one Sunday evening, after he had sliced his finger on a razor blade in his pocket, he played on, the blood oozing out over the keys. The squeals from the Music Group had alerted Peter to the problem. He sidled over and suggested that Bob pop over to the vicarage to let Anna dress it. With a wad of bandaging round his finger he was back in five minutes, ready to play the next hymn.

There were times when his playing seemed inspired. As he played the old familiar hymns so lovingly and sensitively during the administration of Communion the congregation had started to hum or sing along with him.

'When the wife died,' he said to me one day, 'I thought all joy had gone out of my life for ever. Then I remembered God had given me music too.'

Bob was a convinced teetotaller and appalled by the amount of beer consumed in the town. 'I 'ad a mate,' he said to Peter one day in the vestry, as they were waiting for a wedding, and lamenting the effects of too much alcohol, 'who drank eight pints a night. His stomach was out 'ere. He drank that much that 'e went out in the dead of winter in only a T-shirt and never felt the cold. Mind you,' he said, wagging a forefinger, 'it killed 'im in the end.'

'How old was he?' Peter asked.

'Eighty!' Bob shook his head knowingly. He had proved the evils of drink to his own satisfaction.

No, Bob must not be passed over or ignored. So late one night and looking haggard, the PCC decided to disband all present musical enterprise, both choir and Music Group, and form one new team, under the joint direction of Rick and Bob. Bob bowed graciously to this new development. It was a blow, but inevitable. Besides, as the younger people sought out his help and advice he confessed he had never felt so appreciated and it was altogether a very pleasant experience.

One or two choir members followed his lead and made the

transition. Others could not. The pain of seeing their beloved choir pass into history was altogether too great. Ernie Fanshaw, who had been prepared to sing alone in the choir stalls, said he would never come to church again. Ernie fitted quite well into the stereotype of a Yorkshireman, dour and abrasive on the outside, and all soft and sensitive on the inside. As a farrier he commanded respect throughout the entire district. There was nothing he did not know about a horse's anatomy from the knee down. Vets called on him at all hours, seeking the wealth of his expertise. We would miss Ernie very much. Change was more painful than we anticipated.

The local *Gazette*, ever ready to rise up in the cause of the oppressed, took up the story. Angry letters accusing the vicar of iconoclasm filled half a page. One of Grimlington's great traditions had been done to death, wrote some who had not come to hear that tradition for a very long time. 'Modern music is not the same. It won't last,' they said. Who could disagree? But the church was meant to be a living organism and not an academy of ancient music, nor a repository of ancient traditions, preserved in a kind of ice age by the present membership for those who never came.

Edward responded graciously and explained that this was a communal decision, not just his own, made thoughtfully and carefully over a period of time. But the correspondence continued for some weeks and I saw how the personal attack wounded him and the criticism wore him down. Such is the vulnerable position of the clergyman. Unable by the very nature of his job to please all men and fulfil their expectations, he becomes the butt for their frustrations. Marjorie went beyond the duties of a churchwarden and shielded him in every way she could, deflecting every attack on to herself and the PCC. Gradually the hullaballoo died down and the town settled down to its usual indifference to all matters concerning the church.

One Sunday night Ernie Fanshaw and his wife were back in their usual pew for the evening service. Everyone tried to behave naturally, but their pleasure was obvious. Ernie left early. He could not countenance too much of the new music at once. And a man has his dignity when all is said and done. But he came back every week until he was rushed into hospital with a ruptured ulcer. The Sunday after he came out, he asked if he might have the opportunity to say a few words to the congregation.

'If you'd seen the buckets I brought up . . .'

'Yuk,' Jan told me later, wrinkling up her nose, 'it made me feel funny!'

'Well, all I want to say is that I felt yer support and yer prayers and I'm grateful.'

There were those however who would never accept change, and could not countenance the disappearance of the church's aura of middle-class respectability. I was rushing to the service one Sunday morning, marginally late, having miscalculated the time as usual, and as I passed the vestry door I noticed Peter, surplice half-way over his head, talking in a clipped, controlled voice to a rather smart-looking woman. I recognised the signs of pressure and annoyance in him. He hated interruptions just before a service, and so many people barraged him with requests and grouses, not realising how easily it destroyed his concentration. So I went to see if I could assist.

'Oh, yes,' the woman said, recognising at once that I belonged to the curt, unhelpful cleric, still struggling into his uniform.

'I only want to find my aunt's grave.'

The tone was aggrieved.

'We're just visiting the town you see.'

I did not hold out much hope of finding it, but escorted her round the cemetery, making helpful noises.

'By the way,' she said, a little apologetically after about fifteen minutes of unsuccessful hunting when I was beginning to wonder whether I would miss the entire service, 'I am sorry I can't come into church, but I'm not wearing a hat.'

Neither was I. Or did she think I was hiding one somewhere?

'We don't wear hats here,' I said. 'You can wear what you like. Most of the congregation come in jeans or dungarees.'

She stared at me for a moment, took a deep breath, spat 'Disgusting!' at me as if I were a worm which had just crawled out of the soil and marched off down the path.

As I went into church it occurred to me that hats had become such an expense that if they were regulation uniform half the congregation would have to be expelled.

Despite opposition the gradual metamorphosis continued and the new music team blossomed. Chris joined them with his violin, and then, with a nobility of spirit to which I could never rise, began a music group for children. Mary dug out her tambourine and plucking up all her courage, tried it out, faintly, in an evening service. No one complained so she became a little bolder, grinning shyly at first, then growing in confidence. One or two tentatively tried to write their own songs and then there was a sudden upsurge in composing. It became quite common to fall over someone lost in their own little world, humming away happily to themselves. It did little for conversation.

'Don't speak to me, I've got a song, and I have to find Rick or Chris to write down the notes, before I lose it.'

Woe betide him or her who had the misfortune to come upon a song first thing in the morning. It had to be sung all day until Rick or Chris came home from work.

It seemed as if latent creativity, stifled and checked for years, yet never completely destroyed, was only waiting for a new birth to ferment and explode. Julie gathered a group of banner makers together, Kelly started a dance group, and the Drama Group continued to stun me with their ingenuity. It all happened so fast it took my breath away and did more than anything to make me feel that I had at last become part of the scenery. But the greater marvel was that as our creativity expanded, confidence grew, uncloaking a talent undreamed of by those who visited the town.

'The sin of the monied classes in the palmy Victorian days was to condemn the working man to ugliness, ugliness, ugliness. A man needs beauty more than he needs bread,' said D. H. Lawrence. It may not have been in their surroundings, but they had had a glimpse of real beauty all the same. Their eyes had been opened to another world not seen with ordinary human perception and it was that beauty which so inspired them that they could not keep it to themselves. That they could reproduce it in music, dance and art work, creating something of lasting value, was a healing process in itself. Never before had I been so aware of the vibrant, life-transforming nature of Christianity. It was never meant to stifle or strangle personality, as I had seen so often in other places and other people. It made men whole. It made them free. It made them sit more easily in their human skins.

Rick and Kelly visited other churches 'of reputation' in order to glean new ideas. They came back depressed and encouraged all at once.

'They're very professional. We've a long way to go.'

211

'But we're not them, we're us, and for us, we've gone a long way.'

'It's a beginning.'

It was a beginning all right and in an environment where words like 'talent' and 'individuality' were almost forbidden, it was much more than a beginning.

11

We were never given a list of parish addresses and telephone numbers. There wasn't one. It would have been superfluous since all vital information of that nature was stored in Alicia's head. Peter felt at times that he was using a computer.

'Where will I find the Studleys, Alicia?'

'Calderdale Street, off Windermere Road, just past the chip shop. I can't remember the number, darling, but it's fourth or fifth on the right, a bright blue door, you can't miss it. Oh, by the way, if you go during the day you're more likely to find her at her mother's, which is one of the old folks' bungalows on Ashfield Walk, the one with the pillar box outside.'

She was always right.

Walking round the supermarket with her was an experience.

'Hello, dear, feeling better?'

'How's Tommy settling at school?'

'So sorry to hear about your father. It was so unexpected.'

'Which ward is your gran on? I'll see her on Thursday, that's my day for hospital visits.'

After an hour there was very little in her shopping trolley.

'Smile dear,' she whispered to me. 'You may not know who they are, but they know who you are. You represent the church.'

I groaned inwardly. That was what came of having our smiling faces plastered on the centre pages of the *Gazette*: 'Grimlington gets new curate'. Still, I suspected that I could probably get away almost incognito if it were not for Alicia. Everyone knew who she was, and that the community had taken her to their hearts, as she had taken them to hers, there was no doubt. They were proud of her too. She was known to have an aristocratic pedigree, and an aristocrat could get away with anything. Sometimes Alicia did!

Staff lunches at her house were a treat. She, Anna and I took it in turns to make lunch on Mondays for the five of us and our children. Eating together meant that Anna and I could at least keep abreast with the parish news our husbands had forgotten to tell us. This was fairly vital since most of the parish presumed that we had a hot line to the clergy, knew everyone's problems and were a source of all wisdom. In fact we were usually the last to know what was going on. Our husbands fell into bed exhausted when they came in at night. They certainly did not want to talk shop. Without our Monday lunches we would have continued to live in blissful, total ignorance.

Alicia spoiled us. There was turkey, or a roast joint, with mounds of vegetables of every kind. An inventive cook, she was generous with herbs and spices, especially if they grew in her back garden, beneath her imported Scottish thistles. It was not unusual to draw a whole sprig of rosemary from your mouth. And then a meal might be crowned with lemon cheesecake, or 'supervommer' pudding, a recipe to end all recipes, handed down by a previous curate, consisting of coffee, chocolate, breadcrumbs and lashings of cream. By the time the smell of freshly-percolated coffee wafted in from the kitchen, Peter would be feeling slightly liverish and on the verge of dozing off in a corner by the fire. Farewell to an afternoon's work! And no need to feed him again before Wednesday.

Because Alicia's spondylitis impeded her movement and because the house was small, we all tended to get under each other's feet, so we fetched and carried for her, acted as her legs and moved at her command.

'Plates, dear. Place mats. Glasses over there.'

On my first visit I went to what I assumed was a china cabinet to look for some more of her favourite stoneware. I opened the cupboard door, and there, crammed on top of each other in a vast pile, were hammers, screwdrivers, saws, chisels, clamps, drills, anything but crockery. I looked round and everyone else was grinning.

'Just because you don't know one end of a screwdriver from the other,' Peter said, 'don't imagine all women are the same.'

'Alicia has a certificate in mechanical engineering,' Edward said, with a hint of awe in his voice. Mechanics were as much of a mystery to him as they were to me. 'In fact, when the church boiler played up the other day, there was quite a race. I think Alicia got there before Peter.'

'She carries the necessary tools around in her handbag,' Peter said, barely disguising his pique. He had trained as an engineer, graduated during an industrial slump, then went into teaching after several months of unemployment. But he never lost his deductive skills in diagnosing the faults of a dud machine.

'So, you have a rival,' I said to him, 'and a female one at that.'

I caught sight then of a vicious-looking instrument and drew it out.

'This wouldn't by any chance be the mallet,' I asked, 'the famous one which slew a mouse?'

The others examined it at a distance, then turned up their noses. The mouse incident was legend in the church. It was rumoured that Alicia was entertaining the sister of an Archbishop to tea, and who could doubt how lavish the fare, when a mouse ambled across the carpet. Indignant at this interruption, but not alarmed, she ran to her china cupboard, returned with the mallet and landed the creature such a blow on the skull that its tea-party days were over, for ever.

'Is it true?' I asked her, but she refused to comment and disappeared back into the kitchen.

We all drank our coffee huddled over the fire as Alicia's house was cold and in desperate need of renovation.

'How could the church let the house fall into a state of such disrepair?' Peter asked.

'It's not their fault,' Alicia said. 'You must remember that most people don't like to come into our homes. They don't know what they're like. That's pretty typical of the Church of England, or at least it was. The life of the clergy is supposed to be a bit hair-shirt. I don't mind the spartan life. This house is a lot better than many round here. Besides, the PCC did offer me central heating once.'

'You didn't refuse?' Peter asked incredulously.

'The cold doesn't bother me darling. I always sleep with my bedroom window open anyway, summer and winter. You remember how cold January was last year? When I got up one morning my bedroom was full of snow. I had to shovel it back out of the window before I could get to my clothes.'

Peter stared at her in disbelief and she smiled benignly back. There was no reason to suppose she was not telling the truth.

'Speaking of the cold,' Peter said, turning to a subject which had been bothering him for a few weeks, 'how do you keep warm when you do a winter interment?'

Alicia looked at him in amazement. The problem had evidently never crossed her mind. Peter looked to Edward for help, but none was forthcoming.

'The weather is getting colder and colder,' he said, by way of explanation. 'You may think it's a silly question, but I'm a cold–blooded sort of chap and I don't function at my best if I'm perishing. We wear the same gear in the dead of winter as we wear in the summer heat waves. The wind already howls right round that cemetery and blows my cassock up like a balloon. I've tried thermal underwear and it doesn't help. I feel like wearing a parka over my surplice.'

There was a moment's silence.

'Speaking of interments,' Edward said, in a tone of voice that suggested he was not going to be drawn into trivia, 'the undertaker rang this morning with the date of Nellie Hepworth's funeral. Do you want to do it, Alicia? I gather you visited recently.'

'Yes,' Alicia said, apparently quite stunned. 'I visited on Friday. I had such a strong feeling I was to tell her to set her life in order and be sure of God's forgiveness before it was too late. But I never thought it would be so soon. Did I do the right thing?'

'Would we had your courage,' Peter said.

'Well there was such tension in the family, so much to sort out, but I wouldn't want to precipitate anything. This is always happening to me.'

'I should regard yourself as a prophet of . . . I mean a warning angel.'

'You think so?' Alicia smiled, then her brows knitted again. 'I only hope she was ready.'

We left her that day to wonder and hope, marvelling at her concern for so many people.

'How does she manage to give such individual love and attention?' Peter said wistfully. 'With so many funerals it takes me all my time to fit in the visits.'

Michael O'Connor, the undertaker, rang early on Monday morning to deal with the weekend's business. Well might he advertise a lovely chapel of rest. It struck me he must take little himself. With an average of a hundred and seventy funerals a year, give or take an intemperate winter, and that at the Anglican Church alone, without Catholics and nonconformists, Grimlington had a track record which left many other places behind. Fellow curates from college days, with whom we still kept in touch for an occasional commiseration, were staggered at the number. Peter was taking two or three funerals a week before they had done their first.

'It's the air round here,' we joked, 'even the sparrows have to clear their chests in the morning.'

The truth of the matter was that Grimlington was a static community with little new housing until recently, and a high proportion of elderly people. But nevertheless bronchitis and other chest diseases undoubtedly took a heavy toll. The local newspapers informed us that inhaling coal fumes was a hazard. Sulphur dioxide burnt holes in the lungs. Our councillors were concerned. The area had fallen way behind. Something must be done. But nothing ever was. Grants to convert fireplaces to smokeless fuel cost a great deal of money and there was none to spare. The Coal Board could not convert their free coal allowance for pit workers into gas, even for the retired. So new council houses and old people's bungalows were still built with no heating other than coal fires. The elderly humped their coal or froze.

Because of the death rate, visits to the bereaved were often short, hurried affairs and totally inadequate. Peter was frustrated. He could not fulfil his own expectations, let alone other people's.

'It shouldn't be like this,' he said. 'I planned and hoped to continue visiting for at least a year to provide the sort of comfort and counsel which is really necessary.'

The only consolation was that in a town like Grimlington, family and friends usually took over where the clergy seemed to fail. And they were probably more acceptable. Not everyone was glad to see a clergyman standing on their doorstep. He almost had to batter the door down on one occasion.

'Who is it?'

'The curate!'

'What do you want?'

'To come in.'

'What for?'

'Because I'm burying your father on Wednesday!'

But the clergy were gladly received in most homes. After all, a man could cry in front of them. They were different, not like other men. They would not think it sissy.

'I shouldn't cry, I know.'

'Why not?'

'Because men don't.'

'Who says?'

Peter found himself constantly giving families permission to express their grief naturally. We were a nation, it seemed, which released our emotional energies at football and rugby matches, but at funerals kept them tightly buttoned up. Everything had to be dignified and respectable. There were few areas of our national life that struck me as being so totally un-Jewish. Judaism gave space to grieve. There are seven days' compulsory mourning, and most Jews take advantage of the opportunity.

One young miner that Peter visited marched round the house, swearing and cursing.

'I loved me dad. Why did 'e 'ave to die, the stupid old sod?'

'Sssssssh,' whispered his mother out of the corner of her mouth, smiling at Peter, 'don't swear in front of parson.'

'Let him swear all he likes,' Peter said. 'It's one of the healthiest expressions of grief I've seen in a long while.'

The saddest visits were to stunned and lonely spouses, who sat vacant and alone in their misery.

'We kept ourselves to ourselves. We never bothered anyone. We never went into other people's houses, never mixed. We were happy just with each other.'

And now there was nothing to fill the gaping, empty void the partner had left behind.

Peter often felt the inadequacy of his own words. The Christian burial service seemed almost meaningless and out-of-place for those who had had no interest in Christianity in their lifetime. But there was no secular alternative. He did not like eulogies. Coming from the mouth of someone who had never known the deceased, they sounded hollow. Instead he preached as forcefully as he could of his own certainty of resurrection for those who followed Christ. And he grieved for the many who still walked away, locked in their own despair, unable and unwilling to reach out and take hold of the great hope he could offer.

Most mourners gave no instructions about the service, but left it to his discretion. However, one or two were quite specific.

'None of them futuristic services,' said one man, once a regular church member.

'I don't understand,' Peter said.

'No guitars and that. She didn't like 'em when she were alive. She certainly won't like 'em now.'

Peter did not know how he could be so certain, but assured him that we had not yet introduced guitars into the funeral service.

One woman was so determined that every detail should be perfection itself that she rang several times to check. Unfortunately for her, on the last occasion I answered.

'I wanted the curate, but you'll have to do,' she said.

I was beginning to get used to being a disappointing second best.

'Your husband is burying my mother.'

'Oh!' I said. Well I could hardly say, 'Good!' or, 'I'm sorry!'

'Could you tell me what comes after the anthem?'

I faltered. It amazed me that while a person would never dream of consulting their bank manager's wife about the state of their financial affairs, or the doctor's wife about the state of their health, yet the clergyman's wife is presumed to be a repository of wisdom in all matters clerical.

'I don't know,' I said. Then thinking it best to be honest, 'I've never been to an Anglican funeral.'

Honesty is not always the best policy, for it almost begged the next question, 'What kind have you been to then?'

'Jewish!' I said.

There was a moment's silence.

'Could you get your husband to ring me then? It is your husband, I presume?'

Given the number of funerals, it was inevitable a mishap should happen at some time or another. We were all enjoying a staff lunch at the vicarage one day, tucking into one of Anna's speciality Bakewell tarts, when all went dark as a funeral cortege slowly passed the dining-room window. Edward, Alicia and Peter watched it in silence. The Catholic Church was in the other direction. So were the Methodists and the Baptists.

Edward swallowed hard and cleared his throat.

'Whose was that?' he asked, as casually as he could.

Peter's eyes suddenly looked twice their size.

'Mine!' he said with horror, rushed from the table, and out of the door. The last we saw was a human whirlwind, chasing a hearse down the street. Fortunately there is a short-cut through the cemetery. So by the time the procession drew up at the church gates, Peter had opened the church, put on his gear, put out the hymn books and service sheets and was waiting graciously at the doors as if he had been there for at least the last twenty minutes.

So all was well. At least that was what he thought. But unfortunately one of the town councillors was there and he complained to the Council, who told the mayor to do something about it. So he instructed the town clerk to write to the vicar to tell his curate that the church doors must be opened at least half an hour before a funeral. And the vicar replied that any criticisms of his curate should be made direct and was the Council stuck for pressing business!

Peter laughed in disbelief when he saw the letter. The councillor lived nearby.

'Couldn't he come to me himself and tell me face to face? I could have at least had the chance to explain. I know the doors should be open earlier. Can't a man make a mistake?'

'Definitely not!' I said. 'Only perfection is acceptable, and especially from a clergyman!'

Peter never forgot to attend a funeral again, although there was one where he forgot something else and the response was just as unforgiving. The autumn continued bitterly cold and the nip in the air became a sharp penetrating bite, with no respect for several layers of underwear.

'For this funeral I am going to wear my parka over my cassock,' Peter muttered, tearing round the house in his usual hurry. The ground outside was covered that morning in a sparkling white frost. 'On second thoughts, I'd better not,' he said, as he got to the front door, then rushed back to the bedroom and put on another vest. It was a fight to fasten the buttons of his clerical shirt. He was so well padded he could have rolled to the cemetery. Halfway through the service, as they were gathered around the grave he noticed that the mourners appeared to be staring at his feet. He followed their gaze and saw to his horror that he had forgotten to change out of his new, luminous red shoes. Being size tens they refused to disappear under his cassock.

'That'll teach me to worry about the trivia of this life,' he groaned. 'Perfection is just out of my grasp.'

'Don't worry, love,' I reassured him, 'I don't expect anyone will have noticed.'

I spoke too soon. The following night was drama night. Linda was barely through the door when, with a huge grin stretching from one side of her face to the other, she said, 'Hey, what's 'e been up to now?'

I couldn't guess. 'What now?'

'Well, I was in the newsagents at the top of the High Street yesterday and I overheard the woman who was serving telling another woman in the shop that she'd just come from her cousin's funeral and you'd never guess, but the vicar was wearing bright red shoes. "No decorum, these days, the clergy," she said.'

Linda giggled, so did the others.

'It's about time someone brightened up the church's image,' Jan said.

'His reputation ruined and all for a pair of shoes,' I said ruefully.

'Take heart,' Linda reassured me. 'Clergy have lost their reputation for less. Just tell him to be 'imself.'

'Just being yourself' was something for which Grimlington people had a great capacity, a state of existence we were to see in its most uninhibited form in the very near future.

12

November was heralded in with great excitement, not just because of bonfire night, but because that first weekend by long tradition was the parish weekend away. Peter and I had been on church houseparties before, and enjoyed them enormously, but none of them had ever been quite like this.

In Grimlington church outings of any kind were always a problem, as we never had enough cars between us or at least enough that were on the road. Conveying one hundred and fifty people to Filey was therefore a mammoth headache.

'I want to go with me mam.'

'I can't sit in back, I'll be sick.'

'Me shift doesn't finish till seven.'

'I'm not going with him, 'e kicks.'

Eventually, by squeezing three adults with children on their knees into the back of every car, no one was left behind.

Despite all pleadings that luggage be kept to the minimum, suitcases were the largest I had seen, bulging with enough clothing and provisions for a trip to the Himalayas.

'I thought we were going to Filey, not the Antarctic,' I said to Peter as he wrestled with cases, rugs, tins, flasks, guitars, projector and screen.

The sarcasm was noted. He threw me a withering look.

'It can be cold,' Lucy said, obviously feeling that Peter needed moral support.

With every stop to collect more people, the contents of the boot had to be rejuggled, with loud expostulations from Peter which I hoped none of them would hear. Then at last we held our breath as the final bag was stowed away and the boot slammed shut. We were off. No we weren't. Gladys had forgotten her mac, her slippers and the plastic bags, just in case. Back we went and her neighbours appeared at their sitting-room window to wave us off with as much excitement as they did the first time.

Then, as far as any vehicle is able, struggling under such a weight, we raced with twenty or so other cars down the A62. Not one treasured moment in Filey was to be lost. About a third of the party had set off early in the morning, taking a day off work and keeping the children off school, to have those few extra hours eating mussels and candy floss on the sea front. After all, for some it was their only annual holiday. If it was not, it was certainly their only experience of staying in a hotel and a rare chance of a weekend away. And they had been saving up for months, putting away a few pounds a week in the envelope in the kitchen drawer marked 'Filey'. There were lots of envelopes in the kitchen drawer, marked 'coal' or 'electric' or 'milk' or 'rent', and though mother added to them every week from the contents of the pay packet, they were never very full. But once autumn came round again those marked 'decorating' or 'kids' shoes' would have to stay empty. It was a difficult choice. Shortage of money imposes many hard decisions. The soot in the air meant that houses really needed to be decorated every year and the children's feet would keep on growing. But for that weekend in Filey you could put up with a sooty house, boots that pinched and leaked, and tights with darns in them for that matter.

And if, when the time came, despite the sacrifices, there was still not enough in the envelope because of other unforeseen necessities, the money could sometimes be borrowed from Mum and Dad. Or a smile might just melt the heart of Bill, the treasurer, and he might give a few weeks' grace.

'Come on, Bill, only nine weeks to Christmas. I'll get lots of overtime and soon pay it off.'

'My cash flow! I don't know how we run this church!' He would lift his eyes to heaven in mock despair, and the matter was settled.

Poor Bill had just cause for alarm. We were already dipping into our special discretionary fund for families such as Phil and Mary and their children. Phil was an attendant at the swimming baths and his income was incredibly low. Although he and Mary cleaned the church every week, which helped, there was no possibility of a family of five on Family Income Supplement affording a weekend away. Several families were in the same predicament, but we insisted that financial hardship should not prevent them from coming. So the settling of our hotel accounts could be a little wearing on the treasurer's nerves.

Our debts were not his only source of concern. Tradition had somehow forced him into the unenviable position of chief organiser and it was his lot to ensure everyone had a bed for two nights. We fought our way into the hotel through a lobby piled high with high chairs, pushchairs, hiking boots, guitars, suitcases and stray children, all abandoned in the hunt for a bedroom.

'My key doesn't fit in the door.'

'My room doesn't exist. There's no number ten.'

'Yer on the wrong floor, yer wally!'

'Somebody's in our room already!'

'Just pray they don't snore!'

'Thanks!'

Standing in the hall like a traffic warden, Bill dealt patiently with the mounting racket of complaints and misunderstandings and pointed people in the right direction.

Above all the other din a voice was heard.

'Who wants my gezunder this year?'

'Your what, Alicia?' I asked naively.

'What goes under the bed, darling,' she explained, then seeing my surprise, 'These corridors, dear, they're so long and draughty. Someone usually needs it.'

I looked round, but no one came forward.

'Looks as if it might be yours this year!'

My first sight of the upper floors of the hotel confirmed her words and I was in half a mind to go and take her up on her offer. When I had been told with great excitement, 'We stay in a hotel with a swimming pool', I never for a moment imagined the London Hilton, but nor was I prepared for this vast, old-fashioned building with its art-deco furnishings and corridors so gloomy that they seemed gas-lit. They were silent and empty and I marvelled that they seemed to swallow up over a hundred people, turning the raucous noise into a few eerie, floating sounds. But we soon realised that the bedroom walls were often plasterboard and paper thin, putting paid to any privacy. Before long people were discovering all kinds of things about each other they never knew before. But then that is what a weekend away is all about, or so I gathered.

The swimming pool turned out to be a sort of nine foot by six foot brownish green hole, filled with tepid, steaming water and surrounded by murals of golden beaches and palm trees. But it was wet, so the children loved it. So did the one or two who succumbed to the suggestion that this might be the Canaries and donned their bikinis. This was a feat of some daring, since the pool was on full view to the hotel's main corridor and thorough-fare through a large glass window. And no detail, however personal, ever escaped frank comment!

We all spent the first evening putting our children to bed, then putting them back to bed at half-hourly intervals. Some of the spouses, coming because it was a family occasion and not because they anticipated any involvement in the more spiritual content of the programme, had found the bar and sat giggling like a gang of naughty schoolboys who had dodged an RE lesson and dreaded being caught. We joined them after the first talk and the atmosphere relaxed considerably, especially as night wore on into the small hours of the next morning, and the combination of time and the beer loosened many tongues.

We regretted our folly at five-thirty, when Joel and Abby bounced out of bed, demanding towels and swimming costumes. At seven we finally let them loose on the world, with everyone else's children. Alicia had by then been in the pool for some time. Parents arrived for breakfast, their hair uncombed, their eyes half shut. A vast mural of Filey in Edwardian days, yellowing with age, as if Edwardian itself, filled an entire wall. The women were dignified in their long skirts and bonnets, the men stiff and erect in immaculate suits, as they supervised their offspring on the Yorkshire sands. As we launched reluctantly into the kippers, they seemed to mock us with their eminent respectability and the discipline of their well-ordered world. For some time I glowered back at a particularly smug-looking gentleman with a curling moustache, the conversation floating around me as in a mist.

'Guess what I heard last night?'

Grunt!

'Well I never thought those two rowed like that. It just goes to show, we're all the same really.'

With our stomachs full of toast and hot coffee we began to wake up. In fact the morning's discussion about our involvement and potential influence in the Grimlington community became rather animated. It was a subject which touched some raw nerves. We had little influence in the town, we were forced to confess. We showed little practical concern for the council estate. Even the curate was pulling out, if the house ever sold.

'Typical,' the inhabitants said, and they were right. As a missionary church we were a damp squib. If we cared about our town then it was time to show it.

Ideas were batted back and forwards across the room, run the playgroup more often, start a toddler club on the council estate, expand the youth work, which was virtually non-existent. They were all exciting possibilities, but each ended in a blind alley. Our buildings were inadequate, our manpower already stretched to the limit of its resources. Then Linda launched an attack which left us temporarily in a state of uneasy silence.

'The real trouble with the church is that it's too middle-class,' she said, and there was a cutting edge to her voice I had never heard before.

I felt a thud in my middle. I had been unaware of her pain. I had thought, naively I suppose, that what I was enjoying was working-class warmth and spontaneity. But it was not enough, as far as Linda was concerned. These were superficialities which solved nothing. They merely masked the real problem, which was apparently much deeper.

I looked around the room. A few people were nodding vigorously. Some smiled uncertainly. Others wore the set expression of those who have retreated in hurt self-defence. It was almost time for lunch. Since food for the body usually wins any battle with food for the mind, the meeting stopped. Where it would have gone had it continued I would never know. I was left guessing what Linda meant, but one day I would find out. Of that I was determined.

The children had been swimming for most of the morning and were exhausted and ravenous. But feeding a child is like putting petrol into a car. By the time their parents were ready to sink into an armchair for a snooze they had mobilised themselves into an army and, armed with buckets and spades, commandeered us all on to the freezing, windy beach.

Saturday's climax was the Grimlington Follies, awaited all year with avid anticipation. Every joke, foible and funny had been stored up for this one-hour cabaret of all-round entertainment. No one was spared, churchwarden or vicar and certainly not Alicia, who was played that year by a man. After that it was even harder to settle the children in bed and almost impossible to concentrate on a speaker.

Later, yawning, I suddenly remembered I had been invited to room nine for coffee and, against my better judgement, made my way there. There were people crammed into every available space.

'Always room for another one,' they said and shuffled along the floor.

'Oh heck,' said Pat, our hostess, as she moved several disjointed legs to get into a cupboard, 'I've remembered the milk and the coffee and the tea bags and the sugar, and I've brought some home-made biscuits, but I've forgotten the electric kettle. This is the first time in eight years.'

'Now don't worry,' Betty said, 'aren't health visitors always equipped for any eventuality?'

She produced a device which is left in a mug of water until it boils and by midnight there were only a dozen of us still waiting for a drink.

The highlight of the whole weekend was Sunday morning's Communion service. The lounge seemed very hushed and still, especially after the noise and the laughter of the night before. It was not a heavy silence, imposed merely by a sense of the occasion, but one which made me feel deeply at one with God, myself and the world.

As the bread and wine was passed from one to another I looked around the room. The children sat at their parents' feet, quiet for once. The spouses who had refused to come in to any other meeting, sat beside their wives or husbands, relaxed and at ease. The service said we were 'one body', a meaningless platitude in so many churches, where people were alienated from each other by indifference. To be one body was to be bound by a blood tie, more family than family. And this was one of those rare occasions when we knew it was so. The Jew in me always participated in this moment with a sense of wonder, that those whose paths might never have crossed, who might once have had little in common, separated by race, culture and prejudice, now belonged to each other because of all that this act symbolised. But that morning especially so. What if I had never come to Grimlington, never known these people? It seemed unthinkable. How much I would have missed. Now their hurts, struggles, hopes and fears were mine and mine were theirs. We were relatives, whether we liked it or not. We were stuck with each other for the rest of eternity. But I did like it. In fact I was very, very glad.

13

It was a source of immense relief to me that Grimlington Parish Church was not a monstrous Gothic barn, built by the sentimental Victorians, who raised monuments to the glory of God that were cold, austere and inhibiting all human contact. After the beauty and colour of the synagogue my Jewish nature rose up in protest at such icy sobriety.

But Grimlington was passably pretty, small, cosy and part Norman. On a board at the front of the church, beside the old stone altar, which had been smashed in half in Cromwell's day, vicars were listed from 1180. Every time I went out to take Communion my eyes were drawn to it. For hundreds of years men and women had worshipped here, standing on the same flagstones, when there were only hills and fields and they had brought the first-fruits of their crops and cattle. The world changed, generations came and went, but the Church remained. I had a powerful sense of my Christian, as well as my Jewish heritage. Like the rest of humanity, I would vanish, but others, belonging to another age, would take my place.

The church was even mentioned in an encyclopaedia of Britain's treasured heritage for its beautiful Flemish glass. When the sun streamed in through the windows the building was fused with a myriad of coloured lights. Banners now hung gaily from every pillar and children's artwork, friezes and collages, decorated the bare stone walls. This was home. We loved it.

But any building is a burden and one of historical interest carries its own penalties. Woe betide us if we suggested the slightest alteration. We were pursued with all the fury of the preservationist societies, who were more interested in the authenticity of the building than the comfort of the congregation. It was all right for them. They never turned up for a service. And when it came to the constant losing battle which so many churches face, against damp, dry rot and woodworm, with the added problem of subsidence, there they were again, aided and abetted by the Town Council, urging us on from behind, with support that was often moral rather than financial.

Not that we were happy to stand back and see our building fall apart. We were not. It was simply that there were so many other, vital demands upon our spending. It was hard to get our priorities right. The average income of the congregation was so low that if every member gave a tenth there was still nowhere near enough to meet the annual budget. As unemployment rose, and employment became a matter of desperation, so wages could be kept to a bare minimum. Many church members would have been better off on the dole, but they had their pride. Any work was better than none at all, and Family Income Supplement or long hours of overtime could make the basic wage enough to live on.

And yet they would give away all they had, without a thought, to a mate in need. In fact, their attitude to money was refreshingly novel to me. When I first became a Christian I was amused at how embarrassing most non-Jews found the subject. Like death it was taboo, never discussed by nice people. The only thing to do with it was to amass it slowly and carefully, then hide it away for as long as possible. Peter was already trying to do the same, without much success. 'Otherwise,' he said, 'we shall never be able to afford our own house in retirement.' Saving was the cardinal virtue, more than that, the cardinal Christian virtue, at least I thought it must be, until we came to Grimlington. Then I realised that it was a middle-class tradition and not Christian at all. It may have grown out of the Protestant emphasis on hard work and thrift, but when I thought about it, the New Testament did seem to me to encourage giving away rather than storing away one's surplus.

In Grimlington what a man earned by the sweat of his brow he was entitled to spend with equal gusto and as much pleasure as possible. And spend he did! He could be as rich as Rockefeller on payday and poor as a beggar for the rest of the week, but what did it matter if he had enjoyed the spending of it? The town suffered a minor epidemic of videos, microwaves, expensive toys and all the other symbols of the materialistic age. In some cases it was a sign of prosperity, in many it was not.

Most of the church members were unaffected by it. Some were still without fridges, washing machines and other modern conveniences which I took for granted. I felt rich by comparison, uncomfortably so at times. Owning a car suddenly seemed a luxury, not a necessity and a right. Yet what little they had they gave to the clergy. Our car and petrol allowance was such that we were able to live on Peter's stipend without being worn down by continual scrimping like so many other clergy we knew.

'But you can't afford it,' we said to Bill, the treasurer.

'We're only being realistic,' he said in his matter-of-fact way, and that was that.

So the church budget was incredibly tight and Peter and I laughed when we saw the Church newspapers extolling the virtues of a parish administrator – it was the only way to cope with the idea.

'What wouldn't I give?' he said wistfully one day. 'Imagine being free to pastor, counsel, visit, do the job I'm paid to do, I long to do, instead of moving chairs, laying out hymn books and . . . and this lot.' He waved at the mounds of letters and papers, littered all over his desk, correspondence and lists of telephone calls about broken boilers, damp rot and repairs to vandalised property.

'And somewhere beneath that lot is my sermon preparation,' he groaned. 'There seems no justice. We, in a church most needing administrative help, are least able to afford it!'

The idea of an administrator was a beautiful dream, and that was all it was. So was more secretarial help. Peter was forced to admit it every time he trailed five miles into the diocesan centre for a few handouts because we had no photocopier of our own.

Early in November the PCC met to discuss our financial difficulties and the approaching annual Gift Day. Edward stopped the usual speculative ramblings on how much we might get by asking them how much they intended to ask God for. Ask God! Everyone looked sheepish. Consulting the Almighty about matters financial, much as a businessman might consult his bank manager, was not what anyone had had in mind at that moment. They turned to Bill. He had the treasurer's knack of bringing matters down to earth. He consulted the books and cleared his throat.

'We usually get about a thousand pounds on a Gift Day,' he

said, with an impassive face, which in fact hid the driest wit this side of the Pennines.

There were smiles of agreement.

'And how much do we need?' Edward asked relentlessly.

The smiles melted on the spot.

'Well, what exactly is the debt on the renovation of the parish hall?' Bill consulted the books again and without looking up muttered, 'Six thousand pounds.'

An uneasy silence fell.

It had taken the PCC some time to adjust to Edward's revolutionary attitude to the budget. Church funds, he maintained, were a family affair, not to be requested, raised, or earned outside. For too long the Church had appeared before the world as a charitable institution, always in debt and always on the scrounge so that its real ministry had been totally undermined. It appeared to prefer a man's wallet to his person. With their cardboard barometers out in the porch and their 'Please save our roof' appeals, churches looked like discarded, unwanted relics. Besides, fund-raising could become a clergyman's full-time job and an unpardonable waste of time and emotion.

Edward had only been in Grimlington a few weeks when he suggested that twenty per cent of the church's annual income be given away to missionary work, on the basis that their need was always greater than ours, however it might appear. That would be increased to thirty per cent when the congregation could stand the shock. Then he suggested that the proceeds from the annual church fête, the main fund-raising event of the year, should henceforth be given away to deserving charities. The PCC had been wondering what he would suggest next.

'We haven't got six thousand pounds,' someone whispered loudly, 'because we keep giving it away.'

The laughter died down when Mick began to speak. He said little as a rule, but what he did say was always worth hearing.

'Well,' he faltered slightly as he realised everyone was watching him, waiting for a pronouncement. He did not enjoy the limelight. 'It's like this, right. We've no money. We need six thousand pounds. We can talk all night, but that won't get us it. So let's ask God. He'll show us what to do.'

For a while everyone looked at everyone else, until someone said, 'You mean now? This minute?'

'Yes,' Mick said, 'now.'

So they sat in silence for some time, a heavy, uncertain silence. The minutes ticked slowly by and then gradually, imperceptibly, the atmosphere began to change. Silence gave way to an expectant hush. The room became charged with such a sense of God's presence that they caught their breath. Confusion and scepticism melted away and excitement took their place. Unable to contain himself any longer, Frank said, 'If he's our God and the whole world is his, what's a mere six thousand pounds to him?'

He looked around and this time everyone was nodding enthusiastically.

'If he's our Father 'e'll give us what we need.'

'Right,' said Edward, 'how much do we expect then, three thousand?'

'No,' everyone shouted.

'The lot!' said Frank, speaking for them all. 'Our faith could do with a bit of stretching.'

On the following Sunday Edward climbed into the pulpit, cleared his throat and informed the church in a matter-of-fact kind of way that in preparation for the Gift Day we would be praying for and anticipating six thousand pounds to clear our debts. A ripple ran through the congregation and he started his sermon. But everyone was ready to express their opinion as soon as the last amen of the service was said. An older woman in front of me was indignant.

'The PCC must be mad,' she said. 'This is Grimlington, not flippin' Brighton an' 'Ove. Who's got that kind of money round 'ere?'

Frank was at her side and he put a fatherly arm around her shoulder.

'Yer haven't, love, yer haven't. I haven't. No one has. That's the point. But he has.'

He pointed to heaven. Her eyes followed the direction of his finger and she stood looking up at the ceiling for some time, then went out shaking her head.

I felt a certain sympathy with her as I looked around the congregation, most still in their pews, stunned by the announcement. There was Mary, talking animatedly as she usually did, tossing her head as she spoke. How far could her Family Income Supplement stretch? Jan was kneeling on the pew, her head resting on her arms, chatting to a new family behind her. Like so many others who could not share their faith with their spouses, she would only be able to give a tiny proportion of her housekeeping money. Joe, Linda's husband, was standing at the back with his hands in his pockets, deep in conversation. He was small, with a heart so full of kindness, that it more than compensated for what he lacked in height. He enjoyed a good chat, but his smiles could barely conceal the lines of worry and tension which had suddenly appeared around his mouth and eyes. There were rumours of huge redundancies in the iron and steel industry and the only craft he knew was welding. There was a mortgage to pay. Things were very tight as it was.

Everywhere I looked it was the same story. There was no way our congregation would find six thousand pounds between them. I shook myself, feeling slightly ashamed of my rationalism. After all Peter and I had survived two years at theological college with no fixed income at all, and still had some savings! God alone knew how. But this was different. The people were so vulnerable, so unspoiled in their faith. Was it right to put that simple trust to the test? What if the six thousand pounds did not come?

'Stop it!' I commanded myself as I made the long walk home. 'The truth of the matter is that they are just as excited as Edward and the PCC. It's you, you cynic, who has the problem. You can't believe and have to justify it.'

My mother was waiting for me at the front door, arms folded, looking as smug as a businessman who has just clinched an important deal. It was my parents' first weekend with us. We had converted the tiny dining area of the kitchen into a bedroom by hanging old sheets over the glass partition. It was hardly private, but they had made themselves quite cosy and at home. It amazed me how happy and amenable they were, especially after all the threats never to come and stay with us once we lived in church property.

'So!' my mother said. 'Aren't you going to ask me what I'm so pleased about?'

'Mum, what are you so pleased about?'

'I thought you'd never ask. I've sold your house for you, that's what.'

'What?'

'You'd barely set off when the doorbell rang. It was a woman asking to see round. So you take your chances when you can, and I showed her round, using my best sales technique. And, I think you've got a buyer.'

My father nodded happily. He was looking so frail these days, and he had become very forgetful. I felt uneasy, but pushed it to the back of my mind.

'So you see,' my mother said, following me into the kitchen and obviously waiting to deliver her punchline, 'even the Church of England has to send for the Jews when it wants to sell anything.'

I hardly dared to hope that my mother was right. I was beginning to feel we would never move. The longer we stayed the more disheartened I felt with the temporary nature of our housing. It was not home. I could not relax. I was not an especially private person, but being constantly overlooked began to wear me down. I was becoming quite tense and the children bore the consequences.

'Oh, Mum, I do hope you're right,' I said, then felt ashamed. Who was I to grumble when so many of the church families lived in conditions far worse? If we thought we were cramped, it was nothing compared to Paula, one of the young people. Peter suggested in a sermon one morning that people would find it helpful to begin the day with quiet and an opportunity for prayer and meditation.

'I'd be lucky,' Paula chuckled, digging him in the ribs as she often did on the way out, 'with all my sisters.'

'You share a bedroom?' Peter asked.

'We share a bed, you mean! Never mind, as each one gets married it leaves more room.'

Privacy was a luxury all right. There were Phil and Mary in their tiny, damp two-and-a-half bedroom house with three teenage children and no prospect of a move. I had to admire Mary's simple acceptance of her situation.

'I want to move so badly. I pray for it every day, and for one for you too. But meanwhile we're still here, so this is where we're meant to be and I shall have to be contented with what I've got.'

She was right. There was no point in getting into a state about something outside our control. Even if our house sold there was nothing else in the town to buy. Most of the houses were too small to provide a clergyman with three bedrooms and a study.

Anything larger was a rarity and snapped up almost before it was vacated. Since most of the larger-sized housing belonged to the older members of the community there was some discussion about how long it was likely to be before a house appeared on the market. It was a wonder there was no queueing at the doors. Still, my mother's news made me feel that a move was a little more imminent. It was as well that I had no glimpse into the future. Patience is not one of my qualities.

Gift-day Sunday was a bright, crisp November day. Peter and I walked home from the morning service at a brisk pace in an effort to ward off the icy chill of the wind and our own anxiety.

'One thousand five hundred pounds isn't bad,' Peter said, more to himself than to me.

'No, no, it isn't,' I reassured him, 'especially for us.'

'But it isn't six thousand,' he said, and my heart sank.

We stopped and waited for Joel to catch us up. It was hard work on his little two-wheeler bike.

'That means there has to be four thousand five hundred in the collection tonight.'

'I know,' I said, 'I still remember how to do subtractions.'

Peter drew a long breath. We had even left Edward chewing his nails in the vestry.

It was a long Sunday. We could settle to nothing.

'You go tonight,' Lucy had said to me, 'I'll sit for you. Dad doesn't always appreciate that I could do with some time alone.'

Evening came at last and the church seemed unusually full. The chatter was louder and more excited than ever. The atmosphere was charged. It reminded me of a first performance or the opening night of a West End play. The service seemed agonisingly long and once over, Edward gave the blessing and dismissed the congregation. No one moved. He looked round, unsure of what was happening or what to do about it.

'Yer don't think we're going home now, do yer?' someone shouted. 'The counting's only just begun.'

Everyone nodded happily and made themselves comfortable. They would wait all night if necessary.

Bill appeared at the office door and asked for more help. It was a good sign and the excitement mounted. Dorothy leant across and whispered to me, 'I hadn't anything else so I put me milk money in.'

'What'll you do when the milkman calls?' Jan asked from the row behind.

'Worry about it then! I'll make it up somehow. Cut back on the electric or summat. The kids have put their pocket money in too. It was their idea. They wanted to.'

'My husband would go bananas if he knew how much I'd given,' Jan sighed. 'He reckons ten pence a week is more than enough for any church. Anyway, he won't know. I'll just have to do without those new boots this winter.'

One or two people started to hum, then sing. Others joined in until there was such a loud noise that I wondered how Bill and his helpers were managing to concentrate. The office door opened and as if it were some magic signal, the singing stopped instantly. Edward emerged and with every eye marking his steps, made his way slowly into the pulpit. His face gave nothing away. There was no trace of a smile and my heart sank. I could hear the blood pounding in my ears and noticed that Dorothy's knuckles were white as she grasped the pew in front. There was a hush such as I had never known in Grimlington before, not a cough, creak or a rustle.

As Edward made his announcement the suspense was almost unbearable.

'With various covenants and promissory notes . . .'

'Get on with it,' I whispered.

People began to fidget.

'. . . today's collection amounts to . . . nine thousand, nine hundred pounds!'

There was a moment's stunned silence as the news sank in. What did he say? Was it good or bad? Then suddenly he shouted, 'Hallelujah!' and the place erupted. People were clapping, cheering, laughing, crying and hugging each other. Edward leapt down from the pulpit, ran to the bell tower and rang the bells. Alicia hobbled up and down the aisle, waving her arms in a dance of victory, like Miriam, the sister of Moses in the Old Testament.

'Eeeeeh, but this is better than being in club on New Year's Eve,' Marjorie shouted as she was lifted off her feet. 'Give up will yer! I'm not as light as I once was. Yer'll do yerself a mischief!'

'I bet the noise can be heard at the other end of town,' I said to

Mick, who was suddenly caught in a bear hug, which temporarily winded him.

'Dance, Mick,' the people shouted.

He looked round and blinked.

'Me? I've only just become a hugger!'

No one wanted to go home, so eventually, at about ten o'clock, Marjorie and Brian, the other churchwarden, shouted, 'Time please,' in a good-humoured sort of way and ejected everyone out into the cemetery. Some of the young people set off down the street singing loudly.

'If they don't get arrested for being drunk and disorderly tonight, they never will,' I said to Peter. We watched them for a while and laughed.

'Come on,' he said, slipping an arm around my waist and looking up at the stars, 'there's a full moon. May I walk you home?'

'Should a clergyman be so forward?' I said archly, looking up at him out of the corner of my eye.

We set off towards the estate. Peter breathed in deeply.

'You know,' he said, 'there are times when this job has its rewards and I wouldn't swop it for any other, not if they made me the richest man in Britain.'

'You're sure about that, are you?' I asked.

'Well, the temptation might just overcome me. That's why it's never likely to come my way.'

We giggled like a pair of teenagers, all the more so when our island home came in view.

The Church First School was buzzing with the news when I dropped Joel off the following morning. A large crowd had gathered for a chat as it usually did, only it was larger than ever.

'Nine hundred pounds in one collection,' Milly said, impressed. 'That is good.'

'No, no, it was nearly £10,000.'

That was more than good. It was unbelievable.

'Where the 'eck did you get that lot from?' Milly asked, suspiciously.

'We've got a rich Father!'

The crowd dispersed reluctantly to the shopping, cleaning and washing with much laughter and shaking of the head.

A few days later Peter came home from staff prayers with the news that in the extraordinary and apparently coincidental way these things happen, Edward had just received an estimate for repairs to a crumbling wall in the parish hall. It was much higher than estimated, almost £4,000.

'So that's why we needed the extra £4,000,' Frank said the following Sunday. 'It's a good job God sees our bills before we do.'

That night the phone rang. It was a friend, a curate in Sussex. Still in the first flush of excitement, Peter poured out our news. I watched as his face slowly fell.

'What's the matter?' I asked as he put the receiver down and shook his head.

'Well, he wasn't exactly impressed. It seems they received over fifty thousand pounds in a night for their new hall.'

'But love,' I said, 'that was Sussex. Let them have their plush new hall, just like that. It doesn't detract from what's happened here.'

Peter smiled. 'You're right. You know it reminds me of something.'

I nodded. The same thought had occurred to me.

'You mean a certain parable about a widow who put two coins into the collection?'

'Yes. Jesus commended her, not the others who had put in more, because those two coins were all she had.'

14

Discovering wildlife on or in the human body always comes as a shock, no matter how common the experience may now be. Like a prophet of doom, Betty warned us about the inevitability of head lice, rampant in the schools, but she never alerted us to certain other hazards.

Joel had been complaining of acute itching for some time. Since, taking after his mother, he always had a flair for the dramatic, we ignored his antics, the jumping, screeching and leaping up and down. Until one day, for a bit of peace, I went to apply some zinc and castor oil cream and could not ignore what I saw wriggling defiantly before my very eyes.

Shaken, I called the doctor's surgery immediately, fighting to control the tremor in my voice.

'Worms?' said the receptionist cheerily. 'Oh yes, there's a lot of them about. Can you come and get a prescription straight away?'

Could I? I could not collect it fast enough. I rushed to the chemist, where the assistant impassively handed me a large white paper bag. I had hoped for some glimmer of sympathy, a sign of commiseration, but she was well trained.

Abby got away lightly with a teaspoon of medicine morning and night. Our treatment and Joel's became a rugged endurance test. Six of the largest tablets I had ever seen had to be chewed and swallowed every day for a week. The taste was passable at first – a sort of combination of raspberry sherbet and vitamin C – but the initial flavouring quickly wore off, leaving the sickening bitterness of the drug. The aftertaste was unbearable. I was not sure whether it was me or the worms in my intestines which were being poisoned. But we persevered.

The following week I popped down to our Wednesday

afternoon toddler club as usual, and by some strange coincidence Betty and Penny, her fellow health visitor, were there, delivering their annual talk on bugs, lice and nits. As always I underestimated the walk down from the estate and was a little late, so I crept in unobtrusively and squatted down at the back. Betty saw me.

'Come in, love, come in,' she shouted. 'I'm glad you made it. But what a shame, you've just missed the bit that's relevant to you.'

So now I could be sure that by four o'clock the whole of Grimlington would know our guilty secret. The joys of living in a small community! Wherever I went for the rest of the afternoon there were shouts of, 'Unclean! Unclean!' Fortunately there was no longer any real stigma attached to our condition. As Betty and Penny reassured us with graphic descriptions, colourful illustrations and great relish, we would all succumb sometime or another to head lice, body lice, bed bugs, fleas or scabies. We scratched our way through the tea and biscuits.

The fortnightly toddler club was known as 'Mums and Babes', though it always struck me that 'Babes and Mums' would be far more appropriate as there was no doubt to whom the afternoon belonged. Some Wednesdays as many as thirty toddlers – it seemed like many more but they were never still long enough for us to count them – piled into the parish hall, trod on and tumbled over mounds of toys and several intrepid helpers. Screams of pain, pleasure, anguish and frustration split the air and shook the walls. The main hall was packed with bikes, pedal cars and scooters and in pride of place stood Alicia's home-built wooden slide. She explained to me in detail her problems of design, the angles of the hinges, the added safety devices, but it was all a mystery to me. All I saw was the terrified pleasure of an eighteen-month-old, whizzing past us at incredible speed on its nappy-padded bottom, making joyful gurgling sounds all the way down.

The mums themselves huddled in a little room, as far away as possible, vainly trying to follow a speaker, despite the din and constant interruptions. In the few months I had been in Grimlington the programme had been varied and imaginative, tempting the wider community in. There might be anything from flower arranging or dental hygiene, to family planning or delousing your pets, or children! A demonstration of economy cooking provided the opportunity to sample tuna pizza and bean sprout casserole at three o'clock in the afternoon. Bean sprouts had only just arrived in town and were still an object of some suspicion. As were courgettes, and avocados.

'But what do you do with them?'

'I don't know if I fancy them.'

'Are they nice?'

Jan, who with her international experience, was giving the demonstration, shook her worldly head and sighed.

An afternoon of book reviews lacked a certain sparkle. The stories were told from cover to cover and I decided gratefully that there was little point in buying the books. But the effect was soporific. We semi-slumbered, until Cynthia, whose taste is a little more intellectual than the rest of us, reviewed *The Great Divorce* by C. S. Lewis.

'Hell', she said, and we stirred, 'is a depressing, grey town, where it rains all the time and the inhabitants keep falling out with each other and move further and further out into the suburbs.'

There was a moment's pause as we absorbed this information, then it became apparent that we were all thinking the same thought.

'In fact,' she said, grinning suddenly as the thought occurred to her too, 'it's just like Grimlington.'

'Let's face it, it's much like anywhere,' Linda said loyally, as the laughter died down.

'Well, I think I'll stick to me Mills and Boon, thanks,' said Pam, a divorcee, struggling to bring up two children alone. She could be relied on to say exactly what she thought. 'I need a bit of romance and light relief in me manless life these days.'

Jan nodded. 'Linda and I like a good "bodice-ripper" every once in a while, don't we Linda?'

We watched Linda with interest, but she refrained from comment. Cynthia sat with her C. S. Lewis on her knee, looking a little crestfallen.

The afternoon which caused the greatest hilarity was a lecture from a member of the St John Ambulance Brigade on First Aid.

'Next time there's a death in the family,' he said, 'your mum, dad, aunty or whatever, go and have a good look and familiarise yourself with a dead body.'

We all swallowed hard. Yorkshire bluntness can go a bit far, even for a Yorkshireman.

The life-size resuscitation model he had brought with him was laid out on the table in front of him in a grotesque pose.

'I,' he said, 'shall now demonstrate the mouth-to-mouth technique and simultaneous cardiac massage. I shall then be asking for volunteers to do the same.'

'That's all right,' Pam called out, leaping to her feet, 'I've kissed far worse than that.'

But none of us anticipated the antiseptic solution he kept sloshing over the dummy's mouth between volunteers. It tasted more like the kiss of death than the kiss of life, and lingered for ages after.

'I can't decide if it spoils or improves the taste of the tea,' Pam said.

At three-thirty the schools finish, and most of the mums disappeared in a flurry of buggies, baby bonnets and mittens, leaving the parish hall looking like a bomb site. Bits of toys and games were strewn from wall to wall and the last few valiant helpers collected them together and played at doll's house, jig-saw puzzles and post-box toy to make sure everything was complete and ready for the playgroup on Friday morning.

It may have seemed like madness, but we longed to be able to meet every week, or even twice a week. Facilities in the town for young mums were hopelessly inadequate. Betty was always telling us how many were lonely and trapped, with nowhere to escape from the screams of a demanding toddler, and no one to talk to when post-natal depression descended in a frightening cloud. Some were desperate. In Manchester, where we had lived when Joel was small, there were council-based toddler clubs in every local park and they saved my sanity. Grimlington relied on self-help and voluntary groups, but it was not an area where they were likely to be very forthcoming. It was an unbelievable opportunity for the church. We enquired about the possibility of starting a toddler club on our estate, but the only location we were offered was the library and we were asked to give assurances that the children would not touch the books. No one was prepared to give assurances of that kind, and even if we were, the real problem was that we did not possess the manpower to run it.

The toddler club was an arm stretched out into the community. It met a need, and it also provided a safe way of observing the church without coming too close. Linda first went when she was suffering from post-natal depression herself. For the sheer relief of getting out of the house it was worth putting up with a bunch of religious weirdos.

'I laughed at them. I called them a load of nuts behind their backs. Well, I knew deep down that for all their funny language and quaint ideas, I was the mug. For them life was really worth living. But I wasn't going to let them get to me. At least, that's what I said.'

But before long her Tuesday nights out with the girls had become an endless heated argument about the existence of God and the merits, or defects, of Christianity, with Linda, to her surprise, vehemently defending the cause.

'She's got it bad,' they said, seeing the single glass of lager untouched on the table and Linda waving her arms around, too absorbed to remember her drink.

'I can't explain it like they do,' she said to her friends, 'so you'll just have to come with me. It's better than being stuck in at home.'

So they came, Katie, Carol, Wendy, Dorothy and Jan, Jan whom Linda met at an ante-natal class, lonely, homesick and still suffering from culture shock. She was married in Canada to a Grimlington lad and he promised he would never want to go home again. But the firm for which he worked closed down and she was pregnant by then. It was a case of follow him or lose him, so she left her family, friends and furniture and followed him. Not to the quaint little Yorkshire cottage, which she saw in her dreams, but to his parents' house, the end terrace next to the gasworks, with a caravan in the back yard. Soon they had their own business and a house, but part of her always yearned for Canada, even after their second child was born. In the town she was always, 'that foreign woman' or 'the Canadian'. She never felt she fitted, not until Linda half dragged her to 'Mums and Babes'.

From there to the church was a natural progression, like caterpillar to butterfly. Alicia saw to it that it was. Dorothy's husband began to come with her; so did Joe, Linda's husband, looking around uncomfortably at first, then growing in confidence when he realised he quite liked the place and that we had taken to him.

But still the toddler club met only once a fortnight. We lacked the necessary leadership. Many of the women went back to work as soon as they possibly could to supplement the family income. To stay at home was a luxury, not a choice. Others were stretched to the limit, involved in countless other activities and caring for relatives or their children. Those at home with pre-school children often felt too diffident about their own abilities.

'I'll help, but I won't run it.'

It was always the same story. It amazed me that so many gifted, creative people could not believe in their own gifts. But false assumptions enforced by years of experience could not be driven away overnight. Self-confidence is a tender plant which grows very slowly.

At first I could not accept that we could do nothing but stand back and watch such potential pass us by. I felt like a child whose bag of lemon crystals has burst. Try as she might, she cannot prevent the precious golden powder from slipping through her fingers. 'We must do something,' I insisted.

Peter smiled. 'Oh? What have you in mind?'

'Pay one of the mums to be a community worker. Then she won't be forced to find work elsewhere.'

'With what?'

My frustration was acute.

'With anything! Many churches are managing to employ an extra worker these days. Just think what we could do with a youth and community worker.'

My imagination began to run riot.

'A playgroup every morning, toddler clubs or a day care centre for the elderly in the afternoons and a youth club in the evenings.'

Peter took a deep breath, then shook his head sadly.

'Carry on dreaming, but we still have to be realistic. This is Grimlington. Even the Gift Day money was swallowed up the moment we got it.'

'Manpower Services?' I tried.

'You have to be unemployed for six months to qualify. So many of our women get temporary work here and there that they're never technically unemployed for long enough. Besides the grant is meant primarily for retraining and I don't know if we could justify it. And what if it were stopped after a year?'

The urgency of the situation was compounded by the fact that the playgroup which Julie and Karen had started was heavily over-subscribed with a long waiting list. Gone were the days when a social priority area could expect nursery places for three-year-olds and ours was one of only two playgroups in the town. It was only open for one and a half hours two mornings a week and the other catered mostly for children outside the town. But Julie and Karen were teachers and both wanted to go back to work. In the event, teaching jobs were hard to come by and Julie stayed in charge, though there were times that winter when she lived to regret it.

One such occasion was the day Tracy disappeared. Tracy was Linda's youngest, a bright-eyed little monkey and far too canny for a three-year-old. By the time she could walk she had developed an insatiable passion for hide-and-seek. No one noticed her absence from the playgroup that morning, not until Linda, who had just slipped out to the High Street for a bit of shopping, arrived back to collect her.

'Where's our Tracy?' she asked, as all the other mums were buttoning their offspring into their coats.

'She's here somewhere,' Julie said breezily, looking around the hall.

Karen sidled up to her and smiling at Linda, muttered under her breath, 'Julie, I've not seen Tracy for ages.'

'Oh,' Julie said. 'Anyone seen Tracy?' she shouted above the din.

One or two people heard and peered at the children at their knees.

No, Tracy was not one of them. The realisation that this might well be a crisis dawned slowly. But once it did the atmosphere became charged with a sense of barely-controlled panic. They scoured every room, every corner, every space large enough for a child to squeeze into, but there was no sign of Tracy. Linda bore it all with a certain stoicism. She would be rational, sensible, but then someone appeared from the cloakroom with a mackintosh and a small pair of shiny red wellington boots. Her bottom lip trembled and all noble resolve crumpled in that instant.

'My baby,' she sobbed, pointing to the glass doors, 'she's out there, alone, without a coat and nothing on her feet. She'll die of frostbite.'

By then several people had rushed past her and out into the street. Weeping bitterly and too distressed even to bother with a handkerchief to catch the drips, Linda trudged up to the police station. She must have moral support. So pushing one child in a buggy with one arm and carrying another kicking and screaming under the other, the tears pouring down her face too, Vicky went with her.

'Please, God,' they both wailed all along the main road, 'let her be safe.'

Grimlington's entire police force, all four of them, heard them coming, stopped what they were doing and were waiting for them when they arrived.

'Now then, lass,' the sergeant said, 'don't you worry. She'll be all right. She wouldn't talk to strangers, would she?'

'She'd talk to anyone!' Linda howled.

One policeman rushed to his panda car and issued a description. Another leapt onto his bicycle. The search was on in earnest.

Karen alerted the Church School headmistress in case Tracy had gone to find her big sister. Half the staff ran out to their cars to join the hunt. Dorothy informed the vicar through his sitting-room window as she crawled on hands and knees through the undergrowth in his garden. His meeting disintegrated in a moment. Peter, who was in the kitchen washing up the coffee cups, came back and found everyone had gone. Sue unrolled the carpet in the parish hall normally reserved for the tiny babies of the Sunday morning creche. She felt a little stupid, but with Tracy, you never could tell. Carol ran on to the High Street and checked every shop. Business came to a standstill. Jan ran half a mile home for a car, but it broke down on the way back and none of the passers-by would stop to give her a push. They were all too busy looking for a missing child.

After an hour or so, overcome by exhaustion and the urge to spend a penny, Julie went back to the parish hall. In a fit of despair she flung open the toilet door, and there before her, knickers round her ankles and singing happily to herself, sat one little girl.

'I counted to ten,' she said, 'but yer didn't find me.'

15

No one ever discovered how it was that Tracy was not in the toilets, nor anywhere else for that matter, when the parish hall was checked from top to bottom. But it turned out to be an experience which drew the women into a closer camaraderie than ever. Motherhood was a common bond which made them stick together. They all understood about teething problems, nappy rash and sleepless nights. But for Julie, Linda and the others that was not a lasting basis on which to build relationships. They were more determined than ever to share their faith with their friends, but how? That was the problem. Such was their alienation from the church that persuading them to come was a minor miracle. And besides, every now and then, in order to please the older members, the service was more traditional. What if the women said, 'Come to church. It's not like you think, it's changed,' and then it was exactly what their friends imagined. All would be lost. They would never dare ask them again.

So a Guest Service was planned, with all the words and hymns printed on a sheet. That way no one need feel embarrassed that they could not follow the liturgy or find the place. Anyone who found reading a trial was sent into a panic by the mini library of service and song books heaped into his hands as he came in through the doors. And we would not invite an outside speaker. We had Edward and after all there are some advantages in the familiar.

The Drama Group began to rehearse in earnest. This was to be our first performance in the church itself and we felt a little daunted. We chose a piece called *The Long Silence*, not original, but we had not yet branched out into script writing. A group of angry, belligerent people gather on a great plain at the end of time and accuse God of being ignorant of the depths of human suffering. He lives in heaven, untouched by pain and misery. In his absence they put him on trial and condemn him to a terrible death, despised and betrayed by his friends. Then there is a long silence as they realise that God has already served his sentence. It was powerful stuff, at least it would be if we could do it justice.

We congregated in church for a rehearsal one Tuesday night late in November, oblivious of the fact that it was vestry night and that one of the clergy would be available for consultations in the next room.

'Let the legitimacy of his birth be doubted,' Angela shouted from the pulpit.

Next door a couple were asking about the baptism of their baby. Alicia's head appeared round the door wearing an astonished expression.

'Sorry, Alicia, I'll keep my voice down,' Angela apologised.

The door closed and we giggled.

Angela took a breath. 'Let him,' she shouted, then remembering, lowered her voice, 'let him be born . . . a man.'

She paused for a moment. 'Couldn't I say, "let him be born a woman"? It would mean that God had a much richer experience of human suffering.'

'Get on with it,' I snapped and to my surprise she was about to obey, when we were interrupted by a loud hammering on the vestry door.

'I think you've locked me in, or out,' Alicia shouted.

I groaned and picked up Peter's vast bunch of church keys.

'Which one is it? Anyone know?'

After fumbling for a few minutes we found it and Alicia appeared, brandishing a flask and half a quilted sleeping bag.

'I always come prepared for the cold,' she beamed. 'This is my leg warmer. Anyone want a cup of coffee?'

'Ooooo yes,' they all said and that was the end of the rehearsal.

'We'll never be ready,' I moaned at Peter, when I told him what had happened.

'Yes, you will,' he said soothingly and I privately lamented the fact that so few really appreciate the trauma of those involved in the creative arts! He was far more concerned about the number of people coming to the vestry to ask for the christening of their baby.

'We're going to have to do something,' he said.

I looked at him quizzically.

'You mean because there's such a superstition attached to it?'

'Yes, but that can be a good and a bad thing. On the one hand it does mean we have contact with families we never normally see. On the other hand . . .'

'It jars to hear them make vows in public they have no intention of keeping, though they don't realise they're doing it,' I finished for him.

My non–Anglican background made me suspicious of indiscriminate infant baptism and less sympathetic than Peter. If the parents had no faith, it seemed as meaningless a ritual to me as the countless enforced baptisms of Jews during the Crusades and at other inglorious times in the Church's history. It was supposed to make them Christians but it achieved nothing because baptism without faith is meaningless. Grimlington was a God-fearing community on the whole, fear rather than faith being the operative word. Many people were genuinely afraid that if their baby died unbaptised, it would not get into heaven. I could not conceive of that kind of a God and felt sad that they could.

'We've so many christenings now,' Peter continued, 'that quite a number of the congregation are making noises of protest. They feel it's all a bit of a mockery. And you know what it's like round here, they vote with their feet.'

I had noticed, how could anyone not, that attendances at the monthly baptismal services had dropped dramatically. But that was also true of the formal civic services. On Remembrance Sunday earlier in the month, when the Mayor and other town dignitaries had processed down the aisle with their wreaths of poppies, very few regular church members had been there at all. For some reason the brass band did not think it necessary to come into the service either. Instead they sat, crushed together, in the doorway of the parish hall, out of the rain and under the feet of the parents leaving their tinies at the crèche.

The service seemed to lurch from one mishap to the next. Our MP stood to read the lesson and announced four chapters of the Old Testament. The congregation groaned. Lunch would be more than late that week! Then he read the wrong lesson anyway. The two minutes' silence lasted at least three or four, as we all waited for the bugler, who was sitting happily in his pew, apparently unaware of the fact that everyone was waiting for the reveille. In the end Edward announced a hymn instead.

Every formal service seemed to be blighted in some way. We were simply not given to slick professionalism. The human factor disrupted every attempt. But no one seemed to mind. There were no angry recriminations. In fact it was a source of some amusement. A man was allowed to make a mistake, wasn't he? Perhaps it was God's way of stopping us becoming smug. Mistakes were forgiven, hypocrisy was not.

That was why the membership resented having their services taken over by those who never normally came. They would have welcomed visitors, but this was different. The guests imposed the form of service and made them feel like the visitors. Their church was no longer recognisable. They felt they were conniving in a downright dishonesty. And the Yorkshire temperament is given neither to subjugation, nor dishonesty.

And then sometimes the guests complained. That hurt. That was rude. No one would come into our homes and criticise the amount of dust or our choice of decor, or our manners, but in they marched in finery fit for a wedding, tutting at our jeans and casual clothes, moaning about the new services and grumbling if we used guitars or tambourines. They felt it to be a personal slight that 'their' church had changed in the twenty years since they were last there. Many of the regular congregation were new members. Such criticism came like a slap across the face. It was hard to swallow. They could not understand that the visitors were probably feeling threatened by an alien environment, which they thought should be familiar and were embarrassed because they could not distinguish between the Old and New Testaments, let alone follow the service. Church members got up and tried to help them find the place. They had struggled once too. For some the Bible was the first book they had read from cover to cover, 'The only thing I've read apart from *Daily Mirror*,' someone said. It was an achievement.

Sometimes, usually at christenings, their help was refused. The baby and only the baby was the centre of attention. Relatives clucked, cooed, chattered and giggled their way through the service. One zealous mother decided to change her baby's nappy during Peter's sermon. Unfortunately she was not too well equipped. With their usual spontaneity and generosity the congregation rose to the occasion, passing handkerchiefs and tissues along the pews. But the baby, aware that it was the centre of some great commotion, yelled with a fury that brought the service to a temporary halt.

'All right, Margaret,' Peter said. He had been trying desperately hard to concentrate and continue whatever the distraction, believing it was important that people should not feel unwelcome because of their children. But he knew when to admit defeat.

'We'll just wait for you to finish.'

No one minded a disruption like that. Everyone understood the horror of handing the clergyman a dirty, smelly baby at the great moment. What jarred were comments such as, 'Thank God that's over and we never have to come again,' made loudly on the way out. And just a quarter of an hour earlier everyone had heard vows made to the contrary.

'Well if that's all baptism means,' Rick said, 'I'm not having my two baptised.'

Several other families agreed and a state of mini–mutiny was declared. How else has change of policy come to the Church of England down through the years?

'What do we do?' Edward asked.

'We haven't much choice,' Peter said, and so did the PCC. Edward agreed. He respected Rick and was not a man to feel threatened when his congregation came of age and expressed their own opinion. On the contrary, people were used to doing what the boss told them and it was an exciting moment when church members no longer deferred to the clergy. Besides they were only pushing him towards a crisis he wanted to tackle anyway, but had postponed.

But whatever decision was made, poor Edward would alone bear the consequences. People saw a strong, confident leader, not a sensitive, vulnerable man, already bruised by the struggle to bring change. The constant barrage of angry letters and phone calls accompanying any change upset him. But he refused to give in and took the responsibility for all unpopular decisions, even when they were not his own. It was the same for Anna, who had to stand by and watch. Sometimes she herself was a more accessible target. I wondered how Peter and I would react when our turn came. The job of vicar was not for the man who coveted popularity or the quiet life.

So Edward suggested to the congregation that it was neither polite, nor charitable to withdraw their presence from formal services. They were missing a golden opportunity to demonstrate the real life and warmth of the church. On the other hand, he conceded that those services should reflect the more normal Sunday worship and not seem such a performance. And he promised that the PCC would look into the whole question of baptism when it met the following Monday.

That Monday night the new 'baptismal policy' was born. It sounded very grand, but simply meant that couples could have an immediate Thanksgiving service for their baby on request, but baptism only after a course of four one-hour sessions. It was not very onerous but the repercussions resounded through the town.

'Do you know what Vicar's done now?'

'No more christenings!'

'Whoever heard of such a thing?'

'Go into someone else's home, not likely!'

'Why do I need a course anyway? I was baptised, so I'm a Christian.'

'No you're not,' Edward said. 'That's why you need the course.'

The great controversy once again filled the letters page in the local *Gazette*. At least the church was providing a story, even if it was built mostly on rumour and hearsay. In a week, custom at the vestry hour was halved. Every couple that came received a visit as before.

One night Peter went out at seven-thirty and was still out at midnight. I began to feel a little uneasy. He said he was going to do a baptismal visit and would be back within the hour. Perhaps I had misunderstood and he had several visits to do, but who could he visit at that hour? At about twelve-thirty I heard the key in the door. The door slammed shut and Peter's footsteps were heavy on the stairs. He came into the room, saw that my eyes were still open in the darkness and snorted loudly. He kicked off his shoes and they landed on the floor with a thud.

'Never,' he growled, taking off his clothes and flinging them into their usual heap in the corner, 'have I met such a belligerent pair in all my life.'

He sat down on the end of the bed.

'They argued about everything. If I'd said the moon was made of blue cheese they'd have insisted it was green. He said he believed in God, like most miners, and that made him a Christian. "No it doesn't," I said. "Anyone can believe in God." Then he said he didn't have to go to church to be a Christian. I agreed, but told him that "if he was a Christian he would want to." "No he wouldn't," he said, "because they're a snooty lot." "How do you know?" I said. "You haven't been." Even his wife agreed at this point. We've been going round in circles for four hours,' Peter groaned, 'and my head hurts. I hope I don't get any more like that in a hurry.'

Peter snuggled down in bed that night, little guessing that from such inauspicious beginnings, special relationships are sometimes born!

The following day was one of those days when I wondered why I had bothered to get out of bed at all. Joel ripped the knee of his brand new jeans, the vacuum cleaner exploded in a cloud of black smoke and the television played up just as the children's programmes were about to begin. We were calming them down when the phone rang. It was Anna. Edward was running a high temperature.

'Don't worry,' she said, 'it's probably a twenty-four-hour chill and I'm sure he'll be fine for the Guest Service on Sunday.'

Peter felt chilled too.

'I hope he's all right. We can't cancel now.'

But when he was summoned to the bedside the following afternoon, one look at the coughing, shivering form was enough to confirm his worst fears.

'Edward,' he said nervously, 'what about Sunday?'

Edward laughed hoarsely.

'Oh help, but I've never thought that kind of preaching was my gift.'

'Well now's your chance to find out. You'll be given the words.'

Peter nodded and walked home through the cemetery with a new confidence. Hadn't John Wesley said that every Christian should be prepared to preach, pray or die at a moment's notice? He had only been asked to preach. Things could be a great deal worse! Then he bumped into Dorothy.

'Is it true that Edward's ill?' she asked him.

'Bad news travels fast around here.'

'Well, who's going to preach on Sunday night then? I've invited me Aunty Maisie, and she hasn't been for years so it had better be good.'

'I am,' Peter said confidently.

'You!' she said with such incredulity that Peter decided to ring the Bishop the moment he got home to see if he was free.

He wasn't. So the preparation began and for two days the children and I crept around the house like mice. I was glad when Sunday came.

The Drama Group was in a worse state of nerves than Peter before the service began. Stationed at different corners of the church they nibbled their service sheets all through the hymns and readings. Then the great moment came. They leapt to their feet where they stood and railed at God for his heartlessness and cruelty. In a moment it was over. Some people were obviously moved. Others were not.

'When I heard you shouting your heads off like that in God's house, I got down on my knees and asked him to forgive yer,' Nancy said later, as we were drinking coffee in the parish hall. Jan and Linda were crestfallen, then suddenly they saw the funny side and tried to hide their grins behind their coffee cups.

'I suppose it was a bit shocking, us yelling like that from the pews,' Linda said, 'but they'll get used to us.'

I left Peter to come home on his own as so many people were waiting to chat to him. When he finally arrived he was tired out, but very happy.

'So many people said they were helped,' he said with disbelief. 'One woman had tears in her eyes as she thanked me. It never ceases to amaze me when my preaching has that kind of effect.'

'Was it that bad?' I asked.

'Oh you!' He grinned, then the smile died away. 'I've been thinking. A Guest Service is all very well, but it isn't enough, is it? One or two people understand what Christianity's all about for the first time in their lives and we're beside ourselves. But it's a drop in the ocean in this town. Why should we expect people to come to us? There's such a gulf between us. Despite the new music and easy atmosphere, church is alien territory. It's terrifying to walk through those oak doors. We're expecting people to make some great cultural leap.'

I could not help but smile to myself. This was familiar territory to a Jew who had come into the Church, with so many cultural boundaries to cross.

'So where do we go from here?' I asked Peter.

'Jesus never stayed cocooned in the safety of a religious establishment. He would go into the market and the clubs, meet people where they were. They came to find him once the word got round that he had something to offer. We must go out into the community with our playgroup, toddler club and whatever else we can manage to offer. And we work at developing a church that meets the needs of the people here.'

'Joe keeps inviting you to go to his club,' I reminded Peter.

'I'll go, I'll go', he laughed. 'It would do me good. One thing I miss is a large group of colleagues. You have no mates in this job. It's a lonely life. Maybe that's why so many clergymen become eccentric. There's no one to point out their foibles.'

He got up to go to bed, then suddenly turned to me.

'If I do begin to go a bit eccentric, you would tell me, wouldn't you?'

'What do you think? Oh go on with you,' I laughed. 'You've had too much excitement for one day.'

16

By the beginning of December the shops were full of fairy lights and cardboard Father Christmases. Every organisation, great or small, had its carol service and expected a clerical presence. We almost drowned in sickly sentimentalism. But several events prevented that Christmas from becoming too glib and saccharine.

Joe received his redundancy papers. He was simply handed a letter one morning which thanked him for his years of service, but in the light of the present economic climate . . . And that was that.

'Thank you and goodbye,' he said. 'After all this time. No job, no future, no nothing, all there in those few typed words.'

He folded the piece of paper and tossed it onto the table. 'Funny, isn't it? That's all it takes to get rid of a man, that tiny bit of paper.'

Reluctantly he picked the piece of paper up, unfolded it and read it again, as if by magic the words might have changed in the last few seconds.

But they were exactly the same and he shook his head. 'Don't mind me, I'm just being morbid. We've enough redundancy pay to see us until after Christmas, if we're careful, and on Monday I'll go up to the job centre. I'll soon be fixed up, you'll see.'

On Monday morning Joe leapt out of bed and went down to the Social Security offices to sign on.

'I was feeling cheerful and hopeful, but they soon knock that out of yer. I mean, couldn't they treat yer like a human being? I just seemed to become a number. No one had a smile or a hello or a kind word. They made me feel it was all my fault and I was a nuisance. I suppose they were just doing their job, and being efficient like. But that was to file me away as quickly as possible! It's bad enough being in a place like that. It's daft. You know everyone else is in the same boat, but yer say to yerself, "What am I doing in a place like this? I don't belong 'ere. What must they all think of me?" It does terrible things to yer pride. Going to Social Security's like begging. Yer asking for a hand-out.'

'You've earned it, Joe,' I said. 'You've been paying your taxes and National Insurance for long enough.'

'Ay, but yer don't see it like that. The' give yer all these papers to fill in, hundreds of 'em and some of the questions are right personal. I felt like a convict. I don't see any man has the right to know those things about me. I felt ashamed. If it wasn't that I needed money for mortgage I'd 'ave walked out.'

Joe began to pace the room. His Marx Brothers moustache seemed to droop more than ever now that his smile was gone. He was a gentle, sensitive man and I felt angry at what the experience had done to him.

'And then,' he said, shaking his head at what was totally beyond his comprehension, 'the questions are all in fancy language and they treat yer like an idiot if yer can't understand them. They pass yer from counter to counter like some kind of garden gnome on a conveyor belt.

'And what about a job?' I asked him.

He stopped pacing, smiled at me sadly and shrugged.

'Not much hope. But I'll not give up. I'll keep looking. Maybe it'll be better after Christmas when things get back to normal.'

Linda brought two mugs of hot tea into the sitting room and sat down.

'It's funny how yer world can be turned upside down over-night,' she said. 'Here I am wearing exactly the same clothes as I wore two days ago and I suddenly feel shabby. Maybe it's because I'm frightened there'll be no more. I feel as if everyone is staring at me as I walk up town, and whispering, "See her, poor soul, her husband's unemployed." I know they're not, but it's just how I feel.'

'That kitchen yer've been wanting, love, it'll have to wait,' Joe said apologetically.

Linda laughed, but it was forced. 'Oh that, it can wait.'

'It can't, yer know it can't. There's no room to turn round in there. But I'll make it up to yer one day, yer know I will.'

She nodded at him and blinked back the tears.

'I dreamed of central heating too. This place is freezing. Ah well,' she said and tossed her head. 'For the moment the State seems to own us. Joe thought about making wrought iron gates for some of our friends, but they'll only deduct whatever he makes from his unemployment pay. From now on we're trapped, our income's fixed. The State doesn't allow for any hard-earned extras or life's little treats.'

The tears welled up again and she bit her bottom lip.

'Well,' she said, shaking herself, 'we've a lot to be thankful for. We've our kids, we're fit and healthy, and God'll take care of us. Though I sometimes wonder what he's up to!'

So did the rest of the church that Christmas, for a situation developed which was to stretch our faith to its very limits. The first I learned that anything was wrong was the beginning of November when we went to lunch at Mick and Karen's. They were both unusually tense and were struggling to make polite conversation. It was unlike them.

'Do you mind if we get dinner over as quickly as possible?' Karen asked, laying the cutlery on the table in a jumble and disappearing back into the kitchen.

I followed her out.

'It's just that we have to go up to the vicarage to see Edward and Alicia. It's about Paul, my sister's little boy. You've seen him at church, haven't you? The Sunday School teachers know him very well. He's a character! He's never really been well. Janice took him to the doctor's on Friday and the doctor could feel a lump just above the groin. He's going into hospital tomorrow for tests.'

We sat in silence while Karen was busy in the kitchen. There was nothing to say. I wondered how I would be feeling if it were our Joel. Mick sat in the armchair playing with their little boy in a distracted kind of way. Karen brought in the roast meat. There were no serving mats and the table was still only half set.

'I'm sorry,' Karen said, 'I don't know where I am today.'

We ate half-heartedly. No one had any appetite.

For ten days there was no news, just tests and more tests. Every morning, after the mums had dropped their children at school they congregated in the church to pray. Anyone working a late shift joined them. It was a large group. Little Paul was an appealing child with an elfin quality and was greatly loved.

Then suddenly one day he was rushed to Leeds and a malignant tumour the size of a large grapefruit was removed from his liver.

For some days it was touch and go whether he would live or not. He had been weak for so long that he had little fight left. If he lived there was no certainty that the cancer would not form elsewhere.

The group at church went on praying, longing for God to heal little Paul and let him grow up to laugh and play like other children. We were novices in the whole area of prayer for healing. We knew God could do miracles and heal people for whom the doctors held out no hope. But sometimes he did not. How could we know in this instance which it was to be? We wanted Paul to get well so badly that it was impossible to be objective.

Mick and Karen sought out all the help they could get and, with Edward's support, contacted a community of Sisters, known to have experienced healing in many amazing ways. One of the Sisters was absolutely convinced that Paul was going to be healed and we all took fresh confidence from her faith. We were certain. It seemed an affront now to suggest there might be any alternative. And then Paul began to get better. It was slow at first, then with every new day there was a fresh marvel. He spoke. He sat up. He ate fish and chips. He played with his toys, got out of bed, walked, ran and was stronger than he had ever been. He would be home for Christmas.

Amidst the many other frantic activities which increased with every successive day as Christmas drew nearer, the headmistresses of the town organised a 'Search for the baby'. Just as the shepherds and wise men had followed the star, one class from every primary school would follow the clues left all around the town, until they found the baby Jesus. Their final destination was not to be a stable, but Grimlington Parish Church, a much grander substitute.

The headmistresses met there the night before the event to finalise the plans. For six headmistresses to agree requires an exceptional amount of goodwill, but after lengthy debate about where Joseph would stand and the shepherds would kneel and what the wise men would do, the Christmas spirit finally prevailed.

'Oh yes, dear,' one of them said, turning to me at last, 'what we want you to do is announce all our honoured guests, a bit like a TV presenter.'

'Like Jan Leeming?' I asked hopefully.

'Well, you'll have to wear the dress of the time.'

'They didn't have TVs in those days,' I pointed out. 'I'd rather wear modern dress.'

'Couldn't you dress up as a Jew?' another headmistress suggested, then suddenly realised what she had said. 'Oh, I'm sorry, I didn't mean . . .'

'That's all right,' Miss Murdoch, the headmistress of the Church School said, with a wink at me, 'she'll just be herself.'

It was all a huge success. By the time the children arrived at the church door they were breathless with excitement. When they saw Mary holding a real baby they found they had enough wind left to make such a din that I could barely make myself heard. The public address system was not yet ready for use. Mick had been working away, night after night in his spare time, but each piece of equipment was so expensive. He kept asking the PCC for money, but we suspected that in the end he resorted to his own pocket and had to wait until he could afford the next precious part.

So I shouted until I was hoarse. 'Look, children, see who's coming, special visitors from the far corners of Grimlington, all bearing gifts for the baby. Here are the shepherds!'

I suppressed a smile as Peter walked past me, wearing our best bath towels. He hated dressing up and at six foot three was hardly inconspicuous. Someone had persuaded the vicar he would look more authentic if he rolled up his trousers under his tunic. I was distracted from the sight by the arrival of Betty and Penny.

'And here are our health visitors, bringing tins of powdered milk and strained apple and packets of liver and bacon. Just what a baby needs to help it grow big and strong.'

Betty winked at me as she passed. I suddenly remembered her telling me that she and Penny made up the packets of baby food and ate them for lunch when they had nothing else. They could have been giving away their own dinner!

'Who are you, the librarian?' I whispered to a striking-looking gentleman at my elbow, who was carefully balancing a large pile of books.

'The Director of Education,' he said curtly.

'The Director of Education,' I announced hastily.

'The Mayor and Mayoress!'

The photographer from the *Gazette* started flashing his camera.

261

'Get those legs,' Betty shouted at him, pointing at the vicar, 'for posterity.'

He did and for a while pandemonium reigned. Only the baby was quiet and dozed happily, oblivious of all the fuss. The teachers ushered their children out.

'Phew!' the headmistresses sighed. 'Thank goodness that's over. The children seemed to enjoy it.'

'It was certainly unforgettable,' I agreed.

Then, as I thought about it, it seemed to me that it had made its point quite forcibly. Every member of the community had an offering to bring to the Christ-child. Gold, frankincense and myrrh were fairly meaningless, but books, baby food and toys the children understood. No, they would not forget it.

But whether I would have a chance to catch my breath and remember was another matter. The parties began. Alicia was as excited as any child.

'Come on, Edward, do get a move on,' she said, dragging him out of a staff meeting. 'We'll be late for Father Christmas at the nursery.'

'But we haven't finished planning the services yet.'

'Yes, but they're expecting us. They'll be disappointed if the clergy aren't there.'

'Since when did Father Christmas need a chaplain?' Edward asked wearily, but too late. Alicia was out of the door and half-way across the road.

Frank gave three annual performances as Father Christmas for the Church School.

'I always take time off for the Lord's work,' he said.

And Alicia watched all three and the children's faces with unconcealed delight. I must admit it was one of the most convincing performances I had ever seen. No wonder Frank's son was an actor. The talent was inherited. With a tinge of regret I had to keep reminding myself that I did not believe in Father Christmas any more. Alicia obviously did not bother and I envied her capacity for child-like enjoyment.

'Hello, children. Did you see them hailstones? Rudolph thought it was icing sugar and tried to eat them.'

The children loved it. He invited them out to tell their favourite jokes, gave them their presents and had a special comment for each child.

'Now then, children, it's a funny thing. On our birthday we get presents. And on Jesus' birthday we still get the presents. Well, that's just like him. I know that because he's a special friend of mine. So then, children, teachers, and mums and dads, you won't forget whose birthday it is and why he came, will you? Now then, Miss Murdoch says you lead her a bit of a dance. So I'm going to lead her in one now. Music please!'

And out they danced.

Then there was the staff tea and after that, on a stomach full of trifle, chocolate gâteau and wine, carol singing by torchlight round the parish. We visited the elderly and shut-in and everywhere it was the same, nightclothes and supper had been laid out ready by their children. Some were still there, caring for their parents, washing them, tucking them up in bed and seeing they were locked up for the night. And woe betide us if all was locked up. No amount of carolling on our part would move the bolts. We sang three verses of 'Angels from the realms of glory', outside one house and although there was a light on and a shadow behind the curtains, no one came to the door. The TV had won. Undaunted, Betty had an idea. She nipped into the call box opposite and we heard her shouting down the phone, 'It's us, love, from the parish. We've just sung yer three verses of a carol. Do us a favour and come to the window for the fourth verse.'

The curtains were pulled back and a beaming face appeared. Then, our fingers numb and our voices cracked, it was back to the parish hall for hot soup and mince pies.

That was a quiet evening compared to the Christmas girls' night out. We met at the brand new pub, built just off the motorway at the bottom of the town. It was called, euphemistically, 'The Hamlet', because it stood where once there had been a bustling community of tiny, cobbled streets, which had sprouted around one of the pits. The pit closed. The old 'hamlet', all buckled and cracked with subsidence, all but demolished itself. A whole way of life vanished and in its place was built a large, lavish red-brick palace, with a glass sun lounge, filled with palms and cheeseplants, offering a scenic view of the main road into town!

For Linda, Jan, Dorothy and Carol this night out, or 'fuddle' as they called it, was a long-standing tradition. Everyone brought a small present, numbered it and put it in the centre of the table. Then we each drew a number out of a glass and took the corresponding present. Mine was a piece of rock with plastic eyes in it.

'I thought someone would like it,' Jan said.

Linda shrieked with laughter and held up a frilly suspender belt and a pair of black fishnet stockings.

'Good grief,' she said, her eyes as wide as beermats, 'what will Joe make of these?'

'Cheer 'im up no end, I shouldn't wonder,' Dorothy said.

As we sat among the palms, watching the lorries trundle past, giggling like a gang of teenagers, the responsibilities of woman-hood and the tribulations of motherhood were temporarily suspended. All girls together, we could say anything. We were young again, joyous and carefree. It was a marvellous, heady experience. And we went on shouting and giggling all the way home.

Peter was snoring gently as I snuggled down in bed in the small hours of the morning.

'Oh by the way,' I whispered to the Almighty under my breath, 'wherever you take us in the future, let it be somewhere where the people can laugh. I couldn't bear it otherwise.'

Christmas coincided that year, as it often does, with the Jewish feast of Chanukah, the Feast of the Dedication of the Temple. The night before Christmas Eve I took down our brass menorah and gave it its annual polish. When the children gathered around the table we told them the story of how Solomon had built a great and wonderful Temple in Jerusalem. Then in 169 BC the Syrians desecrated it by offering pigs upon the altar. But Judas, the Maccabee, drove them out and they rededicated the Temple to God. There was only enough sacred oil left to burn the eternal light of the presence for one day. But a miracle happened. It lasted eight days, until more could be made.

Joel watched me wide-eyed as I lit the small 'servant' candle at the front of the menorah and used it to light one other candle. Tomorrow two would burn, the next night three, and so on until all nine were ablaze, and it stood on the window-sill, letting its light shine out into the darkness, reminding us of a very special miracle.

Long after Joel had opened his Advent calendar and disappeared munching his chocolate money, I sat on, gazing at the single flame and enjoying its symbolism. The similarities between Chanukah and Christmas became more significant to me every year. Christ was God's Temple who came into the world, and would never be destroyed. He came as a Servant. He came as light too. His coming at all was the greatest miracle of all time.

All the celebration and the laughter were fun. But celebration without meaning was artificial, a cheap cracker full of promise, but empty after the bang. For many, Christmas was like that, all noise and festivity and a bitter disappointment. And seeing it, Christians were often restrained. Christmas was too secular. It was an embarrassment. But when celebration and worship were intertwined, then man and God could enjoy each other to their fullest capacity. It was a delicate balance, but for me, Grimlington came very close to getting it right.

The Christmas Eve Christingle service had a special magic.

'Who's Chris Tingle?' people asked.

They knew Fred Tingle, the local plumber.

'What's a Christmas tingle?'

We explained that the Christingle was an orange, symbolising the world, the candle being Christ, the light of the world and the red ribbon, encircling the orange, Christ's blood, shed for the world.

'Oh!' they said uncertainly, but still they came in their hundreds. We packed the people into every available space until it seemed that the church walls might bend. Each child received a Christingle and at last the great moment came when, beginning with one candle at the front, the light would be passed down the church. Some child picked that moment to be violently sick and the proceedings were disrupted by mops, buckets and the smell of disinfectant.

The little boy in the pew in front of me was wracked by spasms of coughing. Every time he coughed, out went his candle. How this happened was a total mystery to him. He kept looking round to see if he could catch the villain who had the effrontery to blow out his candle when he wasn't looking.

At last every candle was alight and out went the church lights. A hush descended. I looked around at the extraordinary sight of hundreds of tiny flames, flickering in the darkened building, casting shadows across the ancient stonework. The children sang 'Away in a manger' and there was wonder on their faces as they glowed in the candlelight. A lump rose up in my throat.

'The light shines in the darkness and the darkness cannot overcome it.'

I thought of Joe and I thought of little Paul and his parents. It was the year of the bomb in Harrods in London. And I looked again at the single flame in my orange, bright, alive and inextinguishable. None of us knew what was hidden in the year ahead. But one thing was clear. Because of Christmas, Emmanuel was with us and we would not have to face it alone.

17

The snow came, covering trees, rooftops and the distant slag heaps
with a delicate, crystal-white coating. On a picture postcard
Grimlington might almost have passed for the Yorkshire Dales,
but for the lack of trees. I walked to church in the strange, eerie
morning silence which always accompanies the first snow. There
was no sound except my own breathing and the gentle crunch-
crunching under my feet. It seemed as if the whole town were in
hibernation.

Then gradually, as I crossed the cemetery, the sounds of
children's voices floated through the gravestones, distant and
distorted. By the time I reached the church all solitude and quiet
meditation was rudely driven away by a hail of snowballs. Along
with everyone else I ducked and ran for safety, and we stood in
the porch shaking the snow off our coats and stamping our feet.

Inside all was warm and cosy. Seeing the first snowflakes the
night before, Peter had had the presence of mind to alter the
clock so that the heating came on early. He thought of things like
that.

'People are miserable if they're cold,' he said. 'It kills the spirit
of worship. They don't feel welcome. They stay huddled in their
overcoats, unable to relax and meet each other.'

By some strange irony, his sermon that morning was about
manna, that strange powdery white substance which the Israelites
found covering the ground when they woke up one morning.
They collected it up into jars. I wondered whether it ever occurred
to them to roll it into balls and throw it at each other . . . probably,
knowing my ancestors!

As soon as the service was over, the congregation rushed out
into the cemetery, drew up battle lines, and the fight continued.

Alicia had a lethal right-hand volley. I surrendered and we put the children on the sledge and towed them home for dinner. Not before one old lady had complained bitterly that the pathway had not been cleared.

'Dreadful, isn't it?' Peter said with a twinkle in his eye, 'I quite agree.'

She nodded, then stopped, realising that her veiled criticism was having no effect.

'Sorry, but in Grimlington at least, the days of the verger are over,' Peter said to me on the way home. 'I've done two services this morning and clearing paths will have to wait.'

On Monday Peter again had cause to lament the passing of the verger era. The snow had fallen all night. The wind caught it up and swirled it round and round the cemetery, then blew it in mounds up against the church's old oak doors. But Peter was oblivious of the fact as he prepared for a lunchtime funeral. He let himself in through the vestry door at the side, checked the heating dial, robed, laid out hymn and service books and unlocked the front doors from inside. He was all ready, or so he thought. It was only when he was leading the procession up the church path that he noticed the one-foot drift piled up in the porch. In normal circumstances it would have been manageable. In a cassock and surplice and for six pall-bearers it was an undignified climb.

Just as the service was over, Alicia arrived with an ingenious home-made plough. She dragged it along the ground and to the astonished and admiring gawps of a group of onlookers, soon cleared a path right round the church. Unfortunately, by the time the schools came out, the temperature had dropped below freezing and it became an ice rink. Grannies, mums, teenagers and tinies staggered along or clung to each other in a desperate attempt to stay upright, some laughing helplessly as they found themselves prostrate on the ground.

Within another day the banks of snow on either side of the pathways, the thick white carpet on roof and garden, were covered in tiny black speckles. Wherever it was trodden underfoot, the snow had turned grey. What soot and litter failed to spoil, the dogs completed. And soon any illusion of living in the Dales was gone.

One afternoon in that freezing January week, I trudged through slush and ice to collect Joel from school. Linda was there, waiting for Kathy as usual, but her face was very pale and her eyes were blotchy as if she might have been crying. I said nothing. Neither did Jan, who was waiting for her little girl. We just stood there, wondering what to do.

Suddenly, without looking at either of us, Linda said, 'I've a lump.'

I felt as if someone had dropped a piece of ice down my back. No need to ask where the lump was. Every woman lives with the same dread.

'I thought it was nothing,' Linda said, trying to force a smile, 'so I didn't tell anyone. I was sure the doctor would tell me not to be so silly and send me away. But he didn't. When I went this morning he just said I had to see a specialist, straight away. He was so abrupt it frightened me. He wouldn't say any more.'

'You know that the vast majority of breast lumps aren't cancer?' I said to her.

She nodded, without expression, probably thinking as I was, that there was still a chance she was one of the minority.

'You know, it's funny,' she said, staring at the ground, the tears welling up into her eyes, 'I was just thinking that God was good, a real father. Since Joe was made redundant we haven't missed out at all. We've been given food and all we've needed just at the right moment. Christmas was great. We even managed to buy presents for the kids.'

She stopped for a moment, fighting to regain control. It was hard to talk in such a public place.

'But this! This is far worse. It's the not knowing that is so awful. I keep saying "Why?" over and over again. Don't get me wrong, I'm not afraid to die. It's the kids,' she said, looking up as the school doors opened and out poured a tangled mass of arms, legs, boots, mittens, hats and scarves. 'They're still so little. They need me. And I do so want to see them grow up.'

I forced back the glib and easy words which came so quickly to my lips. 'Don't be so premature. Stop talking about death.' Like the advice of Job's comforters, they would have been a rejection of her honesty and a reflection of my inability to cope. She was not being morbid. I loved Grimlington people for saying what they felt, and not what they thought they ought to say or what others wanted to hear. It was better for Linda to express her fears and face them, than for us all to connive at sweeping them under the carpet. Out of sight was not out of mind in this case.

So Jan and I were lost for words. There was nothing to say. We simply stayed close, to let her know that she was not going to face this ordeal alone.

At home that evening I tried to keep myself busy and fill my mind with anything but Linda's lump, but it would not go away! I resisted the urge to check myself at first, then gave up. What must Linda be feeling?

'Haven't they got enough on their plates?' I shouted at the ceiling, but my question hung round in the air, unanswered.

She went to see the specialist the following week. She waited several hours, naked from the waist up, and was shivering by the time he came into her cubicle.

'If this is just an ordinary cyst,' he said to her, wielding a syringe, 'I should be able to draw off some fluid.'

It was painful, but none came, which was worse.

'I'll have to have you in, I'm afraid,' he said, 'and as soon as possible. And I think you would be well advised to sign a consent form agreeing to a total mastectomy if it turns out to be necessary.' He left quickly with a friendly smile and she found herself alone, feeling dazed and slightly sick.

'It's all so easy for a man,' Linda said to us later. 'It doesn't seem to mean anything to him. Well, to be honest with you, apart from feeding babies, they were never much use to me before either. Then someone said to me, "It doesn't matter, you can just have them lopped off," like pruning branches of a tree. And I realised how much I wanted to keep them. It's an amputation and it's gruesome. I'm only twenty-eight. I don't want to be half a woman.'

She shook her head. 'Poor Joe, as if he hasn't enough worry.'

Joe had applied for dozens of jobs. It was always the same. He set off in such high spirits, then slouched home and sank into his armchair when he received yet another rejection. It was a terrible blow to his self-esteem.

'We'll let yer know,' he mimicked, then groaned. 'If I hear that again I'll go mad. Why don't they just say, "On yer bike, lad." I'm always too young, too old, underqualified, overskilled. What do they want? Yer can't win.'

When a job was advertised for a caretaker-cleaner at the Post Office, Joe was among the first to apply.

'I've always wanted to work with people,' he said and I understood. He did love people. No favour was too much trouble. But there were twelve other applicants for the job and Joe heard nothing more.

One night, while Linda was still waiting to be admitted to hospital, my mother rang in some distress. My father appeared to have had a kind of stroke.

'I'm frantic with worry. He can't walk, he's totally disorientated, he talks such nonsense and he seems to be incontinent. I can't bear to see him like this.'

When Peter and I got to Newcastle he was already in hospital, frail, but shuffling about. What was unbearable was his apparent inability to interpret what he saw, so that he thought my white anorak, rolled into a bundle, was a baby.

'Will things get any better?' I asked my mother.

She shook her head. 'Apparently not. The scan shows a great deal of brain damage. Things can only get worse.'

I felt numb as we travelled home. It was like a recurrent nightmare I had had as a child. People that I loved the most had changed so much that I no longer recognised them. How was it possible that this fine and dignified man should come to this, the one thing he had dreaded beyond all others.

'I never want to be a burden to you,' he had always said. But he wasn't a burden, just a terrible, terrible ache. It seemed so cruel. Why couldn't we have our allotted years in full command of our faculties? The more I thought about it the more I saw how helpless and insignificant human beings were. In one way it made me angry, in another it was almost a comforting thought. I could not accept that God was a callous ogre, destroying what he made. He had reversed the cruel destiny of man, not condemned him to it. To decay might be an inescapable part of our lot. But it was progress to a new beginning, not an end in itself.

Linda was admitted into hospital, smiling and at peace, but feeling 'a bit like a jelly'. I could not apply myself to anything the day of the operation, but wandered round the house with the vacuum cleaner in a half-hearted kind of way, muttering semi-prayers. I was doubly anxious because Peter had received news that little Paul was very unwell again.

At four o'clock I could bear the suspense no longer and rang the hospital. Of course all the efficient nurse would tell me was, 'Mrs Jameson is back from surgery and sleeping.'

I rang Joe.

'That's all they'll tell me,' he fumed, 'until I go in at seven for visiting.'

'Ring me as soon as you know anything.'

'I will, love, I promise.'

It was nearly ten when he rang, but he was elated.

'She's OK,' he shouted, trying to control the tremor in his voice. 'It's not . . . I mean she's still got her . . . Oh, yer know what I mean. I was beginning to think nothing was ever going to go right.'

'Thank God!' I said to him.

'I am. I am.'

A few days later Linda walked into Drama. I stared at her as if I had seen an apparition.

'Are you all right?'

She grinned.

'A bit washed out, but fine basically. Anyone want to see? It's very pretty, every colour of the rainbow. They didn't use stitches. They used a laser instead.'

She opened her cardigan and we all gawped at the top of her chest. As she had said, it was a colourful sight. We ooohed and aaaahed appropriately, while Linda smiled and blushed.

'Wait while I tell yer what happened.'

We listened with the ghoulish fascination which hospital stories always seem to create. Besides, Linda was a wonderful storyteller.

'I came round from the anaesthetic,' she said in a hushed voice, 'and slowly remembered what I was in for. I groped around frantically, but with all the bandages it was hard to tell what was what. When I realised I was all there, I wanted to cheer. But then I found something else lying on my chest. It was an open hymn book. A nurse came over and she told me I was fine. There was no cancer. "What's this for?" I asked, picking up the hymn book. "Oh, we thought you might be needing it. You've been serenading the entire ward with your hymn-singing for the last hour. It's been better than *Songs of Praise*." Well, did I feel stupid! But the nurse said, "I shouldn't feel embarrassed if I were you. You should hear what some people shout as they come round from an anaesthetic. I'd like to think my subconscious was as pure and holy as yours."'

'When I got out of bed a while later and staggered down the ward to the toilet, everyone was shouting, "Hallelujah, Linda!" "Praise the Lord, Linda." I nearly died! I laughed so much I almost burst the wound.'

'Well,' I said to her, 'I kind of hoped you'd be a comfort to others, but that's ridiculous.'

We never did do any drama that evening. Angela and Frances had come prepared for the occasion. I was about to begin a rehearsal, when they interrupted the proceedings.

'Do you mind if I take over?' Angela asked.

'Be my guest,' I said, 'I'm getting used to it!'

'It's just that we've planned a little something, haven't we, Frances?'

She gave her sister a knowing wink, then delved into her bag and pulled out a bottle of wine. Frances opened hers carefully and took out a chocolate cream gateau, paper plates and cups and plastic forks and spoons. We were stunned into silence for once and just gawped as Angela poured the wine and Frances shared out the cake. She had even remembered serviettes.

'Well,' Angela said, 'shouldn't we give thanks?'

So we did, joining hands.

'Thanks for Linda, for looking after her and keeping every bit intact. And thanks for the cake and wine.'

'Cheers!' we all said, raising our glasses. 'Here's to you, and her!'

18

Although February is the shortest month in the year, it always seems the longest. Each grey and bitter day drags on from the next as if winter were interminable and spring will never come. There was a weariness about the town. No buds had yet appeared on the few trees to give a semblance of life to their tired-looking spindly branches. The first crocuses had sadly surrendered to the mounds of black mess the snow and slush had left behind. A selection of unwelcome viruses left people looking wan and drained. They trudged up the High Street, heads bent, with heavy step.

But it was not the time of year which cowed their spirits and thrust them into such a heavy gloom. Winter came and went every year and life continued. But this winter the news was ominous. The Coal Board announced more and more pit closures. The talk was of mass redundancies, unemployment and men of thirty who would never work again. A strike began to look inevitable and everyone knew what that meant. The women faced it with dread.

Every morning they clustered together on the High Street corners or in the supermarket.

'I knew it would come to this, I knew it. All over again! We nearly starved the last time. How the hell will we manage?'

'What else can we do? If they're made redundant it'll be as bad. Our Keith was hoping to start when 'e finished school in summer, but there's no 'ope now. What's 'e goin' to do?'

'They say there's plenty work in Selby.'

'Ay, but for 'ow long? It'll be just like last time. They moved me Uncle Wilf not two year since and now they're shutting that pit too.'

'Well I'll not go to Selby. I've all me family 'ere. Better starve together than survive apart.'

'But what good will a strike do, I ask yer? Since when do they ever listen to likes of us?'

'They don't. But we'll stand by us men, like we always do.'

A strike would affect the entire community, and so the church experienced its share of anxiety too. The congregation was made up of people who depended on the mines in some way or another for their livelihood. They employed electricians, engineers, carpenters, and plumbers. Every shop, every small business needed the custom the pits provided.

But at that time the major anxiety was not the strike, although it was there at the back of everyone's mind, it was the fact that little Paul no longer seemed to be improving. He had appeared at family services, bright-eyed and alive again, but now he was listless and constantly complaining of pains in his legs. When he drew pictures of himself, he drew a little boy without legs. Not given to hiding their emotions, the congregation expressed their heartache and bewilderment quite openly. Some broke down and wept during the time of intercession.

Mick and Karen took him and his parents to see the Sister at her community again. She anointed him with oil and reassured them that she was as convinced as ever that Paul would soon be strong and well.

Many church members felt the same. Others were not so sure. It created a problem for the clergy.

'How do we counsel everyone?' Peter said one evening, his head in his hands, resting his elbows on the kitchen table. He had been sitting there for quite some time after he finished his evening meal. 'More than anything I want to believe that Paul will get better, but there's a constant niggle of doubt which won't go away. So many people have pictures in their minds of Paul at school, or Paul running and playing, that I don't know what to think. If we try and prepare everyone for his death, we're accused of having no faith. But once our emotions are involved like this, how can we distinguish God's will from our own wishful thinking? I feel utterly at a loss.'

'Do we need to know the future?' I asked Peter.

He looked at me blankly.

275

'Isn't that God's prerogative and not ours? I thought faith was to do with not knowing, yet still trusting.'

He nodded.

'I suppose all we can do is wait, and trust. But I have the awful feeling that we're shirking our real responsibility.'

There seemed to be an increasing number of evenings when Peter felt angry or helpless. Any illusions I had had that he would slip into the life of a clergyman with the rapture of someone who finds the job he has seen in his dreams, were rudely shattered. He often felt controlled, even driven by his work. It was endless. It was a yawning pit and no matter how much he poured in, it never began to fill up. He could never sit down at the end of the day and say, 'I've finished.' There were always mounds of papers lying on his desk – unfinished administrative business, the half-written sermon, notes about repairs left unmended, visits not made, counselling postponed and the relentless forward planning, that needed time and creative thinking. And he was still only the curate. Edward never treated him as the 'junior boy', yet he was aware that the vast majority of emergencies never came his way. Nevertheless, all his best plans to change the basic work patterns of the clergy and have reasonable time off began to disintegrate under the pressure. And at the end of the day there was still nothing to show for his labour, no sense of completion or satisfaction.

'I take no exercise,' he growled, pacing the house. 'I have no leisure activities. Soon I'll have no conversation either. I'll be boring. How did I get like this? I promised I'd take an evening or an afternoon off a day, like most civilised human beings.'

'I don't see how the clergy dare work a six-day week anyway in a time of unemployment,' I said, trying to be provocative, which was not altogether helpful.

'If the three of you did a five-day week it would provide three days' employment for someone else.'

'Tell that to the powers that be,' he barked. 'Most clergy won't let go anyway. They're driven by guilt. I know now why so many become workaholics. It makes them feel better, I suppose, as if they must be achieving something. At least they can't be criticised for sitting around. It's easier to give in to pressure than fight it.'

But as he prowled round the house like a bear with a sore head things became clearer. He was someone whom pressure drove into reverse, rather than the opposite. His whole body and mind resisted it with fury. He would not give in.

'I will fight it. A clergyman must be able to experience a certain measure of normal existence. I know one thing, if I don't, I'm not going to survive in this job for long.'

I had my struggles too. I missed the relaxed, easy routine of the teacher's wife, when every week was gloriously the same and mine to arrange. I had started to write and I resented the constant interruptions, Peter's to-ing and fro-ing which unsettled the children, the physical restraint required to keep them out of his way, and the stopping to make lunch when I had just settled Abby in bed. Many wives would be only too pleased to have their men around all day, I thought guiltily, especially those whose husbands worked long hours and were rarely there. And here was I suffering from over-exposure! But he was around, yet not around, because he was always on duty. Sometimes I felt like a glorified house-keeper, seeing to the curate's every bodily need and sending him on fit and fed to fulfil the next demand.

There was that inevitable loneliness too. Some of our deepest heartaches over people we loved could not be shared lest we breach their confidence. If one of the children were ill, or it was my turn on the crèche rota and I missed the morning service, I missed church altogether that week. I sometimes went for weeks without being able to take Communion and it was a loss. Grimlington, being a static community with its close ties and inbuilt support system, did not identify easily with those who were forced to be mobile and found themselves without loved ones and family nearby. We missed our friends from Manchester and Nottingham. We no longer had weekends off to see them and they were working on Thursdays, Peter's day off. Many precious friendships were left unnourished and began to wither and die.

Frank Field, the MP, published his report on the plight of divorced clergy wives. We were saddened by the high clergy divorce rate, but not surprised. The Church promised to do more for the destitute, disenfranchised clergy wife. That was something but I still felt uneasy. Wasn't it dealing with a symptom, rather than a cause? As a doctor's daughter I knew the best medicine was preventive. Would no one ask why it happened? Perhaps not, because the clergy knew that a solution would have to be so radical that the behavioural pattern of years would have to change. And the clergy wife had no voice.

Peter and I tried to plan our own mini-revolution. Against all the odds we would hang on to our marriage, our family life and our sanity. We also intended to preserve our creativity, enjoyment of life and our sense of humour too. Having Jewish roots helped. Judaism, with its philosophy of the joy of life, its acceptance and value of man's humanity and all that that meant in terms of the richness of family life, was the perfect foil for the Protestant work ethic. Man might well be meant to labour and toil, but the Haggadah, the Passover service, insisted he was also made for 'seasons of gladness, rejoicing and festival'. These were God-ordained, compulsory, vital for his mental and spiritual health, and not just some unnecessary extra, nice if the time can be spared, but dispensable if work makes a prior claim. That was why, for most Jews, the Sabbath was special and began the evening before.

'Everyone prays for a Jewish judge in court on Friday,' we were told by someone in the congregation who worked in the Leeds law courts, 'you can guarantee you'll be home early.'

We decided that our Friday family night, our 'Sabbath celebration' as we welcomed the weekend, should be sacrosanct too. It was a struggle. There were so many other demands on Peter. The youth group were expecting him. He would have to let the leaders down. But it was more important to say 'Kiddush' with the children, light the Sabbath candles, eat, sing and tell stories by candlelight, then take the bread and wine, reminding ourselves that Christ had said, 'When you do these things, remember me.' We tried to invite others and draw them in too.

Edward and Alicia were puzzled by the importance we gave these occasions. The home was not the traditional place for Christian worship. They were doubtful whether the Church had anything to gain at all from the traditions of the Jews.

'The Church is the new Israel,' Alicia often preached.

'Where does it say that in the New Testament?' I asked her. 'Show me chapter and verse.'

'Well, darling, you know what I mean. We are the chosen ones now.'

'And God has finished with the Jews?'

Alicia smiled graciously. She was far too wise to get embroiled in a subject so packed for me with emotional content.

But I was saddened that Christians so often dismissed Judaism which was their own heritage. It was their own loss. Christ was Jewish and the disciples and the apostles and the Church began as a Jewish sect. Then, in a fierce rise of Jewish nationalism after AD 70, the Jewish Christians were thrown out of the fold. And Christianity was swallowed up in the Greek, Gentile culture where it grew and spread. It lost a certain colour and vibrancy, vigour and joy. For the Greek philosophers the human body was seen as a negative force warring against the spirit. The early Church fathers felt the same. Sacred and secular were divided and pushed poles apart, until, as in present-day Grimlington, church and community seemed to have little in common. Emotional repression suited the British middle-classes with their stiff upper lip. But a working-class community was more volatile and much freer with its emotions.

The relevance of its Jewish roots for a church like Grimlington became more and more apparent to us. The Jewish culture with its sense of family and community had a lot in common with a town where everyone knew everyone else. When a man had been lying in the same position all day, digging coal out of the earth, when a woman had stood sorting nails and screws into the same little cartons for hours on end, they did not wish to stand rigidly in a church service. They needed to relax, unwind and let their hair down. Worship had to be full of colour, movement and excitement, as well as have its moments of quiet stillness. An intellectual exercise, requiring an effort in concentration, was not enough if it was to be a real reflection of the life and needs of the people of the town.

I was excited by the realisation that here was a possible key to bridging the gulf between the church and the town. We had to escape from the hidebound attitudes which had imprisoned the British Church for years. We needed to break down the cultural barriers and go free. But I could not impose my ideas by force. Peter and I could work out our own family life in terms of our Jewish heritage, but when it came to the church, they would probably say, 'Her again! She has a vested interest!' and they would have been right. I would have to wait.

Meanwhile Edward planned the Easter services, filling the week with a series of meditations, culminating in a Maundy Thursday Communion.

'I wish we could do a Passover instead,' I said to Peter.

'So do I, but be patient.'

'When are we going to fit in our own Seder night?'

It was not a proper Easter for me without celebrating the great Jewish festival of freedom which had meant so much to Christ.

'Don't worry, we'll do it,' Peter reassured me, 'and we'll invite Edward, Alicia and Anna to share it.'

'But when? They're busy all week.'

'If we have to wait until midnight, we'll do it.'

I was just about to dash out to a joint meeting of the Music and Drama Groups to plan for Easter when the telephone rang.

'It's Mick.'

The voice sounded flat, totally devoid of emotion.

'Tell Peter, will you, that Paul died this afternoon.'

I was totally at a loss for words.

'We can't believe it, we just don't understand,' Mick said and in the desperate weariness of his voice was a hint of despair.

I knew this was no time for discussion or explanations.

'I'll tell Peter,' I said, 'and Mick, we'll be thinking of you all. I only wish there was more we could do.'

Peter came into the kitchen as I put the receiver down. He sat down slowly and shook his head.

'I've been expecting it for some time,' he said, 'but I wish it didn't have to happen like this, with everyone so unprepared.'

'Do you want to go round?'

He rang the vicarage, but Edward had already gone.

'You'd better go to your meeting,' he said and I agreed, reluctantly.

My feet felt like two great blocks of lead as I walked through the cemetery and up to the vestry door. There was no sound from inside the main body of the church. Perhaps the meeting had been cancelled. Then I heard the coughing and muffled sobbing. I tiptoed in and joined the little group, huddled together in a corner with handkerchiefs on their laps. Linda followed me in, and looked at me in bewilderment when she saw the little group.

'Paul,' I mouthed to her.

She understood and sank on to a chair.

'I'm not surprised,' she mouthed, looking in concern at the little group.

We sat there for some time, perhaps half or three quarters of an hour, the uneasy silence broken only by an occasional sob or the sound of someone blowing their nose. I could not help contrast it with those early mornings when everyone had prayed with such hope and fervour. But I began to feel uneasy. There was a weeping for sheer grief and a weeping for our own disappointed hopes and at some point the latter had taken over from the former. We were teetering on the brink of self-pity. I caught Rick's eye and he was obviously feeling the same. It was time to move on.

'When we were at College,' I heard myself saying, 'one of the student wives died. She was twenty-three. We had all prayed so hard and she had been making such progress. That evening was the first Communion service after Easter. We all felt miserable, just like we are tonight. The Vice-Principal got to his feet and he said, "Of course we all grieve for Chris and her family. It's only right we should. But if all we do tonight is grieve, then we make a mockery of Easter and all this College stands for. Why train to be a clergyman, why bother being a Christian at all, if death isn't defeated for ever?"'

'This isn't the end for Paul,' Rick said gently, 'it's a beginning. His pain is over and he's safe and happy now. Whatever our questions or our confusion, that's all we can know for now and we must hang on to that. So, to work!'

Edward had to announce Paul's death to the church on Sunday morning. My stomach muscles tensed for him as he fought to keep control.

'I feel I must say,' he said, with a slight tremor, 'that this is no time for recriminations. It makes no matter now who said what and who believed what. If you want to point the finger, point it at me. I failed you in that I did not know how to advise or lead you. The whole matter of healing is a mystery. We all make mistakes. I know God heals, but for Paul, this was the best form of healing.'

Joel, sitting next to me, scribbling in a note-book, suddenly looked up. 'Has Paul gone to heaven?' he asked.

I nodded.

'The lucky thing! I bet it's got the biggest adventure playground in the world. There'll be dozens of swings and one of those pulleys that whizz you through the air. And his legs won't hurt any more. Do you think he'll find Chica?'

Chica was Granny's dog who had died a few months earlier. 'I hope he does. He can take him for walks till I get there.'

I looked at Joel and marvelled. A child had a much clearer perception of truth than the rest of us. We were simply too sophisticated.

19

It was almost Easter when the miners' strike began. At first the effects seemed to be minimal. There were more men out shopping with their wives or playing with their children in the park. The women wore a constant anxious frown as they bustled around the supermarket, trying to make the vital cut-backs in the house-keeping. All mortgage, rent, gas, electricity and HP payments were frozen. Nothing else could be done. And life continued, much as it always had, except for a certain foreboding in the air, which everyone tried to ignore. Easter eggs were bought sparingly and handled with care. It might be the last taste of chocolate for a very long time. The future hung like a heavy storm cloud on the horizon, too far away to worry about yet, though burst it must some day soon.

Joe had found a temporary job humping boxes and crates at a local storage depot. On Good Friday he was laid off.

'Don't worry,' Linda said when she told me. 'They'll take him on again on Tuesday. They don't want to give 'im 'oliday pay, that's all. They do it with all their temporaries.'

I was incensed.

'I can't bear it,' I said to Peter, as we cleared away the tea dishes. I clenched my fists and dug my nails so deeply into my palms that I suddenly became aware of the pain. 'They just shrug it off, but I could go and throttle an employer or two. We're going back to the days of Dickens. The injustice of it. It's unfair.'

Peter nodded and put an arm around my shoulder.

'I know, love, but there's nothing we can do.'

'Nothing!' I said, brandishing the washing-up brush. 'Just let me catch any of them and I'll give them nothing.'

When it came to defending the flock I had a kindred spirit in

Edward. The previous week, as we walked into the vicarage for a staff lunch, we heard him shouting, 'How dare you!' down the telephone. There was steel in his voice.

Peter flinched and caught Anna's eye. She grinned back knowingly. They were made of much gentler stuff. Edward was a wonderful ally, but a fearful opponent.

'Well!' he said, joining us in the dining-room a few moments later, 'I won't have anyone talk to Lucy like that.'

'Who was it?' Peter asked tentatively.

'Someone in the Housing Department. Lucy's been going almost every Saturday to ask for a new house. He told her to get married, or pregnant. It was the only way to get a house in a hurry. How insensitive! I won't have her hurt like that. Some officials seem to have no feelings at all.'

But no matter how loudly we shouted or how great a fuss we made, Peter was basically right. There was little we could do to protect people at the mercy of an apparently uncaring system.

On Good Friday evening the hail eventually stopped, the ice melted away and the skies cleared to give a fine, almost spring-like feel to the end of the day. Just as well, for I was looking forward to the Council of Churches' torchlight procession through the town and I hate the rain. There was a spring in my step as I walked to church, enjoying the masses of daffodils in bloom in the cemetery. Stella, a friend who had come to stay for the weekend, was with me and we stopped for a moment and looked around at the familiar landscape, the higgledy-piggledy brick housing and uneven back yards, joined together like a misshapen patchwork quilt.

'You know,' I said to her, 'when I think of all the beautiful places I could have been. Funny isn't it, but there's nowhere else on God's earth I'd rather be.'

A beautiful new banner in shades of lilac and purple was hanging above the pulpit and we sat enjoying it for some time. A cluster of grapes dripped their juice into a goblet and underneath was written. 'Yours was the suffering we see in the wine.'

It reminded me of the third cup, the 'Cup of Blessing', at the Passover service, which we had managed to share as a family with Edward, Anna, Alicia and Lucy on the Wednesday evening. That was probably the cup which Christ used to institute the Communion. 'I'm going to drink a bitter cup of suffering, so that you can drink the Cup of Blessing,' was what he was saying. Passover and Easter merged as the great celebrations of the freedom which God gave to man. It suddenly occurred to me how tremendous it was that Joe, Lucy, those caught up in the strike, all of us there in the church, were no longer victims of our circumstances. Inner freedom was far more important.

My meditation was disrupted as everyone prepared for the march, collecting torches and extra woollies and spending that last penny. With the troops assembled and our ranks swelled by the Baptists, we all set off to collect the Catholics and Methodists.

'Pssssst!' Dorothy whispered. 'Not mentioning any names, but there are certain individuals I wouldn't go near if I were you.'

She nodded in various directions.

'Last year I ended up with wax all down the back of my best coat.'

Silence fell, for us a major feat of self-control, and we marched, torches held high beneath a clear, starlit sky. Doors opened and people stood, silhouetted in the light, as we passed by. It felt strange to say so much without using words. As we reached the pub at the traffic lights two young men came out and bawled, 'Christian bastards!'

Stella looked at me, her eyes wide with astonishment.

'Did I hear right?' she asked.

'I think so.'

'I've never come across anything like that before.'

'Me neither, but it seems quite a healthy reaction.'

She nodded.

'Better than suburban indifference.'

'Oh, there's none of that around here.'

I smiled to myself as we walked along. Grimlington people can be belligerent, abrasive and maddening, but they're never bland or dull. I was to remember those words a few weeks later when an event occurred which provoked that belligerent spirit to its full fury.

It had been apparent for some years that Cuttlesworth, the last remaining daughter church, would have to close, but no one had been prepared to take that final drastic step. Even Edward kept putting it off. There was a limit to how much criticism a man could shoulder at any one time and there was no doubt that the decision would hurt. The congregation was tiny, but vocal and fiercely loyal. Angela and Frances of the Drama Group, fighters to the last, had joined them to give their moral support. It was almost a holy war.

The arguments for keeping the place open were emotional rather than rational, and had more to do with legend than fact.

'They're stuck-up at Parish. They're unfriendly, unwelcoming. They're all professional people.'

None of it was true, except of course a larger church could not offer the intimacy of a congregation of twenty. But gradually we picked up various impressions, memories and stories, which slotted together like pieces of a jigsaw puzzle to create a picture of years of division and mistrust, all rooted in the church's inadmirable history.

Grimlington's vicar was once exceedingly rich. The church had owned vast areas of land all around the town. Glebe, as it was called, was a means of paying the incumbent. All rents went to him. That made him a squire of some importance, with a large staff, coach house and a farm, and not always too popular with his tenants. The system persisted as late as the 1950s, when all land reverted to the diocese and was sold. The stipend became uniform and overnight the clergy became the poorest paid of professionals, which always seemed to me far more in keeping with the spirit of Christianity. 'The Church' was no longer a career with prospects. The clergyman might still live in a semipalace, but whether he could now afford to heat and furnish it was another matter.

However, this was not the problem at the turn of the century. Grimlington's vicar was wealthy enough to resist the division of his living into several parishes of equal size, the tendency in most fast-growing industrial towns. He could afford curates and the building of daughter churches. The Methodist threat made it imperative.

Methodism was the working man's Christianity. Chapels were appearing in every pit village so fast that it was hard for the Church of England to compete. There were almost as many chapels as there were toilets and more chapels than there were trees.

In 1903 a local squire lent the vicar a piece of land for a religious establishment and Cuttlesworth was built. Like the other daughter churches it fared well at first. Attendance at services was average, but exceedingly good at the mass of social events which quickly became its prime function. West Yorkshire never experienced the religious fervour of the Welsh mining communities. Gradually, although the Sunday School was quite large and women attended the meetings almost as faithfully as ever, the malaise set in. In face of war, pain, poverty and suffering the Church had little to say. It offered dances and social evenings to try and disguise the spiritual void, but in the end they were not enough and the congregation dwindled.

The huge social gulf between the parish and the daughter church persisted. In the 1970s whenever the Parish Women's Society had tea together the Cuttlesworth women came and did the washing up.

'How kind!' a newcomer was heard to comment. 'And I suppose we go and do it for them.'

Her companion coughed politely.

'No, no, but we do give them a little something for doing it.'

'Did the men ever go to church?' I asked Jack, as he was sweeping the parish hall one day.

'Not really, not the working men. Not so's I'd remember,' he said.

Jack was a retired carpenter, a master at his craft. I had a soft spot for him. He was a gem. He cleaned the parish hall, checked and kept it, gave hours of his time without a word of complaint. And if anyone had cause to complain, he did. It could be left in total disarray.

He seemed to welcome an excuse to stop, leant on his broom and chuckled. He had an infectious chuckle and my endless questions about the past amused him. His body seemed a weight and he was breathing heavily. I wondered if the cleaning was becoming too much for him, but his face, though flushed, was as bright and alive as ever. He thought for a while.

'Yer see, Michele, what yer have to remember is that yer life were not yer own. Yer belonged to boss, body, soul and spirit. He were always right. And 'e could make yer work as many hours as 'e wanted.'

'Not Sundays too!'

'What! He could make yer work all day and all night if 'e 'ad a mind to it, if there were a job to finish. Yer work was yer life.'

He rested his chin on his hands, which were balanced on the

broom handle, and suddenly he was miles away in another world. Then he chuckled again. 'Listen' he said, 'I'll tell yer a story which'll show yer what it were like.'

I pulled out two chairs and we sat down.

'When I were an apprentice, many year ago now, I once 'ad to build a cupboard. It were tongue and groove and every joint were done by 'and. It took me days, but when it were finished I were right pleased wi' meself. It were a beautiful cupboard. I called boss to show 'im what I'd done. He looked at it a while, then 'e picked up an 'ammer and smashed it to pieces before me very eyes. "What did yer do that for?" I asked 'im. To tell yer truth I were fighting back tears. It were a terrible feeling. I'll never ferget it, not as long as I live. "Do it again," 'e said, "and this time, 'ow I told yer." '

'What did you do?'

'What did I do? I started all over again, just like 'e said.'

He looked at me and shook his head. 'Ay,' he said, 'that world's gone and I can't say I'm sorry.'

'If the men didn't go to church, what made you go?'

'That were recent. I went as a child, then like all me mates I stopped once I were apprenticed. I didn't see point. It were Madge who dragged me back. She said it 'ad all changed. New vicar, that were last vicar, were different. And then Alicia were on me doorstep, tellin' me I 'ad to go too. That were definitely new. We'd never 'ad a woman minister before and I'd never met anyone like Alicia. I certainly wasn't going to argue with 'er.

'But Madge were right. It were different. The sermons were about Bible and God and how we could know him. I could understand them. There I was, a man in me fifties, and I understood for t' first time what being a real Christian were.'

He threw back his head and laughed. 'Well at least I found out before they were putting me underground. And I'll tell yer this. One day, last vicar said, "Jack, you don't need to call me Sir, or Mr Jones. Call me by my Christian name, like I call you by yours." Yer could 'ave knocked me down. So 'ere I am now, chatting with vicar and anyone. It's a new world, it is. And last week when I went out to t' front to pray, well, that were out o' my realm altogether. Madge and I never thought we were good enough to mix with church people. But times 'ave changed all right.'

I left Jack to finish sweeping the parish hall, amazed. 'Not good enough' indeed! They had probably been shaming the 'religious' in the town for years with their self-giving. Still, I now understood why there was such resistance to shouldering responsibility and coming into the limelight. 'You must not get above yourself' was an unwritten law, buried deep in the sub-conscious.

And the Church of England made sure it stayed that way. Lay reading courses were cerebral and intellectual, requiring a large measure of academic ability. After all, the lay reader must know all about Barth and Bultmann to meet the needs of a congregation like Grimlington! Pastoral gifts and quality of character were important, but education seemed to matter more.

But if it was almost impossible for a working man or woman to become a lay reader, it was even harder for them to be ordained. Dave tried. He felt a strong sense of calling and showed real pastoral ability with the children, but he worked on a building site and had no exam passes. For Dave ordination was a dream, a distant dream, light years away in the future.

If Grimlington Church was ever truly to reflect the life of the town, then local lay leadership was crucial, and not just an optional extra. So we got on with it. Mick began to lead services. He had a liturgy all of his own, full of local colour. Marjorie preached with unusual vigour and handled the banter from the congregation as well as any politician. And yet I realised how easy it was to turn to the more skilfully articulate first, because they were not afraid to come forward. We were in danger of recreating a hierarchy based on status and often missed the treasure sitting deferentially in the pew. How I longed for that age-old tradition to go. It was British, but hardly New Testament!

Class distinction still operated in the Church all right. The Cuttlesworth congregation had a point, but it was no longer concentrated in the parish-daughter church divide. Cuttlesworth was no longer working class. It was simply dying and a poor example to the town of the life it was supposed to represent. Keeping it going required an unwarranted amount of effort. So in May the PCC finally decided on its closure. Two months' warning was given to soften the blow, but the respite was used to launch a campaign. Angela organised a petition to the Archbishop of York. Sue signed it in her corner shop. An old lady told her it was a protest against the vicar's insistence on silver rather than copper in the collection. She was outraged. It was months before she discovered the truth.

Feelings ran high in the town.

'My Granny went there for years.'

'I were brought up at the Sunday School.'

'I enjoy the whist drives.'

Some joined the protest, 'Because,' they said, 'I've never liked that vicar. He's no business changing everything.'

The *Gazette* was full yet again of outraged letters from people the clergy had never seen in the church.

Marjorie and several other people from the parish church went up to Cuttlesworth every Sunday to assure them they were loved and wanted, to listen and sympathise. Her mother had been a pillar of the congregation there once. But the bitterness only seemed to grow.

Frances rang me one night to say that she and Angela would not be coming to Drama any more.

'Well you didn't think we would continue as if nothing had happened, did you?' she said gently.

'I hoped and prayed you would,' I said. 'I hoped that knowing how much we had all come to mean to each other you would feel you still belonged, whatever happened.'

'I'm sorry. It's just not possible. We can never come to the parish church again, not after what's happened, but we will support your performances whenever we can.'

The Drama Group were sad, though not surprised.

'We'll go round and see them,' Linda said. 'They can't let this come between us.'

'They'll come back, won't they?' Dorothy asked.

But no one answered. Perhaps we knew that nothing would make them change their minds. It was a downhearted little group who tried to rehearse that night. I gave up and we finished early.

I stayed to lock up and Linda stayed with me, chatting. The others headed for home.

'You understand about the power of feeling behind the closing of Cuttlesworth, don't you?' I said to her.

'Yes, I do. It goes back a long way. It's very deep.'

It was a soft spring evening, the kind when you want to stay out and breathe in the promise of summer warmth. I had been waiting to ask her something for months and this seemed like the moment.

'Do you remember at the Parish Weekend when you said, "This church is too middle-class"?'

She laughed.

'Yes, that's me, always opening my mouth when I should keep quiet.'

'No, you were right to say it if that was what you felt. I must say it's not like any middle-class church I've ever been in. I think I know what you mean, but I'd rather hear it from your lips.'

She knitted her brow in thought and searched for the right words.

'Well, it's not just one thing, it's lots of things.'

I waited.

'Sometimes, oh sometimes I get so angry. I want to shake people or hit out at them. I feel as if some part of me is being slowly rubbed out. And it's a vital part of me. It's what I am.'

'I know that feeling too,' I said, 'or at least I used to. I found the church a terrible shock. I felt that nobody wanted me as I was. My Jewishness was treated like theft or drug addiction. It was a habit to be kicked.'

'That's it,' Linda said, 'that's exactly it! I'm a working-class girl and that's not something to be ashamed of. I'm proud of it. It isn't all beer and pools and Woodbines. There's good things in our way of life. When I was at school I 'ad a teacher who said to me, "Linda, you're intelligent. Go to university. Drag yourself out of the hole you were born into." I felt like slapping his face for patronising me like that. Who was he to say I was living in a hole? It might seem like that to him. But I thought, "If I'm as wise and contented as me Dad, then that's enough for me." '

She paused and felt for words again.

'The middle-classes think two things about the working man. Either he's unintelligent or he's miserable. We're neither. There's a great deal of natural wisdom in this community and a great deal of contentment too. That's why our lads are on strike, to fight for their families, their homes and the way of life they love.'

I looked at her for a while and could see her eyes glinting in the twilight. No one could easily cow Linda's spirit.

'You won't change, will you?' I said to her.

'Not much chance!'

291

We walked slowly out onto the street.

'So the church has to, but how?'

'Well for one thing, there's no point telling people they're miserable sinners when they're perfectly happy as they are.'

She laughed and I said nothing.

'Do you want a catalogue then?'

I nodded.

'Well the home groups are too intellectual, they're not about real life. The preaching's above people's heads at times. We need leaders, local people who know Grimlington and are trusted. Why must the people who take part in services have posh voices? There are too many meetings about irrelevant things. If it hasn't anything to offer someone like me Dad, then forget it. Oh, and simplify the blooming news-sheet,' she shouted as she ran across the road. 'No one can understand it. What does "Vestry hour" mean to somebody new?'

She was about to disappear down the track behind the houses to the bottom of the town when she turned back.

'Hey!' she shouted. 'I almost forgot to tell you the best news. Joe has a permanent job, in a warehouse. Pay's terrible and he'll have to work masses of overtime, but it's a job.'

She turned again, skipped off between the houses and was gone.

20

As spring gave way to our second summer in Grimlington, I began to find our temporary accommodation an almost unbearable strain. The curtains hanging three inches above the window sills, which had amused me twelve months ago, began to grate and annoy. Everything we needed was always at the bottom of a crate in the garage. And our sleep was often interrupted by the intimate revelations made at the bus stop outside our bedroom window.

Still, compared to the hardship the strike was now beginning to cause, it was very little to put up with. Anyway, like everything else, the house market was at a standstill. Had someone wanted our house, there was still nothing for us to buy, nothing that is except a house belonging to the diocese. The previous vicar had been a rural dean and earned two curates. That was when ours was built. The original curate's house, an Edwardian red-brick semi, had been allowed to fall into a state of acute disrepair. It was so cold, damp and miserable that the PCC refused to consider buying it and when the last occupant left, handed it back to the diocese with relief.

But we loved old property. It was sad to see the old house go to rack and ruin. Alicia's brother was an architect and when he came to stay, Peter asked him if he would mind going with him to have a look round and assess the amount of repairs and alterations.

He was delighted. As we strolled from room to room his eyes lit up. He became so excited by the possibilities that his suggestions took our breath away, especially his idea of a sun lounge extension built on to the south-facing kitchen. Wouldn't we like a little sun trap, he asked. Would we! The prospect painted a happy smile on our faces until we awoke to the reality that this was the curate's house and not a luxury villa on the Costa Brava. Besides, vista there might be, of a school playing field, one of the few 'greenbelt' areas in the town, but the tip which lay beyond it was hardly scenic, although it was reputed to be the highest hill in West Yorkshire.

With some careful calculations, Peter estimated that the church could buy and repair the old house with the proceeds of the sale of the new one. The PCC were convinced at last. They were desperate. The issue was becoming boring. And our move was on the way at last.

'You see,' Peter said to me, smiling, 'you who said we would never have the fun of doing up an old house again once I was ordained, here you are with a house to be repaired and modernised to your specification, and with an architect to command!'

What was more the church was generous beyond our wildest dreams. They would cover the full cost of a professional decorator and a hall and stair carpet. We were uneasy. Their budget was stretched to the limit. But they insisted. They had allowed it to deteriorate. They would repair it properly, even if temporary bank loans were necessary. Then suddenly our house sold and I could have wept with relief.

It was some time during those weeks that I happened to let slip to Edward and Alicia that I had not been confirmed. I knew it was dynamite, but I could not help it. Alicia was complaining about those who came to us from other denominations and did not bother to ask for confirmation. Denominationalism always jarred me.

'Well, I agree with them,' I said, 'I'm not.'

Peter kicked me, but it was too late. Edward and Alicia were staring at me.

'It's totally unnecessary,' I said, 'especially for those baptised as an adult, as I was.'

'That may be so, but it's not the point,' Edward said. 'You see, you put me in a very difficult position. Canon law requires me to urge any regular communicant who is not confirmed to do so as soon as possible.'

'Trust you!' Peter said in the car on the way home. 'Why did you say anything? Couldn't you keep quiet?'

'What's the point of making a protest if you keep quiet about it? You know I'm not an Anglican and I never wanted to be an Anglican. I'm a Jew. I was converted to Christ, not to the Church of England, or any other denomination. Denominationalism makes me sick. It's the greatest failure of the Gentile Church and one which makes it the laughing stock of every other world religion, especially the Jews. So why should your failure be imposed on me?'

Peter looked slightly hurt, then pursed his lips, as he did when he made up his mind that reason must prevail over emotion.

'You know I agree with you entirely. You know I think confirmation is a nonsense, a poor attempt at Bar Mitzvah and without foundation in the Bible, but you do see Edward's point?'

'It's the same for you. You vowed to keep canon law at your ordination.'

'Oh, don't worry about me. I can sort out my own conscience.'

I struggled with the issue for several days. Wasn't it enough that I was a clergy wife? Would I have to abandon my last Jewish protest in a meaningless ceremony? And it angered me that like the Communion service itself, here was yet another ceremony the Church had plundered from the Jews, and ruined! Communion was robbed of its warm family atmosphere, confirmation of its great place in the community. At Bar Mitzvah there is only one candidate, one centre of attention, as he sings the law from the platform of the synagogue and proves he is now a man. Then there is a big party. Confirmation was a poor do by comparison. There were several candidates, all put through the sausage machine at once. None were given individual attention, the chance to say what the ceremony meant to them or even read a lesson. There was no sense of their coming to maturity in the church community. And definitely no party!

Grimlington was neither rigid, nor restrained in any celebration and it was an encouraging consideration. The candidates were older, making a real commitment to the church, and that helped too. I read the account of Jesus' baptism again. He did not have to be baptised. In fact, John seemed reluctant to do it. But Jesus insisted. The law must be fulfilled. It occurred to me that there were times when, for the sake of others, we had to submit to the system. Ideals have to be slightly tarnished every now and then for the sake of relationships.

'I suppose I'll do it,' I said to Peter, with very little grace.

'Not for my sake, I hope,' he said.

'No, for Edward and his flipping conscience!'

Quite a large group of candidates were waiting to be confirmed.

'Date of baptism?' Edward asked.

Baptism was a prerequisite of course.

'Do you mean the one when I was a baby, the one when I became a Jehovah's Witness, or the one when I became Pentecostal?' Ella asked.

Edward looked nonplussed. 'The first will do.'

By contrast, Sid, who owned a fish and chip shop, which was in dire straits because of the strike, and had only been coming to church a few weeks, realised he had not been baptised at all.

'We'll have to baptise you then,' Edward said.

'Ah yes,' said Sid, 'but you will do it proper, won't you? I want it like they did it in Bible. None of your sprinkling bit, not for a grown man. They went right under and that's how I want it. God's changed me completely, turned me upside down, and if I'm going to tell everyone about it in public, I want there to be no mistake.'

Peter leapt around with glee at the prospect. Edward discovered we could hire a portable baptistry. It was an enormous monstrosity, somewhere between an overgrown fishtank and an undersized swimming pool. It held four tons of water and took all day to fill.

'You won't forget your bathing costume tonight, will you?' Edward said to Linda, who was one of the sponsors, Sid deciding he was a bit past the godparent stage.

She giggled.

'Ooooo Edward, you are a tease.'

'I'm serious,' he said, without a flicker of expression. 'I expect the sponsors to get in with me.'

Linda sidled up to Peter and me a few moments later, an uncertain smile on her face.

'Er, what sort of a bathing costume shall I wear tonight?'

Peter and I stared at her in silence. She studied our faces, then muttered through gritted teeth, 'He's having me on, isn't 'e?'

'Don't worry,' Peter said, 'we'll get our own back.'

As they were getting ready in the vestry later that evening, Peter said casually to Edward, 'Have you by any chance noticed the new cracks in the chancel arch?'

Edward looked up, alarmed. Peter noticed things like that.

'I shouldn't worry about it. It's probably the weight of the water.'

He grinned and disappeared into the church, where Bob was playing the organ with perhaps a little more gusto than usual. He stopped and listened. The music was familiar. It couldn't be . . . Wait a minute, it was! He caught Bob's wink in the organ mirror and nearly laughed out loud. When he had jokingly suggested Handel's Water Music, he never expected Bob to take him up on it. But in seventy-five years, despite his serious love of music, Bob had never lost his sense of humour.

The significance of his playing was evidently lost on the congregation, too excited by the novelty of the experience to pay much attention to the organ. I remembered baptismal services from our Free Church days in Manchester and imagined somehow that this would be the same. They were always great occasions, moving, joyous, yet nevertheless invested with a certain seriousness and intensity. But in Grimlington intensity was doomed from the start. Finding the church as full of steam as a sauna was a source of some amusement. The Music Group could hardly see Rick to follow his instructions. The vicar suddenly appeared like a ghost out of the mist. Then, to crown it all, Sid, who was wearing an old pair of trousers he had not worn for years, whispered to Linda in a panic, 'Me fly zip's gone!'

'His fly zip's gone!' she whispered to Edward during the first hymn.

Edward raised his eyes to heaven and whispered back, 'Run over to the vicarage for a safety pin.'

Linda ran and arrived back a few minutes later, out of breath, brandishing a nappy pin. It was all Anna could find. Sid took one look at it and paled.

'I don't have to wear a loin cloth, do I?'

Linda stared at him, realised he was serious and clapped a hand over her mouth to hold her laughter in.

'Yer great wally. Just use it to hold yer trousers up.'

The rest of the service passed off without further mishap. It may have lacked a certain sense of grand occasion, but what we had was much better. It was real and just as moving in its own way. The ripples spread out into the town. A grown man was baptised at the Parish and no one had ever been baptised like that before. 'That takes guts,' they said.

* * *

As the day for the confirmation drew nearer, I felt increasingly tense and unhappy. So many conflicting emotions wrestled to take charge. It was hypocrisy to assent to a ritual in which I did not believe. Yet canon law required it. Why should the Church of England have the last drop of my Jewish blood? Yet that was nonsense. Confirmation would change nothing. My feelings were a mystery to me.

Sitting in the front pew with the seven other nervous candidates I had to fight down a sense of panic and the urge to run. I looked down at the Order of Service and noticed for the first time a passage headed, 'Reaffirmation of Baptismal Vows'. I jumped up, pushed past everyone else in the pew and rushed to find Peter, who was standing calmly at the back of the church.

'Do I have to say this?' I demanded, waving my service sheet under his nose.

He put an arm around my shoulder.

'Yes, why not?'

'Because,' I said, fighting back the tears, 'it makes it look as if I never meant them the first time. And you know how much it meant to me. It was the hardest thing I ever did in my life. It's all right for you and everyone else baptised as a baby. I understand why you should want to own vows made on your behalf. But I knew what I was doing. I risked everything, my family, community, traditions, culture, my very identity. Re-enacting it all just sounds sham and hollow.'

Peter smiled and held me close.

'I do understand. But don't we all need to reaffirm the vows we've made to God, whether it's marriage vows or whatever, just to remind ourselves of the commitment we once made? Goodness, I've had to remind myself of my ordination vows over and over again these last few months, whenever I was tempted to give up and run away.'

I nodded and reluctantly went back to my place, ignoring the puzzled expressions as I squeezed past yet again. Joe was sitting next to me. He touched my arm reassuringly, saying nothing, and his presence was a comfort, I noticed his clenched jaw and realised what an ordeal the experience was for him, though for very different reasons.

From the moment the Bishop appeared, large and genial, the

atmosphere relaxed. The church always responded to his warmth and enthusiasm.

'I do enjoy coming to Grimlington,' he said, leaning with both hands on his bishop's crook and a broad smile on his face. They enjoyed having him just as much. How could they not?

The knot in my stomach began to unwind. For the first time I noticed the new banners, 'the fruits of the Spirit', resplendent in crimson and gold, hanging from every pillar. The Music Group sang at times as if for us alone and I was touched by their encouraging smiles in our direction.

Then, with his arms outstretched, the Bishop invited us to stand in front of him. He knew all our names by heart. I was staggered. He bent his head to us and whispered, 'I want you to understand that when you promise to renounce evil it means no more ouija boards, fortune tellers or astrology of any kind. The Bible is quite clear about that. And no more reading your horoscope. Can we proceed?'

Satisfied with our nods, and then our vows, the Bishop laid his hands on our heads. When my turn came he called Peter out too. 'Come and put your arms around her,' he said. It was an episcopal command. Then he prayed for our family, and our home, and I sensed the loving support surrounding us. It was a privilege to belong to these people, to be part of a very special community. To commit myself to the entire Church of England would have taken more grace than I could muster, but at least I could commit myself to them.

'Do allow us to welcome you into our fellowship,' Rick said, drawing me into a bear hug during the giving of the Peace.

'And about time too!' Ian said, over his shoulder, with a twinkle in his eye.

As the Communion service ended, the Bishop finished the contents of the two wine goblets, then, presuming he had consecrated the wine in the decanter, drank what remained of that too. I watched him in awe.

We brewed our own wine, Mick, Bill and Chris taking it in turns to provide from their cellars, but replacements were not always there on time. Aware that supplies were running dangerously low, Peter went to do the eight o'clock Communion service the previous Sunday with some trepidation. But as he opened the vestry door he saw to his relief that a new demi-john was waiting for him. The writing on the label was Bill's and he blessed him as he yanked off the bung. It came off suddenly, accompanied by a loud hiss, which continued for several seconds. He peered at the dark liquid. It was a little murky. He sniffed it, but it smelled all right. In fact, apart from a gentle fizzing it seemed perfectly all right, especially at seven-thirty on a Sunday morning. He poured some into a goblet, took the service, then drank the drop that remained and cycled home for breakfast.

'Funny,' he said, as he munched his toast, 'my legs feel a bit wobbly today. I really must eat something before I do that service in future. Missing breakfast doesn't suit me at all.'

After the mid-morning service, Bill came into the vestry to count the collection as he usually did.

'Thanks for remembering the wine,' Peter said. 'You saved my neck. The older ones would have been so upset to have missed out. There's just one thing though. You don't think it could be still fermenting, do you?'

'No chance,' Bill said, with a determination that took Peter aback.

'Oh? How can you be so sure?'

'I took pains to ensure it wasn't. Communion wine has to be fortified to keep.'

'So?'

'So I fortified it, with half a bottle of whiskey.'

That was why I watched the Bishop drain the decanter with such interest. But if his taste buds were offended he had the grace to hide it. In fact he did not as much as hiccough. As Edward and Peter escorted him to his car and waved him off they only hoped he would be all right on the way home.

Unknown to me, Peter brought a bottle of wine home to keep for the Communion services he did for the elderly and house-bound. He stood it on top of the kitchen cupboard. Later that week I was making a casserole which required half a pint of red wine and the open bottle caught my eye. 'Can't leave it there to waste,' I thought.

'Where's my Communion wine?' he asked, a few hours later, as he was about to go out on his visits. 'I brought it home especially.'

I thought for a bit and then my heart sank. 'Where did you put it?'

'On top of the cupboard.'

'Well there it is,' I said sheepishly, pointing to the casserole on top of the cooker.

'You couldn't take them round some boeuf bourguignon instead?'

21

Despite the strike, despite the anger when Cuttlesworth finally closed, that summer had its share of excitement, especially when it came to creativity. The Music Group, having amassed a great deal of their own material, decided to launch out into making a cassette. I was invited along to narrate two lines of a psalm which gave me an opportunity to observe the work of great genius in the making.

One sultry Saturday morning at nine-fifteen, and that had to be a test of dedication, about twenty people, complete with music stands, musical instruments, recording equipment and a hired organ, squeezed into the cellar of a tiny terraced house. There was barely room to lift a foot or move an arm. I was not normally given to claustrophobia, but nor had I ever felt so much like one of a bag of marshmallows before. Beads of perspiration appeared on most brows. People began to undo their buttons and remove any superfluous items of clothing, space permitting.

'Open that window,' Tom called out.

He was the local police sergeant and any suggestion carried all the weight of a command. Someone obeyed and the window opened into the coal shed. There was a communal groan.

'Shut that window!' Rick shouted. 'We're about to record.'

At ten-thirty I walked out into the sunshine. It was a relief to swallow fresh air. I gathered later that the recording did not finish until seven in the evening and that apart from an hour for lunch they were all down there together for all that time.

'How did you survive?' I asked Mary.

'With difficulty,' she grinned. 'It ponged a bit.'

'A bit?'

'Yes, but what's that between friends? Those songs mean so

much to us we didn't really mind. That one I wrote came to me one day when I was fed up, sick of cleaning, and the washing and of prayers that never seemed to get answered. Those words came into me head. Yer never know, maybe they'll help other people.'

Rick worked on until the following morning, putting the whole thing together. At last he was satisfied and his painstaking effort had its reward. The cassette sold better than we had ever dared to hope. Alicia almost bought them up herself and sent them to the nether regions of Scotland. It was not great music. We were neither deaf, nor that biased. But it did have a vitality that was special. The words were real, born of everyday experience. It was an offering of ourselves and, more than that, in an area such as this it represented that most priceless of treasures, a finished piece of creative work, a flesh and blood achievement.

We would have been satisfied with that, but there was more to come. One day Rick's phone rang. It was the manager of a Christian record company. Rick's heart missed a beat.

'We like your cassette,' the voice said. 'We've been looking for a new church-based group for a while. We've tried all the big, well-known churches with a reputation, but there's a freshness about yours that appeals to us.'

'Probably because most of the group don't read music,' Rick said.

'That makes it all the more amazing,' the Sales Manager said. 'Well, you're obviously prepared to work. Your songs have great potential. How about our coming to see you with a view to your making a record with us?'

Rick was almost at a loss for words. It was more than he had ever dared to hope.

But there was yet more excitement on the creative front in store.

'Brother Christopher would like to know if we fancy a weekend of dance at Frankhill Abbey,' Linda said, in such a matter-of-fact way that it sounded as if she was inviting us out to the Wilton Ballroom rather than a monastery.

'Well, he said he's going to ring you about it,' she said, noting my astonished expression. Frankhill Abbey was usually recommended for silent retreats, not dancing.

Then I remembered that Linda had gone to something similar there the previous year, with Kelly and one or two others, and they had come back with an urge to dance and a great enthusiasm for Brother Christopher.

'He's a lovely little mover,' she giggled, reminding me of their previous visit. 'No, seriously, he really can dance. He says it's not easy to live in an all-male community, but whenever it gets on top of him, he goes into a little chapel with his cassette and dances his heart out. Once, he didn't bother to switch on the light and it was only when he switched on the cassette and they started groaning that he noticed the two Brothers prostrate on the floor.'

I could hardly believe the Brothers there would want us after that, but Brother Christopher assured me that they were all agreed. Would our church welcome the idea of a weekend of dance? There was room for twenty-five but which church could muster an entire corps de ballet? Not Grimlington!

'We've only three or four dance enthusiasts,' I said, 'I think it would be a bit of a waste of your time.'

'Wouldn't some of the others come and have a go?'

I tried to imagine Mick or Frank or Tom leaping gracefully through the air. 'I don't think so,' I said, 'but we do have a Music and a Drama Group. Could we have some sort of creative weekend with workshops, and could the Brothers provide some input with guidance on creativity and contemplation?'

'I think so,' Brother Christopher said. 'Yes, it should be possible.' And so was born the idea for the most extraordinary weekend I had ever spent.

The organisation was a nightmare. No one ever signed lists and I could not find out how many people wanted to go.

'Why are the people of this parish allergic to signing pieces of paper?' I said to Peter.

'Because they're not used to planning so far in advance.'

I had the faint suspicion that it was also something to do with the number of notices which bombarded them every week. It was apparent that the notice-sheet was not always read, let alone digested, and I remembered Linda's comment.

Finance was a real problem, but, to my astonishment, the PCC offered to cover the cost. There was the feeling in the air that people needed a change and at last I gathered twenty-four names.

We set off one evening in a flurry of great excitement and arrived in time for Evensong. We had to sit a long way back from the Community, as did all the visitors. The heady smell of incense and the sound of the distant chanting made the Grimlington gang goggle. For a horrible moment I thought one of them might let the side down. Anything was possible! But we all fumbled our way through the old prayer books, disintegrating with age, and pretended that this was how we did it every week. Once we gave up trying to find the place and follow, something of the awe and silence which seemed to hang in the atmosphere touched and stilled us. Even the children of the theological students who were present sat perfectly still. We were amazed. None of us had ever seen a child sit through a service without uttering a sound before.

Later that evening, after tea and a chance to meet some of the Brothers, Christopher explained the ground rules, silence in the corridors, promptness at meals and the like. 'Some hope,' I thought and so evidently did Rick, as he chose 'Let there be love shared among us' as our opening song. Everyone held hands as they usually did and gazed rather sheepishly into each other's eyes.

'You call that love, do you?' asked Brother Marcus, who had joined us to talk about contemplation, 'It was nothing but sentimentality.'

We shuffled on our chairs.

'Love is doing good to those who hate your guts.'

His words cut through any illusion we might have had that this weekend was going to be happy and comfortable. He was right. It was too easy to substitute sentimentality for Christian charity, but he also underestimated the importance of feelings of solidarity and mutual support in a mining community, and just how much real support there was behind the gesture.

'We won't be singing that again in a hurry,' I thought, 'at least, not without thinking carefully about the meaning of the words.'

Brother Marcus spoke to us of the mystery in God, the days of darkness when he seemed unknown and unknowable and all we seemed to have were so many uncertainties. His words mirrored my experience of the last month, when I had longed to say to Peter, 'Leave this silly job and go back to something sensible with routine and long holidays,' but could not; the times I had cried out to God about the estate and how to get close to the people there, but no answer came and soon we would be moving; the days when the darkness of the area felt as if it rested on my shoulders like a leaden weight and I could not shake off the sense of weariness.

'But if we're in darkness all we have to do is switch on the light.'

Ian jolted me into realisation that some members of the group were struggling with a very new idea. Or perhaps the words were the problem. Brother Marcus knew what he meant by the 'dark night of the soul', but was not aware that they had never heard the term before. We were talking at cross purposes.

'But we can know God,' someone said indignantly.

'Yes,' I reassured them, 'but that's not what Brother Marcus is saying. Look, when Paul died, how did we all feel?'

The silence that followed was oppressive. I knew I was taking a risk. Paul's death had become a bit of a taboo subject which no one wanted to discuss. But at some point we would have to face it and then seemed as right a moment as any. No one spoke for ages. Everyone stared at the ground, as if it might suddenly split open and spare them this ordeal.

Eventually Rick said quietly, 'Well, I can only speak for myself, but I think I was confused at first. Then it seemed to me I had been trying to push God into a box and he just wouldn't fit. He was far too big.'

We talked for a while, but it was hard and difficult. Several people kept trying to close the subject by saying, 'We're being negative', or 'We're being morbid', but instinct told them that we have to persevere, and not just shove our bad feelings into a drawer, because they were too untidy to have on view.

'I realise,' Brother Marcus said gently, 'that this is a very painful area for you all.'

Everyone went on staring at their feet.

'So I'll say goodnight and leave you to continue. But I see that you do know what I've been talking about.'

By Saturday morning spirits had risen and we all worked very hard in our workshops. Here and there, in ones and twos, the debate from the night before continued. Brother Christopher felt that that evening's entertainment should be a little lighter and suggested a party. Grimlington people have the capacity to turn just about any occasion into a knees-up, but given the invitation, the result was bedlam. One by one the Brothers poked their heads around the door to see what the noise was all about. They were either dragged in or disappeared fast. Two people arrived with suitcases for a silent retreat, and I felt sorry for them. It would have been quieter at the Wilton Ballroom. They stared in disbelief as Brother Christopher whizzed round in an Israeli dance at a great speed, faster and faster, habit flying, until the music ended and everyone fell on the floor in an exhausted, hysterical heap.

We tiptoed late to bed and it was a shock to be woken at seven by a Brother with a bell. As he passed down the corridor one or two people managed to stagger to their doors to grin or wave at him, and he responded with a friendly smile. It took us all our time to stop Paula saying, ' 'Ey up, chuck,' to every Brother she met in the corridors.

The Eucharist was the highlight of the weekend. We had all prepared for it in our workshops and were ready to make it a festive occasion. The Music Group had added to their setting of the Communion service. The Dance workshop had prepared the Gloria and the Lord's Prayer. The Drama Group had interpreted the reading instead of a sermon.

Frank and Marjorie had driven over from Grimlington and were waiting for us in the chapel. Betty was already with us. She could not resist a weekend away and had temporarily joined the Drama Group to justify her coming. As I walked past Frank into the chapel he was grinning from ear to ear and whispered to me loudly, 'Betty doing drama! This I have to see!'

One or two of the Brothers, their visitors and some of the students joined us too. It was an unusual service, to say the least, and we were sad when it came to an end. The Music Group went on playing in an attempt to prolong it a little. Brother Nigel, who had officiated for us and disappeared, suddenly reappeared without his alb and waltzed into the centre of the chapel, hands held high above his head. He danced on his own for some time. Then he held out a hand to Linda, who looked around for advice, and receiving none, shrugged as if to say 'I can't be rude', and got up to join him. One by one everyone got to their feet, including the Brothers and students, and were leaping, jogging and swaying. One of the students did a Cossack dance, or it might have been a 'cassock dance', as, cassock flying, he could have outdanced any Russian. We encouraged him, clapping and cheering. It was a marvellous feeling to let go of every inhibition for once and worship with our bodies as well as our voices. No one was watching. Everyone was too caught up in the joy of the occasion.

'Hey kid,' Betty called out to me as she wafted past, arms outstretched, 'I've always felt I wanted to do this, but never dared.'

I looked round to see Frank's reaction, but he could hardly disapprove, swaying round the altar as he was.

'Do you do this every week?' Brother Nigel asked, when the music finally stopped and we were all lying on the pews panting.

We shrieked with laughter.

'It was you who started it, mate! We'd like to occasionally, but we haven't, not since the Gift Day.'

I suspected the Brothers were not too sad to see us go, though some special friendships were made. Kelly was thrilled with a South African Bishop, who, when she asked him where he had come from, said, 'prison'. He had refused to inform on the flock. Paula could not get over his having a toilet all to himself. 'Reserved for Bishop' said the sign over the door.

'Where do all your wives live?' someone asked at tea one day.

Brother Marcus guffawed, then realised it was a serious question. 'We're celibate,' he said.

'But the children at the services!'

'They belong to the students at the theological college here.'

A whole new world had been opened up to us. We shook hands with the Brothers. Some allowed themselves to be hugged.

'You must all come again,' they said, smiling and we knew it was more than just a formality.

'We'll come next week,' Linda said, teasing them as she climbed into the back of the car.

They raised their hands in mock despair.

'One of them asked me at tea if we were evan . . ., evange . . ., what's the word?' Jan asked as she got in next to Linda.

'Evangelicals?' I suggested.

'That's it. Well are we whatever it is?'

I hesitated, juggling a while with my seatbelt, aware that how I answered could destroy for ever a certain precious innocence.

Linda came to my rescue.

'Does it matter?' she said, waving madly. 'All I know is that I like them such a lot.'

We drove home exhilarated, yet pensive too. In the final session we had discussed how hard it was that a few traditional church members still resented and rejected our creative efforts. The Music

Group found it hardest. Most of the hostility to change was directed at them and it could be difficult to sing to such stony faces.

'Then here's your chance to love,' said Brother Marcus. 'Don't patronise them or try to force them to change. The world does that, but it isn't the way of Christ. Look and see what they have to offer and learn to receive from them.'

Once we were home and back into the normal, daily routine, the exhilaration wore off. But Brother Marcus' cutting words, with their challenge to love where we were hurt, lingered and stayed in our minds long after.

22

We moved, but it was not without a certain wistfulness and sense of defeat that we left the estate behind for the centre of the town.

'I used to come down back of this street when I were a kid,' Lucy told me, stopping to reminisce as she helped me unpack. 'It were regarded as posh part of town because the 'ouses were so big and pit bankers and the like lived here. We used to come and hunt in dustbins round back because yer could find some real fancy stuff. One day, I must 'ave been about eight, we found a box, lined with white satin, a canteen without the cutlery. We thought it were beautiful, real treasure. We played with it for hours.'

The houses were no longer quite as upmarket. In fact Joel discovered the first day he went out to play that it was a good deal rougher than the estate. Some child grabbed him by the throat and that had never happened before.

Lucy was not the only one who came to help. Church funds were becoming precarious, so what work on the house we could do ourselves, we did. Lots of people joined in, working day after day and night after night, sometimes into the small hours. Lucy and Betty cleared away mounds of rubble and plaster and mopped the floors with such vigour that the water poured down the staircase. Chris cut out hardboard to cover the splintering floorboards, Joe did whatever he was asked, Alicia performed miracles with a screwdriver and Jack used all his creative skills to assemble the kitchen.

'Where is he?' Madge shouted down the phone in the small hours of one morning.

He looked at the clock, then at us, chuckled as he put on his coat and cap and disappeared quickly down the road.

I felt so grateful to the wives who gave up their husbands for all that time. Some came between shifts or just popped home to eat, or they came all day on a day off or if they were on strike. Nothing seemed too much to ask. The house often rang with laughter. It was a good start to a new home.

By the time another autumn crept up on us, we felt more settled than we had felt for a long time. There had been three moves in as many years and it had taken its emotional toll. I longed to put my roots down deep. I began to appreciate why the miners resisted being moved about. To have a mobile workforce might be economically advantageous for a nation, but people's emotional well-being was surely more important. In Yorkshire there was no tradition of mobility. They were not used to the trauma of it, to the effort required in making new relationships. It was a terrifying prospect. They could see that temporary relation-ships were superficial, compared to those they had now. Their one wish was to live and die where they had been born, where they knew everyone, and parents, brothers, sisters and cousins were just up the road. Was it so much to ask? After all, it meant that the community was almost self-sufficient. It halved the load on the Social Services. People cared for their elderly and infirm and their handicapped children at home, because of the inbuilt support system. But move the men, take the props away, and the community and all it stood for would collapse like a pack of cards.

Nancy was tiny. The bones in her legs were brittle and had to have a series of major operations, which put her in a wheelchair for several weeks at a time. Because her sisters were nearby there was no need for her children to be taken into care.

'We did try going to Selby once, like they said. The pay was much better, but I couldn't stand it. I cried for me mum and me sisters every day. We came back after six months. Just as well. What would I 'ave done up there without me family and friends when I went into 'ospital?'

The Coal Board had been moving men around the pits for some time. It was always a hard uprooting. A year or so later they would close that pit too, and tell the men to move again. It caused a great deal of bitterness. No one trusted the Coal Board's offers of alternative employment with high financial remuneration any more. All the money in the world could not replace a man's roots.

It seemed to me that there was a natural wisdom about living in a close-knit community, sharing one's life and resources. Though the world tries to deny it, a man is his brother's keeper. My Jewish upbringing taught me that. A Jew may not feel love towards his brother, he may not even like him, but he knows his duty. Birth and identity bring responsibility. With the world against us, in joy and in sorrow, we must stick together, they say. Self-preservation requires it.

The miners said the same. And their freedom to choose that way of life was under threat. Men and women who had never experienced communal commitment of that kind could never understand the strike.

'If they don't agree with the strike, let them go back to work,' friends from a distance said to us.

'You don't understand, they can't,' we replied.

'They're just frightened of intimidation.'

Afraid of intimidation, yes, who was not? But more afraid that once the sense of corporate identity began to crumble, there would be no end to it, until nothing was left of an existence that dated back over a hundred and fifty years. Whether they agreed with the strike or not, miners had stuck together in famine and plenty from the beginning of the nineteenth century.

But sadly, few are left in Britain today with any sense of history or community. The unidentifiable masses live in vast anonymous cities, in ribbon developments, alienated from their neighbours, fiercely self-reliant, enclosed in the nuclear family and trapped within their own privacy. And yet they believe they are more advanced than the Grimlingtons of this world. But how is progress measured? Who knows? In fact such people are blissfully unaware of the poverty of their own lives and do not know that there is a better way to live, for if they did, they would not condemn Grimlington to destruction and its inhabitants to the same lonely, anonymous kind of existence.

The wonders of economics were a mystery to me. I could not understand all the arguments for or against pit closures. But one thing was obvious. With a new industrial estate at the bottom of the town, with our location at the junction of three major motorways and London only two hours away by train, if the pits had to close there was no reason why money should not be invested in many alternative industries in the area. After all, countryside which must have once approached the Dales and the

Moors in loveliness was already a treeless wasteland. There was nothing to lose. The train journey to Leeds revealed mile upon mile of bleak, barren landscape, churned and charred, spattered with bricks and rubble, pieces of broken-down fencing and tattered barbed wiring. There was little hope of reafforestation. This was not Sussex or Surrey. No voice of protest would be raised. New industry was therefore sensible and essential. But who cared enough about the North? The 'oppressor', he who would rob us of our jobs and our homes, and leave us with nothing, was seen as a faceless, mindless man from the South, the successor to the landowner, the pit owner, and every other lord and master, who had owned men, patronised them, treated them as cattle and left them to starve in the great depressions.

Temporarily the oppressor acquired a face. Since there was no one else to be the butt of so much anger and bitterness, since he represented Coal Board and Government, was a foreigner who had no understanding of miners and their ways, Mr McGregor would do. The fact that Mr McGregor was also the name of the nasty farmer who chased poor Peter Rabbit for pinching his radishes meant that Joel's familiar bedtime story took on new meaning altogether.

My heart ached for the town as it fought for its life, bruised, battered, weary and confused. McGregor said one thing, Scargill another. They stood in the middle, uncertain whom to believe. There was no trust. The Coal Board had always let them down; managers could be hard, vindictive and impersonal, and had not cared for their workforce. Yet did the Union leaders really care? Would a strike achieve anything? They were helpless, pulled one way by old loyalties and another by hunger. They were pawns on a chess-board in a great political game of power and most of them knew it.

But few families could bear the stigma of 'scab'. Some streets were still known as 'Scab Alley', fifty years after a strike. There was no greater shame to pass on to your children. It was the worst possible betrayal. I suppose it was a bit like the way the Jewish community felt about my becoming a Christian.

Perhaps there was a chance that a strike might work. After all it had always been their only effective weapon against exploitation. If a man had no other control over his destiny, he could at least withhold his labour, and it gave him some sense of his own worth and dignity. This time he was not asking for more money. All he wanted was a job, his home, family, community and future. If there was the slightest chance that a strike could preserve all those, then it was worth any price he might have to pay to achieve it.

Autumn seemed to reflect the mood of the town. It was sad and wistful, with more than its usual hint of farewell to the halcyon days of summer. An insipid, watery sun gave out little warmth and as I walked the children to school through the cemetery, our extremities were frozen before we were half-way there. The bleak and icy prospect of winter was not far away. Families would soon need coal and there was none to be had and no money to afford an alternative. I shivered at the prospect.

The path through the cemetery was the nearest thing in the town to a woodland glade. It was bordered on either side by a few spindly ash and cherry trees. Few people dared walk there alone at night. With its dim yellow lighting and long wispy shadows it looked like a Hollywood set for a Dracula movie and there were rumours of glue-sniffing and other strange goings-on. But by day, if I closed my eyes to the gravestones and piles of litter stacked against the walls, I could almost imagine I was miles from civilisation. The tips of the leaves had turned russet and gold and the effect was quite picturesque.

Then Peter discovered that most of the trees would have to come down. They had Dutch Elm disease. I grieved for my 'woodland glade'. It was hardly beautiful, but I was learning to take beauty where I found it. And there was something infinitely precious about a poor, single tree, which had stood resolute through the years, defying vandalism, pollution, development and industrialisation. Each tree became a kind of symbol to me of the unchanging, undefeated glory of God and all he made, despite man's worst. Autumn always made me a little sad anyway. I hate goodbyes of every kind.

Harvest festival was chaotic. Children juggled their oranges, rolled down the aisle over melons and marrows, munched their way through bananas and got a slap for eating the offering. Despite the strike there was an amazing display of harvest gifts. Why was I surprised? I already knew that people would give away their last potato.

Frank, who had recently become churchwarden, along with

Tom, who was doing hours of picket duty, eyed two large boxes of potatoes.

'At least this lot's ready,' he said.

I looked at him quizzically.

'I thought everyone in the town knew. Someone down at the allotments harvested all their potatoes too soon. He left 'em in a mound to rot, but when 'e came back next day, they'd gone. They think some miners must have taken them. They're getting pretty desperate. They've asked around, but no one admits to it. You see, the thing is, if they eat them, they'll poison themselves, poor souls.'

Frank shook his head, then he laughed. 'Eeeh, but I don't know how they got in. So much fruit and veg vanishes that the allotments look like Colditz. I can hardly get in meself and I've got a key!'

'Where there's a will, there's a way,' said our police sergeant with the full weight of experience behind him.

Alicia had the unenviable job of sorting the harvest gifts into parcels and commandeering the workforce who turned up on Monday morning to deliver them. The clergy phones had been ringing all week.

'You will give to the miners, won't you? They're starving and they've always given to the church.'

'You won't give anything to the miners, will you? My business has had to close because of them.'

On the whole community spirit prevailed and the distribution of the parcels was left to Alicia's discretion. She had started a church food cupboard years ago, keeping it well stocked with tins and giving them away when she knew someone was in need. Several church families had had cause to bless her in difficult days. But by the time that harvest came, the shelves were bare. She had been delivering food parcels and seeing to the needs of the various families affected by the strike, especially those connected with the church, for some time.

'I did encourage people to give tins this year,' she said. 'You see we can store tins and give them out as they're needed.'

But there were still relatively few and she rang Mr Mason, the greengrocer, and ordered tins of steak, mince, pease pudding, baked beans and whatever else was cheap and nourishing. I gathered from their discussion that he was quite used to an order of this kind from Alicia.

After much sorting, packing, repacking and debate about what an aubergine was and what you could do with it, and whether green peppers would go down well at the Old Folks' Home, twenty or so volunteers set off on their errands of mercy. Linda arrived back with her parcel half an hour later.

'I knocked and knocked for ages,' she said, 'but no one came to the door. Then a face appeared at the window of the next house. "She's not 'ere, love," the neighbour shouted. "She's in Ossleforth General 'aving 'er legs off." '

Linda laughed nervously, but she was as green as the peppers in her parcel. 'It sounded as easy as 'aving her teeth out,' she said. 'I wonder why it's getting so common to lose bits of yer anatomy these days!' With an uneasy smile, she set off with a new address.

As the helpers came back for more parcels the story was always the same. Many of the regular recipients complained as usual that there was not enough, they didn't eat bananas, they would have rather had something else. But mining families were grateful for the tiniest offering. Everyone who went to a miner's house came back very moved. Lucy went to Ginny's and Ginny almost broke down when she opened the door.

'I can't believe it,' she said, 'it's a gift straight from heaven. Yer timing's incredible. We only 'ad so much money left and it were food or coal. Well the baby 'as bronchitis, so it 'ad to be coal, didn't it? I didn't know what we were going to eat.'

Ginny had been coming to 'Mums and Babes' a few weeks. I noticed her straight away. She always sat with her hands in her pockets, swinging on her chair, with an amused nonchalance which could not hide her interest in every word that was said. She had a ruthless honesty and a determination I admired to settle only for the truth. No platitude was going to satisfy someone with that kind of perception.

'I nearly died of cancer a few years ago,' she told me. 'I was engaged to Doug at the time. You're never the same after that. I don't regret it. It alters the whole way yer see things.'

I told Peter about her. I found her abrasive dismissal of all dishonesty a challenge.

'What did you say her name was? Where does she live?'

'Right opposite the parish hall.'

Peter threw back his head and laughed. I watched him, bewildered.

'Well, well,' he said, 'come to think of it. I thought it was her I saw in church the other day, but I told myself I was seeing things. Don't you know how I know them?'

I shook my head.

'A certain baptismal visit?' he prompted.

Suddenly it clicked into place. Ginny had talked about wanting the children baptised. They were a special gift to her. She was told that with so much of her insides missing she would not have any.

'The most belligerent pair you had ever met?' I asked.

Peter nodded and laughed again.

'Well, I think it's time I visited them again.'

He did, and again, until popping in on Doug and Ginny was such a regular occurrence that I always knew where he was if there was no sign of him at midnight.

Doug hated receiving the parcel from the church. His bulky frame and tough exterior were just a front for the more sensitive character inside.

'We're not reduced to taking charity, y'know, Ginny.'

'I know, love,' she said, 'but yer've got to admit the timing's right. Can't we accept it this time, for the kids?'

'Ay, well, this once,' he said reluctantly, then he grinned a broader grin than she had seen on his face since the strike began.

'What's up with you?' she asked him, surprised.

'I'm just thinking, it is nice to know that someone cares.'

23

'There's smoke coming out of boiler. I don't suppose it's serious, but he ought to know.'

'Thanks for ringing. I'll tell him,' I said wearily.

'Peter!' I called out into the hallway.

He was half-way out of the front door, with a long list of visits he had been intending to do for ages.

'Boiler's on the blink, again! There's smoke coming out of it, this time.'

'There always is these days,' he called back, unimpressed, and sighed.

'Why must things always take up more time than people?'

'Perhaps because you have a way with things you don't have with people!' I said, smiling at him sweetly.

He acknowledged my sarcasm with a snort.

Peter's reputation as a do-it-yourself, mend-anything whizz kid had quickly spread through the parish. One week he walked in from his home Communions with an alarm clock and two vacuum cleaners. All kinds of parish repairs, unmendables, broken appliances and other bric-a-brac began to gravitate in our direction and since I refused to have them anywhere else they ended up in a great heap in the middle of Peter's study. I could always tell when sermon preparation lacked inspiration by the whirring or tinkering sound which escaped from behind the closed study door.

As he visited round the parish, doors which had never shut properly before, shut for the first time. Lights which had not worked for ages lit at his touch. Drains unblocked and boilers staggered into action. There was no way we could gauge his pastoral effectiveness, but as a handyman he was past master. Twice the phone rang calling him out on matters of the greatest urgency. Had a marriage broken down? No, it was the central heating. Still, it was all part of a clergyman's day.

'You know,' I said to him, 'if you had the same effect on people as you had on things you'd be the Archbishop of Canterbury in a year or two.'

'Thanks!' he said. 'I'd better go and have a look at the boiler, I suppose. I might as well go to the parish hall first.' He sighed and the door slammed.

It was as well he did. By the time he arrived, black smoke was pouring out of the building. An excited gang of Scouts were standing outside, laughing and shouting.

'Who's called the Fire Brigade?' Peter shouted. As he approached the doors he saw the flames leaping under the floorboards.

There was no reply. He ran for all he was worth up the vicarage drive past Anna, who had been summoned to the scene, and dialled 999.

Grimlington's part-time fire brigade arrived swiftly, but it look them some time to get the blaze under control.

'Why did no one phone them earlier?' Peter asked. Sparks from the boiler had ignited litter left under the floorboards when the hall was modernised. The fire had been smouldering for some time.

'The boiler's been blowing smoke signals at us for so many months that no one realised what was happening.'

Peter sadly acknowledged the truth of it. He went inside and stood for some time assessing the damage.

'We're insured, aren't we?' Anna said.

Peter nodded.

'But insurance never covers everything,' he said slowly, looking round at the damp, charred building. 'And the inconvenience! This place will be out of action for ages. No playgroup or toddler club. And we've just had it decorated after dealing with the damp.'

'Buildings!' he muttered to himself through gritted teeth, 'Buildings and boilers! They're nothing but weight round our necks. A drain of time, manpower and resources. Why don't we just get rid of the lot of them and hire a hall or meet in people's homes?'

He was in no mood for his visits. There was only one place to go. He saw the light in the window of the house opposite and found his feet carrying him across the road.

'By, yer've 'ad some trouble tonight though,' Doug said, as he opened the door and saw the dejected form on his doorstep. 'Come in. Get theesel' warmed up and 'ave a cuppa.'

'It's all that money I mind most,' Peter said, the feeling coming back into his hands as he clasped a mug of tea. 'There are so many other needs at the moment.'

'Ay, well, that's life,' Doug said, settling himself heavily in his favourite armchair. 'I shouldn't worry theesel' too much about money. It comes and it goes.'

Peter smiled.

'You're quite a philosopher in your own way.'

'Well, 'ow I see it is this. I've 'ad weeks when there's been plenty and weeks when there's been nowt. When I've got it, I spend it and when I 'aven't, I do without. Yer 'ave to tek what comes. No use worrying about it.'

'But isn't it hard to be without? I thought miners had quite a good wage.'

'Face-workers do, ay. That's why it's hit 'em hardest now. But not us surface workers. We're lucky to take home ninety pounds a week. But Ginny and I don't complain. We've never starved.'

'We nearly did last week,' Ginny said, with a child under each arm, as she came into the room. 'If God hadn't looked after us and sent us a parcel at right time.'

Doug grinned at her sheepishly.

'She'll not let me forget, will she?'

Peter got up.

'I have to go. The wires under the floor might still be smouldering and the fire brigade says they must be checked every hour through the night.'

'Listen, mate,' Doug said, following him to the door, 'I'm no great sleeper. I'm up with kids every hour or two through the night. I've no work in the morning. So get to bed and I'll keep an eye on parish hall.'

Peter's relief was beyond measure. He could have hugged Doug, but taking another look at his large form, he changed his mind. Doug would think him altogether soft in the head.

It was a Communion service. I looked up during the administration of the bread and wine and realised that at the altar rail, in a row, were miners who were on strike, some who had left the pit in disgust and found other work, Tom, weary with hours of picket duty and Sid, whose fish and chip shop was only just surviving. Such is Yorkshire integrity that I knew that if there had been so much as an ounce of hostility among them, they would not be kneeling there, shoulder to shoulder, waiting to take Communion together.

'Sid, did you realise you were kneeling next to striking miners at the altar rail?' I asked him out of curiosity after the service.

'Was I? It makes no difference to me, not here.'

'There seems no resentment among you.'

'Resentment?' he laughed ruefully. 'This time last year I'd 'ave killed 'em, ruining me business like that. That shows yer 'ow much I've changed. These are me brothers. How can I 'ate them?'

'What are you going to do, Sid? What will you live on?'

'Don't you worry, lass,' he said, patting me on the shoulder. 'Someone's looking after me. I've managed to get a job on a building site for now, so I'll labour by day and fry by night.'

'You'll be shattered.'

'I'm not afraid of hard work. And I'll take Wednesday evenings off so's I can come to the fellowship.'

I marvelled at the spirit of mutual support which seemed to grow daily within the church. Neighbouring towns became frustrated and aggressive, with increasing outbursts of violence. A handful of men from Grimlington went back to work, and the town began to despair. As a Christian community, sharing all we had became a necessity. We learnt to throw nothing away, nor hang on to what was no longer useful. Someone, somewhere, needed it. We sometimes felt we had been given a special chance, which few churches are given, to see how much of our love was real, and how much the sentimental sham Brother Marcus had spoken of.

'Christians should never strike,' a well-meaning woman said to me at a meeting in Sussex.

She had never met a miner, never been to West Yorkshire. Would that life were always that easy, that right and wrong were emblazoned in the sky in illuminated letters. A law for every occasion, so that we would no longer need to think for ourselves.

The freedom God gave human beings was a heavy burden to bear. Life would have been easier if we were puppets, so that all the divinity needed to do was pull the strings, but it would never have been so rich and colourful. We would never have wrestled, struggled or prayed.

In the midst of this crisis, one thing was clear. Politics were irrelevant. We could not stand by and watch our brothers starve. As we dashed up to Newcastle on days off and I sat by my father's bed, watching his slow deterioration, I remembered words he had so often spoken when I was a teenager.

'Principles are very important, but people must always come first. When that isn't so, fanatics are born, and fanatics are dangerous. They are without mercy. Politicians and religious people are always the worst offenders.'

Dear Dad, he would never have understood the strike, but I discovered the wisdom of his words over and over again. Perhaps Christ was saying exactly the same thing when they dragged over to him the woman caught in the act of adultery: 'Let him who is without sin cast the first stone.' Principles that never bend for people give a false sense of security and self-righteousness.

We stopped worrying about the church budget, vital repairs, the redecoration of the parish hall and we fed and clothed whoever needed it. And the demand grew with each successive day. Peter encouraged our striking miners who were tempted to go back to work to stay at home. The repercussions for themselves and their families were too enormous. Every day an armoured police van drew up outside the church and under police guard the handful of working miners got out and ran the gauntlet into the cemetery through a jeering crowd. Grimlington had experienced nothing like it.

One Wednesday evening, Barbara broke down in the mid-week meeting and began to sob.

'Let her have a good cry,' Peter said. He could see she was in some distress and three or four pairs of arms were about to smother her. The sobs continued for some time, then gradually subsided.

Eventually she managed to say, 'It's my brother. He went back to work on Monday and yesterday his house and car were smashed to pieces.'

She broke down again and several others began to cry too,

either in sympathy or because the strain of the last few months had suddenly become too much to endure alone.

'It's not that property matters,' Barbara said, 'it's that the kids are so frightened. They don't understand what's happening.'

'Neither do I,' Ginny said, 'the world's gone mad.'

Peter made no attempt to call the meeting to order and the crying continued. The wives in particular had had months of hiding their feelings, of coping, of being strong for their husbands and children. Someone had to be brave and keep the home going, find food to put on the table, even though their nerves were taut and their spirits almost broken by the shame of begging and buying rubbish from the butcher's and greengrocer's. Instinctively Ginny, Mavis and Barbara moved together and stood with their arms round each other, swaying slightly and wiping their tears away.

It seemed somehow right and natural and no one interrupted them. The meeting continued. Gradually the tears stopped, they blew their noses, wiped their eyes again and went back to their places, not before Ginny had remembered to go over and give Sid a big hug. It was a kind of apology and he acknowledged it with a wink.

None of the wives had any time for self-pity. It was not in their nature. Once the tears were out of the way, that was that. Life must go on. Support was plentiful, but sympathy was limited and ran out fast. Almost everyone had had some hardship to contend with. That was life. It made them tough and resilient. But the wives at the church not only coped. They began to see the strike in quite a positive way.

Mavis, who came to help Peter with some typing to supplement their income, said, 'If you'd told me this time last year that we'd have gone all these months without a wage coming in, and I'd still cope, I'd have laughed at you.'

She reluctantly accepted the coffee I put into her hands. She was a shy, gentle person and her husband Ron was not really in sympathy with the Union. They lived a quiet life, enjoying evenings in with their records, and I could imagine how much the disruption to their peaceful routine must have upset them.

'The hardest thing I find,' Mavis said, 'is that you feel that everyone else outside the community is against you. I mean, the newspapers and TV make the miners look awful. We're all condemned without a hearing. They don't seem to understand we've no choice. Of course Ron wants to go back. We're ashamed of the pickets. We're ashamed of all the violence. We're a bit ashamed of ourselves for not having the courage, but what would anyone else do? How can we put the children at risk or have them live with their dad being called a scab?'

I nodded and she went on sipping her coffee, thoughtfully. After a while she said, 'Do you know, the Union rang the other day about some fire-fighting Ron was doing, with their consent, to keep the pit safe. Well, when they said who it was, my legs turned to jelly. Daft, isn't it? But that's my trouble, I'm a born worrier.'

She put the mug down on the table and was about to go back to the typewriter, when she turned suddenly.

'But d'you know, I think these last months are teaching me to stop worrying. Ron and I never realised how much material things had come to matter to us, the house and things like that. You don't, not until you have to do without. I've been thinking about Joe and Linda, watching them give to miners' families. He was unemployed all that time and we did nothing for them. We just didn't understand. We'll never forget though.'

She paused for a moment, then her face suddenly lit up. 'The funny thing is that now we've nothing, we've never been so rich. We get what we need as we need it. I've been down to my last tin and something always turns up. We don't take basics like food for granted any more. So,' she said as she stood smiling in the doorway, 'maybe this strike hasn't been all bad. You always ask yourself whether your faith is real or just a delusion, at least, I do, or I did. You wonder whether it's strong enough to survive a real crisis. Well, I don't regret the chance to find out.'

Nancy's attitude was almost the same. She had had yet another leg operation when I went round to see her and was sitting in her wheelchair, running her home with her leg stretched out in a plaster cast in front of her. She and her three girls were all huddled round a coal fire, the only one in the house.

'These girls,' she said, 'had no coats for the winter, so what was I going to do? I couldn't send them to school with no coats. Someone from church offered to buy 'em one each. That made me feel worse, because she'd no money either. I didn't know what to do, and I thought, "God's supposed to take care of the sparrows, so what about my girls?" The next day there were a knock at the door. It were Dorothy. Now this is honest truth, what do yer think she 'ad in 'er 'ands? Three coats what 'er kids 'ad just grown out of! "Are these any good to yer?" she said. Any good! Each one fitted one of my girls perfectly, as if they were made for 'em. Now yer can't tell me that were coincidence. I wouldn't believe yer anyway. It's been like that all through strike. Our Alf can't get over the way people have given to us without expecting anything back. It's changed 'is whole attitude to church. Maybe we 'ad to 'ave a strike to learn to give and receive.'

It was the week I saw Nancy that the news of the famine in Ethiopia broke. It put Grimlington's plight into a strange new perspective. One after another mining families urged us to bring them no more food parcels, but to send the money to Ethiopia instead.

'At least we've enough for bread and potatoes with the occasional sausage,' Ginny said. 'I can't sit and watch that screen and do nowt. If I could adopt some Ethiopian kids I would. We 'aven't got much in the way of food, but it's more than they 'ave. And yer can starve much quicker without love, than yer can without food. If I've learnt anything these months it's that.'

'And that,' I thought, 'is more than most of us learn in a lifetime!'

24

In October my father died. Initially I felt an enormous sense of relief. I could hardly bear to watch his slow disintegration any longer and nor could my mother. Why should such a fine, intelligent man have to spend the end of his days weak, helpless and totally dependent on others? The standard of nursing at the small cottage hospital just outside of Newcastle helped us all to cope. To the end they ensured he was treated with great dignity and respect.

My mother, brother, sister and Peter and I were with him most of the time. I was glad we were able to say goodbye and tell him how much we loved him and what a wonderful father he had been. He need have no cause for regret. Although he was in a coma, his eyelids flickered in response to our voices and we knew he could hear and understand. In a strange way, although one was a sad farewell, and the other a joyful welcome, I felt there were similarities between this moment and Joel's birth. I felt the same awe, the same sense of wonder at being face to face with infinity, the mystery which lies beyond man's limited perception. My father had never feared the moment of death and he went as gently and peacefully as he had lived.

It was later, when the initial relief and numbness wore off a little, that I realised how bereft I was. I had cried so much over the last months and behaved so irrationally at times that I supposed I had done much of my grieving already. But now I became aware of an aching void which no one would ever fill again.

'You know you need never worry about anything,' he would say to me, despite my not making his ideal marriage, despite everything, 'I'll always be there when you need me.'

But it wasn't true. I still needed him and he was no longer there.

I felt angry he had left me, though it was no fault of his, angry with God for the few paltry years we were allowed, and angry with the ageing process, both my father's and mine! There was no one left to shield me from my own mortality. As the older generation died, and my children grew, I was slowly and inevitably becoming the older generation. I had already lived half a lifetime and accomplished so little. The only comfort was the certainty that my human perspective was inadequate, that probably, once we knew what lay beyond the horizon, we would not say, 'Why did you only give me threescore years and ten?' but, 'why did you leave me down there so long?'

For the seven official days of mourning known as 'Shiva', I stayed with David and Sandy, my brother and sister-in-law. As well as the sadness, there was much laughter in the house too. My father would have enjoyed that. He was not a morbid man. As close family, we were not allowed to cook at a time of bereavement, according to Jewish law, so we waited to see what would arrive at our door and watched in wonder as Sandy's freezer filled from top to bottom. There were chickens, fresh salmon, apple pies and luscious cakes. They so whetted our appetites that David said he had not eaten so well since he got married, and from the look on Sandy's face, I doubted he would eat as well again! We had no heart to shop or cook and were glad it was forbidden anyway. But at the end of a hectic day, with constant visitors and phone calls, it was bliss to sit down and know the food was there and ready. In the Jewish community food is the cure for all that ails you, and in this instance, it certainly helped.

It seemed to me that the way the Jewish community coped with bereavement was wiser and more wholesome than any so-called Christian approach. For one thing it was practical, rather than sentimental. Perhaps the problem was that, apart from sending cards and flowers, Christians have no tradition of how to comfort the bereaved. They feel lost and embarrassed because there are no guidelines, no obvious thing to say or do. It is much easier to visit with a tureen of chicken soup, or a bowl of chopped liver in your hand.

A loss in the Jewish community is not just personal, the whole community feels it. Day after day friends of Sandy's came to take our children out. My mother held court and people came to sit, laugh, cry and remember. They came to join in the prayers every evening, the women in one room, clustered around my mother and me, who sat on low stools, and the men in the next room, reciting 'Kaddish'. The rabbi was present every evening too. And I thought Peter worked hard! But then my mother could not get over the fact that Peter was not invited to the parties after the weddings and funerals at which he officiated. As an Anglican priest he was a functionary, not a focal point in the community.

We awoke every morning to the sound of the memorial prayers again. An act of worship requires the presence of ten men. The rabbi would be leading morning prayer at the synagogue. So David had to rely on ten of his friends and relatives coming to pray before they went to work.

Many non-Jewish friends came to the house too. In fact there were so many at the funeral that the rabbi resorted to reading half the service in English. There were representatives from every organisation my father had served in some way. The St John Ambulance Brigade wanted to lay their cross on his coffin as a sign of respect. We appreciated the thought and Dad would have loved it, but the rabbi said it was not possible.

There were no flowers at the cemetery. There never are at Jewish funerals, but the house was full of them, sent by non-Jewish friends. Sandy worried about what to do with them at first. The rabbi said that there was no law, it was simply a tradition, so we relaxed and enjoyed them. We were all quite puzzled about what the laws actually were and what was just tradition. David wanted to be right so he asked the rabbi endless questions, and in the end was given a booklet so he could look the answers up for himself. Many were sensible and healing, designed to give a mourner space and time, others seemed a bit irrelevant. I was amused. My father had paid scant attention to the written laws himself. His only law had been his conscience, and that he had lived up to it to the best of his ability was evident from the number and variety of people who came to pay their respects.

The rabbi quite obviously found my presence a bit of an embarrassment. After all he could not be seen to condone what I had done, but nor could he slight the bereaved. He was reserved, yet always gracious. I wondered how Sandy felt too. I knew that 'marrying out' and to a clergyman of all people was an affront to her orthodoxy, but she had never said so and always welcomed me lovingly into her home. We sat up late night after night, enjoying the stillness of the small hours and getting to know each other for the first time. The situation drew us together in a new way. We talked for hours, so much so that when I left to go home, I felt that though I had lost a father, I had found a sister.

Peter had brought me many loving letters and cards from Grimlington, but going back was like coming out of hibernation. With a jolt I was catapulted from my safe, quiet cocoon to a world that was weary and wounded. I went into the kitchen, walked over to the window and looked out at the now familiar sight of the pit head wheels in the distance, unnaturally still and motionless. Something was different.

'Peter,' I called, 'was it my imagination, or did the Council put up a brand new fence around the field at the back a few weeks ago?'

He came up behind me, looked over my shoulder and nodded.

'Thank goodness for that. I thought I must have been hallucinating. Where is it?'

He grinned. 'Every morning when I got up, a little bit more had disappeared. I expect it makes very good firewood!'

I had to laugh.

'Ah well, it was only a fence after all.'

I had managed to push the strike out of my mind for a fortnight, but Grimlington could not forget, not for a moment.

'When it's over . . .' were the opening words of every sentence, as if saying it often enough would convince people that some day life would return to a measure of normality.

But the fact was, it was beginning to seem a never-ending nightmare. Grandparents were sharing their pensions. Retirement savings had long since gone. That little 'nest-egg', a little something put by for the future, had evaporated into the air. No more plans were made, no dreams were dreamed. Life was temporarily suspended and we lived a strange kind of limbo existence.

Jan finally announced that she and her husband were getting divorced. The gulf between them which he said the church created had grown too wide. But there was no chance of a separation until their house sold. And houses were not selling during the strike.

Then, with the worst possible timing, both the DHSS and the binmen went on strike too. According to Linda, the binmen's strike was something to do with a black scab, but whether that was one of the men, or something one of them found crawling out of a dustbin, no one was sure. The dispute started over their refusal to use the black bin liners the Council were now supplying and it continued for weeks. Dustbin bags full of stinking rubbish were thrown into the streets or left in mounds on the street corners. The cats and dogs tore them open and their filth spilt out onto the pavements. Despite the threat of vermin, the Council did nothing. Grimlington once again slipped through the bureaucratic net. A strange stomach virus broke out, and some people, already weakened by a poor diet, were quite badly affected.

The DHSS strike compounded the general hardship and caused chaos. Since I tried to postpone collecting my Child Benefit until I had saved enough to make it feel worthwhile, I was totally oblivious to the problem for some weeks. On a chill November day, when I had just about recovered from the nasty tummy bug, I crawled round to the Post Office, feeling wobbly and washed-out. To my horror the queue went out of the door and half-way up the street. With a sinking heart I joined the weary pensioners and frazzled mums who were trying to keep their bored toddlers off the street and away from the traffic. It began to rain. We huddled against the wall, vainly trying to keep warm and dry.

'They've closed all the blinking sub-Post Offices,' an elderly woman complained. 'I've had to walk nearly a mile from the bottom of the town to get here.'

My turn came at last.

'You'll have to start coming every week for your emergency payments,' the postmistress barked without looking up.

'But I don't need emergency payments,' I said.

'I don't care. I can't be paying out a month's benefit in one go. It mucks up my cash flow. And there are no new allowance books, so I can only give you one week's payment at a time.'

'Have you seen the queue outside?' I persisted, mustering all the strength I had. 'Why should anyone have to wait an hour in the rain for thirteen pounds?'

'If they need it, they'll have to. I can't help that.'

I knew she was under pressure too, but it was hard to sympathise with someone who had simply become a mouthpiece for the system. Why did bureaucracy dehumanise its officials, even in a small town? I walked out and the queue was even longer than before. It reminded me of films of the queues at the soup kitchens in the Depression of the thirties. No pension or no Child Benefit would mean no food. So they waited. There was no choice.

'One of these days there'll be women miners,' I said to Doug. I loved teasing Yorkshiremen about their traditional attitudes to the male and female roles. But with Doug, it rarely worked. He was far too quick for me and Ginny went out to work anyway. He looked at me, his face a mixture of amusement and supreme patience and said, 'Eeeeeh lass, but thar't daft! Where would they pee?'

Now I had not thought of that. Up until that moment it never occurred to me that there were no toilets down the pit. How could there be? I suddenly felt very naive.

'And anyway,' Doug said, grinning, 'no woman would last long down there with all them mice.'

'Mice?' I whispered.

'Ay, if yer don't tie yer snap to yer belt, yer've 'ad it. Mice eat it.'

'Snap?'

'Yer lunch box. Yer can't put it on ground. The mice came down in the 'ay what they used to give pit ponies. By, they must be havin' a lean time of it now,' he chuckled.

I thought for a bit.

'Doug, is it cold down there?'

'No, hot usually, though it should be ventilated properly. It's dark though, and wet.'

'Then why does anyone want to do it?'

He shrugged. 'I suppose because yer dad and grandad did it before yer and there's nowt else.'

'Do you want your lads to be miners?'

The two boys were playing at our feet. Doug looked at them for a while. The little one, angelic with his bright eyes and halo of tight golden curls, gurgled at us, as if expressing his point of view. Doug laughed, then shook his head.

'No, not if I'm honest. No miner does. He always wants his lads to do better. But there's never been owt else, and especially now.'

'If they built the new airport up here, on the M1, instead of at Stansted, and there'd been the promise of lots of jobs, how would you have felt?'

He threw his head back and laughed.

'But they won't. They've never given the North a chance and they're not going to start now.'

He looked at the children again and a sadness came into his eyes.

'What's for them, that's all I want to know. What kind of future waits for them?'

But on the whole people tried not to think too much about the future. How to survive tomorrow was enough. The thought of Christmas filled most people with gloom. The Union promised every man a turkey, but what of all the other trimmings the adverts said were a necessity? Most people accepted that they would just have to do without that year.

'We're not having tinsel this Christmas,' Mavis said. 'None of the finery, the presents, and all the irrelevant bits. We can't afford them anyway. We'll have a real family Christmas. We'll sing, we'll play games, we'll talk. We might even discover what a real Christmas is.'

No one dared overspend, not even non-mining families. I felt guilty if at the checkout of the supermarket I had chocolate biscuits in my trolley. Members of the Miners' Benevolent Fund sat beside the exit, with a basket at their feet, begging with their eyes for contributions. I suddenly realised how much of my weekly shopping was for luxury, not necessity goods and I became more thoughtful about what I was buying and why. If the strike had not had that effect on the town, I suspected the pictures of Ethiopia would. They took them to heart. Life for all of us that Christmas was altogether simpler and less extravagant.

The church finances were in dire straits. Our determination to keep up the food parcels and the lack of giving took us five thousand pounds into the red almost before we knew it. Everyone was supporting a relative somewhere and no one had money to give to the church. Then came a command from the Town Council to mend the church clock.

'It's a town amenity,' they said.

'Fine,' we said, 'you pay for it then!'

'We've just voted that the church members should.'

'The church members aren't interested.'

'We'll help then . . . but just a bit.'

And so the wrangling continued. Nothing could be done for the time being anyway.

We received our usual mound of Christmas cards and letters from friends and clergy all over the country. Most seemed totally oblivious of what was happening in our part of the world. Some even asked us for money for their ambitious building projects. Their request was like a slap across the face. I smarted. Let them have their plush new buildings. I did not resent them that, but could they not have spared us a thought, a token? Their brothers and sisters were hungry.

One clergyman in the South rang and said his church was concerned. What could they do? Our hearts leaped. Someone did care.

'Send money,' Peter said.

'I meant could we pray? I don't think they'll want to send money.'

'If politics are a problem, don't worry,' Peter said, 'there are plenty of church families in need who have been affected indirectly.'

But we heard nothing and our hearts sank again. It was silly to raise our hopes and we tried not to be disappointed.

'Do they ever think about us?' Linda asked one night at Drama, just before Christmas. We were rehearsing a sketch with a rather cynical feel about it, which seemed to match our mood. She had to stick a picture of a jolly Father Christmas, his sack bulging with presents, over a War On Want poster. She stood for a while comparing the child with its gaunt body and haunted eyes to the rotund, jolly Santa Claus. 'All those Christians in the South, I mean, do they ever think about us or know how we live?'

'I don't think so,' I said. 'How could they?'

'It's just, well, it seems so funny. We're going to be in heaven together, but we don't know anything about each other now.'

She shook her head and smiled wistfully.

'Oh, don't mind me. I'm just sad tonight, that's all.'

It had been a hard week for Linda. She was already upset about Jan's divorce. They were close. Then her brother-in-law, a man in his mid-thirties, collapsed and died while queueing at the pit for his Christmas parcel. There were four children.

'I can't blame the strike,' Linda said, 'his heart would have given way sooner or later. But he was so upset at having to beg like that. He was ashamed. He got into such a state.'

Two days later his near neighbour died too, digging in a local slag heap for bits of coal.

'Better to be cold above ground than beneath it,' most miners said. But his children were cold and he ignored the miners. The coal tip gave way and crushed him. The street was reeling from the shock, while Linda had been comforting Jan and her sister.

Her question stayed with me, perhaps because it was mine too, and I was still thinking about it a few days later when a letter arrived in a strange hand, postmarked Surrey.

'Dear Mrs Guinness, you came and spoke to us a few months ago.'

My initial reaction was relief. Not another invitation to speak. There were so many and it was not something I enjoyed very much. People did not seem to understand how much of a strain it was, though if they were honest, they must, or they would do it themselves and not invite someone else. I read on.

'I sat next to you at the meal and I have not forgotten what you said about the effects of the strike. We have just sold a vase, a family heirloom and it raised more than we expected. Please accept the enclosed as a small gift.'

I looked at the cheque. It was for a thousand pounds.

I threw on my coat, ran through the cemetery and burst into the vestry, where Edward, Alicia and Peter were having morning prayers.

'Look!' I said, waving my letter about.

They looked at me as if I had taken leave of my senses, scanned the letter, and were just as excited themselves. It was not the amount that mattered, although it helped. It was the knowledge that someone had remembered us, and cared. I found Linda and showed her the letter too. She stared at it, then smiled and shook her head.

'Well, you can knock me down. I don't believe it. I just don't believe it.'

It was Lucy and Mary who received the best gifts that Christmas, and from the Council too. Both heard at the same time that they had been given a new house.

'Pinch me, I'm dreaming,' Mary said, wandering round her new house in a daze.

'Look!' she said, pointing at the kitchen counters and throwing open the cupboards.

'And come in 'ere,' she said, dragging me into a large, bright sitting room.

'And what about up 'ere?' she said, rushing upstairs. 'A bedroom each for the kids. And it's warm! No more going to bed in gloves and socks. The radiators run off the fire.'

I followed her round and we ooohed and aaaahed into every nook and cranny.

'I nearly kissed 'em at 'Ousing Department when they told me,' she said. 'I were so happy I didn't know what to do. This is the best Christmas present, it's the best present I ever 'ad. I knew me prayers would be answered one day. I just knew it.'

Looking at the sheer delight on her face, I could not have imagined God holding out on her for very much longer.

Lucy was as thrilled with her new flat. Dad took some persuading that life could be as rich without a coal fire, but once they had moved and he had experienced the joys of warmth at the touch of a button, no more humping, scraping and cleaning, then he wondered why he had made such a fuss. And since the heating was coal-fired, the Coal Board continued to give him the heating allowance they gave to all ex-miners, and he was in his element. In fact he told everyone he had master-minded the whole move. 'Council just 'ad to give in, because wi' me, actions speak worder than louds,' he said defiantly, thumping the arm of his chair to show he meant business.

'Well, Mr Barker, God's good, isn't he?'

A small group had gathered at Lucy's for a guided tour and were now devouring large quantities of her fruit cake, washed down by large mugs of tea. There was silence from the armchair. They tried again.

'God's been good to you, Mr Barker.'

He took his pipe out of his mouth and stared at them suspiciously.

Undaunted, they tried another tack to tempt the old man into discussing his eternal destiny. 'Mr Barker, you're not a drinking man, are you, what do you like doing most?'

'Me?' He stirred at last. A spark came to life in his eyes. 'I like walking, that's what I like.'

'And when you're out there, in the hills, don't you feel as if God is with you?'

There was a moment's reflection. 'No, I'd much rather be on me own.'

And there was no answer to that. Lucy ran out into her new kitchen and clamped a handkerchief over her mouth to stifle the laughter.

Since this was her first real home, Anna organised a shower party for her. There were pots, pans, casseroles and dinner sets. Lucy's eyes filled with tears.

'It's only right,' we said. 'After all, you could put any married woman to shame with your gift of hospitality.'

'Fancy having to wait till yer my age to set up home. Never mind, it's been worth waiting for. I can't thank you all enough so yer must come to my house for yer New Year's dinner.'

I could not think of any way I would have rather started the year.

25

Suddenly, after a year, it was all over. There was little elation, no dancing in the streets. In fact there was no reaction at all. Perhaps people were too tired, or hungry. Perhaps they were too numb to absorb the fact. Besides, nothing had changed. They knew it that first day back, when they were given their first pay packet in advance. After deductions on all their debts, fuel, rent, rates, insurance, Union dues, it was almost empty. Oh they had marched in that first morning, heads held high, to the sound of the brass band, and we all turned out to watch our men and cheer them, but they slouched home, shoulders stooping and that empty pay packet scorching their pockets.

Had it really been all for nothing? No Yorkshireman would concede defeat, but it hung over our heads like a giant question mark, which refused to go away. To acknowledge it would be to open a wound too deep to bear. Crushed and scorned by the South he might feel, but a man still has his pride.

The strain of months of interminable waiting, the disappointment, heavy debts, and fear for the future took their toll. Some of the men became ill. They were anxious and nervy. Mick's cousin had alopecia and lost all his hair.

In desperation a number of men felt there was no alternative but to accept work in Selby and commute there every day. The journey took about an hour, not long by London standards, but punitive at four in the morning on hazardous country roads. Then, when they got there, they knew no one. At home, in their own pit, they knew everyone, whatever shift, working alongside fathers, brothers and cousins. That was what made mining bearable. Now there was nothing to relieve the terrible monotony, only the thought that it might keep the town going. The sixteen thousand pounds dislocation allowance seemed like blood money. Small wonder many turned it down, even though it would have paid off their enormous debts overnight.

But slowly, as the daffodils pushed their way through the frozen earth and the milder weather came, spring was again in the air and life began to regain a semblance of normality.

Doug appeared at our house early one morning in an old pair of jeans with his ladders and a huge pot of cement.

'Mornin'. How are we, then?' he shouted cheerily.

It was Saturday and I had just staggered out of bed.

'What's he doing?' I groaned at Peter.

'The pointing,' Peter said with excitement.

'Oh.'

Repairs never filled me with Peter's enthusiasm, but in this case I was relieved. Huge yellowish-grey patches, covered in an interesting kind of mould, had been appearing on our newly decorated walls and we hardly dared to mention it to the PCC, given our financial situation. But Peter had been chatting to Doug who, being a man of many parts and desperate to pay off his debts, offered to do it for us at an irresistible price.

'Need any towels or bedding or owt?' he asked me when I took him his first mug of tea. He sat down on our back steps.

'No. Why?'

'I'm setting up a little business. If I can get it going I'll finish with pit. I like the daylight, yer see, and I like being me own boss. I'm not daft, I know where it's all going to end. There'll be no jobs there in a few months and I fancy putting me redundancy money into summat that pays. Anyway, our lass'll help keep me at first. She's decided she likes being out at work.'

'Doug, with your cheek, and sales patter, you should have been one of my race!'

He grinned.

'Only difference is they like saving it and I like spending it. I've told Peter, don't whatever yer do pay me, not till I've finished job or I'll never get rid of me debts.'

From then on Doug might appear at our house at any time of day and at any window. When I walked into a room I might see a pair of shoes, or legs or an arm or two, and then I would hear the unmistakable, 'yoo-hoo!' and like the Cheshire cat in reverse a huge grin would materialise before my very eyes, sometimes sideways or upside down. It was hard painstaking work and sometimes the cold bit through his clothes; at other times the sun brought the sweat out in beads on his brow.

'I've put you a pint in the fridge,' I called to him one day. His face lit up.

'And I've taken it out,' Peter shouted from behind me, 'he's on a diet.'

His face fell, but he worked on.

On the first Saturday warm enough to sit out, Doug stayed at home with the children and Ginny came round with Nancy. We sat drinking tea on what would have been our south-facing patio, had Alicia's architect brother had his way. Peter was trying to create some order out of the overgrown mess of our back garden.

'I like to watch a man work,' Ginny said.

'Hmmmm!' Peter said.

It was the fourth garden we were starting almost from scratch and the novelty was wearing a bit thin. One or two church members walked past down the back alley, stopped, amused to see him naked from the waist up, and leant over the fence to offer advice.

We sat in the sun, lethargic and drowsy, gazing into the distance. Across the fields was row upon row of council housing and beyond and above them the great black mountain which seemed to grow larger by the minute since the strike ended. Towering above that was the huge metal cage with its wheels, familiar symbol of a way of life.

'I remember when that field were all prefabs,' Nancy said, 'and just beyond them were Methodist chapel and none o' them council houses were there.'

Ginny nodded lazily.

'Grimlington's grown right fast.'

'Ay, it's not like it were, it's changed.'

'You sound like a pair of old dears in an old folks' home,' I said.

'I tell yer what though, this strike's aged me years,' Nancy said.

My humour never seemed to reach her.

'Ay, we've changed an' all,' Ginny said. 'I feel like a different person to what I were a year ago, but I wouldn't change that!'

'Wouldn't yer?' Nancy said, with a look of amazement.

'No, I'd do it again, tomorrow if we had to. We showed 'em what we were made of. We showed 'em that Britain doesn't stop at Birmingham. We fought for a man's right to work and we put our stomachs where our mouths were. We've proved that there are more important things than money in this life. We showed 'em all that a man can live on next to nothing, and maybe if we all lived like that all the time there'd be no more Ethiopias.'

Nancy listened to Ginny carefully, but whether she heard was doubtful.

'Well I wouldn't want to go back to living like that,' she said finally, 'it's too much of a strain.'

'Oh, I don't know,' Ginny said, cupping her hands around her mug of tea. 'I'm glad for what I learned. Life was simpler. You found out who yer friends were. I felt much freer in a funny way. I didn't crave for what I couldn't have and I realised that what I couldn't have wasn't worth having anyway.'

Nancy still looked doubtful. Ginny's philosophy was beyond her. Ginny saw it, thought for a moment, then said, 'Listen, when I were a kid I envied Janice Fairclough because she were nice looking, but most of all because she had a real bath at 'er 'ouse. Now I've a proper bath and I miss old tin one. Yer could sit fer hours in front of fire and when one end got cold, get out, turn cold end to't fire and get back in where it were warm.'

I shivered involuntarily, just thinking about it.

'Well, that's it,' Ginny said, the way she did when she felt something was obvious, 'there's always someone better off. No point wasting yer time worrying or being jealous.'

We were interrupted by the sound of a horn, tooting loudly in the back alley. It was Doug, sitting at the wheel of an old, but immaculate, shining Volvo. He leant out of the window, grinning from ear to ear.

'Like it?' he called to Peter, who went over to look, suitably impressed.

'Ey up, he's 'ere to show off 'is new toy,' Ginny said.

'I thought you were broke,' I said.

'We are. He reckons with all the debts 'e 'as already another'll not be noticed. And 'e's been dyin' for a car. What'll I do with 'im?'

Peter got into the passenger seat and together they stroked the upholstery, twiddled all the knobs, and admired every square inch.

'Your lad's just as bad!' Ginny said to me, lifting her eyes to heaven.

'Just think, Ginny,' I said, watching their glee, 'what a preacher Doug'll make one day. He'll turn Yorkshire upside down and make Billy Graham look like a beginner.'

'That'll be the day,' she snorted. 'Did I not tell you what he did in Filey at the last parish weekend? You know he came into the Communion Service? Well, he saw everyone whispering something to each other when they passed round the bread and the wine, but he didn't know what. So when he got the cup he turned to Ian to give it him and said, "Get this down thee lad, it'll do thee good." Some Billy Graham him!'

'Mmmm,' I said. 'Writing his own liturgy already, is he? You've got to admit, he was right.'

She watched him a while, shaking her head.

'Ah well, the age of miracles isn't over, I suppose,' and the thought of it making her lips curl into an enormous grin.

'Are you coming, woman, or are yer goin' to sit there callin' all day?' he shouted.

The strike also left the church with a new attitude to money, a new sense of proportion. Alterations to the building which would make life a great deal more comfortable no longer seemed so important. Peter longed to move the old oak door out to the entrance to the porch and build new glass doors into the church. The constant to-ing and fro-ing during every service to the toilet down at the parish hall, or out into the fresh air for a coughing fit, bronchitis being rife, meant the constant creaking, groaning and clanking of the latch. Worse, a closed oak door was hardly inviting to a newcomer who arrived late and we gathered that some came and turned away again because they were too frightened to come in.

But there were more urgent needs than new doors. People still needed financial help. Sid's job on the building site had finished, and everyone, especially the miners, felt it only right we should try and help if we could. What were new doors? We could live without them for now. The parish hall was redecorated, thanks to the insurance money, then gallons of water from the boiler condensed in the loft and poured down the new wallpaper. Which all went to prove, everyone said, that buildings were a vicious circle of financial demand and we were right to put people first. The attitude was relaxed without being complacent. Just as at the

Gift Day, now past history, we would receive what we really needed, not what we thought we wanted. There were frustrations of course, and Bill, who saw the accounts and knew about the sinking roof, was not always as relaxed as everyone else!

There were other crises too, of equal importance. The man-power, or rather womanpower, we had relied on to run the church had gone to work and had no intention of stopping just because the strike was over. They enjoyed working. They never realised before how hard it was, or how boring it could be, to be tied to the kitchen sink until they were dragged away from it. A long-standing tradition was crumbling, and as it did so, many relation-ships crumbled too. Change, like a hurricane, leaves all sorts of debris in its wake, and the Marriage Guidance Clinic tried to piece things together. The church found itself lacking leaders for every aspect of daytime activity and the children's work.

Peter understood the struggle many of the men were facing. We had experienced our own crisis of roles too.

'You will stay at home,' he said winsomely the night he proposed, the lovelight shining in his eyes. 'You don't have to go out to work, you know.'

'Oh yes,' I said, swept clean off my feet and in my heart were dreams of baking, cooking, cleaning and a gingerbread cottage with honeysuckle growing up the walls.

We always had the honeysuckle, but the rest of the dream was not quite the same! And then, as work in writing and broadcasting expanded, we seemed to be catapulted into a new kind of existence. Doors opened that I had never forced, never anticipated and we both knew I had to go through.

'Go on,' Peter said and I knew that for him there was a cost involved. 'Take the opportunities and we'll share out the chores.'

If ever I had wanted to be the traditional clergy wife, it was no longer possible. I was working every morning and people found it hard to understand at first that I was there, but not there, because I could not answer the phone or doorbell. But there were no regrets. I had always been determined not to be driven by the need for approval. It could be a terrible tyrant. And fortunately we had found a parish where expectations were not very high, but acceptance was.

So here we were, discovering once again that our struggles were mirrored in the life of the parish. Or was it their struggle reflected in us? Perhaps our lives were now so inextricably bound together that it was all part of the same struggle, the struggle to keep up with a world that was changing so fast that we barely had time to catch our breath, let alone adapt our ways. All was in turmoil, the old values vanishing for ever. Employment could not be taken for granted. There was no longer a set pattern for marriage. Community and culture were under threat. Nothing was safe. Nothing was sure any more.

In the light of all this, for both our family and the church there were two possible courses of action. We could dig in our heels and determine to hang on to the old safe ways and attitudes at any cost, or we could walk out into the uncertainty and despite our insecurity and occasional panic, forge new ways. Peter and I had already made our decision. We felt that the old patterns did not treat the clergy wife as a person in her own right, that children of the vicarage often suffered unnecessarily. Our home, half-Jewish, was unusual anyway. We had to have a little of the spirit of the pioneer to make it stay that way. But pioneering meant adventure and adventure was far more exciting than the safe way.

In reality the church had little choice either. The strike ensured we could not be just as we were before. Change was inevitable. There were no longer glib or easy answers to anything. People needed a Christianity that was true and real, that worked. And once they began to question the old attitudes there was no turning back.

26

'It's not going to be one of those success stories, is it?' the Bishop groaned.

We were at a party and he had politely asked me what I was writing now. I looked at him quizzically.

'You know, a *How your church can grow* book?'

'Hardly!' I laughed.

That sounded like a handbook for successful gardeners.

'Knowing Grimlington as you do, you know, it would take more than a little poetic licence to stretch the truth like that.'

'Actually,' Peter assured him, 'this is the antidote to a success story.'

As we drove home the Bishop's words continued to buzz round in my head. Was there ever such a thing as a successful church, in the same way there was a successful firm or business? If there was, was it quantified in terms of money, or building projects, size of congregation, number of meetings, efficient organisation or answers to prayer? The idea was nonsensical, yet some churches, like some firms, enjoyed a reputation. Their system worked. Then why didn't ours? We could try to be professional and jet-set too, but someone always let the side down. If it wasn't an ordinary mortal, it almost seemed to be God himself.

I thought back over the past two years. We had prayed, but the child had died. One month our debts were paid off, the next they were worse than ever. Many found faith, and many seemed to lose it. Change was vital, but costly and painful. Sometimes the church was full. Sometimes it wasn't. There seemed no rhyme or reason for anything. In the same way, some Sunday services took off, while others never left the hangar. Either way no two were ever the same.

'Shall I write a sort of "failure" story then?' I said. Like many couples there were times when we followed each other's innermost thoughts without having to express them verbally. 'Not many people write about coping with frustration and disappointment, do they, and it does seem to play a major part in our lives. Is that what you meant by antidote to success?'

Peter thought for a while as he drove along, then he smiled. 'You wouldn't do justice to the Yorkshire integrity if you were anything less than honest,' he said. 'But what is success anyway? A contemporary western virtue, but certainly not Christian. Our society would hardly call death by crucifixion at the age of thirty-three a roaring success.'

We drove along in silence for a while, Peter concentrating on his driving, as the road to Grimlington was winding and badly lit. I was trying to absorb what he was saying.

'When I think of our church,' he said after a while, 'a picture comes into my mind of a ship in full sail. Some of the passengers keep falling overboard and the rest are so busy pulling them back on, that the ship can't get up any real speed. That tells me we don't fulfil our potential, but I don't think it's the same as failure. The people here are vulnerable. They've experienced great hurt. Perhaps we need to go slowly.'

As he spoke I felt as if a vital piece of jigsaw which would never fit had slotted into place. I had been trying to force it in back to front. A picture was beginning to emerge.

'Are you saying that our human understanding is so warped by the society we live in that our values are upside down? What we call success could really be failure and our apparent failures part of a greater plan?'

Peter nodded.

'So that everything,' I said, 'the heartaches and bewilderment, even Paul's death, had meaning.'

I thought about Mick and Karen and the others who had prayed so much for Paul. They had been hurt, disillusioned, but now they were ready to start praying again for anyone who was ill. At first I marvelled at their courage, their refusal to be defeated and readiness to take a risk. But now I saw that their whole attitude was different. Now there was a deep awareness of our total lack of control over life and death, and that had been the ultimate discovery. We had taken our hands off and having come to the end of ourselves, God was still there, vaster than anything we had ever imagined.

'Perhaps that's why no method or system seems to work for us and we've found no blueprint for success,' I said. 'Self-sufficiency doesn't need God, does it? No struggling or wrestling, but no more adventure either, no mystery to explore.'

'And it does keep us from becoming pompous,' Peter laughed.

'Or cold! No slick and smooth performances!'

'The chance would be a fine thing.'

'But you wouldn't want that, would you?' I said, as the lights of the town came into view just ahead of us.

He shook his head. 'I've learned this much here, that a simple thing like stopping to chat to someone in the street can be more important than running the most efficient church in the country.'

Lucy had done the babysitting for us that night, as she so often did. I had left the children curled up next to her, munching her home-made chocolate crispies while she did her knitting, and I realised how much, as a family with no grandparents or relatives nearby, we needed adopted aunties.

While Peter took her home, I sat in the sitting-room in the dark, watching from the window the town's twinkling lights stretching into the distance. On the horizon the pit-head was flood-lit and, silhouetted against the sky, the slag heap looked dark and menacing, like an angry monster brooding over its prey. I studied it for some time. Every night it was a new shape. Too much slag had accumulated and it was being moved, a little at a time. 'No chance to get tired of the view,' I thought, 'it never stays the same long enough!'

I thought about the strike, now receding fast into the past. It had been a kind of symbolic act, a gesture of defiance and pride to show the country that the cultural identity of industrial Yorkshire was unique and worth preserving. It had seemed to fail, yet the people were as resilient as ever and a flicker of hope still survived. How I prayed that hope would not be disappointed and that someone somewhere would see the potential of the town and pour in resources.

The church was still struggling to reflect that special cultural identity, despite the limitations of any institution, and there were moments of elation when progress seemed almost tangible. Anna often stopped to chat to the assistant in the butcher's in the High

Street. She always had an opinion of the church and loved expressing it, though attendance was another matter altogether. One day she handed Anna her chops and said, 'Well I'm glad you've become socialist up there at last.'

Anna blinked and wondered what rumours were rife in the town now.

'I mean,' the assistant said, 'that it's for everyone, not just certain types and classes.'

But, lest we be carried away by the joy of this apparent 'success', we also discovered a strange irony. The more we reflected the life and character of the area, the more that life and character was at risk, because it began to attract professional-class people from miles around. And inevitably they left their own mark, but it was not the mark of the town. Guest services, known locally as 'Parish cabarets', drew some new people in, and Family Services many others who never normally came, but some of our recent growth was by transference from other churches. The two thirds of the town which was council estate was still barely represented in the congregation. When some came, there were so many strangers there that they wondered if it really was their church. Outsiders were hardly aware of the problem, but Linda, Ginny and Ian felt it keenly. Their families lived on the estate and they knew the isolation and rejection people experienced there. The Drama Group planned to take part in the estate's next Gala to say that we did care but it seemed such a small gesture.

'Where do we go from here?' I wondered, as I staggered heavy-eyed up to bed.

But sleep eluded me. I lay awake for ages, trying to answer my own question. Something Linda had said a few days earlier suddenly came back to mind.

'Oh, I used to be all intense once. I tried to look spiritual. I could pray in fancy language, say the right-sounding things, and pretend life was wonderful even when it wasn't. But it got too much. I gave it up and now I'm just me. I know I'm a thorn in the clergy's side, always going on about what this town needs and what the church should do about it, but it is my town and I love it.'

I smiled as I thought about Linda with her uncanny way of expressing thoughts which others buried in the subconscious and hoped would go away. But it was a vital discomfort, like the grit in the oyster which eventually produced the pearl. I knew from that throwaway remark that nothing would make her sacrifice her integrity, submit to the pressures of a middle-class institution and conform to its ways.

It reminded me of my own struggle to come to terms with my identity as a Jew in the Church. It occurred to me that self-acceptance was probably the key to coping with being a clergy-man's wife too. I could refuse the role and the pretence that went with it, disappoint people's expectations, because, whether they liked it or not, all I had to offer was myself.

And I began to wonder whether the Church ever really accepted people as they were, or whether we continually forced them to fulfil our expectations. Perhaps that was a signpost to the way forward.

Slowly, as drowsiness came at last, an idea came to mind, an experiment. The Drama Group was always complaining about the church. Supposing they had a free hand. What would they do?

'Imagine,' I said to them the following Tuesday evening, 'that there's no such thing as the church. An itinerant preacher has visited Grimlington and you've all decided Christianity is for you. But there's no building, no clergy, nothing at all except the Bible and you may not be able to read. It's up to you to decide.'

They sat in silence for a while, letting the idea take root.

'I'm in the Grimlington pub,' Ginny said, 'I've a pint here on table.'

'So have I,' Ian said.

Whether it was there or not, it loosened their tongues and once the conversation got going, there was no stopping them.

'Shhhh!' they all went to Ian, who was holding forth loudly on the effect the preacher had had on him, 'they'll all hear you on next table.'

'Let 'em,' he said. 'They need to hear it,' but he went quiet all the same.

'I think we should meet like this regularly,' Linda said. 'I mean we need to talk together and learn about God. We can use my sitting-room. Joe won't mind.'

And so, for about three quarters of an hour, the newly-formed 'church' met in Linda's sitting-room. Only one of the group decided they would own a Bible and soon the rest deferred to her and treated her as the fount of all wisdom. Until Linda decided she had had enough of listening to someone else. She would get her own, even if it meant learning to read.

Communal prayer caused them some problems. They were not sure what to do. Linda suggested they all put their fingers in their ears and pray out loud together. They laughed at her, but did it all the same. Ian said he felt stupid, so Jan suggested they wrote some prayers down.

The congregation of imaginary people grew, until, they decided, Linda's sitting-room was too small and they would have to rent a hall. That was the start of a long debate on raising money and the slow realisation that it was becoming increasingly hard to get a consensus of opinion on anything. Eventually Ian had had enough of their 'time-wasting' and walked out in disgust to form his own congregation.

I could not contain my laughter any longer and lay on the floor shaking helplessly while they all looked on in amazement.

'Ignore her,' Ginny said.

Eventually I managed to control myself enough to say to them, 'You realise what you've just done?'

They were puzzled.

'For all your complaints about the church, you've just recreated it exactly as it is, with a building, liturgy, clergy, collections, money hassles and even the denominations.'

They looked surprised at first, then they smiled at each other sheepishly.

'Did it ever occur to you, once you got too big, to form two groups, rather than hire a hall?'

'No,' Ginny said. 'We liked being together. It was cosy. I didn't really want lots of new people coming in to spoil it.'

'Only one of you really cared about sharing the faith he had found and you shut him up effectively.'

'That's right,' Linda said. 'We just assumed no one would be interested.'

'That happens to me all the time,' Ian said, shaking his head. 'Maybe it isn't just . . .'

He looked round the group. 'What I'm trying to say is that it isn't just the system that keeps people out, is it?'

'The structure doesn't help,' Linda said, 'but it's us, isn't it? It's our attitude that really counts. That's where we need to start.'

About a week later Rick popped in for a chat. He was obviously excited about something.

'I've been thinking about the future of the church and the manpower crisis we're facing at the moment,' he said.

He was right about a crisis. So many Sunday School teachers were wanting to retire that it seemed we might soon have no children's work at all.

'Well, I began to wonder whether we're not rummaging in the wrong place. Maybe we should be concentrating on the things that matter most in the town, like family and community. Why separate the children from the adults? We could have the home groups earlier in the evening and include children. We could have more communal celebrations in the church, when we eat together and let our hair down. New people feel happy at occasions like that. They're a kind of a bridge. A man should feel as at home in church as he does at his Club. It shouldn't be such a psychological leap. Sunday worship should be just as enjoyable, so we're not saying one is religious and the other isn't. The test for whether our services are boring or not is whether the children can sit through them. Mine want to be in church. They love Family Services. That would solve our Sunday School problem. Perhaps we should have them in every week.'

I looked at him a moment, temporarily struck dumb by hearing so many of my ideals on someone else's lips.

He grinned at me.

'I thought it all sounded a bit "Jewish",' he said.

I nodded, my heart sinking at the thought of having the children in the service every week. Joel never could sit still for long. But I knew my motives were selfish. I loved silence as well as exuberance, but I would have to train myself to concentrate despite the distractions. Besides, it had been an experience to watch little Peta, at eighteen months, stagger out in front of the Music Group whenever they played and dance for all she was worth. Her spontaneity made us feel stiff and reserved. Children have rhythm and movement in their bones. Although there had to be some constraint, too much 'Sssssh', and 'Stand still', drove it out. It made them self-conscious, not God-conscious.

'And is there any chance the children could take Communion one day?' Rick appealed to Peter. 'They are the Church, aren't they? Ours want to so much. How can we deny them?'

'That certainly is Jewish,' Peter said, with a twinkle in his eye. 'In a Jewish home every child shares in Kiddush, the bread and wine, on a Friday evening. That's where the Communion came from. Yes, I think it will come one day, in the Church of England at least, and in other denominations too, I hope. But meanwhile, we do it at home. I think a child understands what it's about as much if not more than an adult. Their perception has not been spoilt.'

'That's what I wanted to ask,' Rick said. 'We want to worship as a family once a week and somehow it seems natural to have bread and wine. Is it all right?'

'You can please yourself in your own home,' Peter laughed, 'but since you ask me, I think it's great.'

'By the way,' I said to Rick, as he got up to go, 'can you do anything with this?'

I took a children's Haggadah down off the bookshelf and handed it to him. 'It's the Passover Service. It's full of psalms and there are dozens of different tunes for them, depending on the family tradition and the country they came from. I see no reason why a church which now has its own setting for the Communion Service shouldn't write a Passover setting too!'

Rick took it, studied it for a while, then smiled.

'Thanks,' he said. 'It's funny, I was going to ask you if you had any records of Jewish music you could lend me. I have a yen to write some of my own. And perhaps one day we could have a Passover.'

As Rick went out the door I had a strange sensation in the pit of my stomach that a new adventure was about to begin.

The Continuing Story

27

Seventeen years have passed since we left Grimlington, but an aching sense of loss still catches me unawares from time to time – a Yorkshire voice, a picture of a pithead wheel, old photos of miners with glistening, white-ringed eyes staring out from grimy faces, like a historic throwback to the 1950s' TV *Black and White Minstrel Show*.

I cried myself to sleep our last night in Grimlington all those years ago, and woke with a start at around 3 a.m.

'I've just had a terrible nightmare,' I muttered to Peter in my confusion. 'I dreamed we were leaving.'

'We are, darling,' Peter whispered soothingly, and as the awful consciousness dawned, I started crying all over again.

To this day I find it hard to say goodbye to the place, as we do every New Year's Day after our annual visit and knees-up at Linda's house. It's always the last and best party of the Christmas season. As we - sometimes with the children, now grown-up - drive that half mile down to the motorway, past the old, familiar landmarks, the raucous laughter dies away and a deep silence descends inside the car. In these days of our middle age, it could of course be due to post-seasonal exhaustion or pre-work shock syndrome, or even simply night-time concentration.

'Road-calming measures' have turned Grimlington's only main road into a hazardous snake pass, undulating around bollards and semi-circles of pavement covered in empty plant containers that stick out into the path of unsuspecting cars. But little else seems to have changed. The rows of higgledy-piggledy terraces have had a lick of paint or two, modern windows with double glazing and a new coat of pebble dash. The corner shops have changed hands several times. Surprisingly, Kookai has set up an outlet shop in a disused factory, but the quaint little red-brick library is boarded up.

The deathblow dealt by the pit closures inflicted deeper, more invisible wounds on the community. Many of the young feel disillusioned and alienated, despite the valiant attempt of their leaders to preserve some sense of local pride or self-worth.

'I know what we could do,' one of the councillors was heard to cry at a council meeting, in a moment of inspiration, 'we could turn our town into a tourist attraction.'

His colleagues blinked. That wasn't an option that had occurred to them.

'Well,' he said, in the concentrated silence. 'We could get a gondola for 't lake' – 'lake' being the large pond the size of a bowling green in the middle of the park.

'Aye,' agreed one of his colleagues, as the penny finally appeared to drop. 'We could that.'

He warmed to his subject. 'In fact we could get two gondolas and mate 'em.'

Not surprisingly, tourism never has arrived in that part of the United Kingdom, but a rather more unwelcome form of progress has – in the shape of 'Port Yorkshire', swallowing up the golf course, the last surviving greenery, and ringing the town with endless container depots and distribution centres for goods invading the north from the Channel Tunnel.

'Give us the land,' cajoled the developers, 'and we'll give you a new library, swimming pool, superbowl and other, lavish community facilities.' No one put up a fight. What was the point? But no one was taken in either, which was just as well, because all the locals got was a massive roundabout network at the bottom of the town, with around twenty sets of traffic lights and a whole load of extra hassle to get on to or off the motorway. For a town that had only ever had one set of traffic lights, this did seem a little like overkill.

Edward and Anna have long since moved on to new pastures, and the church has had a succession of vicars and has waxed and waned, declined and grown and gone on trying to serve what will be – if not for much longer – a closely knit community.

A part of me will always belong there. I had rediscovered some of my childhood roots, left undisturbed beneath the northern coalfields since my parents abandoned my father's GP practice house in Felling, under the looming shadow of the Heworth Colliery, and headed for the dull, anonymous suburbia of greater Gateshead in its pre-Metro shopping days. I had also found a community, an extended family to replace the one left behind when I made up my mind to try and follow Christ – the Jewish community that was the very fabric of my childhood existence, the context for who and what I was.

So leaving Grimlington was, in some senses, a very brutal end to all the securities I had lost, rediscovered, and lost again. I set out reluctantly and uncertainly, like Sarah in the Old Testament - several steps behind her husband Abraham, who strode out, full of faith, focused on his unknown future, while she, probably convinced he had lost his senses, kept saying to herself, 'I only hope he knows what he's doing.'

We were being sent to Coventry, Peter said confidently. His hotline to the Almighty always functioned better than mine. All I felt was a profound emotional chill. Coventry was an unengaging city robbed of its past by Hitler's bombs and then its 1950s' planners. When it came to architecture, post-war Great Britain was anything but great. If only we had known it then, and safely resorted to rebuilding the beauty that was bombed. But no, the fashion for a stark Corbusier modernism didn't do any town any favours. It lumbered Coventry with gloomy concrete walls and characterless dual carriageways that gave way to vast industrial landscapes as barren as the West Yorkshire coalfields, dominated not by pitheads but by the monoliths of the new wealth that manufactured Jaguars, Austins and Rovers.

The people had come from far-flung parts of the United Kingdom, seeking to escape the empty clang of the coalhouse or steel factory door as it slammed shut in their faces, denying them access to making a crust. They came to make money, not relationships. The emotional landscape could be as bleak as its physical counterpart. The Christmas-week carol singing round the parish, so appreciated and such fun in Grimlington, was greeted by silent, empty streets and firmly closed doors. Only the slightest waver of a net curtain at a window let us know that our best efforts were not going entirely unnoticed, as we trudged from cul-de-sac to cul-de-sac and sang our hearts out to the accompaniment of a valiant accordion.

I couldn't get used to living in a 1960s' box on a main road to nowhere. It was a biggish, stand-alone box, admittedly, but still a rectangle with straight lines and uninteresting proportions, several inches on one side from the fifty-foot brick wall of the church, which filled the landing window. The kitchen was tiny – no room for a table, so no room for children doing homework as I pottered – and the dining room, without any furniture other than the table, only seated six people holding their breath. My mother-in-law came to live around the corner, and had lunch with us every Sunday. Squeezing in another couple was an acrobatic feat; inviting another family was out of the question, unless we ate buffet style. It was a terrible denial of the Jewish Mama hospitality gene, and the New Testament promise that I might entertain angels un-awares. The concept of the extended family was manifestly unknown to Church of England architects. This was the new, streamlined, cheap-to-run lego vicarage for the new, strapped-for-cash, stereotypical clergy family, which was manifestly supposed to leave aging parents to fend for themselves, and shut themselves away from their parishioners.

'The clergy don't want big houses nowadays,' said our diocesan vicarage surveyor, when, in a fit of homesickness for Grimlington and our warm and roomy Edwardian terrace, I had harangued him on the matter. Here was a convinced and uncontested expert in the particular foibles and preferences of clergy spouses. 'Can't afford to run them.'

Fair point. I only had to read the letters page in the *Church Times* to see the support he might enjoy from vicarage families tired of trying to heat vast barns on a pittance – but couldn't there be a happy medium, a place large enough to encompass friends, extended family and half the parish? And did the newer vicarages have to look so obviously public service, so red-brick and square, so like a police house, announcing to the world that it was not and could not be ours? How could we, poor church mice, afford such a large, prestigious detached property?

I drew the line at the mustard cupboard fronts he sent for the kitchen, without consultation.

'I am surprised,' he said mildly, as he surveyed the flat packs left stacked on the floor. 'All other clergy wives seem to like them.'

None, it was abundantly clear, were as difficult as this one. But then, there was always one! His look said it all.

The fact that Peter's study was big enough to seat a dozen

round a large table and still find room for a dresser or sideboard, his desk and bookshelves, only added to my frustration. I thought of switching the rooms around, but the study had been built next to the front door, opposite a visitor's toilet, and both were safely separated by a further glass door from the rest of the living quarters. The boundary between work and play was carefully set out.

One of Peter's first jobs was to get himself on to the diocesan parsonages' committee – and from that moment, vicars' wives chose their own kitchen cupboard fronts. To be fair to our diocesan architect, he was surprised at some of the demands that were made. Some clergy wanted jacuzzis or whirlpool spas in their bathroom, some had endless problems with pollution in the pond in the back garden, while others left more behind them than a job vacancy, as their vicarages needed fumigating.

But our four Coventry years were far from completely bleak and barren. Gradually, splodges of colour began to appear on the canvas – many new friends; a fascinating introduction to the rich and colourful Asian community; the dynamic, international cathedral culture; the proximity of a buzzing city like Birmingham; and then suddenly, with a profound sense of shock, I found myself with a career.

28

'English women don't have careers,' my interior-designer German sister-in-law informed me on the phone one day. 'They have jobs. That's what they call their work.' The lack of ambition of her British sisters had always puzzled her. But as a young woman, I had never planned my working life, never considered what I might do once the children went to school. I had dreams. I had always wanted to work in the media, but that had to be a daydream, not an achievable reality, didn't it?

Yet as I look back now, what a long way Peter and I had to travel since those days when I sat with him in a café in Manchester shortly before our marriage, the lovelight shining in my eyes, and said, 'I won't go out to work. I'll stay at home and iron your shirts and darn your socks.' He claims he wasn't asking me to be a traditional housewife. He was merely giving me the opportunity not to go out to work, if I didn't want to. Given the way things turned out, we laugh about it now.

I think in those early days I imagined living in a gingerbread cottage, with honeysuckle growing up the wall, and clean, sweet-smelling nappies wafting gently in the breeze as they hung out in the summer sun. The reality of Manchester, the Yorkshire coalfields and Coventry car factories didn't quite live up to the fantasy. In fact, the baby and toddler years were my wilderness years. I thought I ought to enjoy being a mother of babies, but instead, disappointingly, I was horribly bored. The creative housewife who made her own clothes, jams and furnishings disappeared overnight. My creativity was reduced to finding a thousand ways to fold a nappy, putting away a post-box toy in three seconds – with all the pieces in the right holes - and sleepwalking my breasts into an open mouth six times in the night. I did try, once, to make dinner for six, filling profiteroles with cream with one hand, mixing a feed with the other, while frantically rocking a bouncing cradle with my right foot in a vain attempt to pacify a screaming baby, blue with hunger, boredom and rage. Even going out to see friends was limited because Joel couldn't sit still for a minute, and a slack sphincter at the top of his stomach meant he brought up small piles of food all over the host's carpets, as he propelled himself across the floor as if there were a motor attached to his rear.

If one person had told me I might make a better mother of teenagers than babies, it would have released me from the guilt induced by the stifling boredom I felt. But blessed with the ministry of encouragement, friends simply said, 'Just wait till they're teenagers, it gets worse.' It never did get worse, I have to say. I loved having funny, quippy, bright and loving teenagers. Most of the hardest work was done when they were little. Somehow, they managed to grow into adults I liked and enjoyed, despite the fact I was catapulted into the workplace when they were still quite small.

I certainly wasn't ready to go out to work. My confidence was gone. I didn't know it at the time but I was building, in today's language of the workplace, 'a viable and transferable skills mix'. I only knew I felt invisible the moment I pushed my buggy out of the front door, undermined by a society that did not rate mother-hood. I felt undervalued by the church, which never treated me as if I had brains or ability or a valid opinion.

Yet I often reflected on the fact that never had I heard a Jewish woman say, 'I'm just a housewife,' probably because she wasn't 'just' playing second fiddle, like so many Christian leaders' wives I observed, who were 'backup' for the husband's ministry, running the home and the kids so that he had street cred as a church leader, and was free to rush out to his next meeting with a warm heart and a full stomach. No, the Jewish woman was a power to be reckoned with, mistress of her kingdom. The home is the centre of worship. Woman is responsible for creating the right ambience and smooth running of events, so that festivals can begin exactly at sundown and the whole extended family relax into worship and celebration. It means choosing the right menu, preparing the table, inviting and welcoming the extended family. It means instilling in your children a feel for the Jewish way of life, so that they will grow up to carry on the traditions of their ancestors. This is the key to the survival of the Jewish people and community. This is leadership, for those who do it well have skills enough to run the country.

I didn't seek to escape my lot. I didn't choose a career. It chose me. To get my hands and head out of the nappy bucket, I had begun writing. I wanted to try and convey what it felt like to be a bit of an oddity in the church, when in fact, to my mind, the Gentiles were the real odd bods, while I was strictly kosher – born to be there. But two thousand years of history, of Jewish banishment from what might have been our natural habitat, couldn't be changed overnight - and most British institutions wouldn't revert to their original, immediate post-resurrection culture just because I jumped up and down and demanded they become more Jesus-like, more Jewish. How could I expect Christians to understand just how much they were missing – colour, celebration and around half of the New Testament, at a conservative estimate – because they didn't know its context, or see through Jesus' eyes? It was like asking someone who was blind to describe what sight denied them. Nevertheless, determined and foolhardy as I am, I was determined to have a go.

To my utter amazement, features and articles were accepted, and so whenever the children were at playschool or asleep, at lunchtime, in the evening, in the early hours of the morning, I picked up the pen.

'Will you learn to type,' my dear husband said to me in sheer desperation one day, when the word processor made its debut in our home. 'I'll see to the technology, but draw a line at the typing.' So I got myself a Pitman's, covered the keyboard as instructed, and discovered that, like driving, touch typing is only around thirty hours of practice away.

But the real substance of my dreams was not the print on the page, but the little box that was given pride of place in every sitting room in the land. Surely, I groaned inside, there has to be more to religious broadcasting than *Songs of Praise*. There was a great deal more drama to faith than a couple of hundred well-scrubbed, middle-class, elderly but jolly hymn-singers, the men with booming breasts, the women warbling wide-mouthed, keeping any emotion well away from the camera lens that all but disappeared up their noses.

At a conference I was introduced to the producer of Radio Piccadilly's weekly religious programme that had a built in mid-week repeat.

'You need something to keep your listeners listening,' I said to him. 'A sort of simple soap, a serial of some kind, a story.'

'Write it, then,' he said.

And I did – since the Jews love stories. It was the precursor to *Child of the Covenant*. It ran for twenty weeks on Sundays and Tuesday evenings, and when it was taken off the air during the siege of the Iranian Embassy one Tuesday, the radio phone lines were jammed with complaints. I reworked it for BBC local radio when Peter trained in Nottingham, and then again for BBC Radio Leeds when we moved to Grimlington. In fact, I discovered that recycling could be quite an effective way of building a career in radio.

But when the miners went on strike, I had a vast amount of new and virgin material. BBC Radio Leeds urged me to carry on beyond my own story to tales of a striking people, told at 11 a.m. on Monday mornings, when housewives stopped for coffee. Those were the days before the housewife became an almost extinct species, and before coffee time was a mug of something swigged during a spare working moment.

It was a wonderful opportunity to explain how it really was in Grimlington – the immense bravery in unremitting grimness, the generosity when there was so little to give away, the humour that kept the community alive. It was a bit like the *Archers* set down the pit, with one voice telling the story. Radio Leeds sent a tape to BBC Radio 2, and soon I found myself as a sidekick to ex-*News of the World* editor Derek Jameson, doing 'Pause for Thought' on his breakfast show once a week, and enjoying my own BBC mailbag. We had a rapport. We chatted on and off air, and on the phoneline when I couldn't get to London. He was brought up amongst East End Jews, loved Jewish humour and thoroughly enjoyed the stories I told. Not so the Jewish Board of Deputies, who protested loudly to the BBC religious department that a convert, married to an Anglican priest, could no longer be classified a Jew. What I was, with my looks and mannerisms, if not Jewish, heaven only knew. But freedom of speech is hard to preserve when it clashes with political correctness and the desire not to alienate a fairly formidable group of listeners. However, the Head of Religious broadcasting stood fast and maintained my right to broadcast – for a time.

It was a different matter when Ernest Saunders' lawyers threatened the BBC, shortly after the publication of my biography of the Guinness family and an interview on the Radio 2 arts programme. I was blackballed, while Saunders, the erstwhile Guinness Chief Executive, published his own version of the events that led to his conviction and imprisonment. Jameson came to my rescue and this opened a new door – but that came later.

As the radio work developed, I had been presenting a BBC TV worship programme called *This is the Day*. There is probably no more demanding television on the globe: there was no autocue and scripts had to be learned off by heart, and were often changed at 2 a.m., before a 7 a.m. rehearsal and a 9.30 a.m. live programme. In fact, the script was changing up to sixty seconds before the programme began. I never knew how we ever managed to finalise the details. We sometimes fell on air. I was a nervous wreck and never at my best. In fact, I remember watching the researcher, who responded to the thousands of people who wrote in asking for help, advice or prayer, and thinking that, when the children are older, I'd really like to be a television researcher – the person who searches out the cracking stories, or finds the answers to the viewers' questions, or better still, works on a wonderful historic drama, sniffing out authentic houses and knocking on the door asking permission to film.

Abby had been at school full time for a month when the phone rang in our Coventry home, and the Head of Religion and Education at Central Television offered me a job as a researcher.

'What'll we do with the children after school? How will we manage?' I asked Peter.

'We will,' he reassured me. 'I can be at home doing administration, and if I can't, someone will help out.'

I sat at an empty desk on my first morning back at work, terrified out of my wits, totally devoid of self-confidence. I was used to pushing a pram around for the past seven years, and now I was faced with a blank piece of paper on an empty desk. But slowly the creative juices began to flow; ideas were conceived, programmes born. I not only researched programmes and trotted around after film crews with the biscuits, I also reported, presented pieces, wrote scripts and even billings for the Radio and TV Times, and eventually shared a Sandford St Martin Award for the best regional religious programme of the year – a documentary about Compassionate Friends, a support network for people bereaved of their children, initiated by a Coventry hospital chaplain.

But some strange law governing the universe of working women seems to dictate that as their professional skills grow, their home-making skills decline exponentially, as if it would be too unjust for them to have it all. Peter and I were both totally committed to our home and hospitality, but that meant rearranging our relationship as well as sharing the domestic chores.

'I've cleaned the floor for you,' he said one night.

'No,' I shouted in exasperation. 'You haven't done it for me, you've done it for us. This is our home.'

'Oh, yes,' he said ruefully, as the implications of our new life finally dawned. I couldn't begin to imagine how single people coped, running a home and a job in tandem, on their own. Without Peter's full support and encouragement, without his conviction that I should have as much opportunity to fulfil my calling as he had to fulfil his, even if it meant minding the home fires while I was away filming, I could not have gone on. No wonder a recent survey showed that given the choice, only 9 per cent of women would work full time, especially as 60 per cent were not as fortunate as I was and still did most of the household chores.

I left all the financial accounting and DIY to him, because it bored me silly. He left the cooking to me, because he hated it so much. To be fair to him, he did try to learn, and took a cookery course with another vicar and five elderly ladies, all trying to guess what job two men could do that allowed them a Friday day off. 'I think I might ask if I can start by making croissants,' he said on his first day.

'Well,' I said carefully, 'that would be really nice, but I wonder whether you shouldn't try making bread and puff pastry separately first, before you try to combine the two?'

He appeared to enjoy setting out with his basket, containing little pots of carefully measured ingredients, and coming home with his work of art. He even started showing me how to do things properly, the way men are wont, but in the end, since it took him all day to make a lasagne, and the children half a day to clean his pots, we decided to let go of his culinary services. I insisted, however, that he came and peeled potatoes and chopped carrots, not because I didn't want to be a skivvy, but because it was our only opportunity to talk. Even so, my cooking, all last-minute, was not what it once was, and for a Jewish woman it was hard not to be Mrs Perfect in the kitchen.

But oh, the self-punishing guilt that pursued me for not being there for the children when they came home from school, even though Peter was – most of the time at least. To look at them now, strong, independent, loving young adults, full of faith, I can't think why I worried, except that the traditionally held view in both church and state was that the children of working mothers were in danger of becoming drug addicts, criminals, and reprobates, and if they were from Christian families, pagans to boot. I can still see Abby, at five, barely able to wield a knife, sitting at the kitchen table, making her own school dinner, honey from ear to ear, in her hair, up her nose, down her uniform, anywhere but on the bread.

'It's not that I like being sticky,' she announced one day. 'It's just that I've got used to it.' What a heel I felt, until she said with smug satisfaction, 'The other children complain about what their mums had put in their sandwiches. They're silly. I told them to make them themselves – then they can have honey or peanut butter and jam.' That's when she first realised there could be advantages in having independence early.

'I did miss you terribly when you went away,' she told me recently, 'but your working has opened up so many possibilities for my life.'

What a relief it was to hear those words, belying so much that was said to me or inferred then. My gem of a mother-in-law, for example, who often cared for the children after school when Peter had to go out, implied from time to time that her son and grandchildren were not being cared for adequately. Some church members let me know they would have preferred a minister's wife who was there for them, others hinted darkly at the long-term damage to children of working mothers, and one told me in no uncertain terms that the church could have understood my doing a caring job like nursing or teaching, acceptable professions for a Christian, but not an unproductive and glamorous job in the media. I sat in the bath one night in a state of exhaustion and shouted to all my critics, 'I do not need your approval. I only need God's, and fortunately, undeserved as it is, I have it.'

I often felt I didn't merit his approval. The job wasn't glamorous. Most of it was spent in that demanding and wearing institution, the great British office, and I often found myself drawn into criticisms of the boss, bitching among the colleagues, and the intrigues which are an integral part of any miniature society. Every day I asked for guidance through the shark-infested waters, for the strength to guard my tongue, for protection from the flattering advances of attractive men, and from the temptation to jostle for promotion. Looking back, I was too keen to please, too nice and too passive – a terrible womanly weakness. Like many in our team, I found myself subjected to sexual harassment from one of the directors. His Christian faith was well known, and I didn't feel able to make a public accusation that would destroy not only his reputation and career, but his innocent wife. When the man was finally tempted to fish beyond his immediate usual pool, and try it on with someone outside our team whose husband lodged an immediate complaint, he was suspended instantly. On reflection it was inevitable. I was ashamed I hadn't had the sense to see it, or the urge to protect my colleagues. This was the first time I realised how much the world needs assertiveness – not aggression, nor even outspokenness, but the courage to stick out one's neck and have one's head chopped off, if that's what right requires. Esther and Ruth were Old Testament women who were prepared to risk their reputation and do what they had to do, whatever the cost. And they did it firmly, quietly and without a fuss.

Two years later, it became increasingly obvious that Central TV was in financial difficulty and cutting its staff, particularly in religion. Enter Derek Jameson. When the BBC reneged on promises to publicise the new Guinness biography, Derek graciously gave me the chance for some extra publicity on his Sky TV chat show. Watching from his armchair at home was Mike Marsh, station manager of a brand-new BBC radio station for Coventry and Warwickshire. Having hired an all-male daytime cast, he just happened to be searching for a female lunchtime presenter – a task, he claimed, that had come to feel like the hunt for Scarlett O'Hara when David Selznick was making *Gone with the Wind*. 'And there you were on Sky TV – a Coventry woman. It was too good to be true.'

Within hours I was offered the job. To his bewilderment, I declined. I thought I might be pregnant again. It certainly wasn't planned. He thought I was prevaricating because he hadn't offered enough money and made a fresh offer. This was becoming interesting, but I still couldn't commit. It seemed as if the chance of a lifetime was slipping through my fingers.

When the first realisation dawned that the work at Central TV might be coming to an end, I had sat in the bath and felt the Almighty was initiating a conversation along the lines of, 'Given a choice, what would you like to do?'

'Interview people, all day every day,' I said. 'That's what I really love doing. And I could do it so much better than I do now.'

BBC Coventry and Warwickshire appeared to be a very fast answer to that prayer, delivered on a plate, only to be whipped away before I could get my hands on the goodies. It was a real test of faith. I wish I could say I passed with distinction. I didn't. I was rescued before I found resolution.

Perhaps God knew I never would be able to resolve such a conflict. Perhaps he spared me having to do so, but I wasn't pregnant, felt relief and accepted the job with a whoop of joy. Looking back, I think I was being given a choice – a new baby or a new job. I so badly wanted the latter that I couldn't countenance the former, and got what I thought I most wanted. From my current vantage point I now think I probably turned down the greater gift. The only real regret in my life is not having more children. Nothing compares with the sense of satisfaction my two now give me. But how was I to know that then? Pregnancy really didn't agree with me, and I had nearly lost Abby at birth. But I think I have learnt with age that the things we think we want most may not necessarily be the best.

I did not enjoy presenting local radio. I hated being cooped up in a studio without daylight for several hours a day, like a battery hen. On the one hand, Mike Marsh provided excellent media training. 'Cut the prattle,' his dismembered voice would break from a microphone in his office into the studio, if he didn't like our presenting style. 'Who wants to know the details of your little life?' There are times today, when I listen to local radio, that I wish I had a microphone like that straight into their studio from my car. On the other hand, I was bored by the repetitive nature of the work, and though, after around fourteen guests on the programme every day, I could eventually interview in my sleep, there was little that was new after the first twelve months. I badly wanted to find an exit, but when I did, it wasn't at all what I had in mind.

The wonderful Mike Marsh moved on to greater things, and was replaced, without due interview process, by a new station manager with instructions from the BBC in the north-west to move in presenters from another, rival but defunct BBC station. Mike had tried to arrange a long-term contract for me before he left, but being uncertain about the future, I had refused. I suddenly understood what he had been trying to do. My days were numbered, but when I was finally asked to leave, at my first meeting with the new manager, it was a terrible blow to my pride – and a financial worry. A minister's pay is not substantial, and we did not want to find ourselves on family income supplement again. Nevertheless, it became abundantly clear to me that I had a choice. I could put myself in the hands of the new station manager by railing against his unjust behaviour and seeking retribution through employment tribunal, but that would in effect be saying he was in charge of my life. Alternatively, I could put myself in the hands of God, believing he knew, and may even have decreed this eventuality, and must have a better plan in mind. That meant leaving without a fight – and with all the grace I could muster.

Despite the hard struggle in the grace department, there was no real contest. I knew which were the safer pair of hands. The first course of action left me feeling bitter, angry and resentful; the latter filled me with peace and expectation. I told my boss firmly and gently that I would work out my contract, and made up my mind to clamp my jaw shut and not to criticise him to my colleagues.

One by one, each suffered a similar fate. The station was a war zone.

'You're better out of it,' my ex-PA said on the phone one night. 'The atmosphere is awful – weeping and wailing in the toilets, bitching in the studios and screaming in the corridors. You never did that. Was it because of your faith?'

It was then that Peter saw an advert for a job back up North that seemed to fit the mental identikit we had created of where we felt we should be. Now we were free to go, liberated from the pressure of having to decide whose job was the more important, and which of the two of us would follow the other. It has been fascinating to see the way at different times our different ministries have taken priority. The doors to working in the media never opened in quite the same way again, but an extraordinary and totally unexpected new opportunity arose.

29

Our first years in the new church were extremely difficult. We tend to put our stress somewhere in our bodies, and mine obviously went into my womanly bits and pieces, for out of the blue I discovered I needed a hysterectomy. Knowing what I know now I would have asked for more information, read all the research, demanded a second opinion, and looked at all the alternatives, but being a patient robs us of independent thought and action. Faced with medical professionals and being unwell, we are at our most vulnerable, and allow others to make choices for us which we alone should be making.

I said as much to the nurses after my operation. It was Good Friday and there were no new admissions before the Easter weekend. I was the only patient left on the ward, and they were bored.

'You couldn't have a fit of hysteria,' they asked, 'to make us feel useful?'

'No,' I said, 'but I'll tell you about all the things that worried me that you never explained – like whether this would this affect my sex life.'

Wonderful how the subject of sex whets the appetite. They gathered around my bed, and as we tucked into the hot cross buns I had asked Abby to bring in, we talked about how they could give their patients a better service.

'Why don't you work for the NHS?' one of the nurses suggested. 'We need someone like you to help the patients to say what they think and feel, and help us communicate with them more effectively. We also need someone to improve our media image.'

Within five months, without making a single approach to

anyone in the NHS, I became Press Officer for the biggest hospital in Lancashire. Furthermore, I discovered that working in PR could pay me almost as much for part-time work as I had earned working full time in the media, allowing me more time for Peter, two boisterous teenagers, the occasional speaking engagement, the local church and writing a book or two. Going out to work was a rest.

My only sadness was that my father didn't live to see it. He always believed I should work for the NHS – though admittedly as a doctor, and not in this capacity, which would have never entered his head in his day. I loved it nonetheless and felt it was a vital role, explaining and promoting services, building public confidence that the care they expected would be there when they needed it, and boosting staff morale by recognising their efforts.

Two years later, when my close relationship with the Chairman of the Health Trust, who was never any less than upfront about her Christian faith, began to be used by jealous colleagues as a tool to question her integrity, I felt I had no alternative but to clear my desk and walk – and though I didn't know it at the time, it was straight into a new job in Blackpool which gave me much greater scope to train health professionals in communicating with patients.

I stayed for six years, longer than I have stayed in any job, because the new boss gave me the freedom I needed to continue with my own writing, speaking and broadcasting. But then a new Labour government brought in a host of changes, or 'reconfiguration' as it was called in NHS gobbledegook. Some of it was very necessary, but inevitably there was fall-out, and my boss declined to join the ungainly race for the new jobs.

'Aha,' I said to myself, with not a little relief. 'Time to leave the NHS behind. Thankfully we don't have a heavy mortgage hanging around our necks. That gives me some freedom.'

And then the sly and slippery voice of materialism insinuates itself into the thought processes. 'On the other hand, we will need a house in retirement. And then there's Abby to support. She may want to do a postgraduate course.'

And then a firmer, stronger voice asserts itself into my consciousness, 'You know I care for your children more than you do. You know I have always provided whatever you need when you need it, and when one door has closed another opens. After all we've been through together, can you still not trust? What is it you really fear? The loss of status, the loss of significance, the loss of independence? What are they by comparison with following me?'

I really was ready to leave the secular workplace and the salary – in fact, delirious at the prospect – and then I was told that the new Cumbria and Lancashire Strategic Health Authority was advertising for a Head of Communications. There are twenty-eight Strategic Health Authorities nationally. They sit between the Department of Health and the NHS trusts on the ground, supporting the trust staff, encouraging better, more efficient performance, and creating strategies for the whole area. I didn't see myself as a strategist. I thought I was a doer rather than a thinker, and couldn't see how I could lead around thirty communications managers, until Peter urged me to apply.

'At this stage of my life, I can live without such a huge responsibility,' I argued. I was planning on baking bread, making jam, tackling the garden, and becoming at last a lady who lunched with her friends, not playing she-who-must-be-obeyed. 'Anyway, they need a political animal, someone to fulfil the government's objectives, and I don't want to dance to their tune.'

'Try it. It can't do any harm.'

I conceded reluctantly. I wasn't going to get the job, after all.

In the end I left it too late. The application date had closed. 'But send your CV anyway,' said the friendly PA.

I did as I was told and found myself shortlisted.

There were six of us at the interview and I was so laid back I was ready to say the first thing that found its way to my mouth – and did.

'How will you encourage staff to communicate with patients better?' the Chair asked. She seemed a round, rather jolly and comfortable lady, and I warmed to her at once.

'I'll tell them the Alan Bennett story,' I said. 'One day, he went to one of the London hospitals for an X-ray, and had to ask a receptionist on the ground floor where it was. Without looking up from her magazine, she said, "Second floor." Alan Bennett said he wanted to get hold of her, shake her until her teeth rattled, and say, "You are as important to the wellbeing of any patient as any consultant in this hospital simply by being nice. So be nice – you cow!" '

I thought I had well and truly blown it, and was delighted – until I saw the Chair, grinning.

I rushed back to my office in Blackpool and tried to get hold of Peter. What would I say if they offered me the job? How does one turn these things down graciously? He was busy, in a meeting. He would call me when he was finished. I was on tenterhooks, and then the phone rang. Relief, it was him. I snatched up the receiver. It was the Director of Finance of the Strategic Health Authority. 'We want to offer you the job.'

No, I shouted to myself. 'Yes,' I said to him, quietly, hung up and burst into tears.

I cried for days, yet couldn't deny an inner certainty that this was something I had to do.

Never have I embraced what I believed to be God's will with such reluctance. This was Gethsemane – admittedly on a very minor scale, and with far less at stake and a great deal more fuss made than was the case with Jesus. Laura, a lovely friend who has a degree in social work, cerebral palsy and can barely move a muscle, prayed for me as I sat in a heap in church one Sunday. There was such grace in it. Here was someone who would have given almost anything to be able to use her gifts and qualifications in the workplace, but found herself face to face with an ungrateful wretch fighting a fantastic opportunity.

'Why do it, then?' she mouthed at me.

'I don't know,' I replied. 'I just know I have to.'

It has been the biggest learning curve of my whole life, and at my ripe age. For three years I have felt challenged and out of my depth, frustrated and fulfilled, exhilarated and exhausted – yet so glad to have been given the chance. I have learnt the art of looking knowledgeable, while being completely ignorant, praying hard for wisdom. And miraculously, skills I never consciously knew I had have been there when I have needed them. Or perhaps they simply fell from heaven at the right time like a ripened harvest.

How much longer will this be for? I have no idea. I only know I understand now how many people are condemned to a work-place that is stressful, boring, brings them little by way of satisfaction, hedges them in with nonsensical procedures and policies and fails to make the most of their potential. No wonder they hunt for amnesia at the weekend, stifling the gnawing meaning-lessness of Monday to Friday in binge drinking, drugs, or casual sex. They crave release, recreation, party, celebration, without ever knowing that Jesus extends an invitation to authentic party and real celebration, to a banquet with him that begins now and goes on forever. More than ever, I am convinced that the Jewish Jesus was a man of the party with much to teach us about true celebration. If we shall party with him forever one day, we might as well model it down here.

One morning Peter came back into our bedroom as I was finishing my Bible reading and found me in floods of tears.

'It's all hopeless,' I howled at him. 'House prices have shot up and despite all I've earned we won't be able to afford what we really want in retirement. We'll be condemned to a tiny flat on the mudflats of Morecambe.'

'What on earth are you reading?' he asked, and came to look over my shoulder, to see if he could find any clues. But there was no relation between this great book of hope and consolation and my mood.

'Oh you woman of little faith!' he chuckled.

And then, by way of encouragement, as only a man can, he added, 'Anyway, we might move to Africa, or you might not live to see retirement.'

I may or may not – but it's largely irrelevant, I have now come to see. Like so many others, I suspect, I have spent a great deal of time, beating my breast, demanding to know God's will for my life. Now I understand that the important thing is to stand back and watch as God writes his history of humanity, and then discover my part in it – however small, strange or incomprehensible at the time. And that means living in the moment, not trying to see too far ahead – essential as the years of this life speed forward, like the pages of a good book being flicked at an ever increasing rate to its ultimate denouement.